Secrets of
The Old Woman Who Never Dies
The Ancient Ways of the Moon Phases

Secrets of
The Old Woman Who Never Dies
The Ancient Ways of the Moon Phases

Virginia L. Meyer, M.A.T.

Judy Koons

iUniverse, Inc.
New York   Bloomington

Secrets of the Old Woman Who Never Dies
The Ancient Ways of the Moon Phases

iUniverse books may be ordered through booksellers or by contacting:

iUniverse
1663 Liberty Drive
Bloomington, IN 47403
www.iuniverse.com
1-800-Authors (1-800-288-4677)

ISBN: 978-1-4401-5401-0 (sc)
ISBN: 978-1-4401-5402-7 (ebook)

Printed in the United States of America

iUniverse rev. date: 04/19/2010

Acknowledgements to:

Licia Duryea, Carol Canterbury, and Ana Kobayoshi, for their editing
    insights
Steve Dahmus for his research in ancient star-patterns
Darryl Schmidt for personal photography
Annette Olson and Arron Schmidt for their technical rescue work

Dedications

Virginia's

In memory of my father, who would have understood this
and
For my daughters, who sang the nursery song
"I love the moon, the moon loves me—" to their children,
and for my son, who was born under a full moon.

Judy's

To my father, whose gentleness, strength and sense of humor
encouraged me to open my heart to the world with joy.
And to my 4 children
- Nance, Mike, Jeff and Amy –
who taught me the true meaning of unconditional love.

The words go forth
into the great darkness
on waves that crest and fall.
After many births and deaths
through unknown time
the words come forth again.

Table of Contents

Part II
WINDOWS IN TIME
The Archetype of All Cycles of Relationship

Prolog
A Shamanic View

Grandmother Moon is very old, almost as old as Earth. She was born before people were here, and taught us how to become human beings and do wonderful things. If you go out and stand by the tree that grows by the water, and look out over the water you can sometimes see Grandmother Moon weaving her silver web of destinies at the very edge of the sky. Between here and there are the great mothers, standing in a long row—Mother Bear, Kwan Yin, Sh'khinah, Mother Mary, Blue Lady of the Stars, and many others whose names I don't remember, who will show you the way to Grandmother Moon.

Grandmother Moon is the hands of Grandfather Sun, who is the emissary of He Who Made All Things—that was His original name, but there are those now who say he has 10,000 names, which is to say, an infinite number. But I have four names and by whichever one you call me, I am the same person.

It is the task of Grandmother Moon to make real Grandfather Sun's words, and to point the way to the Guardians of the Sun's path.

Preface
On Changing the World

All the high civilizations of the world are to be thought of as the limbs of one great tree, whose root is in heaven. And should we now attempt to formulate the sense or meaning of that mythological root... that precipitated the image of man's destiny as an organ of the living cosmos—we might say that the psychological need to bring the parts of a large and socially differentiated settled community....into an orderly relationship to each other...must have been fulfilled with the recognition of the orderly round-dance of the five visible planets and the sun and moon through the constellations of the zodiac.

—Joseph Campbell[1]

This book may not change the world, but if those who read it make Grandmother Moon's teachings a part of their personal universe, all of us together can do it. At the time of this writing, the US has just gone through the throes of a 2008 election of which the theme was Change, and the path from there appears to be a long walk in a canyon clouded with mist. According to the outdated philosophy of our culture it was often necessary for each candidate to be defined by the negatives of the other. This philosophy belongs to the worn-out world of nations conquering other nations, when might indicated right. It drowned out the question needing to be asked before creating any future plans: *does it work toward the highest good of everyone involved?* Here at the crossroads of America's directions, we are learning that it does not just take a president to bring change. In the future it will be all or none of us.

The Old Woman's teachings are about bonding with Earth, Moon, Sun, and humankind, about changing Perceptions and opening up Perspectives. Another way of putting it is that the teachings are about tuning in to the dance of your soul and spirit so that your whole being can be united with itself and the soul of humanity. Constant personal growth leads to expanded consciousness and expectations

---

1   *The Masks of God: Primitive Mythology,* p. 149, by Joseph Campbell

of wider viewpoints about what could be the final world drama that is unfolding as we write. This book is about that personal growth, begun by the Ancestors, because better world leaders with better behaviors can only come from raising the consciousness levels of the collective masses from whose ranks they come. If you are one of the many, you are potentially more powerful than you think. Follow the Moon from where you are now, and become a part of the still-invisible change that is pushing all the envelopes out there to bursting. You can do this without ever stepping outside of your house, if necessary, though you might want to look out your window at the Moon.

That said, we often wonder who we are that we created such a departure from the original image. Robert Bly tells us something about that. It is where we begin this journey.

> The drama is this. We came as infants "trailing the clouds of glory" arriving from the farthest reaches of the universe, bringing with us appetites well preserved from our mammal inheritance, spontaneities wonderfully preserved from our 150,000 years of tree life, angers well preserved from our 5,000 years of tribal life—in short with our 360 degree radiance— and we offered this gift to our parents. They didn't want it. They wanted a nice girl or a nice boy. That's the first act of the drama.
> — Robert Bly, *A Little Book on the Human Shadow*
> [see Bib.]

This is the point in our evolution where we think the Moon work takes up an earlier thread. If we all continue on the same old path, evolution is slowed down by the inertia of the past, and very little changes. If we pick up the thread from the original ancestors, we can be a new kind of person, one that is not born of the complete line of ancestors, but of the "first ancestors." As we write about our Ancestral connections, always remember that we are looking at the original, fresh, universe of the beginnings, before the dark ways came onto the scene.

Introduction
Welcome to a Personal Universe

You are the Link between Heaven and Earth,
You Hold the Golden Thread from the First Ancestors
Who Forged the Link

A sacred praise I am making
A sacred praise I am making
My nation, behold it in kindness!
The day of the sun has been my strength.
The path of the moon shall be my robe.
A sacred praise I am making.
A sacred praise I am making.
—Wachpanne, Heyoka Ceremony
from *Black Elk Speaks* [1]

The Stone Age peoples anchored this link over 30,000 years ago at the most conservative estimate. Native Americans, North and South, maintained it, along with the early shamanic cultures of the planet, a few of whom have remained relatively untouched as a reminder.. We need to call on their wisdom, and realize what they are trying to tell us about it right now, in the face of the fact that we have so carefully ignored the real value of their presence among us. Their presence is a reminder of the inherent connectedness between all people and the triad of Sun, Moon, and Earth, together a divine foursome. Their wisdom is the honoring of all of nature and the gift of Sun and Moon without which we would not exist. Honoring does not mean to worship, but to give equal respect to all four, to make a "sacred praise" to them, in whatever we are doing. To do that, we must give up our arrogant assumption that we are superior to Earth and its indigenous peoples, and replace it with respect and recognition. That is all.

Our ancestors maintained a working connection between heaven and earth through a spiritual technology that had kept them and their universe in balance for thousands of years. This system was

---

[1]   *Black Elk Speaks:* as told through John G. Neihardt *(Flaming Rainbow)* by Nicholas Black Elk. U. of Nebraska Press, 2000

taught to them by the natural role model that existed within the world they knew. They learned about time, space, writing, numbers, relationship, life, death, the renewal of life, and divination, from the Moon and its changing dance with Earth and Sun. This relationship modeled a spiritual path—in later, historic, times known as "The Moon Path", or more recently the path of evolution, one that seems to be caught on a stubborn snag.

The Moon path went underground about five thousand years ago, when we began our submersion in violence and death. The aggressive, greedy, arrogant, controlling spirit that had appeared on what we believe to have been a predominantly peaceful planet has now brought us to a critical crossing. This tells many of us that we will live or die according to our willingness to change. Just one person making a step up in consciousness, and adding his/her peaceful feminine Moon energy to the collective consciousness, can make a difference—because, on this path, we will be joining our peaceable energies to the energies of the Moon herself as she sends her eight scheduled "broadcasts" to humanity every 29 days. Imagine if a whole planet reached for the Moon!

This is about the evolution of human consciousness, which does not have time to wait for human nature alone—we need help. This time, in 2009, we know what is happening to us, and that we are responsible for our future. But until you have actually touched the Moon you can't imagine what that can change. That connection will become your most precious possession. To wear the robe of the Moon will set you upon the real path, the one of respect, clear thought, the power of your own core selfhood, and of compassion. It will fill you with the strength of the Sun.

The ancestors' technology is still here— the system which taught them numbers, writing, and time. It had a message so universal and so timeless, that its relevance is unchanging. Are the ancestors ready to reconnect us to Earth and sky, show us the secrets of self-transformation, and reintroduce us to our birthright—the Personal Universe? Are we ready?

We, who are also now two old women, found the Moon on the paths of our youth, before we ever met, and in a lifetime have validated the beauty, integrity, reliability, and spiritual power of the Moon's teachings.

SHE—*The Old Woman Who Never Dies*[2]—is waiting to pick up the shuttle and weave her golden thread again, for you. Her path has re-emerged out of the mists of millennia, in a new and unified form perfectly suited to our "modern" times. She does not bring a religion or a substitute for one or anything else—hers is a path in its own right, but replacing no other.

Read the first chapter right now to learn the four basic steps on the Moon Path, and make your own connection to the Moon. We don't need mystics or gurus or occultists waiting in the wings to "pass the power to us"—Moon belongs to everyone. All she requires is your intent and reaching up. Friends, she is real, she's mystical, personal, and yet so very, very grounding.

If you are curious, please read the whole book and find the deep wisdom of the *Old Woman Who Never Dies*. Learn about the *Gift of Tomorrow Today*, the *Seeds of the Moonflower*, and many never published teachings of our ancestral Moon. We think you, too, will reach up or you wouldn't be here.

—Virginia and Judy

---

2   Many cultures of early times called the Moon "*Old Woman Who Never Dies*", and she is still called by that name in the Navaho culture, as well as other cultures around the world.

Secrets of the
Old Woman Who Never Dies

Part I
The Power of Dark and Light

The Sun is the archetype of cosmic Being. The Moon is the
archetype of cosmic Becoming.
—Adapted from *The Sacred and the Profane,*
by Mircea Eliade

Once every 29 days at the last and darkest day of the Lunar
month we have the opportunity to lose ourselves in the light, to
put ourselves in resonance with, and accept renewal from, the
universe— from the Field of All Possibilities. In the pit of darkness at
the Old Moon, where we can only *Be*, lies our greatest power— to
rise again and *Become* even more.

At the mid-point of the Lunar month we have the opportunity
to become light itself, to align *spirit* and *soul,* to bring together two
opposites within ourselves or in our external world. We can *Become*
in the midst of *Being*, with the total light of the Full Moon.

What is this dark and light, and why is the dark as important as
the light? Where is it in us? What is its secret?

1

1
Look! The Moon is Dancing with the Sun
The Moon Phases as Markers of Growing Consciousness

To seek an understanding of ancient astronomy is to encounter deep wellspring sof religion, life-energizing forces of sex and eroticism, and frequently, cosmic aspects of games and sports.
— David H. Kelly, *Exploring Ancient Skies*[1]

How We Learned the Old Woman's Secrets

When Judy and I began seriously to follow and record our experiences of the Moon Cycles, we initially worked with the four phases only, although we were familiar with the eight phases. While we were investigating the history and pre-history of the Moon cycles we realized how basic the four phases were, and that the ancients initially did not use eight phases either. The recorded recognition of the original four is linked to the late Paleolithic (30,000-10,000 BCE,) while the eight-fold set appeared after writing, numbers, time and astronomy were established[2]. The roots of what we are now as humans are in the prehistoric past. Far back in the Paleolithic, our roots were being lived out within belief systems based on the fourfold structures of seasons, directions, and the Moon cycles, as the beginnings of Lunar calendars. This was exciting, because we came to feel truly connected to our ancestors all the way back to the

---

1   *Exploring Ancient Skies* by David H. Kelly
2   The first historical record of of eight Moon phases is a link to the Ogdoad or eight early Egyption Moon gods in 2700 BCE traced directly from there to the corresponding meanings of the eight moon phases in Hellenistic astrology circa 3-500 BCE. After that, we only find records of the eight phases coded into other systems of thought and divination, until the middle ages. We stress here that chess is one of those. This might be understood as the result of efforts to erase from the mind of the collective all pagan ideas.

Lascaux caves, where consciousness was already more sophisticated than we ever reamed.

It was not until we were halfway through this record of our journey that we realized almost simultaneously, in a moment of serendipity, that we had found in the Lunar cycle the very archetype of evolving consciousness itself! The history of consciousness as we know it, stimulated by Moon energies, turned out to be a natural, universal structure of evolving consciousness. Instead of a linear story, it is a dynamic pattern simultaneously within every human being and the bowl of the sky—a major living archetype—that at every time in history has been stimulating new possibilities for evolution. We did not invent the system or spiritual path we were writing about—*it* seemed to be inventing *us*. In chapter 10 we discuss this structure in detail.

Why is the Number Four So Important?

From here to the section on "The What, How, Where, Why?" questions, we ask you to bear with us as we lay the science and math groundwork for the Moon Phases; they have created the interpretations and meanings of Moon Magic, divination, and aspects of consciousness from the beginning, whenever that was. Your own ability to align yourself with the Moon cycles will be more complete. After all, we will tell you nothing you did not learn in Middle School, but promptly forgot if you don't like math and science. We ourselves did the same, but confronted with the magic of math when applied to consciousness and our relationship to the Sun, earth, and Moon, it suddenly became the unravelling of mysteries.

Four is the basic pattern of the Moon cycles, and the symbolic meaning of manifestation in the three-D world. If you draw a circle with an equal-armed cross in it, you will have the pattern of every Moon cycle. We begin with the basic four phases with which we initially began writing the book. The second half of the book contains the eight phases in entirety. For a more complete visual picture see our fanciful version in Diagram 1 which shows all eight phases, with short labels for the meaning of each phase. We marked the basic four so they are easy to see. We will be calling them either the *quarterly*, or the *dynamic four* phases, while we call the other four *transitional* phases.

Our Paleolithic ancestors probably initially recognized only four phases because those are the most easily recognized shapes of the Earth's shadow on the Moon. It was much later when people divided the four into the eight. The eight phases will be explored in detail in Chapters 11 and 13-21. This four-eight-phase cycle lasts 29½ days, with about 7 days between each of the four phases, and about 3½ days between each of eight phases. The 9th phase in the diagram represents the eternal return to New Moon. This eternal return was the visual evidence that led early cultures to a worldwide belief in life beyond death. The The ancient ones identified their lives with the Moon at their deepest levels: because the Moon

died and was reborn so did they. We believe the Moon is the external archetype of the soul, so such identification with Moon's patterns may be the most significant understanding of the immense influence the Moon had on early cultures.

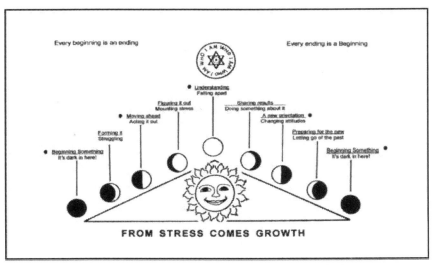

Diagram I. Eight-Phase SoLunar Cycle with the
Original Four Phases Marked by Black Dots.

When you are ready, you can use the diagram in ways that will improve your choices, reduce your stress, and increase your consciousness. It is a conscious process which includes self-observation, combined with observation of the Moon's progress through her phases each month. As you work with the phases consciously, a strange and wonderful thing will be happening to you underneath—you will be bonding to Earth, Moon and Sun in a way most of us didn't as children. Joseph Chilton Pearce tells us in his book *The Magical Child* that at age seven we bond with the Earth, but we have in our many years seen less and less of this happening. Without that bonding, Earth cannot be saved.

With earliest man living in nature day and night, this process had been operating all along at the unconscious level, as they began making it conscious through ritual. The phases of the cycle are created by the dance of the Moon with the Sun. The shadows on the Moon are made by the Earth, but only humans can give the shadows meaning. This dance between *She who never dies* with *He who made all things* can sweep us up into its rhythms and give our lives resonance with the universe. Let's look at the meanings of the Sun and Moon in terms of their relationship to us.

> The Sun represents one's consciousness as a purposeful intelligent individual with the ability to initiate action and make choices.
>   and
> The Moon represents one's reactions and responses to spirit-Sun's direction, and events outside and inside the self as an emotional, caring individual.

Together, they also represent our spirit and soul as spirit-*Being* (Sun) and soul-*Becoming* (Moon). Our connection to the Sun and Moon can become more conscious as we resonate at deep levels to their energies and dance their dance with them. You can even learn to feel the energy changes of the phases. The excitement of discovering the sensation of energy flow and change in one's daily life within the cycle of the Moon to the Sun must be experienced to believe it, though science already knows it.

The Moon and Our DNA

Before we go further, we want to introduce a radical new concept, concerning the effects of this cycle. Science provides information about the elctromagnetics of our Solar system which Science believes can affect all living beings. The information is not new, but until recently scientists primarily have applied it to the moon's phases. It validates what we have always believed about the concept of Sun, Moon and planets having some kind of effect on Earth and vice versa. The Moon path is a true spiritual path on its own, but we, like many others, delight in finding substantial "proofs" of that. We are surprised others have not put the information together. Here is how it works.

All planetary bodies emit electromagnetic frequencies, dependant upon their speed. As the Moon and planets orbit around the Sun their frequencies are measurable here on earth but are too far below the auditory range to be heard. If the individual planetary/Lunar frequencies are multiplied about twenty times, they move into the auditory range. Our first scientific awareness of this fact was in learning that the increased frequencies are found to affect the acupuncture meridians. Tuning forks set to the enhanced frequencies are being used to experiment with the concept. Of course, if there is an effect effect from increasing an inaudible frequency into the audible range, then there may also be effects from the inaudible ones as well, at less obvious levels.. We and others are exploring this interesting possibility. One personal proof of the actual subtle human response is that some of us are able to recognize the times when the moon first enters a phase, and recognize its "feeling". Whole months go by when we have temporarily forgotten to check the phases and we will suddenly be aware of what phase we are in. Given that kind of experience, and the science background, what else have we found in connection with Moon phases?

We now know that something called the epigenetic shield around our DNA registers every personal and environmental stimulus to the body, emotions and sensory systems, and probably other systems outside conscious awareness. The planetary and Lunar frequencies are almost certain to affect us at the DNA level, just as a mother's thoughts and feelings are known to affect the baby in utero, including its DNA, since all impressions are received by and sent from the shield directly to the DNA. New brain research at the Heart Math Institute lets us know just how incredibly sensitive our epigenetic shields are and how much more readily we can change than any of us thought until recently.[3] And just imagine—DNA is made up of millions of groups of four proteins in different combinations! Four is basic to DNA and the basis of our individuality as human beings, even if we cannot yet "read" it completely.

All humans and living beings are affected by the Lunar phases, as are clams and crops. At least, we are all affected at the unconscious level. People who are not especially sensitive to changes in energies probably only register them unconsciously. This is why we believe the Moon phases have always had an effect on all living things on the planet. For early humans and/or humanoid beings, their process was probably an initially unconscious urging toward increased

---

3   *The Biology of Transcendence* by Joseph Chilton Pierce

consciousness slowly over eons of time. At least by the early or mid-Neolithic—through visual information along with the subtle urgings of the Moon—the idea of ritual at New and Full Moons arose to increase the awareness. To us, it is an exciting promise that we can do it faster and more effectively if we know what we are doing. That is what the Ancients did, and as a result, writing, measurement of time, and mathematics appeared and developed far faster than historians feel they can account for it. We know from our own experience that our consciousness level has changed more rapidly than we can otherwise account for since we have been intentionally working with the patterns of the phases.

The Mechanics of How the Phases Operate

The four basic Moon phases, and the four annual Solar seasons, are the primary "fours" found in the earliest patterns recorded by man. They continue in subtle ways to provide the model and timing for our own manifestation in the Earth dimension. The Moon's phases taught early people how to count, write, and measure time, the most basic fundamentals underlying modern civilization. The exercise below captures the elements of the Lunar cycle as we have come to know them in modern times. Our desire is to recapture the awareness of the subtle energies so that we can evolve at all levels.

If you draw a circle and put an equal-armed cross inside it, you can see the Moon's cycle as a circle divided into four equal segments. Imagine the Moon moving around this circle in time, every 7 days crossing one of the points of the square within the circle or orbit.

So now, we can represent the Moon's orbit as a circle with an equal-armed cross within it, a common symbol found world-wide in early drawings, representing elements both of the Lunar cycle and four Solar seasons. Referring to the ritual patterns behind the symbol (described in Chapter 6), a shamanic cosmology arose within it, evoking reverence toward our planet and its spiritual guardians. These elements were recognized as ultimately guiding or mirroring the path of the ancestors' daily life and their need to be in harmony with nature. As such they were also used as protective designs on objects or walls.

The cross's touch-points also create a square within the circle. The square models the dynamics of the four basic or critical Moon phases. The Moon's orbit, or any circle, always contains 360 degrees. Tracing with your finger around the circle counter-clockwise shows how the Moon moves through four segments of the circle to create the four phases—a square with 90 degrees on each side. This square demonstrates a 90-degree angle at each of its corners. As you can see, a right angle of 90 degrees is required to respond to the change of direction at each one-quarter turn of 90 linear degrees of the square within the circle. Tracing the Moon's path with your finger will hopefully clarify what we are writing about. This is "Moon Phases 101." If you do this now, much of what comes later will be more clear.

We remind the reader what we all learned somewhere in probably the 9th grade--that the angles of any square are always 90 degrees. When we draw the square from the intersecting points of the cross to each other we call the square's points on the circle of the Moon's orbit "the angles" of the square. We see this configuration every time we approach a city intersection. We suggest you write "90" near each point. Then draw a dotted line from each arm of the cross to the next one. Write "90" on each line. We call the distance between the cross lines "90" and we call the distance on the circle between the points where the cross arms intersect the circle "90" as well. In both cases the measurements are in degrees. This means they represent a concept of relationship rather than actual distance. Whether the total figure is smaller or bigger, the relationships are the same.

Now we can see just why astrologers tell us that "squares" are hard and they make us work and struggle, which does not mean we have bad luck. They are just part of the rules of the universe and the 3rd dimension we happen to be living in. Since the four phases all begin on the hard 90 degree angles of the symbolic 360 degree diagram, they express tension in moving from one phase to another, requiring effort or struggle, and those positions are therefore in astrology called "squares". When driving down the street, it takes more effort (energy) to make a right or left turn than to continue straight ahead or at a broader angle, because one literally has to stop the forward movement in order to turn at the right angle. Violating that traffic law is called a "California stop". Such angular movements stand out, move fast, push, frustrate, and can get us into trouble if we don't honor that right turn. If we are willing to work at our lives, "squares" are not problems but more like solving puzzles. Exercising brains or bodies increases their strength and abilities. In a fundamental sense the struggles of squares refer to *Manifestation* and the need for energy to make that happen. We and this earth did not appear here out of some deep sleep; billions and billions of mega-tons of energy got us here.

At the beginning of any phase (except New), the Sun and Moon will each be in different signs of the Zodiac and positions on the circle. The Sun and Moon, at the four quarters, always are either 90 or 180 degrees apart, thus relaying that effort theme, each time in a different way. The two quarter-moons of 90 degree aspects, as we call these relationships, generate more pressured action than the Full Moon 180 degree double-90 aspect, called an opposition. This is where the Moon is exactly opposite the Sun at Full Moon. Rather than *pressuring* us to act, this positions tends to *pull* us apart so we can see both sides of an issue clearly in order to make a decision between the two; or it helps us see them in alignment within a larger context, leading to revelations or enlightenments about life at that moment. If you think about it, you can see that these *squares*, called *aspects*, imply *changing relationships*, about which more will be said later.

The reader may want to be aware, as well, of the interrelationship of the Moon's and Sun's related timing. The Moon takes a little over 27 days to complete a full orbit around the Earth through the 12 signs. The Sun takes 29½ days to transit (traverse) and complete the 30 degrees of one sign and enter the next. Meanwhile the Moon must finish the last 2 ½ days by covering one more sign to catch up with the Sun. So the transiting Moon covers 13 signs in order to begin in sync with the Sun after exactly29 days and a few hours.

In the Sun's fourfold annual journey, the fourfold pattern is similar. to the Moon's phases. In its annual journey around the Earth, through the twelve signs of the Zodiac, it encounters four turning points, called solstices and equinoxes. These turning points divide the year exactly into four seasons and we mark our calendars with the dates. The meanings of these seasonal markers will be discussed elsewhere, as an inter-weaving between them and the 13 Lunar cycles.

[We forgot to remind you that in the looking-glass world of Moon phases everything is WYSIWYG or what you see is what you get. In the SoLunar world the Sun orbits the Earth as does the Moon.]

We have now established that the Moon's observable dance with the Sun can be diagrammed as a circle with an equal-armed cross in it. For now, keep the thought that the four quadrants of the circle each equal 90 degrees while the circle represents the Moon's orbit, with Earth in the center of the circle. These 90 degree points represent the quarters of the Moon—the basic four-phase Moon path. At each 90 degree angle, Sun and Moon are in exact 90- or

180-degree relationship with each other, creating powerful spiritual energies conducive to human action and manifestation.

Western metaphysical teachings and Greek philosophy tell us that the square and cube represent manifestation in our 3-D world. This means that we produce in that context a *manifestation* of what our life is about at that moment. That energy spurs us on, either subliminally or consciously. If we are aware of this as a fact, even if we do not consciously feel it, we are in a position to make conscious decisions that help us manifest our lives more effectively. There is also the possibility that many will resist the energy behind negatively perceived effects, which converts those energies into conflict.

Of human interest to the modern reader is a discovery by researcher Rhoda Kellogg (*Analyzing Children's Art.* (See Bibliography) that the image of the cross in the circle is one of the most common figures drawn spontaneously by young children (about 3-4 years old) in cultures all over the world. She also found it in abundance in early and later cave art, which paleontologists associate with rituals held at annual Solar and Lunar cycles. Its deeper relevance to the present subject is a mystery, but it does indicate the archetypal nature of the figure, which we know often represented aspects of ritual done in later times at New and Full Moons, as well as seasonal celebrations. One possibility is that an earlier recognition of the "fours" in nature had become so embedded in the human physical experience from the beginning that it had always been in the human DNA as an archetype[4]. Some controversial pre-historic researchers believe that young children reflect the evolutionary level of so-called primitive peoples and therefore draw symbols common to them.

Here is a good place to add that we believe with many physicists, that everything and everyone in our universe affects everything else. We know the Moon contacts every body in the Solar system through these same angular type aspects, as does the Sun, and leaves its messages in all the planets' mailboxes. We look at our participation as amplifying or mirroring whatever Moon puts out to Earth.

---

4   DNA is made up of groups of four proteins, endlessly repeating the components in different combinations representing characteristics of the individual like brown hair, and everything that makes us humans as well as animals, with which we share most of our DNA. The Moon has been described as moving among multiples of entities, like connecting with the planets, including Earth, through relationships called conjunctions where they pick up information and leave "moon messages". As we grow each month, why might we not broadcast our consciousness to others?

What, How, Where, Why?

These are four basic questions that might occur to a contemporary person watching the Moon for a month, and hopefully give a glimpse of the legacy early shamanism left us. We apologize to the reader who knows about the phases, if we repeat ourselves, here and throughout the book, but we have found that understanding the phases is not always easy for newcomers. Also the geometrics of the phases, as in the paragraphs above, contain symbolisms that must be incorporated into our understanding of the phases. So we want to show how these four phases can be distinguished in the context of our own familiar dimension. They are already familiar to anyone who has ever fished or had a fisherman in the family, and to farmers all over the world. They are also familiar to women everywhere who get their hair cut according to the phase of the Moon. However, to those people, the reality and familiarity has not gone beyond the tides and the growth supporting moments of hair-cutting and planting seasons.

Now for some more geometry. The cycle or "circle" of four basic Moon phases all activate on the "angles" of that circle where the arms of the cross intersect the circle. With the circle representing the Moon's monthly orbit of Earth, the 90 degree points become the "manifestation points". Connecting these points to each other, creates the square inside the circle. The points where they touch the circle's circumference are visual metaphors for "turning points" as visual angles in the month—New, First Quarter, Full, Last Quarter. In terms of *action,* the four points are critical to the creation or co-creation of our lives. Each indicates the critical, turning-point energy of one of the four components of manifestation. These are the basic mundane cyclic energies in physical reality. The type of action at each point is unique, and each one offers us a symbolic right-turn when the Moon crosses a point. The Moon does not cause us to take these actions—its orbital interaction with Earth's orbit in relation to the Sun produces measurable energies that encourage us to take the actions. The kinds of actions are our choice.

1. Energy-*initiating* (New Moon—day one of the cycle)
2. Energy-*forming* (First Quarter—day seven)
3. Energy-*relating* (Full Moon—day fourteen)
4. Energy-*evaluating*. (Last Quarter—day twenty-one)

The four points or energies are a primary formula for the process of unfoldment or manifestation in our physical world. These points also ask for us the four basic questions about our specific and personal actions in a cycle, beginning at New Moon.[5] We will show you how to find them, on the centerfold dial, in your own life, along with new and different meanings each month. Later on, you will see how the meanings of these phase-points parallel the meanings of the four stages of ritual and other "fours" we mention later in this book. The four questions are:

1. *Initiating*—WHAT?—New Moon
2. *Forming*—HOW?—1st Quarter Moon
3. *Relating*—TO WHOM OR TO WHAT?—Full Moon
4. *Evaluating*—WHY?—3rd Quarter Moon

Whoever you are, you are "in these phases in your own life." From the moment the Moon crosses the initial point of any phase, you are "in it" which means it is now a subjective experience which wants to be objectively defined. Unconsciously, at these points you start actively answering the questions by living them. If you looked at the Moon or checked the weather pages of newspaper or website, and asked yourself the first question a day or two after the New Moon, you might have caught a glimpse of the "project" you will be working with for the Lunar month.

With a few simple tools, like the dial in the centerfold of this book, you can also know ahead of time the four different areas of your life that will be receiving the energies of all the above four kinds of activity. However, for that you also need to know what Zodiac signs the Sun and Moon will be in, at the beginning of each phase. All of that and much more you will find in the tools in chapters 7-10. Those chapters contain all the techniques you will need to do an in-depth, detailed "reading" for yourself for a month, and get different information for all the months of your life. You can start to use those chapters now, if you like, but don't go away—you might miss something very interesting between here and there. The chapters in between contain depths of knowledge and understanding of the Moon phases not to be found anywhere else in print. Chapters between here and there also contain important

---

5   The four questions as applied to the four quarters of the Moon cycle, were originally used by Dane Rudhyar in his *The Lunation Cycle* This little book re-opened the ancient discussion of the importance of the Moon's cycles in the West. Without this initiation, the present book would not have been written, nor could it have been received.

information you need to understand yourself, your consciousness, and your relationship to humanity—information intimately involved in active work with the Moon cycles Here are some topics you can expect to find in chapters 2-6

> What consciousness is and how it evolves
> The functions of the conscious mind
> The personal unconscious and the collective unconscious
> The archetypes, what they are and how they affect you.
> How all the above create a foundation for self-understanding,
>   and for personal and   planetary evolution

Answering the Questions without the Tools

We wrote this chapter purposely in such a way that anyone reading this stand-alone chapter could immediately begin working with the monthly Lunar energies. So even if you do not have this book, you can intentionally be putting yourself in harmony with the interlocked energies of Sun, Moon, and Earth.

Without further chapters, we can recognize the four energies at work in our lives just by knowing when they begin a new cycle, and counting the days. We know only what is implied by the new impulse, but it is like a seed that has suddenly germinated and wants to grow. Our first thought is *What is beginning?* At that point the creation is begun, and the outcome is set, but still as a divination so to speak. Half-way through this phase (3½ days), the initial intent begins to take form.

At day seven our next question is *How can I complete this impulse?* In the coming seven days of this phase, we must figure out how, and use our technique for bringing about the completion. In linear time this is the *How of it* that develops during the First Quarter Moon and with which we are meant to struggle and use our own creativity as part of our growth. This is meant to be a joyful struggle, like climbing a mountain, or painting a picture, but not everything you are used to doing seems to work. This is the most important time in the cycle to take individual action, if we are to reach the fulfillment of our seed-intent. It must come at least in part from our own creative being, and not automatically from past patterns we have been taught.

At day fourteen, we arrive at the light of the Full Moon, and we can "see" from outside ourselves what we have created. This is the answer to *Whereto is the New Moon impulse leading?* The full light on the Moon symbolizes insight or illumination of perspective concerning the fulfillment of the New Moon's intent. We need to be clear that whatever we have created can be mental, emotional or spiritual, as well as physical.

At day twenty-one, the 3rd Quarter, we want to explore *What* was the value of this cycle? Value is evaluation of its meaning, the price I paid, why I needed to experience this, and what I learned from it? Should we call it cosmic de-briefing?

Therefore, without any tools we can view our month phase by phase, just by watching the newspaper weather pages or the sky, and consciously living these four steps of changing energies.

Seeing the Phases in the Sky

The visual images you see in Diagram. 1 are symbols of what is happening in the sky Note the waxing moon has the light on its right side and is proactive, moving out instinctually, intuitively or impulsively in a new direction toward fulfillment or completion. The waning Moon has the light on its left side with its energy increasingly inward—moving toward creating meaning of the month's events, integrating the experiences, dispersing the wisdom to others. Above all, it is transforming external light into internal light-the product of transformation.

> New Moon is all dark—creative silence. For some that could be creative chaos for three days. The energy is there, but it is not yet organized around a focus.
> First Quarter is half light, half dark—new ways versus old ways.
> Full Moon is all light—culmination of manifestation, conscious enlightenment, personal growth. Last Quarter Moon, half light, half dark—new values versus old values, and finally letting go of something old.

Later, there will be tools that describe every month in detail, either as you live it or ahead of time for the curious. In the chapters on technique you will learn about imagery and descriptive words that you can apply to your own life—words of divination from ancient sources of collective wisdom; information about the areas of your life that are involved; and information about the most fruitful ways to handle the issues, situations, and emotions involved.

For now, hold that thought and begin looking at the Moon outside to see the increasing light on her right face from New to Full Moon, and the decreasing light on her left face from Full Moon to New Moon. Actually looking at the Moon for a few moments may increase your sense of connection. At each phase point ask yourself the questions, and to some extent you can answer them yourself, as you manifest the answers. It does take some practice, and not all months are as clearly read as some.

1. New Moon: WHAT is my seed-intent primarily about?
2. First Quarter Moon: HOW can I best fulfill it? (manifest it)
3. Full Moon: WHERE is it leading? (to what goal or fulfillment?)
4. Last Quarter Moon: WHY was it of value? Why did I do it? What did I learn from that experience and why is it valuable to me?

Remember that ultimately our own lives give us the answers, anyway. For example, a teacher says after Full Moon, "I had this problem with a student. Then at the Full Moon, the answer just came to me and I tried it and it worked!" (true story).Since we do live the pattern in its natural order, asking each successive question on the first day of each phase during a signs month helps us to be more conscious of our actions; and knowing the unique basic outline of a given month ahead of time, helps us to unfold our intentions more consciously and effectively. At this point, without further tools, you are not working with all the phase-energies, but you are becoming more conscious of what you are doing in relation to them.

We offer the ancestors' wisdom that these phases mark appropriate times to plan details of our personal and group lives and rituals. They are what the ancients would call "propitious" times to explore divination about specific phases as a way of connecting heaven and earth. We can all be shamans, now, if we are willing to be. We need, even more at this time in history, to be, like the shamans, connectors between the Divine and the human. "If not I, who? If not now, when?"

This potential can manifest regardless of your preference of personal spirituality. It does not replace your choice of religion or its repudiation, or your own free will. It merely times your experiences of being part of a purposeful universe, and helps to define the nature of the situation at the right time. The Moon cycle is your tiny wrist watch fractal of the cosmic cycles of the universe.

How to Use the Spirit/Soul/Personality Diagram

Meanwhile, what are the parts of ourselves doing during the four phases? How do our parts—ego-personality (conscious self), soul (Moon), spirit (Sun) interrelate at each phase? Diagram 2 gives the visual image of a Western Metaphysical viewpoint. It shows the dynamics of the three elements of the Moon path—Moon (soul), Sun (spirit), and Earth/ego (Personality.) This diagram does not correlate literally with an astrology chart, and is meant to be viewed as a philosophical statement and experienced first hand. Personality is here defined as the conscious self, and as a personal aspect of the Moon, while Soul is a more subtle part of the Moon all of which will be explored later.

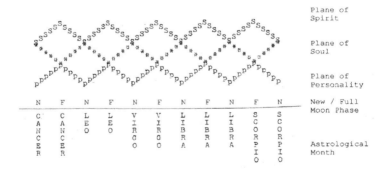

The above diagram is an illustration of the monthly cycle of the spirit, soul, and personality activity in relationship to the New and Full moon cycles.
Notice that at New Moon the personality is on its own plane while soul has risen to commune with spirit. Likewise, at Full Moon soul descends and personality rises for their communion. It appears that the New Moon is a period which is best "sensed" or "felt" by those who are to some degree soul-infused in order to be receptive to the energies of the spirit, which are even more subtle.
Basic Moon Phase practice will open anyone's consciousness of these energies with time.

Diagram II. Spirit/Soul/Personality

Spirit/Soul/Personality through the Phases

We leave it to the reader to contemplate diagram 2. If it resonates, use it, but it is not necessary to the understanding of the phases. We personally find that it helps us to understand why we feel somewhat distant from our inner selves at New Moon, and more emotional than usual at Full Moon. The parts of ourselves, in Diagram 2, represented by the Sun (spirit), Moon (soul), and Personality, all of which play several roles in our make-up, will be discussed in detail later.

While Sun and Moon refer to spirit and soul. Personality refers to how we function, and how people see us, as described by our behaviors, emotional expressions, and communications. It is the "me" that experiences the movements of spirit and soul. The diagram shows how these parts operate on the esoteric or spiritual level, moving from New to Full Moon, with the First and Last Quarters indicated where the diagonals intersect in between New and Full. The paths of these three parts are marked by the letters S for soul (Moon), P for personality, and * for spirit (Sun). New Moon is designated by N; Full Moon is designated by F. As shown by the signs written vertically below, the Moon cycles through about a sign a month, but every so often it slips behind and has two New or Full Moons in a month. The activity described by this diagram is primarily outside of normal conscious awareness. The reason we like the diagram so much is that conscious intention to accept that the activity is happening, tends to help us over time to actually become aware of the more subtle energies. This ability, too, is part of the goal of evolution.

The four phase-points imply strong changes in the type of energies needed and experienced. Without realizing it, we gather or focus our energies at the end of each phase, and release them at the beginning of the next, though this energy change is most noticeable at the end of the 3rd Quarter and the beginning of the New. The nature of the phases is clearly defined here, but real life is seldom clearly defined—our personal experiences of the phases are often subtle versions of the foregoing. At other times we may only see their negative energies and respond with our own negatives, creating unnecessary resistance and struggle. We also don't make major decisions every month, or create on a monthly schedule.

Neither does a Moon cycle always begin at the beginning of a sign. A Lunar month is a continuation of all our previous ones, on different levels, sometimes beginning in the same sign as the last, which this diagram clarifies if questions arise. You can learn to see in this structure the subtleness of life, and through that, the importance of the small. You can see the Moon's phases moving through all the areas of your life in about a year's time, highlighting one area after another.

For now, consider how much information these four phases offer you, without going any further. Unless you live in a coastal area, you are likely to see the Moon often in the night sky, and sometimes in the day. However, nearly every daily newspaper lists the quarters of the Moon along with sunset and sunrise, tides and weather. At the end of chapter 2, we list several books and other items that you will need to fully follow the phases. One of them is an appointment book that lists the Moon phases for the year. If you are planning on doing the "big gulp" reading of this book, get them now before you tackle Chapters 8-12.

Below we offer an example of how one cycle might work out. You may be able to apply the principles you see in it to whatever your own cycle might be about.

An Example of One Cycle

Four to five days after the last quarter Moon, go out for several nights, before dawn, and look up; and when you have noticed the waning moon has disappeared from the sky, you will know that within 24 to 36 hours the Moon will meet the rising Sun, lost in its light. About one day after New Moon, the tiniest fingernail sliver will appear, called "first light". It indicates that you can begin to get a sense about the "something" that is new. For example let's say you realized in the previous cycle that you needed to do a complete housecleaning because you are a "terrible housekeeper". That need may show up at the New Moon. Keep watching, and during the week from New to 1st Quarter, that New Moon intent will have taken form as you impulsively manifest that urge.

At First Quarter (half light, half dark) be prepared to observe what social, parental, or other barriers suddenly arise to confront or delay your activity—dentist appointments, casual company, long telephone calls, a broken washer, a flood... Don't worry—you are supposed to struggle at this point, in order to have strong spiritual muscles at the Full Moon. Get rid of any false beliefs, your own, or others', that frustrate your plans. Move ahead with all speed and direction. You might discover that your mother's methods don't work for you and you have some better ideas.

At Full Moon consider how your activity, now well-defined and partially or fully completed can be of value to others. Even if your New Moon intent was "only" to do spring cleaning, what is a clean house in nice order for if not to share it with company? You decide to invite company for dinner and realize that

you have been missing the social contacts because you felt ashamed of your house—the Full Moon "enlightenment".

Last Quarter Moon, again half light, half dark, is very complex.

A number of scenarios could present themselves. Take one example only, here, that of the thorough house cleaning. Having enjoyed fulfilling feedback on your lovely house and dinner, you could conclude that your lifelong habit of leaving the dirt to pile up for 6 months at a time is not really how you want to live. You realize that you only do that because your mother did the same. You intentionally let go of that habit and that value and go through your house lightly once more, picking up and straightening to practice your new way of keeping house, promising yourself you will continue to keep it in good order. Then you turn away from this month's activity toward what may be coming next. The key to this stage of the month is to mentally "make an offering" of your month's experience, as part of your foundation as a social being. Perhaps in this example, you invite a group to meet regularly in your house. Follow that by considering your present needs that have arisen out of the month's activity, and the desire to attract some answers to them in the next new phase. In some sense you are changing—consider what that might mean. You may have to deal with some unfamiliar situations. Some examples of needs or as yet unsolved problems that could have arisen out of this month's activities in relation to the group are (a) someone you don't get along with will be coming to the group, (b) you have dogs who bark incessantly when you have company (c). Several hours a week of preparation are needed for the host/hostess to prepare for this group. Where will you find that extra time? You will not need to look far at any Last Quarter Moon for future needs.

You can see and know this in your life every month without reading further in this book, without buying anything, without knowing the first thing about astrology. The Moon is out there, you are busy living your life, and you can simply step outside, check the Moon's light-dark balance, and ask yourself, "Am I moving in harmony with the energies I see in the sky?" If you spend a few minutes four times a month observing how your life just naturally flows into these four foci of energies you are "in the flow" and doing what you are supposed to be doing.

We invite you, if you drive, to watch the different kinds of behaviors you see on the road throughout the four phases. They say laughter is healing—this part of your practice is healing for sure. Later as we put the Zodiac signs together with the phases, the commuter behaviors become even more interesting! Health food stores also provide great information about phases and signs, if you ask questions about how their customers behave during any given phase. We are meant to find satisfaction and joy in our lives and to learn to play with our experiences. You may even laugh at yourself. Life is so serious sometimes that we don't accept the lighter side, but playing with the phases helps us to stand outside ourselves and realize "it's not always about me".

Our Relationship to Ourselves

The ritual of honoring the faces of the Moon is my terminology for the re-visioned ancient Moon ritual, and its modern counterpart (See Chapter 7). We see the Moon's cycle as a cosmic ritual played out in the sky. It no longer requires mirroring with a specific shamanic practice. The Ancients used many different rituals, but the key to all of them was that they created Sacred space and while they were in that space there was no-time; they were just Being, and open to the god's energy. We can create our own sacred space through intent and/or ritual in ways familiar to our own lives. It can be simply a practice of intentionally paying attention to the Moon energies. This *becomes the ritual for us* when we stop what we are doing in ordinary time, and notice where the Moon is and the pattern of shadow on its face. We can intentionally tune in to the energies by locating the moon's phase in the sky, reminding ourselves of its energies, then checking to see if we are aligned with the phase energies.

As we connect with the Moon phases in this or other ways, "time stops." We are *Being* in the moment aligning with the energies, as intent, or a meditation. These moments offer the opening to an alternate reality or interstice, where changes can occur, and intent is the most important basis for that. Doing this small intention frequently helps us maintain ourselves in the openness of non-linear time and space more of the time. This is the primary relationship— our relationship to the universe, the Divine, and ourselves—in a world where relationship *is* a major issue at this time. But even more important, because the primary relationship is between Sun-spirit and Moon-soul and by extension Earth itself. We think there are frequencies reaching us from the Moon and Sun, as we discussed above. Focusing on Sun and Moon might enhance our own efforts.

We have a view of the universe as a silver-light web by which every body out there is connected and through which frequencies run free. Some writers, such as Lynne Taggart,[6] are now saying that when we do healing work or pray for a healing, we connect

---

6   Lyn Taggart, *The Field*. Her work will be further discussed in a later chapter.

to an energy focus in the universe to which we have a resonant connection. If we could understand how to use that connection we could call forth whatever we need. The attitude and energy of prayer is one way, and there are others, such as the Moon path. The Sun-Moon connection is our first outpost on the way out to the infinity in the sky. Staying connected keeps us open to whatever gifts the stars may send to us, so look up and reach for the endless potential in the black sky. Let go of all the old fears of night, the unconscious, the unknown, eclipses, dark of the Moon—all are sources of renewal.

2
The Old Woman's Gift
What If...You Had the Gift of Tomorrow Today?

*...if you are living your own myth, you will know what happens
next because the myth will tell you.*
—Joseph Campbell, *Pathways to Bliss*[1]

Joseph Campbell, in *Pathways to Bliss,* asks the reader this question "Are you living your myth; do you know what your myth is? Or do you even have one?"

I don't even know what he means, you may say.

So then he asks, "Have you been seized by something—a symbol, something from one of the great bodies of world mythology and religion, something that can carry you through disaster as well as provide you with inspiration?" This is what myth can do for you. Whoever you are, you are living a myth whether you know it or not, because myth arises out of real life, and it is everywhere. To know your myth is to empower your position in life at a non-verbal, mental-emotional level that integrates all of your experiences into a cohesive whole.

Almost anything can function as a myth—if it *seizes* you, if it does indeed carry you through the hard parts of life and inspire you. There is a classic story most of us remember from high school freshman lit, *The Great Stone Face* by Nathaniel Hawthorne. In this story, a boy with little to inspire him in his life is seized by the magnificence of the face of a great man in history carved out of a mountainside. The rest of his life became a process of walking in the footsteps of that man while carving out his own destiny. You can see something similar in the First Corn Ritual story in Appendix A, as

---

1   Joseph Campbell, *Pathways to Bliss: Mythology and Personal Transformation.* 2004, New World Library, Novaro, California. Published posthumously, it is part of a collection of previously un-published works by Campbell.

the shaman says, "I am walking, I am walking, I am alking in your footsteps, Old Woman."

Maybe your personal myth is something your grandfather said to you that has returned at critical moments to give you a handle. Maybe your myth is being an alcoholic, falling into the pit, coming back out, accepting that there is something greater than yourself, and telling your story at AA.

Story-telling trainers in the AA say the three elements of story are: (1) How I was then, (2) What happened, (3) How I am now—stories of transformation, stuff of myth. What myths or stories or great lives have taken you through a transformation? Maybe it's Jesus or Moses or Buddha, or maybe it's someone you know, or maybe just a poem. It is not the brands of our religions but their stories that change us; and one can have many such stories, perhaps one within another.

The authors' own daily experiences are held together in a matrix of the Sun's 360 degree annual journey combined with the Moon's story of her eight rendezvous with the Sun each month. This symbolic and mythical path speaks daily, weekly, and monthly to transformation and rebirth, giving us new perceptions of the dailiness of things, showing us where the transformative possibilities are right now. These changing celestial patterns of the Sun and Moon embody the myth behind all myths, the one forgotten for thousands of years, the one behind the Corn Ritual. We can imagine ourselves as living a myth in which we have a special meeting with our spirit eight times a month. Clues have remained, held by those cultures which have maintained to this day the original mythic elements of shamanism: the signs (Moon phases to the Sun), and the timing of certain holidays on religious calendars. Within our chosen matrix, awareness of our own individual myths is completely personal as well as universal, both time-wise and geographically. It is about writing our own story while living it, intentionally and consciously. Like all great stories, ours also speaks of darkness, struggle, transformation, and finding the light. It is mysteriously synchronous with the rhythms of the solunar[2] cycles. This structure can include any religious system we or you may already be a part of, or simply your own philosophy.

The Myth of the Old Woman Who Never Dies

There are many myths of the Old Woman Who Never Dies, which is a universal world myth. It is about the Moon acting out,

---

2   Sun-Moon: Solar-Lunar = SoLunar

every month in the sky, the drama of birth, maturation, eldering, death, and rebirth. In early cultures, some myths described these changes as maiden, matron, and crone. The Sioux myth of the first Corn Ceremony (Appendix A) is but one of thousands, through the ages, that addressed the Moon cycle—some, like the Sioux, calling the Moon "Old Woman" and "Old Woman Who Never Dies". She was called Old Woman in Mesopotamia and South America, and other places. If you haven't already, you might want to read the Sioux story before you continue. You will find it in Appendix A. When we read it, we were intrigued that the Sioux identified the Corn Spirit with the Moon, but learned later that this was a common practice in early times. Some of the symbology is opaque to us; but hidden within the First Corn Ceremony is the fundamental message, about walking in the footsteps (phases) of *The Old Woman Who Never Dies* so that the "dead" winter corn will grow again in the spring. The myth is about Corn, but behind Corn is the power and energy of "*The One Who Made All Things*," the Great Spirit, partnered with the fertility and regeneration of the Old Woman. The life of Corn—the most spiritual food of the Sioux—was literally the life of the Sioux and required them to honor the ongoing dance between *The Old Woman* and *The One Who Made all Things*, the Moon and the Sun. This is typical of much early mythology. Moon cycle ritual observance began all over the world in the Old Stone Age (100,000 to 10,000 BCE), not as the symbol of, but as the *power* of, the planting-growing-harvesting food cycle, and of human fertility. Even up until 2000 BCE the Moon was still believed by some cultures to be the actual germinating and growing force, without which plants, and even babies, would not germinate or grow. Even after the ancients realized the role of the male in conception, they still believed that the Moon was ultimately responsible for the actual germination. In truth, there is a mysterious reality to those beliefs hidden in the changing frequencies of the eight phases of the solunar cycle. People often pray for a child and later say, the Lord sent me this one, silently acknowledging an unspoken belief of all time that all things are manifested through the power of *The One Who Created All Things* .

Any one in modern times can still see the Moon cycle as symbolic of the life cycle. Particularly we see it as the daily reminder that while we have many deaths in one lifetime, we have as many rebirths, and after this lifetime is over there is the promise of another.. What might it have been like to live one's life in constant alignment with the Moon's phases?

Beginning the Journey

Judy and I discovered the progressive series of eight very different energies generated by the Sun-Moon dance each month, as a simple pattern for our lives, which soon developed into an increasingly inclusive, changing, interesting, complex and deep practice. Anyone else who chooses can learn to recognize, feel, and incorporate the same into their lives. These energies are discussed in great detail in section II, *The Archetype of All Relationship Cycles.* One can let the practice be as simple or complex as desired, but it is clear that the effort put forth will bring corresponding rewards.

We may not be Sioux, we may often take our food for granted as a part of the give and take and business of life, but we can plant seeds of consciousness and use the Moon energies to grow ourselves in our field of life. In fact, all of us are planting, harvesting, taking a siesta, or tearing down according to the Moon cycles, even if we are not aware of it. But would becoming aware make a difference? This is what we intend to explore in the next 21 chapters.

Suppose we begin by viewing our whole life as a cycle of spiritual unfolding? Then we might choose this Moon-path, among countless paths, including it with whatever path we might be on already, and walk it consciously in the same reverence as the Sioux medicine man who repeats many times in the ceremony, "I am walking your path". This is a sacred path that connects us to Earth and sky, Moon and Sun; ourselves and the Divine; our own several selve being: personal self, soul, Higher Self and spirit. They connect all of our parts to our daily lives. This is about a spiritual technology, created in the beginning to help us unfold our consciousness. If you are not now aware of those parts we just listed, the Moon path will help you become acquainted.

You, the reader, may or may not have a light that draws you, that holds your focus and from which hope and help or direction come. But here is a living myth that can be incorporated into anyone's path—one that you can see and feel, one that is dynamically part of all life on earth, and will enhance whatever path you are already on. The cycles of Moon and Sun each month inspire the entire family of humanity with a new set of dynamic impulses, even though we may often disagree with others' interpretations of those impulses. At the end of the month, when all is said and done and we are sometimes tired, discouraged, disappointed, or depressed, they give us the opportunity to use the energies of healing, transformation and regeneration—and open a new phase. If we are joyfully anticipating or intending a new and higher beginning, we may use the same healing energies to help us begin clearing away no-longer useful reactions or strategies.

If you incorporate this mythical but very real energy cycle into your own life or religion or practice, you will find it tells you what is going to happen next just as Campbell said, and what your part in it needs to be. It is a true divination, but not one related by a psychic human or a deck of cards. It is related directly to us through participation in the patterns of the real Moon in the sky in the immediate moment. This is where you get to write your own myth, and empower yourself. Like all spiritual paths, it is one that must be lived with conscious intent. We do not hear the messages of the moon-phases (or any other spiritual source) if we are not listening (hearing, feeling sensing...,) even though our bodies and unconscious minds are always responding to the subliminal taps on the shoulder. the Moon phase energies are subtle—they reach us from inside as well as outside—in responses of the physical self such as ideas that pop up from nowhere, or changes in mood. We are not taking full advantage of our gift of *free will*, if we do not listen consciously, since free will can only be used at the level of our own consciousness.

The gift is this: the Moon is both inside us and outside of us, and inside she holds our personal unconscious. The external Moon holds our conscious personal selves in that she shows everyone clearly throughout the month just how those two internal and external selves are working. It is a gift and an obligation to ourselves to listen and let our two points meet as they were destined to do from the beginning.

A Bird's Eye View of the Cosmic Pattern

The individual Moon phases describe the nature of all cycles. So we can see the individual stages of our lives, in the same relationship, with each month being a fractal part of the whole life. Both describe a universal quest—the search for our Selves.

W.B. Yeats' writings[3] have given us an insight into who we are, in terms of the Moon phases. In context of a whole life, Yeats gives us the key players, as he calls them *primary mask* and *antithetical mask*—two parts of ourselves which are in a relationship of struggle all our lives, and which we see the Sun and Moon dramatizing each

---

3   W.B. Yeats, *A Vision*

Lunar month. He calls them the primary mask and the antithetical mask.

The *primary mask* (patterned personal self) is the symbol attached to the Moon, which is memory and "remembers" all the parental-social "rules of life" we carry around with us and which determines many of our decisions and actions. Moon also represents the soul behind that manifested socially and parentally patterned self-awareness that struggles with a greater part still—that which enlivens and directs the purpose of the soul's incarnation. This individual spirit is behind the *antithetical mask,* or real Self (Sun), the role your inner, unique, individual Self-spirit wants to play. This is a life and death struggle, as you will see in a moment. This is a struggle we experience each month of our lives, and every lifetime. Our realization of that *antithetical* mask, or our individuality, determines whether we will be fully reborn the next Month[4], or the next 10 years, and ultimately how we will live our old age. Now that is a real and pressing question for Judy and me, who are also "old women". We have been seized by the Old Woman, herself, tasted the depths and the heights she promises, and decided the story is worth sharing. We are coming to know "who" is walking our paths. We struggle with it every day. "Is this the part that was shaped by my parents, or is it my true, core individual self who is making this decision?" Sometimes we wish we had begun this path when we were younger, for reasons you will soon see as we continue through the chapter.. This is not an old woman's path, by any means.

How our two masks work involves our very brains. We have two sides to our brain—left brain and right brain; they are seldom balanced and therefore many of us are not whole-brained. Persons with a left-brain emphasis may be more connected to ideas and to the material world, and be unable to relate easily with others at a personal level. Right-brain emphasis persons may be more connected to the creative, emotional, relational, visionary world, and be unable to make their bread and butter.. *Whole brained persons* find ways to do the work of the core self (antithetical mask) using the appropriate learned patterns (primary mask) and letting go of the rest. The Moon teaches us how to become more and more whole-brained through

---

4   The word, "reborn" is used often throughout this book, and does not in anyway imply religious meanings that may have been ascribed to it by others. Rebirth in any context may be encountered on the Moon path. The Moon or Sun do not cause such experiences, they time them.

the practice of living. There is precise timing for integrating our brains, free of charge, every Moon cycle.

The Moon Cycle as Life Cycle

Here is the Old Woman in the life story of everyone. We find it most interesting that both C. G. Jung and poet W. B. Yeats were interested in the Sun-Moon pair. In reading Yeats' description of the life cycle, which he posed in terms of the Moon cycle, and which Campbell quoted in *Pathways to Bliss*, we realized again how all-encompassing the phases are. In this larger context, every life demonstrates the symbolic four-fold pattern of the primary monthly phases. Other Jungian writers, such as Erich Neumann[5], have shown us how the same patterns underlie the evolution of humanity itself. This gives us pause, as it becomes clear that the monthly phases, their lessons, and how we deal with them are fractally tied to—and vital to—not only how we live our whole lives, but how that can be important to humanity, even for the least of us. That seems especially important in considering how we might want to live the last quarter of our lives.

Eric Ericson, a major foundational writer on developmental psychology in the twentieth century, encapsulated his discoveries in his now famous (in the field of psychology anyway) Eight Stages of Life. To help you review your life, or to see it as a whole, I include the following Table 1 of these stages below. Look at your life as you read Ericson's *Eight Stages of Life*, and determine what stage you are in the cycle, where you have been, and where you want to go. Then when you finish this book you can see how the exercise affects your practice of the Moon path, and why each month is so important to your whole life. Note that ease of achievement of each goal depends upon the fullness of achievement of the previous goal.) Also please note that the extra 9th Stage (Beyond-hood) was added by Michael Story, PhD Psychology, of Seattle, Washington.

---

5   Erich Neumann, *The Origin and History of Consciousness*: Princeton University Press, 1954

THE LIFE CYCLE STAGE	THE TASK Where You Learn the Following	DEVELOP-MEN-TAL GOALS of the Tasks	THE RESULTS in Old-Old Age of failure to Achieve Goals of the Previous Stages (Naomi Feil)
1. INFANCY	Basic Trust versus Basic Mistrust	HOPE	BLAMER to PARANOIA
2. EARLY CHILDHOOD	Autonomy versus Shame, Doubt (Self-trust)	WILL	ALWAYS RIGHT – MARTYR
3. PLAY AGE	Initiative versus Guilt	PURPOSE	*Not included in Feil's work
4. SCHOOL AGE	Industry versus Inferiority	COMPETENCE	*Not included in Feil's work
5. ADOLES-CENCE	Identity versus Identity Confusion	FIDELITY (Sense of True Belonging)	HYPOCHON-DRIA – Guilt, fear of losing body parts, death
6. YOUNG ADULTHOOD	Intimacy versus Isolation	LOVE (Family and Intimates)	DEPRESSION, WITHDRAWAL
7. MIDDLE ADULTHOOD	Generativity ver-sus Stagnation	CARE (For the Larger Circle)	DEPENDENCY – Need for a sig-nificant other to exist
8. OLD AGE	Integrity versus Despair or Dis-gust	WISDOM	HOARDING
9. OLD, OLD AGE [Introduced by a later writer, Dr. Michael Story.]	Immersion versus Dispersion into The Unknown— the Achievement Of Continual Change	BEYOND-HOOD Resolution vs. Vegetation	DENIAL AND FANTASY

Table 1. Eric Ericson's Eight Stages of Life with Author's Additions,
Including Those of Naomi Feil (see Bibliography)

In my work with the elderly in the late '70's and early 80's, I learned that the earlier developmental goals show up in the elderly as problems if they have not achieved some degree of effectiveness during childhood and mid-life. If one has not achieved enough experience of one or more of the goals, be assured that there are opportunities to make up for that. Each month the Moon phases will be presenting an old, uncompleted part of yourself for healing. Each life stage will also give you opportunities to catch up with unfinished business. The Moon is a good therapist, and there are also therapists "out there", whether they have letters after their names, or they are unsung helpers of others in this world. Don't be surprised to find that the boundaries between the following phase descriptions are fuzzy. Nature is not exact, nor is human nature, and we are all different because of a lifetime in society. The phases as successive stages of a lifetime are relative to each other, and more so as one ages.

The Beginning. At the New Moon of life you are born in darkness. The first part of your life is pretty much in darkness (not remembered), gradually getting lighter, as you grow and become aware of yourself as a separate being from others and your environment. About 15 years pass, represented by the first seven days of a Moon cycle. During that time you have primarily been under the thumb of those who rear you, and their societal orientation, and you are wearing their *primary* mask, or mindlessly rebelling before you know why. Half-way to the First Quarter, is a time, according to both astrology and psychology, when we become aware of the potential inside ourselves, the *antithetical mask* (or the individual within, in its context of the world around us)[6]. A flash in mid-adolescence around age 14-15, brings us images or ideas about what we could do in life, and they are usually not what the expectations from outside have told us. In terms of the monthly Lunar cycle as well as our lives, this is the potential of the Full-Moon-to-come, and the role we see for ourselves coming from our true individuality. Choice will be required. What will we do? Which mask will we choose to follow when we graduate?

The First Quarter. At this point, we have approached the First Quarter or "half-Moon" which is half light and half dark, and known by the Moon as *crisis in the outer world*. Are you seized by the desire to break through the barriers or walls around you, to think and act outside the box? Can you do it without creating World War III or IV

---

6   For Astrologers: This is a (Uranus sextile to its birth moving out from the Sun, Uranus is the first of the final three planets beyond visibility. It represents the struggle for individuality, progress, the new, etc. Its orbit is 84 years, representing a possible human life span. It moves 30 degrees (equivalent of one sign) in seven years. Therefore it moves from a birth position of 17 degrees Aries to 17 degrees Taurus in seven years. When the person is 14, the same Uranus will be at 17 Gemini, and so on. Each seven-year point throughout life is of significance to a person's recognizing and living out his/her core self. Eight phases times seven years = 84 years.

or XV? Have you left behind your dependency on what you learned from your parents in the past and become responsible for your own decisions and actions? This is where you build personal foundations for your mature life. By age 28 you hopefully have learned how to become your true self without necessarily rewriting society. You are now a responsible, creative member of the collective, working toward creating some goal for your life.

Full Moon. After seven more days, we reach the Full Moon and peak of midlife, around 45. We are now either relatively successful in living out our unique individuality, or we are anchorless, bored, unfulfilled, living out our parents' unfulfilled desires. Did we fulfill our potential so we are prepared for that great peak experience of reaching for and touching the Sun, assuming we have reached our full individuality and some understanding of why we are here? This is what midlife crisis is about. Apparently we do get other chances if we didn't fulfill our sense of potential, although there are consequences. The universe is kind (although we realize many would disagree). This is the social phenomenon in which someone you know either gets that important promotion of his life, or whatever he/she was reaching for, or quits a successful (or unsuccessful) career and becomes an artist in a garret, or goes back to school in a different field of endeavor.

We mention here that the age-dated periods become more variable the older we get. Some people live 60 years and complete the four phases. Others live 80 years and the phases may not feel finished. For the next seven days—or from 45 to 65 years of age—if we have lived our real self role, we use what we have become to build a foundation for ourselves in the outer world, to deepen our work and lives, to share some of the creative wisdom we have gained, to complete or nurture something of lasting value that carries our own mark on it. Meanwhile the Full Moon light is waning down to the last Half-Moon.

Last Quarter. We are now at the last quarter of the Lunar cycle, or the 21st day. Dark and light are again equal on the last half-Moon. This begins at the culmination of our lives when we are ready to retire, and we have the most influence we will ever have, perhaps our last burst of glory, or our sense of truly understanding what life is about. Just at the beginning of this 21st day of the Last Quarter Moon, we also have another crisis like the first quarter, only this time it is an internal crisis, *a crisis in consciousness*. We must choose between the past and the future. Did we learn anything in our life worth taking with us? What was it? Can we use it where we are headed? Are we looking at hiding away in our living room reminiscing with no one to listen, or do we have plans to do something we always wanted to do—maybe something downright outrageous? Our external work done, we face the darkness, now daily overcoming the light on the Moon and heading toward complete dark at the end of the 29th day [7]...and make a decision, or not, as the case may be. Have we discovered that the darkness contains a deeper wisdom? Some fear it and some don't, but to face it full on is to achieve the spiritual status of "elder" (whether the outer world recognizes it or not.)

The real situation is that we may be caught between the past and the future. We may be tired, perhaps even disillusioned, maybe we feel our vigor and youth and health fading. Do we judge ourselves incomplete, as though we had missed our ship when it came in, back there in our youth? What do we have to look forward to? If we allow ourselves this luxury of dwelling on what we may have missed, our horizons narrow, our primary mask begins to take over as we sink into old age and must again follow society's dictates. We have taken care of others all our lives, now it's time for someone else to take care of us—dangerous words, if they come from the primary mask—because we will live the rest of our future life in the past. Who knows what we could miss, what final piece of magic could come to us between now and that 29th day?

Are we going to let the darkness take over, and sink into something fearful and only too real because the 29th day is our last? This could be a very scary moment. We think that we are no longer useful. If we let our primary mask take over our life, we may become focused on inappropriate youthful pastimes, ignoring the wisdom we have gained, in a desperate hanging-on to the past. Or we may play out the unfulfilled developmental goals in exaggerated dependency, paranoia, or complaints over small things. We can obsess that "young people are not friendly to old people like they used to be; they don't respect us." We mourn our lost youth, lost opportunities and so on. All of these above may be true. We don't imply that any of it is an illusion. We realize that aging is a struggle in many ways, including

---

7   Jung and Yeats appear to have referred to the Moon cycle as a cycle to its own position at a New Moon which is $27^{1/2}$ days. We refer to the Moon cycle as a cycle of the Moon to the Sun which takes 29 days and some hours. Day 29 is therefore the last day. In astrology 29 degrees always carry a critical finality in their meaning. In either case the symbolism applies so we legitimately take the liberty of changing the other authors' number of days.

illness, difficulties with interpersonal relationships, and losses, especially those of friends and independence,. However, we admire those elders who have accepted the inevitables, kept their integrity, and even found the gifts in the difficulties. By and large, they are happier for understanding that it is not what we experience but how we deal with it that allows us to leave a fragrance of character and selfhood behind us.

This crisis beginning the aging process is a rite of passage, *croning* as the female elders call it. W. B. Yeats[4] asks this disquieting question *Are you just going to wind down? Or in the moment of the full moon did you make the jump to the Solar light?* Reaching for the Solar light would have been reaching for your deepest most integral self, grabbing it and hanging on, knowing who you really were and taking it with you.

Even here there is a last chance. Belatedly, even now you can make that jump. These last seven days (or twenty years or so) of the cycle can be deeply rewarding, full of adventure, deeply healing, for one who makes peace with his/her life, and reaches for the transformation. It may even be the time and opportunity you now have to share your hard-earned wisdom with the world through writing or speaking volunteering, or other means of sharing. Because, wonder of wonders, "transformation," like "reborn," is a key word. In this last phase, touching the Solar light will be a different experience than touching it in midlife. But everything is appropriate to its own time. There is magic in transformation, early or late in life, enough to fill books, or heal, or recreate this moment, or even the past.

Remember that the teaching of the solunar cycle rests on eternal renewal. It speaks to how the Stone Age ancestors had carried their observations of the monthly cycles all the way from when the first ancestor looked up and noted the return of the lost sacred light of the night. A golden thread, perhaps in our DNA, has carried that knowing to us in the present. We *know* there is a new light after this one fades.

The stages in the table above may offer some insights to this Last Quarter Stage, as well as to the whole cycle, because they look specifically at what you really must do at each stage in order to live the next fully, and how that affects the last stages.

Our Final Task. It is this 9th stage to which I wish to pay most attention; it belongs to the end of the Last Quarter phase (in the Palsamic), just before the Old Moon ends and the New Moon returns. This is the stage we most fear. Some patients losing their memory have said to me these most poignant and powerful three words "I'm losing *myself!*" This stage will have a surprising relevance in the monthly final phases.

Here in Ericson's table this is called "old, old age". Shockingly, have we spent a whole life trying to find ourselves, only to lose ourselves at the end? What can we say of value or comfort to this elder being? Neither I nor the reader has been there, but all of us have experienced moments of loss of memory, for one reason or another, and known someone who lived through this last stage. We have imaginations, and they are too vivid at this point, as we look ahead from any age to this dreaded possibility.

Do you wonder where the person goes during the times of confusion? Apparently many have asked this question, as I did, watching my father drift and wander in and out of the present reality during his last year. Intuitive, trained clinicians, familiar with Ericson's famous stages, (and apparently with this mysterious 9th stage) are clearly telling us that our final task is to find a greater selfhood—a *beyond-hood*, withdrawing from the self that is no longer fully present, but is either *dispersing into the* unknown or *immersing in* it, which are key phrases for the Last Quarter Moon. I find this truly awesome. I hope I remember it if and when I get there. It means reaching out to embrace the unknown new identity and belongingness at the New Moon whatever that may mean.

Every month, at the end of the cycle, we have an opportunity to apply this revelation in some way to our current life, as a key to transformation. For the old-old one, as for us, there is a greater wisdom and a greater sense of Self waiting there in the unknown, the next cycle— the sense of chaos, or still-unfounded hope, or whatever any individual experiences at this point. In terms of the monthly or lifetime phases, we are at the end of one set of energies and not yet arrived to the next set, and sensing a kind of creative chaos, or lack of direction. To watch for this moment with openness each month is to find a place of familiarity on the 29th day *whenever* it occurs. The 3rd Quarter phase is a time when at the monthly level we actually do disperse some of our personal consciousness into the mass consciousness, as opposed to the collective unconscious at the end of life.

If these are sobering thoughts, they do anchor us into our personal reality and make us wiser than we might have been. The human birth, unfoldment, maturity, and aging processes are archetypal, whether in terms of a whole life, or in terms of one month. Perhaps if we can find our personal archetype for this Ninth Stage, we will find an unexpected gift or joy here. In the 21st century, lives have been so disrupted that the outlines of the life-stages or phases, have often been obscured. We may have to look deeply within in order to see them, which is critical. Knowing *how* to live at a given time within our own pattern is more important than the "what" of the matter. It is our belief that if we live each day of each Moon cycle using the natural energies that pattern both our daily lives and our lifetimes, then both our daily living, and life's last stage, will be transformative. We *will* know what is coming next, just as Campbell said. We *will* have wise guidance from the ever present inner Spirit about how to deal with life.

As a further comment, we will sometimes be using the words darkness, unconscious and the unknown interchangeably throughout the book. It is the unknown which we fear, whether physical darkness, the darkness of the collective mind, or our own hidden darkness. Perhaps, as you travel with the Moon, you will discover that the unknown carries within it the gift of life. Magic and transformation can only begin in darkness. We never see how the magician does his trick. Learn how to recognize the "pregnant darkness", encourage it, and welcome it, lest you miss it entirely. Have you ever considered how this darkness factor contributes to the fascination of games, mystery novels, wild carnival rides, haunted houses, Halloween, and the moment before the curtain goes up on a long-anticipated movie? Do you remember Kelly's Chapter 1 quote about encountering deep wellsprings of...cosmic aspects of games and sports?

Knowing this progression of phases tells us to some extent what will come next in this month or this life. Using the tools to follow the actual current phase meanings gives us much more specific and individual information— the gift of tomorrow today. It is the universal myth, and when it is integrated with our personal information, that universal information becomes personal.

* * *

As we move on, you will learn how to use the Moon phases to synchronize your daily and monthly energies with those of Earth, Moon, and Sun, and to use special tools for knowing how and where each phase fits into your life. Using other tools, you will find the meaning behind everything you do, how it fits into your life purpose, and much more.

We recommend the following materials for readers who plan to follow the Moon path as we teach it in this book. You will need these books by the time you reach Chapter 5. You will also need moveable sticky-dots or other small markers of varied colors. We suggest yellow, orange and blue. These are to be used on the centerfold dial in this book. You need to have xeroxed, cut out, and put together, the 2 wheels as per instructions, also by Chapter 5.

If you have access to the web and to our website, you can do without these books to start with, because we have an abbreviated list of the 360 degrees in Appendix E, and our website carries a current calendar of the Moon Phases. However, as we explain in the chapter Veils of Prophecy you may ultimately need the books, since access to the web breaks down periodically for everyone. And for students who get through this book able to track their own phases, the added information of the degree books will become a perceived necessity. The appointment book becomes a great way to jot down the months' experiences and see how they fit the phase interpretations, as well as to track one's own appointments.

Jim Maynard's "Celestial Guide" yearly appointment book

An Astrological Mandala (degree symbols) by Dane Rudhyar, and/or

The Sabian Symbols by Diana Roche (degree symbols) recommended for beginners if you have to make a choice. We use both all the time).

The above specified books contain materials necessary for the practice detailed herein. There is no substitute for the two degree books. Also necessary for everyone is Jim Maynard's appointment book. It contains several items you may already have if you are an astrologer.

- Monthly phase positions of the Moon, plus eclipses, and their positions*
- An ephemeris for the year.
- Detailed information on the signs and Sun and Moon..

*If our website is available, the monthly and phasal positions of the Moon will be available there on a calendar page.

3
Shadows on the Moon
Personal and Collective Unconscious

Unlike the Personal Unconscious, the Archetypes and racial memories contained in the Collective Unconscious never become fully conscious.
—A Jungian concept

When we connect with the Ancestors, we get entry to the wisdom of the Collective Unconscious.
—Stephen Karcher

Most of the philosophical/psychological background of this book is based on Jungian concepts. Modern psychology does not include mystical concepts that deal with the collective unconscious or Moon cycles; whereas Jung's psychology has room for all of it, including ancient Greek philosophical ideas that often were used in alchemy. The inclusiveness of this logical, as well as mystical, system has made Jungian psychology the primary background for writers and teachers of most Western and even some Eastern spiritual philosophies. In terms of the Moon cycles, Jung's writings about various levels of consciousness are especially appropriate, since they speak not only to our personal consciousness but to the deep well of ancient humanity's collective wisdom. Whether you favor the genetic or spiritual/psychological transmission of such wisdom, this approach fits. We think both are part of one aspect of unfolding human consciousness. We also want to be clear that this is a symbolic philosophy in which we find a language and a structure that includes our story in a logical way at every level. Science may never find a place called the Collective Unconscious, or an archetype, but these concepts are acknowledged as existing outside of practical left-brain existence.

The premise of *The Old Woman* is that the shadow on the Moon's face is representative of the proportion of personal unconscious in relation to the personal conscious that is available within everyone in the world at any given time. We believe that we understand what this means for us as individuals, but how that affects the Collective Consciousness is much beyond our understanding as yet, other than to say that, whatever the shadow proportion is at any time, it contains information that could be read both in the signs and the degree Symbols (See Chapter 10) and also compared with what we see in the news. However, although the Collective Unconscious has already been explored by Jung and his followers, including Dane Rudhyar, no one to date has been able to fully explore its possibilities. We base our ideas about the Collective, conscious and unconscious, on those of Jung who is still the fundamental source for such information. We, like many others, have extrapolated some of his basic concepts into the Moon Phase information.

We believe the Collective Unconscious (C.U.) is represented by the dark side of the Moon. We also believe that this dark side connects, in some momentous way, to humanity during Solar and Lunar eclipses, which are dealt with in Appendices C and D. We also believe deeply that each of us does contribute something, however small, to the Collective Unconscious and the Collective Consciousness which is the state of consciousness of humanity as a whole at any given period of time. It takes a finite number of drops to fill a bucket or an ocean; and so whatever increase of consciousness we gain for ourselves, it will help increase that of the Collective. Part of this process may include morphogenetic fields which are said to respond to something called the "hundredth monkey phenomenon".

Collective Unconscious as the Foundation of Personal Consciousness

Freud wrote about conscious and unconscious in his psychology. He referred to everything not conscious simply as "the unconscious", making no distinction between personal and collective. It was a large bone of contention between him and Jung who explored the concept of a Collective Unconscious and went on to describe two parts of our unconscious—the Personal Unconscious (P. U.) containing our personal memories, and the Collective Unconscious (C. U.) containing archetypes and racial memories). According to Jung, we are all born with the C.U., we create the P. U. as we live our experiences. The personal unconscious contains personal memories and emotions belonging to the present lifetime, most of which are available to the conscious level without much effort, however some of it is only available with quite a bit of effort, usually through dreams, art work, and therapy. Other parts appear to be irretrievable, such as the first few years of life. Later you will see how Moon work helps us know what part of our P.U. is ready to be brought into consciousness as a positive conscious energy heretofore unavailable except as an uncontrollable mental or physical reaction.

We access our personal unconscious every day—for common memories such as what we had for breakfast, what we planned to do today, how much that computer cost, definitions of unusual words, phone numbers, what people we recently met look like and what they wore, data behind a decision we made last week, the daily news stories, and so on. Science believes we can be aware of only about seven facts or items simultaneously, though that can be improved with practice. So to carry on daily life we are continually pulling familiar things out of our PU, which is like a handy little closet that contains things we can't bother with at the moment. At a little deeper level, the long-ago birthdays of one's grandchildren may be easily accessed with a little digging, but one may truly have forgotten the birth times. That means the brain's little tracking lines to the information, called neural pathways, have been obliterated by time and disuse. They then need a piece of associated information to trigger the piece you have completely forgotten, and even that may not work, so they need to be re-introduced. Deepest of all are those things we can't remember because they are too traumatic, painful, or fearful, or simply too early in life. Some memories are lost through denial—we choose not to remember them because they are embarrassing or undesirable, or we just don't want to accept their factual nature, such as grief over a loss; but when we are confronted with the truth, the memories may unexpectedly return with shocking impact. That is because we intentionally "forgot" to guard the pathways to them.

The memories lost because of fear or pain are the ones back of the instinctive reactions you either are not aware of or that you wish wouldn't happen. These are like undue grief over events and people not related to you because you did not grieve fully over an earlier loss. If the reactions bother you or someone else, and you are really upset by them, it's time to get therapy, or figure them out for yourself if you can. These kinds of issues along with denied material are discussed at greater length elsewhere, and may come up during Moon phase practice.

These are the points where Collective Unconscious and Personal

Unconscious cross boundaries in ways we do not clearly understand. But we observe that life does not let us live a whole lifetime doing as we choose about these locked memories and their effects on our behaviors.

In the following pages are listed four basic urges with which we are all born, all archetypes coming from the C.U. The fourth urge is the urge to transform. Transformation is necessary to change, as in the above examples, as well as in general evolution. As you will see, that urge, an archetype, lives in the Collective Unconscious, to which we ordinarily have no conscious access. We think that when it is your time to recognize and heal one of these memories, the transformation urge or archetype pushes you into situations where that can happen. You finally agree to therapy, or you spontaneously remember the memory in a related situation, which may immediately explain the problems you have had over the repressed memories and their effects. We have found many such memories while doing Moon Practice, and learned to understand ourselves so much better as a result. However, the more traumatic the "lost" memory, the less likely it is that it will resurrect itself without therapy. We don't recommend tinkering with this concept, but allow life to happen, and then if it seems too difficult to deal with this sudden new emotional information, get help. It is legitimate and healthy to seek help, regardless of what some of your family or peers might think.

The Archetypes

Ideas about archetypes and racial memory are scattered throughout Jung's works, and those of writers of many fields. Various elements of both are used in interpretation of astrology and are relevant to any discussion of the Moon Phases. In fact, the Moon phases cannot be fully understood without reference to archetypes because the Old Woman myth of the Moon is herself an archetype. Sun, Moon, Planets, and the symbolic 360 degrees of the Zodiac all identify or reveal archetypes of the Collective Unconscious which can stimulate us to change through the principle of resonance, through stirring of deep feelings and repressed emotions. We are designed to evolve without external instruction, through our conscious relationship to the Sun/Moon cycles, and all the hidden memories we carry, which are in themselves embodiments of archetypes. This is part of a larger picture which cannot be dealt with here. It speaks simplistically to our being born with an internal guidance system called instinct.

It is critical, and interesting, to note here that C. G. Jung defines

Archetypes as *urges or instincts* operating out of the Collective Unconscious[1]; while Astrology defines planets, Sun, and Moon in the horoscope as *urges, instincts,* or *archetypes.* By that is meant that the planets represent or symbolize these instincts or urges, which are therefore activated or triggered by the planets in transiting the sky through one's chart.

The Four Basic Archetypes

Dane Rudhyar also saw the role of planets as instincts represented by the planets in our horoscope. As such, he says, all persons are born with four basic instincts (archetypes), which he describes as combinations of planets in his book, *An Astrological Study of Psychological Complexes.* He lists these as four basic instincts born in all men and women, to which we added a new one of our own, number five. We list the planets representing each urge for any astrologers who might be reading this. However, we do not deal with planets in this book, so readers can ignore the parenthetical matter.

1. The urge to be a particular being (Saturn-Moon)
2. The urge to maintain its characteristic form or temperament (Mercury-Jupiter)
3. The urge to reproduce that particularity (Mars-Venus)
4. The urge to transform it (Uranus-Neptune-Pluto)
5. The urge to return to the unity from which we came: New Moon, which represents the return of Moon to Sun

These basic five instincts are pure, basic, universal archetypes. Rudhyar says they operate in every human being at the unconscious, instinctual, and psychological levels. Think of any urge you might have, whether toward good or evil. The planets in our parenthetical list characterize our personal way of living out the five archetypes. In your birth chart they provide the templates for how you as a particular being will express those urges. Therefore the number of

---

1   To make it simple, Archetypes, mysterious as they are, seeming not to exist until someone embodies them, are the patterns of all individual and collective life. Racial memories are the records of the archetypes lived out—of human and collective history and pre-history. They are therefore inseparable from each other in a non-linear way. Our racial memories are not of specific events. But if they are in our DNA, they exist as potential.

archetype-forms may be virtually unlimited, but each will be personal and individual variations of one of the basic four (or five).

Archetypes and the Four Moon Phases

Much of mythology describes these urges/archetypes in terms of the cultures wherein they developed. The truths behind our own familiar stories and popular or religious beliefs may be found in earlier times and cultures, but in different forms.

Each of the four urges parallels one of the four phases of the Moon. The urge that is most important to The *Old Woman* is the fourth and last, the urge to transform. When you begin to work with your own centerfold dial, you will be able to see how a New Moon in one area of your life experience will characterize your current activity in that area; you will be working under the archetypal urges of that area. Thus, a New or Full Moon happening in a specific area of your life will trigger some activity from that urge. That urge already existed in your life, and the New Moon provided the timing and the general supporting energy for that archetype.

Science generally agrees that collectively we all have a natural urge to connect with something greater than ourselves—the urge to be religious is one expression of that. Following the Moon phases is one way to fulfill that urge—we believe it is the original urge to become part of the universe we live in, by reaching for something greater than ourselves and our personal worlds. This urge may be related to the fifth archetypal urge above—the urge toward unity or connection to the divine. Religion today is much more organized, specific, and full of long accepted rights and wrongs to make decisions easier, and define limits and demands. Some of these religious and cultural "dots" and "tittles" are clearly becoming less helpful as our knowledge about the universe grows rapidly broader. We are perhaps "growing up" and discovering, as my grandmother said, that there are more ways than one to cook a goose— or live a life. Our own truth grows only as we transform or make ourselves more whole by incorporating parts of our P.U. and C.U. into our conscious. Remember we said the C.U. can never be fully conscious. But to be conscious that fulfilling an urge is living out an archetype, such as Joan of Arc, or Loki who found fire, or Sedna who let go of her victim complex, and then knowing what your archetype is, raises its potency in the personal conscious and the outside world.

The Old Woman tells us each month which of 360 sub-archetypal symbols is operating in the world at that time. Whether you know their names or not you will recognize your own archetypes, and as we mentioned in the second chapter, if you know your myth you will know what comes next. Sometimes these revelations leave us breathless with astonishment, and sometimes they actually contribute to healing of something we are working on. Archetypes are the "deep stuff", but they can be fun, exciting, uplifting, as well as a bit scary. They keep our interest in life moving, like a good story.

Racial Memories

Racial Memories, the other part of the Collective Unconscious, are a great gift to all individuals, along with the potential development of particular individuality which we believe turns out to be related to Free Will, of which more later. Racial memories contain the record of our collective history of the world we live in, and our connection to our ancestors. The fact that our DNA traces the evolutionary timeline of our ancestors suggests that we contain and use their legacy as potential, carried in the fourfold structure of DNA in our very cells.

Archetypes, as part of the Collective Unconscious, have been called by some since Greek times, *thoughts of the Divine*. Like trees, with roots forever in the collective soul, they grow branches into the personal soul. Branches and leaves in symbology represent thoughts and ideas. In the body-mind they are instincts translated into human ideas, hunches, etc. The soul as we define it includes all of ourselves, interpenetrating body, mind and emotions, as it emerges or manifests out of the Collective. As thoughts of the Divine are overarching patterns that we express through our lives and through many generations; some can be seen as forms behind whole cultures. Whole cultures change over long periods of time during which religions, technology, customs, mores, and taboos change, as a result of creative human actions that slowly change the way archetypes manifest.

Since archetypes are only seen through people living them out, it appears that we ourselves cause cultures to change as we introduce creativity— individuality and new ideas—into the old patterns of the culture. There are many instances of our creative ideas emerging simultaneously in different parts of the world. Could this be the work of the Collective Unconscious? The phenomenon may be far more widespread than we know, because there are others who claim that, when a society begins to change, new archetypes emerge through those persons who can attract the attention of enough others to push the energies in new directions. Rollo May, in *Love and Will*, says that our artists, poets, and musicians always heralded great social changes—somehow they picked up from the collective the still unformed urges working their way to the surface of human consciousness via the arts. Of course! Music and art are primary communication—pre-verbal information, not yet put into words. They can be understood at the emotional/physical levels by anyone. Their primal messages enter the personal unconscious directly, bypassing the left brain's limited interpretation. Such messages move people far more than verbal information, providing a subliminal push to those who would just as soon continue in the old patterns.

So we can see how archetypes in the Collective Unconscious can, at the mysteriously right moment, begin the process of social transformation via musicians and artists through their beguilingly beautiful and fanciful—even enthrallingly ugly—imagery of music and art. In turn, exposure to this music and art, now so available through the ethers, begins increasingly rapid paradigm shifts in listeners, at the unconscious levels.

The Soul and the Divine

Jung and the Greeks called the C. U. *The Anima Mundi* or "Soul of the World," (meaning soul of planet Earth and humanity).[2] So we are being told that Earth, and/or humanity as an entity, has a collective soul, as we believe we have a personal soul. At the individual soul level, we individually participate in the whole of the *Anima Mundi*. Some writers interpret "world" as the whole universe. Jung did not, to our knowledge, define that possibility. We do here suggest that there are many levels of consciousness and of soul. We take *Anima Mundi* to be collective humanity's soul level on this planet, as a planetary soul. When humans advance to higher levels of consciousness, such as galactic, someone will write about that and call it something else.

Archetypes (the word is often attributed to Plato) are said to be universal patterns or forms (blueprints?) behind all living beings. Some say these patterns are created by the Divine, which humans

---

2   Jung seems to define the Anima Mundi in more than one way, and philosophers all the way forward from the Greeks who created the idea have all differed in their definitions. One reason may be that the universe became more inclusive than the "world" of the Greeks. For simplification, this is our definition, allowing that there are others out there. We have the right as did other writers to use our definition as long as our conclusions are consistent. If you can catch us deviating from it you may cite us for inconsistency!

express from the soul level into their individual lives. Jung finds the archetypes as themes in mythology, and as instincts in a person. The fairy tale of Beauty and the Beast is one example, only, of the Shadow archetype. The Shadow is a container for our personal dark side, in this case the "beast"—the externalized part of Beauty in the tale. When Beauty kissed the beast, i.e. learned to love her rejected dark side, he turned into a handsome prince and married her—was integrated into her whole self (i.e. she accepted her sexuality back into herself). When we accept the things we dislike about ourselves (Shadow), they become a power or asset in our lives. This is a major teaching of *The Old Woman*.

The Importance of Creativity

Jung attributes Creativity to the Urge for Transformation. It is what distinguishes us from the animal kingdom. It comes with the urge to change—ourselves or the world. We don't remember any of this if we have lived many cycles of reincarnation, but as members of societies and cultures we carry the racial memories of when we lived out changing forms or themes of particular archetypes. We now carry with us common instincts or instinctual patterns of behavior from those lifetimes, and as we often say, "times they are a-changin". A tentative example of this might be the choice of the American people in choosing Barack Obama as the 44th President and the instrument of change. His self-professed hero and model is Abraham Lincoln, and his tasks have many connections to those of Lincoln—there are many parallels between the two periods of time in our culture.[3]

There, we've said it. Archetypes are the forms and patterns in the C. U. which people live out in their lives instinctually. The wild card which prevents humanity from forever repeating all its mistakes and any other patterns is creativity. As creative persons live out their archetypes, they change the "usual" way of things. Sometimes that introduces permanent changes to how we all live the archetypes. For example George Washington Carver totally changed humanity's view of the lowly peanut. That was an archetypal change affecting agriculture, economy, health, and many other areas of human life.

But the archetypes themselves remain unseen or unknown, within the C. U. Racial memory is simply the group memory in humanity's

---

3   Our own researches into the astrology of the two presidents have revealed numerous strong connections between them indicating that Obama may be a reincarnation of Lincoln.

collective unconscious, of people living out the archetypes over long periods of time through creativity —the expression and gradual change of how archetypes are expressed. Some scientists now are agreeing that such memory may be passed down the generations via DNA through the epigenetic structure.[4] If this is true, history will gradually be written in new ways, and we may better understand our role in this world. We will all see that some values of earlier times need to be used as guidelines for today, while others eventually need to be left behind as our creativity builds on the creative changes of the past.

Living Archetypes

Archetypes are of a deeper order of consciousness than even our own individual unconscious, because they are universal principles rather than things. Racial Memory is the record of how humanity has embodied the Archetypes over time. Each of us at birth arrives with a folder entitled Collective Unconscious on our brain's hard drive (or possibly in every cell). This folder contains two permanent hidden files—one titled "Racial Memories" and one titled "Archetypes". Even though these files are inaccessible on our individual "computers", they appear to us in artistic expression, dreams, urges, instinctual knowledge, feelings about humanity, sexual attractions to individuals, and various drives that command our various energies. *The Old Woman Who Never Dies* and *The One Who Created All Things* are the two largest, most visible and obvious Divine expressions of our primary archetypes, the fundamental duality of Male and Female, Yang and Yin, and the rhythms of their cycles. Sun is still the visual archetype of the Creator-God of all religions including Paganism. Moon, as the feminine side of divinity works with that *first duality*, without which form could not exist. Moon is the manifestor, the female Mother of All Forms—Shechinah, Mother Mary, Kwan Yin...

Here lies the living connection between the Archetypes in the Collective Unconscious and us as human beings—the Moon's cycle. What we see outside of ourselves and feel inside ourselves are the archetypes at work. Wars, criminals, heroes, saviors, beauty and ugliness dance with each other continuously, to the rhythms of the Moon cycles, as humans resonate to the archetypes and play parts

---

4   Epigenetic structure, a recent discovery. (See Chapter 1.) A kind of highly sensitive sheath around the DNA spiral which transfers every emotional, physical, mental reaction of the person to the DNA, and changes the spiral in the process.

of them out in their own lives. Through walking the Moon path we can gain more consciousness of these mysterious, divine processes, and begin to cooperate with the universal process involving all of humanity.

The personal Moon, in astrology, represents the soul of the individual, which manifests his/her inner self in the outer world. The personal Sun represents both the Creator and you the co-creator. In your chart it indicates through the degree Symbols, the major archetype of your individuality. In primitive terms, Sun represents the same God as *He Who Created All Things*, the God of the corn ceremony. In Western thought, He is often now called "I Am". The personal Sun ("I am") over time reveals to us our Selfhood and the slow wheels of destiny, planted there by "I Am". The personal Moon over time represents our participation in the Collective Unconscious, as a seamless part of the physical, mental, emotional, and spiritual living-out of our particular soul destiny.

We will see how the Sun and Moon's movements together provide the rhythms and themes (Archetypes?) of the dance. The phases indicate, through the Houses and signs on your centerfold dial, the content and choices of archetypes of your individual life, and the way in which you choose to express them, which of course is much more complex than we can possibly imagine. With all this in mind, we have been gifted with immeasurable clues to everything we might ever need to know, and will know, in its proper timing. The eternal repetition of the cycles of "the eternal return" allows us to do it all over and over again, with a different answer each Moon cycle, until in some life-time if not this one, we finally "get it". However it is becoming clearer to everyone in this 21st century that we must all get the message this time.

We can now see that our personal soul is described by the Moon, which reflects the light of Spirit, and the shadow of personal unconscious. We suggest that the dark back side of the Moon which we never see represents the C.U. where the collective memories and archetypes reside. The Moon's cycle is our path to transformation, one individual at a time, and also our potential unity with the Divine (as in the fifth major archetype, above)! Moon is as the ancients said, the Great Mother, the lovely feminine manifesting part of God, and the dark mother of which more later. Finally, the Sun, archetype of archetypes represents the destiny behind one's life story, and our true spiritual consciousness at any point in our evolution. The Moon's (soul's) ultimate urge is to re-unite with the Sun from which we separated ourselves at birth to become an individual. That separation is the division of our unity into masculine and feminine or Yang and Yin, in order to manifest. It lives in the so-common attraction of female for male and male for female.

And so we now turn to the dark side of the Moon—forever dark, forever hidden, the *Anima Mundi*, and Soul of the World, never to be seen, never to become fully conscious. How can we understand that which we can never see or know? Once we are shown a place we are forbidden to go, does not human curiosity drive us to seek entrance, like Bluebeard's heroine? Isn't that a fundamental archetype in everyone? Why is it forbidden? How can we enter the locked room anyway? Where is the key hidden? Physically, one might say that a person could not survive on the dark side of the Moon, and perhaps that is the metaphor.

Stephen Karcher tells us the secret in *The Total I Ching*. We must learn to connect with the Ancestors. At least that is how the ancient ones did it. He says:

> *When we connect with the Ancestors, we get*
> *entry to the wisdom of the Collective Unconscious.*

That is a story for another day. And quite cagily he fields an answer, saying we will access their wisdom, but not the ancestors themselves. But let us briefly mention who "The Ancestors" are in terms of this book. For our personal purposes primitive peoples and Native Americans say ancestors are people in your genealogical or ethnic lineage who were advanced in consciousness—wise enough to walk on the Milky Way or river of light, the honored who in each generation become absorbed into the light in order to be forever remembered. In our time, they may be the people who are said to have chosen after death to go into the light. The others remain in the field of earth as "ghosts". We probably don't know, nor will we remember, many of our own individual ancestors except through meditation or shamanic journeying, but we may honor them in our thoughts and rituals, religious or not. After all, they live on in our very cells, contributing to our lives! To recognize or honor them is to empower them in our lives.

That said, making friends with Stephen Karcher's books and those of Mircea Eliade are places readers might begin their search for the connection to the Ancestors (See Bibliography). These books describe the ancient rituals in which the ancestors are invited to join the celebrations. The principles (archetypes) of ritual at Moon times are clearly stated in Chapter 4 of this book; and with what we teach in this book, someone could create a modern ritual based on those principles. Or, one might find ways to begin by contacting organizations who teach journeying techniques for modern shamanic work if that is one's particular interest. As we progress through these first hundred years of the new age, we will find others. And perhaps *The Old Woman*, herself, the archetype of archetypes, will teach us as we learn her patterns.

4
Dark Mirror
The Way of Transformation

'My son,
look, and know yourself you shall appear in this mirror'.
Then Quetzalcoatl saw himself, and was filled with fear...
—Virginia Meyer, *Wheel of the Winds*[1]

The Problem and the Promise—the Eternal Return

Transformation has been a universal human issue in all times and belief systems. The Ancients may have learned about it from watching the never-ending cycles in the sky. They appear to have been obsessed with this connection and perhaps thus learned to see their own experiences or those of leaders as modeling the heavenly cycles. In fact, many early myths have star gods acting out taboos, with disastrous consequences. Their myths nearly always offer us larger views of different aspects of our lives, and tools for walking ourselves through them. But the transformation urge or archetype seems to have captured their thought most strongly—perhaps because a successful transformation evokes such a powerful, soul-stirring, transpersonal feeling. Also it nearly always involves the universal problems of death, pain and suffering, for which they and we still write books, preach, and struggle with at our own levels. It permeates ideas from ancient pre-history to contemporary times and religious writings. It is one of the greatest of all mysteries and often the spiritual power behind promises of the founders of religions. Nearly all of them point to transformation as overcoming these inevitables. Yet, the original promise lies in what Mircea Eliade calls The Eternal Return, the mystery of the last phase of the signs cycle and the eternal return to unity or New Moon, forever beginning

---

1   Author's unpublished children's novel, adapted from Vol. 18, *Landa's Relacion de las Cosas de Yucatan, Papers of the Peabody Museum of Archaeology and Ethnology.* Harvard University. The quotation is from that volume.

again on a higher level. Renewal of life is the essence of *The Old Woman,* herself. The Moon is the ultimate living myth of rebirth.

However, lest any of the poetic wisdom of the Moon deceive you into believing the transformational process is easy, we here put the really hard part right up front where it belongs, after the journey into the foundational worlds of the personal and collective unconscious. We all have to get through the hard stuff somehow, and much of the process is in the personal unconscious, waiting for a form of the transformation archetype to shake us loose from our inadequate foundations.

Intellectually, the path of transformation can be idealized, but physically and emotionally it is not that easy, and we dread it enough to resist stepping into it. The first step for most of us is a major crisis—family, job, health, addiction, loss, or any other. You have heard people say, "It was the worst thing I could have imagined at the time, but I learned so much from it". Often a crisis will trigger something unpleasant from childhood. Resolving the old memory as well as the present is the nature and purpose of that transformation. Another type of crisis might be one in which more is demanded of someone that he/she believes they can handle, as though it is an initiation of some sort where your consciousness needs to move on to another level.

If you are old enough to be reading this you probably have had a crisis, or will be experiencing one in the future. It immediately plunges one into unexpected sometimes overwhelming emotions. Whatever the emotions, we advise strongly that you let them happen and find someone to talk to. The next step is to go into logical mode, assess the situation, find out what your resources are, and take care of yourself and/or any others for whom you are responsible. Do what you can do and attempt to let go of the rest. These days some people find themselves living in their cars. Others have had to confront an addicted family member. Some get cancer. In all these situations, your solutions may not "fix" things back the way they were. The world we see around us is not helpful, either, unless we have friends or family to support us. Unlike the ancients, most of us are not embedded in the society around us, or an extended family. Unless we have some kind of group to which we belong, being a separate individual is a disadvantage. Depending on our basic attitudes, we may come out of this crisis bitter, depressed—or healed in some permanent and wonderful way.

There are also minor crises, which have less overall impact, but since they happen frequently, they need to be addressed in the same manner. These will usually be mirrored by the Moon in its phases, which has become our resource for such events. Each one, be it criticism, getting our family buttons pushed, getting the "flu from hell", losing our purse or having our identity stolen, etc., begs the question Judy always asks first "what is the gift in it?" Those questions apply to the larger crises as well, but if you aren't ready, begin with the little questions. This is where the Moon Phases so often begin for us, and they can help you figure the answer out, whether the crisis is great or small.

Even a small crisis can be a disruption of one's life, but we guarantee it can bring transformation and evolution of one's consciousness if one has the will and the desire to deal with it effectively.

For seven years, Hercules had to clean out the Aegean Stables, and apparently immortal horses leave the same messes around as mortal horses. He stayed with it, and so did Jacob[2], in the bible. Both had their resolution or transformation. Myth is not for the timid, fairy-story-like as it may seem. Like Beauty and the Beast, it "gets under your skin" if it fits your situation. Much myth is about the ugly, the painful, the scary, the dark, the unknown, and only eventually the transformation of all that into light and personal power. Dying as transformation, which is most often ego-death, and only physical once, is mostly painful until one finds one's sea legs. So let's look at the mythology of that process.

The Aztec Myth of Quetalcoatl

For years, our models for transformation came from other countries on other continents, often from religion and myth. Ironically, so-called primitive Central and South American cultures became great civilizations before they disappeared, and their myths—as meaningful as the Greek and Roman ones so often read in the Western cultures—were ignored till recently, while we had our own heritage right here on our own continent.

The Aztecs, from long before Cortes arrived, had inherited from the earlier Olmecs, a transformation model so crystal-clear it may seem familiar even if this is the first time you have heard it. This major

---

2   Genesis 29:21-30. Jacob worked for 7 years to marry Leah, but was tricked into 7 more years before he could marry her.

Aztec myth describes, step by step, the process of transformation, in terms that are understandable in Jungian and related psychologies.

This is the story of the feathered serpent god which spread all over Central and South America and influenced many North American native cultures. Ethnologists believe, from details of different versions, that the feathered serpent god was originally a very ancient human spiritual leader who became a legend and finally mythically a semi-divine man who brought light to the darkness of earthly men. He was known as *Quetzalcoatl,* the Feathered Serpent, Lord of Light, who was also Venus as the morning star; his dark brother *Tezcatlipoca* was Venus as evening star. Events during Venus' transit as morning star were favorable, while those during Venus' transit as evening star were unfavorable. Quetzalcoatl became a god through a very human transformation experience. His story is that of every human who walks the path of transformation. Myth of course has its own language of symbols, which we will translate briefly as we go along, and in more detail at the end.

In this story *Quetzalcoatl* began as a half-human half-divine leader, just as all of us have a bit of divinity within us. As the story begins, he is called "Lord of Light", code for "he is already what he will become." He had a twin, or double—a shape-shifter often called *Xólotl* (pronounced "Shólotl" or "dog.") because *Xólotl* often took the shape of a dog when he visited the underworld."). He was also called *Tescatlipoca,* the dark or smoking mirror, and Lord of the Dark (the Land of the Dead in the Underworld), and of all the pleasures and riches of this world. Europeans call him a "Doppleganger"; Jung would have called him Quetzalcoatl's shadow, or "the trickster." Whereas *Quetzalcoatl* lived and taught that one should live a pure life, *Xólotl* enticed people, and introduced them to the addictive materialistic things of the world. They were not forbidden, even to Quetzalcoatl, but people became darkened by their excesses which were taboo. *Xólotl* carried a "smoking mirror" around hidden in his clothing and when people were guilty of transgressions, he would flash the mirror before them and they would have to look at their true selves. He called it "giving them their face".[3] As in all of us, these two opposites of light and dark (consciousness and shadow) continually tried to undo each other. One night, during a great festival, *Xólotl*

3　"Face" to the later Aztecs equated to something like the ego which was the part of a person who was overly attracted to the pleasures of the material or external world. One's true face included what we call the shadow, or the evil memories in the personal unconscious.

turned himself into a wise-looking old man and tricked *Quetzalcoatl* into drinking too many cups of pulque and becoming drunk.

"It surely can't hurt to taste it with your little finger", *Xólotl* said.

Under *Xolotl's* influence, Quetzalcoatl drank many cups, and slept with a visiting dignitary's wife (BIG taboo). Next day he awoke having forgotten what he had done. For some years he went on with his life, but felt great internal conflict and became old and ill. *Xolotl,* as the wise old man, approached and offered to show him the mirror, which he claimed would help. When *Quetzalcoatl* saw himself in the mirror, he was stricken to see his true face, and recall the memory of what he had done. He "repented" (according to the translation of the Catholic priest who transcribed the story) and left his people. No longer feeling worthy of his leadership, he stripped himself of his holy feathers and garments, and went to the Western Sea, where he immolated himself on a funeral pyre (purification). Then he went to the land of the dead and "preached" to the dead for nine days, after which he ascended to Venus, where he became fully divine, god of light. He made an agreement with *Xólotl* that when Venus rose in the East as morning star, *Quetzalcoatl* would rule the people, while *Xólotl* ruled at night when Venus set in the east as evening star.[4]

The Interpretation of the Myth in Personal Terms

We can see here the process of transformation, and one way we might deal with our human frailties. Our unconscious tricks us into doing something which either our own conscience or the social conscience defines as wrong, or someone has done the same to us. We try to suppress awareness of it because it is too painful to think about. However, we suspect something is wrong, and often our health is affected. Our unconscious tricks us again, and we do or say something in an unrelated situation that evokes a response from someone "mirroring" to us, who says, "You sound angry at me. Who are you really angry at?" Memories flood our conscious, which can

---

4   When planets are in 'direct' motion, they rise in the East and set in the West. When they are retrograde (appearing to go backward in the sky) they rise in the West. Both Quetzalcoatl and Xolotl were associated with Venus, which dominates the horizon just before sunrise or sunset with her size and beauty. Indeed if you watch the sky over time, before sunrise Venus will be conspicuous as morning star, and at sunset as evening star. Xólotl, who was associated with retrograde Venus as evening star, was a backward sort of god, whose feet were on backward, who unraveled time, and blocked people's forward-moving activities.

be shocking to the very core. Our defenses are destroyed, and we regret perhaps many things deeply all at once.

We have several options at that point: stuff it back down, seek repentance and try to atone, run away, or seriously consider changing. In Aztec culture, self-sacrifice was often the solution, and, like Hara-Kiri, greatly honored. In our culture, suicide is an illegitimate form of running away, so we could try to atone by doing good deeds but we can never do enough, or we use it to cover up the pain of what we stuffed. However there are indeed many people who do commit suicide in our culture, so we are not so different, after all. (We remind those in desperate situations that self-sacrifice of the body prevents our ever changing anything in this life, so we must come back after this life and do the process all over again). Neither do our acceptable forms of self-sacrifice through doing good quell the inner pain. Even certain religious rituals sometimes do not work for us. We are finally driven to look at ourselves in the mirror and recognize the past, so that we can let go of the hidden emotional reactions, hard as that may be. This letting go is Quetzalcoatl's funeral pyre. Fire is an ancient universal symbol for cleansing. We can see this fire as symbol of complete cleansing of our negative thoughts and feelings, of letting them go. Water is also such a symbol, used in our myth of Sedna. We will discuss these concepts in the chapter on the Balsamic Moon phase, showing how following the Moon phase energies of transformation can prove so much more fruitful than choosing other phases to time this part of our self-work. We could use the example of the nine days in the Land of the Dead as a custom in AA, in which the new member, fresh from his recognition of need to change, tells his story to the members, many of whom are still vulnerable to abandoning their rehabilitation, but who might become encouraged to find their strength to continue rehabilitation, which seems to be the purpose of Quetzalcoatl's dark journey.[5] This is an excellent parable for alcoholics. They become examples to the "spiritually dead" (non-recovering alcoholics). This principle can work for other problems, through one's own belief systems, or through working the Moon Phases.

---

5   Native peoples of the South West US, as well as the Aztecs, believed that when honorable people died, they went to join the ancestors walking on the Milky Way. Others were consigned to a sunless, depressing place in the underworld, called the Land of the Dead—in modern plain-speak, depression for those not physically dead. Western non-ethnic people often talk about "going into the light," which seems to have a similar connotation, since the Milky Way is about light.

Sometimes even our divinity is repressed—our ability to express love, our power to heal or create, or our self worth. Responses and reactions received from others concerning the good we don't see, and inviting us to let go of the limitations we have placed on ourselves help us re-define ourselves through mirroring. Sometimes others even give us permission to define ourselves in these more complete ways, by acknowledging *for* us those life-enhancing abilities and emotions we have falsely learned not to acknowledge for ourselves. This is the positive side of transformation. I had a friend who was in deep depression. She said, "I feel like I am dying inside." She was in a marriage in which her partner would not allow her to follow the customs of her chosen religion, or be a part of its community, and she was feeling her soul being starved for what it needed. Neither one of us had an answer for her at the time—her resolution only came after a divorce. Some things are insoluble unless the total situation changes.

And what of the final step, ascension to Venus, planet of love for self and others? That, too, is available when we understand that, in mythology, becoming divine means raising our consciousness to something greater than ourselves. In our time, we might term that as our super conscious from which we can live a transpersonal life. Quetzalcoatl, like every one of us, was semi-divine to begin with, therefore attracted to earthly things, but the divine part allowed him not only to make the mistakes, but to find a way, suitable to himself individually, to use the mistake to carry him further in his quest for greater consciousness. We saw the same pattern in the story of Sedna (which you will find in Appendix B). Transformation is an inborn urge in everyone. It is not only for people of particular religions, it is a piece of everyone's equipment from birth. We all create a shadow that contains the memories of unfortunate experiences, but the memories also contain their own healing.

So, here are the bare steps of transformation. It can happen quickly or after years of living with lost memories such as childhood abuse from another person, in which case, our inner suppressed pain, anger, and often either a "victim" or "victimizer" attitude may suddenly confront us in a marriage relationship during a critical exchange. This is often because one who was abused later attracts abusive partners. Each needs the other as a mirror, and in cases where they both see themselves for who they truly are, they can work together to repair both the abused and the abuser. I have seen this happen successfully, but I have also seen the years of intense struggles to face and let go of their personal memories in order to change their patterns. I have also seen the new consciousness emerging, sometimes a day at a time, sometimes suddenly, casting major joy into the unhappy part of the mix.

We add that suppressed grief over a childhood loss, followed by years of depression, is a common cause of the need to find a re-birth experience.

No matter what techniques and inspiration we hope you will find in the following chapters, you are the ones who will have to go through the gates of death/transformation/and rebirth alone with your own soul and spirit. What, really, is the hardest part? Ask yourself what is the worst thing that could happen to you. If reliving these scary memories happened, where and who would you then be? You would have to admit that you would still be here, intact. So try reliving some early emotions that have gotten out of hand (with another person present). That fear, grief, or anger came from somewhere. You hid the most important things from yourself because they were too hard to look at. Is it possible that the inappropriate emotions that are now overflowing are reminding you of something you had forgotten in your early life? The medical profession is now beginning to consider the possibility that some traumatic memories may trigger the cellular DNA process that leads to cancer.

Carl Simonton[6], who in the '70's pioneered a new approach to adjunctive Cancer treatment, found that major early childhood traumas appeared to be connected to several major cancers in mid-life, and if the patients engaged in psychotherapy for about 18 months many of them were permanently healed. In many cases, therefore, we would recommend that if your crisis is so deep you cannot find the source of your symptoms (mental, emotional, physical) yourself, you get help.

One thing about this life is inescapable and it is that every person in our life is a mirror of things in our unconscious that hold our joy and energy hostage and need to be made conscious. They also can bring out the best in us, and qualities we did not know existed. It

---

6   Carl Simonton, whose research profoundly affected the field of social oncology, and the attitudes of many patients toward their disease. His work suggested that some cancers emerged many years after early childhood traumas from the ages between 18 and 36 months. Such deep-rooted memories involved rage, terror, hate, and other major buried emotions, requiring at least 1 to 1½ years of therapy. They documented cures of people only weeks from death. You can read about his work in his book *Healing Journey*.

would take volumes to list the convolutions of them all, so take our word for it, for now. But take a moment to ask yourself who do you dislike the most? Or of what are you most fearful? That person or event is mirroring a similar person, or event, from your past. As you follow the Moon Phases you may sometimes be able to tease out the memories and feelings within the context of a cycle of phases. It is not for nothing that the Moon is so often associated with mirrors and reflections.

The Mirrors

Why are relationships—individual with self, or self-other, or self—collective, so basic to consciousness and evolution? Myths are mirrors that speak to us, and so are people, as when someone who has nothing to do with a situation triggers a strong emotion inside you. You need to ask yourself why. Sometimes a piece of music, the effects of your own actions on others, or watching how another handles a similar problem, can trigger an insight into yourself

Imagine being alone in the world—we would never be able to see and therefore know ourselves. Something of that nature has been suggested in religious literature concerning God's aloneness in His initial Oneness or unity. We can only grow and learn who we are if we have at least one other person in our environment to reflect us back to ourselves. Is the divine in ourselves calling out to the divine in the other? We need them as mirrors that do more than show us what we look like on the outside. We need mirrors that help us define our inner selves through the reality check of others, the reflection of our impact on the external world. In the process of our self-definition, assisted by others, in that dance of conscious with unconscious, our inner light grows brighter and our awareness of ourselves, initially separative, expands to include others, represented by the decreasing light (increasing wisdom) on the waning Moon. We are being enveloped by, absorbed by, overwhelmed by, or accepted by the larger group, depending on our viewpoint. At this point we can tentatively suggest that another way of seeing the shadow on the Moon is as the inner self. After all, the "shadow" is the sum total of what we are unaware of inside, not only those things that are there through no fault of their own.

How one learns about one's personal unconscious is nicely described by the wake of an invisible boat. The unconscious is the invisible boat, but it leaves effects in its wake that both you and others can see. An individual can believe and say she is not angry, but her hands or teeth may be clenched. Others can see that and remark upon what their senses are telling them. This is mirroring, a very powerful tool. Individuals can accept or not accept the mirror, but that's often hard once they have observed the results of their hidden emotion through the eyes of another. For the individual it is something like being invisible and only able to see oneself in a mirror, while all the time you are feeling that "everybody's looking at me!" Only then is one able to recognize the hidden angry, grieving, or victimized but powerful part of oneself, bring it into consciousness, and transform it into its original and legitimate form—power used in the pursuit of wholeness. This is integration. Mythology is full of it.

Again we suggest you read the myth of minor planet Sedna, head Goddess of the Inuit People (Appendix B). Read deeply and see how Sedna (daughter of a very dysfunctional father) refused to "let go" of her part in that life. At sea in a small boat and a great storm, her father shockingly cuts off her hands that hung on for dear life, because the boat could hold only one person. Sinking to the darkest depths of the ocean (her deepest subconscious), a mystery of purification and transformation through water, instead of fire, happened, and she became a goddess. No one knows how transformation takes place, but often in such major ones as Sedna's, one has had a vision. Perhaps after the worst has happened there is nothing left to fear. Perhaps she gazed into the eyes of her own Higher Self after she had given up all the frightening memories. That is a mirror that often appears to us when we believe ourselves to be completely at the end of our rope with no hope. We are not told, but probably she rose to heaven like Quetzalcoatl and thereafter was a tiny, invisible planet only now discovered, with her contemporary message of the need to abandon our victimized and victimizing actions and attitudes; and what will happen if we do, and what will happen if we don't. In fact, there seems to be a widespread growing awareness (consciousness) that there actually aren't many options, just as there were not for Sedna. We waited too long.

But the circles spread as we become more inclusive of our own selves and therefore of others. This is what relationship gives us, without which we would remain frozen like a crystal in our limited self-knowledge, either balanced in the direction of an unrealistic ego or in the opposite direction of self-denial. Of course in reality, we all have many people in our lives, and we all have exactly that many opportunities to learn how to relate to ourselves and others.

Actual relationship-deprived people are often seen among those who have been defined by society and medicine as mentally ill—schizophrenic, or autistic. These people are unable to relate to others or to have realistic self concepts. Many others to a lesser degree have similar problems because of early childhood deprivations. It is as though they grew in a bubble of isolation. Often their actions seem to us chaotic, or their responses irrelevant to our reality. Is it frightening to know that this is how the rest of us might be if we grew up without the opportunity of relationships? There is never a time when the Moon and Sun are not in relationship. Nor is there such a time for us in normal life, but what we do with the results of those relationships is critical to our growth.

Projections

We call mirrored information *projections*, a common topic on the psychiatrist's couch. We encounter them everywhere all the time but they tend to come up more glaringly at Full Moons and Lunar eclipses. They create road rage for example, and the man who shouts invectives from behind you on the road is shouting at someone else from his buried past. Emotions repressed in the shadow become active at Full Moon because the light on the Moon acts as a form of denial, at the same time as the Moon-ruled emotions have intense instinctual need to express. Usually such emotions do not express themselves at the original object. Instead they blow up over anything another person does that aggravates the hidden piece of shadow. Or, if we are obsessed with a hidden fear we become "afraid of our shadow" so to speak, paranoid at its extreme, because we don't know what we are afraid of, therefore it can be everywhere. If we feel victimized, "it is always someone else's fault." There may be someone who consistently irritates us for no obvious reason. Maybe it is the tone of voice, or the sense that someone is constantly criticizing, when in fact the person hasn't said anything critical. One may or may not actually be doing that out of one's own inner shadow, which is irrelevant. What is relevant is one's reaction. If you are consistently irritated but afraid to ask the person why she is critical, you are dealing with your own projection. If it turns out that she reminds you of your mother, perhaps she is actually repeating similar patterns of her own mother. This happens often and when it does, you have found that serendipitous pairing of two opposite shadow mirrors! How fortuitous! You would have so much to teach each other! However, in real life, "divorce" often happens before the teaching can begin.

In short, projections are reacting with old emotions when certain people unknowingly trigger the unconscious memory of old experiences behind the emotions. This unresolved emotion causes us to perceive another person as like someone from the old experiences of the past, so that we can then reenact whatever it was, equally unknowingly. Just remember the wake of the invisible boat and when you see your effect on others, or theirs on your own, it is an opportunity, particularly at Full Moon, to see yourself objectively, or to mirror another person. We help each other become whole when we recognize and give them permission to let go of that piece of shadow. The chapters in Section II will offer specific ways to do this. We have found that persons who intentionally address these projections find the transformation part easier and more joyful. Hanging on, like Sedna, to some beloved lie about yourself—well, you read it above. It is as though you keep saying, "If I just hang on long enough, this will go away." The results could actually be rather grisly.

Ideally, *the Full Moon is the time to "reach for the Sun" (spirit, purpose) and achieve wholeness, while New Moon is the time to experience internal unity.* This is you, recognizing the higher path of your spirit and aligning your way of doing things with that higher path. This is you, accepting the whole of yourself, even not knowing what your unconscious holds. New and Full Moon together create both an internal and external dance. Unity in wholeness is a natural urge of humanity toward some far goal, modeled by the signs cycle which is relationship modeled for us, but only our own relationships will get us there, no matter how bitter the struggle. That said, this way of, and attitude toward, life has brought us a piece of joy in the midst of problems we are working on. Searching for wholeness is a very joyful dance. Do you know someone who has major life-problems, but who manages to truly radiate joy in life? That is where we are going. The journey never ends, but we can realize that the journey is more important than the destination, because if we cannot find joy here and now, we may never find it.

The Moon Cycle and Transforming Consciousness

In a very general sense, *conscious-ness* depends on the degree of ability one's ego has to transform. If you could practice this on little things every month do you suppose the big ones might be easier? Can you see the Moon cycles in that process—the monthly outline of the transformative process? Here is what we found— that every

Moon cycle gives us a small practice in carrying out the intent to do something important for ourselves. In the process the Moon energies often trigger recognition of something inside us that we suddenly realize is not helpful in the current situation.

(1) <u>New Moon</u> rebirth into initially accepting "not knowing" as part of our wholeness. In a few days, the new seed of the month's project or lesson will shoot up a tiny stem and leaf representing the form of the new project accompanied by some old attitudes or other pieces of the shadow.

(2) <u>First Quarter Moon</u> incorporating the new form into, and expanding, the conscious self; empowering the self with the new energies available. The old pieces of shadow or one's social/parental patterns challenge one's creativity in moving forward. The success of the Full Moon depends upon one's previous intent to follow their creativity beyond their own personal socially patterned self.

(3) <u>Full Moon</u> the personal aspect of the initial seed idea is fulfilled here, becoming part of one's outer life. If the old patterns at First Quarter dominated the action, then it may spoil the fulfillment, or get out of control. Look for mirrors—people or events which point to the problem or its solution. The actual energy used here is toward "reaching for the Sun" or being able to use the guidance of spirit to manifest that completion of the New Moon intent.

(4) <u>Last Quarter Moon</u> struggle between what new values you learned from the past three weeks, and the old attitudes. If you let it, this struggle involves using your High Self, or Solar Self's highest values. Make sure the new not the old ones are going to help you in the coming cycle. The second half of this phase is the transformation. Accept the unknowns of the future cycle and reorient yourself toward them, with the intent to use the new attitudes or values; acknowledge the old attitudes and let go of them. The energies at this time help promote the process, and will be described in more detail later.

Being able to accept what is not yet known is one of the signs of a mature ego and strong consciousness. When a relationship is ended without closure, one may be left clueless and obsessively grieving. In an actual case, I had a client who was in persistent depression and grief over a lost relationship. She told me that while meditating at the Full Moon, an inner voice gave her the clear message "I don't have to know why". When she accepted those words she felt a great relief and as though her personal power became more whole, and felt stronger. She had what we call the Full Moon enlightenment or realization. She only later realized she had had a transformation, though she may have done the work on the problem at the previous Last Quarter Moon and finished it as a revelation at the next Full Moon. Remember this about transformation: accepting loss is an ego-death, but a friend states that "if you know it is an ego-death, it is not an ego-death!" Transformation takes place in the deepest parts of your unconscious, probably partly in the collective unconscious. You only find out afterwards. Remember that the urge to transform is an archetype and archetypes live in the world of the C.U.

Through her realization this lady was able to take back a part of herself she had unconsciously allowed another to hold hostage. Moon's changing reflected light symbolizes the changing proportion of personal self-awareness and unconscious or "shadow". As personal awareness grows, like the Full Moon, it begins to yearn for or reach toward the "Sun at the center"—our Higher Self or individual spark of divinity behind the antithetical mask. When other people reflect, attract, magnetize (polar opposites), and comment on our personal selves, we are assisted in our reaching. What we see is that our Sun-*individuality* and Moon-*personal self* must be at least aligned in intent. Ultimate unity or actual alignment may take many generations, but *intentional* alignment is possible for everyone. Remember, that despite ego's bad press, ego is the part of ourselves that has to express that intent and bring it about through its own choices and willingness to grow more inclusive.

5

The Alchemy of Sun and Moon
The Alchemy of the One who First Made All Things
and the Old Woman Who Never Dies

> Alchemy: *A medieval chemical philosophy primarily* [and metaphorically] *concerned with the conversion of base metals into gold.*
>
> —Webster

> *One of the chief statements of Alchemy is that this Great Work is performed by means of the Sun and the Moon through the aid of Mercury. The Sun is the Pineal Gland; the Moon is the Pituitary; and Mercury is the thinking lobe of the brain, the Intellect. It is performed, then, partly by the self-conscious and partly by the subconscious, with Mercury steering the ship. It is the thinking lobe of the brain supported by Mercury who, by the steady pressure of his will is giving his suggestion to the subconscious, which does the indispensable work. Everything is explained back to Mercury and it is he who forms the images.*
>
> –From *The Rabbi's Tarot*[1] by Daphna Moore.

How does transformation come about? Daphna Moore tells us that conscious will and intention connects to the unconscious by giving it messages or images. The mind by forming the words and images is responsible. Where do these images come from and how will we find them?

Humankind has always found a place to gather spiritual information and find group support. All over the world people come together in nature, sacred spaces, homes, churches, temples,

---

1   *The Rabbi's Tarot* by Daphna Moore. Llewellyn,1989.

synagogues and mosques to worship and give thanks. Now it is time to take our spirituality to another level by using the words and images from these gatherings as one source of potent words. The next step requires that we actually use our belief systems out in the world at home, at work, and in the streets. We must fan the divine spark in each of us and learn to communicate to our unconscious and to others with understanding and compassion. We all have a contribution to make because the collective is us, and evolution of consciousness requires our individual conscious thought, conscious speech, and conscious action. *The Old Woman* brings us a spiritual technique that integrates spirituality, consciousness and practical living in a new way, one created out of the past but made relevant for this time.

    In case you hadn't noticed, the story of Sun and Moon, in its largest sense, is a myth about how Spirit or God interacts with the third dimension or material world in order to create. The process is an alchemy, a transformation of one substance into another, of one level of consciousness into another.. God doesn't do this alone; this is the step where we become partners in co-creation of our own lives.

The Early Transformational Path

    It is said that in the great transformation of soul-merge where soul meets and merges with the spirit or God, the two mysterious glands in our head—Pituitary and Pineal—merge in their functions. They represent our masculine-feminine sides as personal Sun-Moon. In another sense, whichever we are on the outside we have the opposite on the inside, so our outer self merges with our inner, or our conscious merges with the unconscious. Kabbalah has a word for this: *Toku-Kovaro*— outside like inside. Another term in popular political use is *transparent,* and recently transparency is being demanded of our public servants and major financial world players, a strong indication that the collective is ready for more on this topic of a personal nature. We add that the Pituitary represents the Lunar feminine polarity, while the Pineal represents the Solar masculine polarity. The secret no one has ever bothered to tell you is that this unity of inner and outer does not mean the unconscious becomes conscious, only that *the motivations of both become the same*, a transformative process that cannot be consciously arranged, but can be intentionally accomplished. Another way to say this is that "soul-merge" is the merging of one's soul with one's spirit, through the purification of ones personality, which is the first step on the Moon path, in order to reach the Sun. That merging is said to unify one's whole being and prepare one's several bodies for 7th dimension energies and 12-strand DNA initiations. These concepts are currently being presented by many individuals under many different terminologies. We are here attempting to present a sort of perspective or common link between concepts among which our Moon story may find a relationship of some sort.

In this book we see the transformational or alchemical process as a gradual transformation, taken in many steps, though not always completed in this life at this time. We see transformation for everyone in the smaller changes we all can go through frequently, even monthly, on our spiritual paths. The tools, words, and suggestions herein, provide a context and a language with which to motivate the conscious self to stimulate the unconscious to do the transformational work that is our personal alchemy.

Shamans, enlightened teachers, gurus and mystery schools have been the guides by which many humans in the past have traveled the transformational path. Many have walked the path of the mystics through the major religions: Christian mysticism, Jewish Kabbalah, Islamic Sufism, Esoteric Hinduism, and Western Metaphysics (based on Tibetan mysticism). All of these paths owe their core wisdom to the Moon cycles. The percentage of such students has been extremely small in terms of all humanity; but we now live in a time when the whole of humanity needs this path, not just the forerunners—the spiritually elite. We need it for humanity's survival, both physical and spiritual.

The *Secrets of the Old Woman* mark out the original, natural path of transformation for everyone. It can accompany anyone's religion, or metaphysical system, or it can be followed on its own. We are talking about a conscious, intentional, daily "directed", evolutionary path toward what is everywhere called enlightenment, based on the Moon's natural timing. Its essence is in intentionally reconnecting ourselves to the universal rhythms of evolution through the Sun and Moon, re-synchronizing with the changing four-fold energy pattern as the Old Ones did. It is a daily practice of cosmic timing for learning to observe, understand, and direct our actions and beliefs in terms of our own inner truth. Its purpose is to create a better world for ourselves and humanity. It is an alchemy one studies using one's daily life as the book, and the Sun-Moon-Earth energies as the tools and the timing. Even though the First Ancestors are our teachers, their system is never out of date. We believe they held rituals with divination on the Moon phases throughout the long age of shamanism—more than 30,000 years. Divination—which was basic to the rituals— began developing the vast data bank of Moon phase information. Religions incorporated some of it, which few recognize today; the alchemists saw the symbolism and created complex mysteries around the symbols, which often lost connection with nature. By our time much of the meaning has become unintelligible. You can't pick up a book at the library and become an alchemist.

According to archeologists no one knows how far back the earliest shamanic practices existed, or the ritual use of Moon Phases, although there is a famous but disputed bone with 28 marks with every seventh mark exaggerated, carbon-dated to 30,000 BC. There are many others found in the caves in France. Until recently we ourselves could find no proven dates of first use of the eight Moon phases. However, we have found in China the beginnings of a set of eight archetypal principles from around 6,000 BCE, which are very suggestive of our Moon phases. We call your attention to the later eight Buddhist principles called "The Eight-Fold Path", which we incorporated into our Eight Phases in Part II of this book. Buddhism began in China around the 5th century BCE in India with the teachings of Siddhartha Gautama, commonly referred to as "the Buddha", who introduced the eight principles as part of the four noble truths. It is likely that the basic principles were in a widespread simpler form already pre-existent in the belief system of the time and place of Buddha. Religious leaders often introduce new teachings based on earlier ones. The Christian teachings are a good example. As we have stated earlier, everything in our world today has roots somewhere in the very ancient past.

How can information from primitive people of the past suddenly become our future hope? Could millions care about signing up for Kabbalah or Practical Mysticism or Alchemy--all strenuous, time-consuming, and now expensive, ways of spiritual life? A relatively very small number do sign up, and Kabbalah is being popularized and is currently drawing more people. Could this be because Kabbalah contains more of the ancient shamanic wisdom? Can religion fill that role?

Religions are various versions of outer paths to the Divine. Their external, codified forms can support one's expansion of consciousness. We believe institutional religions hold and support people in basic patterns of reverence to the Divine and seldom deal extensively with the metaphysics of the inner life, which are found in each religion's mystical teachings. Nevertheless, from the religions come the foundations for evolvement—first the urge to reconnect with the Divine in our lives (religion = *re-ligio* = Latin for "re-connect"). Then come the basic, necessary rules of self-government—one's rules-for-living—most of which come from religions and underlie contemporary social laws governing our moral and ethical relations toward others; the models for that living—such as Abraham, Buddha, Mohammed and Jesus are behind the experience of group worship and individual prayer.. The exoteric or outer forms of religion provide collective guidance for a long, slow path that affects whole societies and their history, and contain all the keys to misuse.

Since the esoteric, or inner, teachings originated with the Sun and Moon, we are returning to that source. We are presenting it as an integration of inner and outer, and a direct way of bringing both sides of ourselves into unity as modeled by the New and Full Moons. In our book there are no restrictions on what you can learn because we no longer need the division of exoteric and esoteric paths. Here, there is neither *inner* nor *outer* in terms of what you can learn. There is only the interweaving dance of the inner-and-outer-you that finds here timing (a rhythm in the sky) and pattern of steps (signs and phases.) These two move you along your own spiritual paths at your own speed. We don't promise it is easy, though! Just that you can go at your own speed until your unconscious or super conscious takes over. After that, enjoy the ride. When you trust yourself and the universe, and accept life as it comes, a lot of conflict is gone.

The Moon Path of Transformation

We will find our inner-directed self, the empowered individual, by practicing the original resonance with the universe, one who *Becomes* within his/her family and society. This person *Becomes the drop that maintains its identity and integrity within the ocean.* This individual retains his/her individuality and personal meaning within any social context, while fully recognizing and honoring his/her unity within that context. *Who we are meant to be i*s our spiritual evolving self—fully functioning in our daily life and relationships. This way of life is the major difference between the early shamanic versions of the Moon path and the present version

In early or tribal times and in the shamanic roots of eastern religions, people were/are not encouraged to develop individuality. They experienced themselves as a unit with the group and functioned according to the group rules, for the good of the group. That was only half its destiny—*Being*. The other half—*Becoming*—has been the task of the West. Now East and West must meet and fertilize each others' creativity.[2]

We are proposing a path on which anyone can consciously and intentionally develop and maintain his/her unique individuality within the group, here and now, while purposefully making choices "for the good of the group as well as the self." This is a world of difference, creating a fertile ground for soul growth. It is especially important at this time, as we see people in general too harried, too stressed, too pressured by outside demands, to know or think about whether they are operating from their real self or their parental patterns. And yet nearly all, if asked, would tell you that they know there must be something more if they only had time to look for it. To all of those people we would say, "Watch the Moon and the Sun. Set your physical and mental watches to synchronize with the two lights. Take advantage of the right energies when they are available. Learn to draw from their wells of wisdom. Do it on your feet."

Since the Teachers of all ages have said in extremely complicated ways that the Sun and the Moon are key ingredients on the spiritual path, how about letting the Sun and the Moon teach us directly? What a liberating idea! Everyone on this earth sees and experiences the energies of the Sun and the Moon, and most of us take them for granted. Though we all are influenced by the two energies, we miss some critical parts of their messages when we are unaware. To say it in another way, although we let the Sun and Moon rule our hours of sleep, work and occasional fishing trips, most of us have no idea that by including the Moon-Sun relationship we can incorporate both Lights into a holistic personal Lunar calendar, and re-bond with our *Sister-Moon and Brother-Sun* (St. Francis of Assisi).

How the Alchemy Works

The fundamentals of our personal alchemy include the idea

2   For example, there is a Japanese doctor, Johnson F. Yan, with degrees in both Japanese and American medicine, who wrote a little book called *DNA and the I Ching*. Its theme is about one way to combine Eastern and Western medicine in a seamless way that will multiply the benefits of both to the patient. We do have Eastern medical traditions here side by side, with American medicine. However, the AMA has never figured out how to make one medicine out of the two. Neither has it figured out how to include Native American medicine except as expensive synthesized drugs.

that spiritual growth requires not only unity of conscious and unconscious, but conscious words to connect them. Mercury—the innermost planet of our Solar system—is a dual planet, representing our logical thinking processes and the mythical winged messenger of the gods. It represents the conscious mind and higher mind, and communication between them. Long before Egypt's Thoth and Greece's Hermes (both culture gods believed to be incarnations of the planet Mercury), an unknown god represented the planet Mercury. He symbolized the original shaman, who went into trance, shape-shifted into a bird, and flew to the upper worlds (heaven) to receive the spiritual message (usually a divination) and bring it down to the waiting community. Even today, the NW Indians have a widespread story of the white raven that brought the Sun and a bit of its fire to cold and hungry first humans, and taught them how to lift the sky so that they could stand up on their two legs. Many such stories have brought early cultures the power and spiritual inspiration that comes with consciousness They tell us that there is a winged Something that opens up communication between the subtle parts of our minds, and soul or spirit, transforming us. We don't call it Hermes or Mercury, but it represents a most powerful experience for those to whom it has opened an inner door.

This Something is what we can find or use at the practical level with our own minds in our own time, in our own way—directly, without trances, mantras, rituals, meditations or other esoteric practices; although such disciplines intensify and speed up the process, and come naturally as a result, to the evolving person, and we will mention them occasionally. What we offer here is a path anyone at all can follow if they are motivated to do so, and can read. We personally have found that incorporating basic shamanic trance, meditation or religious prayer practices greatly expand the Moon path for us, and we recommend such practices to those who are inclined. But our basic key is the use of words.

Part of the process is putting our insights, emotions and reactions into familiar words that our unconscious mind can understand (a function of Mercury as the whole brain/mind.) We need to talk to ourselves about its content in order for the unconscious to be transformed. However the actual work of transformation is not our conscious task. That work belongs to the special wisdom of the unconscious—personal and collective. It needs to be fed new positive words, like those in the 360 archetypal Sabian Symbols[3], of which more in Chapter 11. Such words may also be found in the keywords of the several zodiac tables scattered through this book. You will notice that some of the degree symbols, and all of the signs, include negative words and ideas, also related to the archetypes. Pay close attention to these, because the Collective Unconscious contains both the Divine and the Demonic, speaking poetically. Both need to be brought out, the latter to be transformed, the former to illuminate, uplift you, or re-establish your own lost divinity in your conscious self. Often the divine deceptively appears as the Shadow, the dark side, simply because we mistake its warning signs as bad or negative. You won't know until later which they came from—the dark or the light, Shadow or personal divine. The more you don't like the negative words, the more you need to find out why you don't. Whichever it is, it could be holding you back. Sometimes you can find the exact opposite positive word for something negative, feed it to your own unconscious and receive important insights about yourself as a result.

Feeding the personal unconscious the right words at the right time has extraordinary power to transform the unconscious and externalize its gifts into our lives. Words can get us into trouble, but they also are the mind's way of expressing the deepest experiences we can have, and of redirecting old limiting unconscious mind-stuff. We, like the shaman, can meditate or cast a divination, or follow the methods in this book to find the words of divination or direction for your next phase. Within the Moon path context, a particular but always different archetypal *Sabian Symbol* is the key to each Moon phase. The position of the phase in the Zodiac designates its own primary energy focus; and the Symbol gives us the words that apply to the area of our individual life visited by the phase. When we find a word that resonates, and use it, we let our unconscious know that we are ready for transformation. Amazingly, the unconscious applies its own structure and organization to bring about the needed change. The secret of the system's effectiveness is that the timing of the words matches the needs represented by the Moon phases.

By our intimate and complete connectedness with nature, its timing is also our personal timing. The system points toward the way of connecting with the C.U. As we said earlier, *our connection to the*

---

3   A set of 360 universal symbolic imageries which characterize each of the 360 degrees of a cycle or the circle of the Zodiac. See Chapter 11.

Divine is through the Collective Unconscious; and we connect with the *wisdom of the C.U through the ancestors.* The Divine and the Demonic are in our shadow, which we create ourselves, but which nevertheless came out of ways people have used and misused the archetypes, so at bottom the original archetypes behind the Shadow exist with the archetypes in the C.U., along with the misuses in the racial memories. Here we are in muddy territory, but it's something to meditate on if it interests one. A still more interesting meditation might be on the initial statement in this paragraph, which completes a deep three-step process in our spiritual life. One goes through the ancestors to get to the *wisdom* of the Collective Unconscious, and through the C.U. to get to the *Divine.* But what does that mean? Here that means the collective memories from the Ancestors who manifested belief systems and lived the resulting experiences activate the racial memories and archetypes within our own cells. If we view the ancestors as existing in our racial memories or the DNA, we can understand that we also activate the wisdom the ancestors learned that may also exist in our very cells (instinctive wisdom) to connect to the C.U. (group sense or urge toward group spiritual activity (religion?) to connect to the Divine. If you are religious, somewhere within it you will find a way to do this. If not, you will find it within yourself as we go along the basic natural path. Now for the words that will empower our journey.

Potent Words and Timing

Daphna Moore calls transformative "words" *potent suggestions to the unconscious.* She states three qualities required for their success, taken from the initial chapter quotation above 1. *It must not be anything abstract; it must be concrete*; 2. *It cannot be anything neutral, it must be emotional*; 3. *It cannot be anything passive; it must be active.* All of these qualities will be found in the Sabian Symbols as well as many other places. But these symbols are keyed to the timing. We add a fourth quality, that it also should contain a visual element—that is, mental imagery, with a feeling attached.

Correct timing is of the essence in the transformation process, which is why this path is so powerful and effective that at times we are almost stunned by the results of our efforts. The Sun and the Moon provide an ongoing rhythmic pattern of four (and eight) frequencies, keyed to the symbols, perfectly timed for healing and integrating ourselves. It really makes a difference when we do things in the correct timing. There are still farmers today who plant according to the Moon's phases. Sometimes one will tell you how different his results are from those of his neighbor who plants when he wishes. We are about planting, too. We are planting seeds of consciousness. The cycle moves us from New Moon when we have no words for something that is beginning in a specific area of our lives, to Full Moon when it is fully defined, because what began at New Moon, two weeks later either is fulfilled, achieved, or destroyed. It is "out there", objectively seen or known by ourselves or others, and described by the archetypal degrees. As the Moon begins to wane, energies urge us to put these new words to our experience, share it, place a value upon it, internalize it...and manifest a difference in our lives because of that understanding.

Whatever our source, we need to find, inside or outside ourselves, words of realization, inspiration, love, peace, despair, regret, grief, protest, every human emotion and understanding of conscious and unconscious life factors. Verbalization leads not only to understanding what is in our depths now, but also to putting carefully timed and chosen transformative words back into our unconscious to trigger future internal action and awareness. As we have said, these words often can be the archetypal (see Chapter 10) meanings found in the particular Moon phase zodiac degrees. Every New Moon and each of its phases begins on a Zodiac degree. Each Sabian degree's symbol operates first as a verbalization of the energy of that phase, and then as a divination or description of the situation that exists at that moment. If one wants a divination, one can also look up what the rest of the month is about, although often we find it is like reading the last chapter of a book first. It doesn't always make sense at the time.

The personal unconscious contains the totality of what we don't know consciously, including the personal divine, demonic, and early social/parental patterning. The problem with unconscious living is that it keeps recycling all the learned patterns so that one's negative reactions continue. "This always happens to me!" We feed the same old words back into our unconscious. Judy calls it "if you keep doing what you're doing, you keep getting what you got." The phase keynotes allow one to look at the situation from a larger point of view, at a distance so to speak. For a few moments one can step back and take stock or put a conscious intent or word into the situation, which begins to change us unconsciously and therefore begins to recreate the outside. Some psychologies call this breaking the feedback loops. We say it is the archetypes, attaching to and projecting on, the outside world something in our personal unconscious that needs to be revealed, and/or transformed.

The rhythmic dance of the Sun and Moon with each other provides the exact timing and specific words each of us individually needs and is ready for, that will stimulate the "directed" or conscious intentional growth we spoke of above. Once we intentionally align ourselves—conscious mind (Mercury), and body (Earth), and with the dance of Sun and Moon, we can see that it automatically mirrors the dance in our own lives. Or perhaps it is the other way around, for both may be part of a much greater universal rhythm. If that is so, as we believe, then this alignment can have awesome significance for how our planet will make the great crossing that is happening in our time.

At New Moon, if we so intend, we can have a three-day practice in unifying our inner and outer selves. At Full Moon we are offered a three-day practice in unifying our selves with humanity. Between New and Full, and between Full and New, are the three steps each that lead toward personal transformation, however humble, subtle or minimal. Each month is a new adventure for everyone who wants to change. It requires only conscious intent. All the work is what we have to do anyway, but *how* it is done is what makes the difference! Whatever life offers us becomes whatever we created for ourselves to experience and grow with, and all of it is an adventure in knowing ourselves.

Struggles, Intention and Their Reward

We who are writing this have been walking/writing this path together for six years, and much longer separately. The challenge of trying to stay conscious and present in the now, all of the time, has brought us incredible changes and insights. By now, we can say unequivocally that our lives are vastly different than they could have been had we not committed to these challenges. This can be true for you six years from now if you want it. We are not promising that it will be easy, but neither is the other way. If you live intentionally, you will be fully engaging with life itself, "down in the trenches" as Judy says; "and we often lose it [our focus], but we always get it back"

There are few failures on this path, and we accept that fully even though there are days when one of us has said, "There may be hope out there, but I don't feel like it right now." There are few failures because when you think you did something "wrong," it usually is because you didn't know how to do it right, and you are here to learn it by doing. Also, you may think you have failed because you are buying into another person's idea of what is right or wrong. Intentionally doing something wrong may be a different issue, but that too may come from one's not knowing any options. We see the purpose of being alive on this planet as being about learning what you didn't yet know. The world over, there are many differences of opinion about this purpose, but your truth is your own, and it must be honored if you are to evolve.

You will find remedies on this path for those occasional times of despair, pain, or sense of failure. This honest grappling with external reality while remaining connected to spirit, can be hard at times. But you will feel better about yourself when you realize that the struggles and missteps are fundamental to the growing process, itself. One changes very quickly with each successful encounter. The brain sciences assure us that what took years to learn to do incorrectly takes only a few minutes to re-pattern by changing the neural pathways! It is not widely known that our personal struggles with "doing it wrong" often speak to unborn gifts, strengths, and spiritual insights, of unimagined potential power in our lives

Stay with us through the following pages!

A Reminder. Moon patterns are not the same thing as the alchemical teachings, but Moon patterns were the basis for the "Moon-mysteries" of early times. Religious teachings are imposed from without, mysticisms have their own inner teachings, and mystery schools teach practical occultism. All were based in the Moon cycles, but none of these systems will be found on our Moon path. In a sense, we (both authors and readers together) are creating our own, contemporary mystery-teaching.

For impatient readers who ask, "When do we get to the meat of this?" we answer "We already have, by first introducing the philosophy behind the teaching." The Moon cycles contain the most profound wisdom on earth. This profundity must be understood and appreciated in order to approach the contemporary path-work that emerges out of the old teachings. Because the phases need to be reverently approached, with appreciation for how our universe is set up to teach us, we share a basic foundation that we hope inspires the reader. Also, the phases are just plain difficult for many people to apply to their lives because they require a major paradigm change from outer focus to inner focus. Therefore each chapter also adds a small amount of the technique so that when you get to the technical part in chapters 7-12, you will not find the contents completely unfamiliar.

6

The Old Woman's Ritual
Honoring the Faces of the Changing Moon

Out of the past into the now,
Honoring the faces of the changing moon.
Out of the old into the new,
Bringing the feminine into the all.
Out of the darkness into the light,
Calling the shadow to yield up its power.
Out of the day into the night,
Reaching for the light awaiting our call.
Filling the Crescent vessel of light
Becoming the vessel, becoming the all.

--VLM

Personal Ritual

The Moon's cycle is itself a cosmic ritual—a pattern we all can and do live our lives by in some mysterious way. What do you think of when someone says "ritual"—morning shower, coffee, a cigarette, maybe candles and incense? Do you wear your lucky red shoes every Friday? Mankind compulsively gravitates to ritual. We believe it is part of the Divine Design because it fills such a deep need. But the spiritual, psychological purpose behind much of it seems to be largely forgotten. The dictionary says that a ritual is a set of actions thought to have symbolic value, yet today many holiday rituals have been abandoned or perverted into money making ventures. People tend to go a bit crazy during winter holidays just because there are so many easy ways that one can participate in a "ritual". Anyone can buy and send cards, bake cookies buy gifts, light candles, or decorate a tree, all of which are enjoyable. However instead of feeling peaceful, joyful and secure after the holidays many of us are tired, overwhelmed and let down after all the "fun" is over. Was the need for the ritual fulfilled?

Starbuck's has literally created a new national ritual—or rather, people have grabbed onto it to fill a need—the cup of coffee on the way to the office. Each person I see walking along, briefcase in one hand, paper cup in the other, is absorbed in a private world, and I envy the aura of intimacy between his/her outer and inner self that I cannot enter, and would not, since that secret communion would cease to exist. But I imagine that I see a feeling of some momentary belonging in another world, in that person walking along with his/her cup. What need is being fulfilled?

What is the missing piece from the Design that encourages the use of rituals to help us evolve? Read about the Rituals and the Moon phases in this chapter and you will find out.

Ritual has been a part of everyone's life since the beginning. Conscious ritual began as a community practice. At one level the importance of primitive ritual was to keep the individual subject to the group, and the group's connection to the natural world, initially probably for survival reasons. Since then we have evolved into awareness of ourselves as individuals, and gradually lost the centrality of group consciousness, although we see it in religious services in our time. No one knows how, why or when it began. We see it even in animals, and most markedly in some primates. Our group rituals have changed and we have cultural rituals, religious rituals, social rituals, business rituals, mating rituals, family rituals, work rituals, corporate rituals. These rituals were created to help us integrate our individuality into some segment of society. The importance of that is seldom mentioned because we associate ritual now with "outdated" traditional practices. Personal and private rituals are becoming more conscious, but we still often do not recognize them as such. Nor do we recognize their importance, which is to integrate us into a larger, more universal realm and world view.

Because these stages of ritual have been with us from our very earliest prehistory, we know they have value; they are worth experimenting with as a structure around which we create our own rituals, however minimal, or make a personal connection to the divine. Patterns or rituals based on the Moon's phases may well suggest an activity fundamental to human evolution. It is interesting to note that in the mental health system one encounters many clients with obsessive compulsive behaviors that are ritualistic in nature, such as constant washing of hands. Compare that with Lady Macbeth (Shakespeare's play, *Macbeth*) who washes her hands to rid them of an imaginary spot of blood, during sleepwalking, as the result of her guilt over encouraging her husband to kill the King of Scotland.

These are attempts by the individual to control an otherwise socially and personally unacceptable outbreak of some kind.

Underlying the obvious uses of ritual, a possibly more fundamental issue may link ancient and modern ritual at all levels. The above compulsive behaviors are considered to protect one from a personal incurable, persistent, unconscious guilt or other threatening emotion. If one looks closely, all early ritual was for protection, from evil spirits, drought, and anti-social community mis-behaviors. Perhaps nowadays we would call them something else if we are among the "normal" segment of the population. But what of those who go to church, or those who don't, but need that vague sense of comfort of personal daily rituals we all have, the comfort of the predictable that shields us from an uncomfortable perceived change? Note that "four" is prominent and fundamental in DNA. Some scientists now say that our thoughts can affect and change our DNA. How much can ritual affect our DNA? If science is correct in the results of its recent studies of the epigenetic shield, appropriate ritual could be a powerful way to not only increase our current consciousness, but to add consciousness to the gene pool for our younger readers. In any case, contemporary life is never free of restrictions upon natural behaviors and we seldom have control of the rules of society. Rituals can help us be more comfortable with our artificial lives, help us control anti-social urges (we all have them) and even help insomniacs sleep.

As autonomous individuals we all have personal rituals that we still do more or less unconsciously, mixed with many we do intentionally—for a purpose. When we lose our personal rituals, we are "at loose ends" or feel disorganized. We need ritual for good reasons, such as comfort, emotional peace, belongingness, organization, connection and so forth. It makes bridges between different activities of a day, gives us a "time out", and prepares us ahead of time for something stressful. Most of all, as our world is losing its formal group rituals, and the purpose behind them, we miss the connection to *something beyond our selves*. In that still-new isolation of our individuality, we make our own connection—with a cigarette, a drink, a foot massage, or whatever will give us a feeling of satisfaction, not realizing that we are trying to reach for a connection inside of ourselves—a whole new evolving orientation—that connection being to the individual's version of *He Who Creates*

All Things. The popular book-movie-calendar, *The Secret*[1], tells us something about what we are reaching for..

> *You are not alone. Within you is the infinite creative power and presence, guiding you, loving you, and waiting to give you anything and everything you choose. You have access to all that is, to all that has ever been and all that will ever be—and it is the creative power within you.*[2]

Rituals are anchors for our daily lives. They momentarily take us out of daily reality and focus our attention inward. Most are practiced without being aware that they are inner-reaching, or even that they are rituals. Here is what a conscious ritual looks like. My younger daughter has been creating rituals since childhood, consciously. One of them is making her children's breakfast every school day from kindergarten through 12th grade. As a school nurse she was shocked at the number of children in the grades (50%) who came to school without breakfast. But from personal experience she also realized how hard it is to get teen-agers to get up in time to eat before leaving. So she added more elements to a natural household "chore", breakfast. She lit candles, turned on music, and continued the never-ending work on getting the children all in place, in time to eat the whole meal together. Her children were somewhat resistant to and unaware of this effort being done for them, but if perchance one day it didn't happen, they were upset and clueless. But when they have children of their own, they will understand what was done for them and probably repeat it. I had done the same (without the frills) for that daughter and her siblings, but without the conscious awareness of its importance other than as a health need for all children. It was not a conscious ritual at that time, but simply one of the three meals my family has always served for many generations. It gives me great pleasure to watch the repetition of this small household task becoming a true ritual in the next generation. In this age of disconnectedness in children's lives, such family rituals provide an anchor for the future.

We are not including formal and group ritual in this book, since many forms of that are well-known to everyone. Like my younger

---

1   *The Secret* by Rhonda Byrne Nov 28, 2006
2   *The Secret*

self, however, many may not realize they have personal rituals which, like most practices in this book, are often more effective when practiced consciously. Everyone has rituals and, if they wish, they can create new ones to fill a new need. Judy and I will share a taste of our own experiences with other people's rituals.

Virginia. When I was in my 50's, a close friend, Eleanor, was dying of cancer. She had chosen alternative treatment and had an outwardly peaceful final year. At the beginning of the year, she separated from her husband, rented a room, began to do some art work, and listened to classical music, which had not been possible during her difficult marriage. She spent regular periods of 7-10 days at a rustic cabin in the woods up in a mountain range. She was finding herself for the first time. At one point I was invited to spend one of those times with her. I asked her what she had been doing up here. She said, "Creating new rituals." I was puzzled since I had never really thought about rituals at that time in my life. She told me that when first living alone she felt "at sea" about herself and her life. In her reading she learned about ritual and realized she had lost all her rituals, or their relevance. She spent time in nature creating new ones in order to feel order in her life. As she had planned, this order made it possible to face and prepare for her ultimate loss. I was blessed to have learned about ritual from such a master while she was creating her own. From her I learned much about myself, my personal rituals, and making them more conscious and intentional.

Judy. My aunt, uncle, and cousin were as close to me as my mother and father. They lived in a woodsy area just outside of Bremerton and I always felt loved, welcomed, and happy when visiting. However there was one thing I missed. The three of them had a family greeting and no one else was ever included. There were no exceptions, not even for me. When any one of them left the house or came home they were given three quick kisses, usually on the cheek or forehead. This was my first introduction to personal ritual (although I didn't even know the word at the time) and I really wanted to be included. The facts that they cooked my favorite foods, played my favorite games, and were more than generous with their hugs and attention didn't lessen my feeling of being left out of something very important. I loved all three of them so much. Shouldn't I have been included in the "three quick kiss" ritual?

My aunt spread love, warmth and joy everywhere she went. So even though I was a young adult when she died I was totally unprepared for the feelings of grief and pain. After the funeral, as

I looked around the room, I saw my uncle and cousin. They had their arms around each other exchanging three quick kisses on each other's cheek. My grief deepened as I realized the three of them would never do that again, but what a tribute it was to a tightly knit and loving family. I have to confess though; I felt a pinch of sadness that I would never be part of their three kiss ritual.

Early Ritual Sacred Space and Its Construction— The Personal Universe

This section and the next are about how rituals began; and how they are behind our long evolution into individuality. It is about how we still have group rituals that fit our different lifestyles, but how we have to find our way back to the universe through our inner selves as integrated, individuated selves. Finally, it is about how the Moon Phases help us do that.

The Shamanic tradition where ritual began required a carefully chosen and specifically constructed sacred space. This space appears to have become nearly universal, lasting into present times both among native cultures, and non-native shamanic groups in contemporary society. The early shamanic sacred space required a cosmic geography, one based on the number four—does that surprise you?

Prehistoric records tell us that the number four represented the four distinct moon phases, four seasons, 4 directions, and the four corners of the Earth within which sacred space was measured for rituals. Essentially, four has historically represented everything that is created. To the ancients, what was created was not divine; therefore sacred space had to be made in order to do ritual. Four represented the known earth-plane for early peoples. It was a horizontal plane representing *the middle world* (the surface of our physical Earth and normal reality.) The circle you drew while reading Chapter 1, with the cross inside of it, shows the same figure.

The ancients also had a concept of three-dimensionality, completed by the World Tree, which they represented as a vertical pole piercing the center of the Earth-plane of the *middle world*, down through the earth plane to *the lower world*, and up to the sky or the *upper world* which led to heaven or the Great Mystery. Some version of this belief is found in early cultures all over the planet, and is still active in many contemporary groups who are learning how to reclaim their connection to Earth. You can visualize this as a tree which is observable in our reality, as the World Tree or a tent-pole. Its roots penetrate the lower world, while its branches reach up toward the upper world in the sky

In this geography *the middle world*, to be safe and in tune with the spirits of nature, needed to mirror *the upper world's* star-patterns.[3] The *lower World*, where the dead, dark spirits, and mythical creatures lived, mirrored geographically both the *middle* and *upper worlds* where the shaman flew or climbed a tree to commune with the gods, through a hole in the Northern sky tent. The hole was occupied by the North Star, while the constellational circle of the *Great Dragon* wound around it, chasing *"The Pearl"*—a small constellation in front of the dragon. This hole in the sky was also where the souls of the dead were taken, but only if they had finished their fate for this life. Otherwise the dragon in the constellation surrounding the hole prevented the soul from leaving. It was important to the ancients to know that when they died, it was the right time.

This was also the specific location called the center of heaven where the shaman could enter the realm of light behind the stars and receive guidance and divination for his community. Fragments of the world of the gods could be seen by everyone in the lights of stars shining through holes in the roof of the sky tent. In rituals, a real tree or a tent-pole represented what became known as *The World Tree*. In mythic descriptions, we can see the mathematical formula for 3-D in the shaman's metaphor when he calls *the spirits of the six directions* to make sacred space at the beginning of every ritual. Modern mathematics recognizes ten dimensions, each with its formula of directions for constructing it. The formula for our 3rd dimension contains six directions. It is implicit in the universal children's chant, "right-left, front-back, up-down," and in the shaman's six directions—East-West, North-South, Upper World—Lower World. For perhaps 30,000 years or more, that ritual formula was and still is depicted on rocks and other ancient surfaces, as an equal-armed cross in a circle, each arm representing a direction. The center or seventh

---

3   Stonehenge, Chaco Canyon, and many other ancient landmarks all over the planet, mostly from the late stone age, are clearly mirrors of some pattern in the sky. Various caves elsewhere in the world seem to have been altered as well, to represent *underworld* mirroring. For example, the Milky Way is mirrored in the *Lower World* of China as the Ghost River, a river the dead must cross to reach the land of the dead, and across which new souls being born must cross to reach the *middle world*. In many cultures a local river of the *Middle World* was considered to mirror the Milky way. Such mirrored images had the same protective and spiritual powers as the sky images, themselves.

direction, called the *Center* evolved from the up-down direction occupied by the World Tree. In a flat view of earth, the center might be represented in a drawing by a dot or a small circle in the center of a larger one. Another pattern is a square inside a circle, obtained by connecting the four intersection points on the edge of the circle. These points were obtained by extensions of the four directions, the circle itself being the horizon. Some cultures have seen that as a magic square protecting those gathered for ritual. Perhaps that was a mirroring, telling us that the four directions of heaven were meeting and connecting with the four directions of Earth, on the line of the horizon, the line between heaven and earth..

The *Center* itself (a function of the three axes of the four horizontal, and two vertical, directions) was a seventh or spiritual direction. The ancients saw The *World Tree* as that spiritual direction which held everything together and connected the three vertical worlds. Only after these six directions with the center were marked out and their spirits recognized and in attendance, could the ritual begin.

With some creative movements we can use these seven directions to focus our own personal universe and tie ourselves into Earth, Moon, and Sun. Visualizing ourselves as the tree, feeling our roots sink downward and our hands or thoughts reaching up toward the sky is a common device for relaxation or centering before entering meditation, prayer, self-hypnosis, or other practices involving going within.

We suggest you pause here and imagine the shaman's cosmology. This visualization can be modified as the pattern for personal ritual. Think of a tree growing out of a mound. The ground on which you stand was the middle world, the familiar place of our ordinary daily life. The ground below, containing the tree's roots, was the shamanic underworld, full of dark spirits, souls of the dead and often frightening mythical gods and goddesses. High in the sky above the tree's branches was the upperworld or heaven, home to other gods, fantastical creatures, and the souls of the honored dead. The tree is the Center, connecting the lower, middle and upper worlds. This image models the formula for our ability to function as the center, ourselves, if we are living from our spiritual center. This is that golden thread described earlier by which we connect not only to our own centers but to a universal center of humanity and also backwards in time to our ancestors.

As the shaman looked out from his center position under the

tree, he saw the east-west axis extending out in one direction and the north-south axis at right angles to the first two, creating a cross with himself at the center. The ground level thus had four corners created by the four directions intersecting the horizon. The four corners modeled the cross of right-left and front-back. This was sacred space—the daily world bounded by sky at the horizon, and the underworld which today we accept as our own unconscious, calling our angry or fearful emotions and thoughts our "demons".

The vertical tree, at the center, models the up-down direction, and also the universal concept of spirituality as an upward moving human dynamic. Humanity has always looked upward to the domain of the divine. Other than imagery, not much has changed, has it?

The Shaman's Ritual

Shamanic rituals were always about the community's inter-relatedness among themselves, with Earth and the spirits; all of this was in the context of the Unknown, with which they were surrounded and deeply connected. Divination was the intent of the ritual in most cases, since it would reveal to them some aspect of the Unknown necessary to their survival.

The shaman began by presiding at the altar on a mound at the *Center* of our familiar *Middle World*, usually modeled by a tree growing out of the top of the mound. Sometimes, particularly in cold, northern climates, the same enactment was around the tent-pole in a shaman's dwelling or a community lodge. The intersection of the pole or tree with the ground in which it was rooted became the *Center* of the *three worlds* wherever the tree or tent-pole was established. The center pole, where the two axes of the four directions intersected, held all things together, right to left, front to back, up to down. (In modern Western shamanic work, the *Center* is extended to be an individual's personal center or spark of divinity.)   From this position the shaman honored the spirits. Specific spirits ruled the directions and kept the space sacred. They protected the middle world from spirits or beings considered evil or dangerous. It was the shaman's way of acting out the formula for this three-world reality and declaring that through this ritual he was magically making space sacred, penetrable only by the Divine.

Since early times, most shamanic rituals worldwide have been held in this seven-fold directional context. This was the world most late Stone Age peoples lived in, and similar practices continue today in many native cultures. Most communal rituals were celebrated on

New and Full Moons, and equinoxes and solstices—the Sun's four seasonal markers.

First, the community gathered. After calling the directions, a sacrifice was offered and cooked, to be eaten later by the community; and propitiations and thanks were offered to the gods to ensure good divinations, good harvests, good hunts. The communal meal was served, including the animal sacrifices or harvest grains, vegetables and fruits; and Great Ancestors were invited to share the feast.

When the meat was tender enough to remove a flat bone (usually a scapula), the bone was thrown into the fire where the heat produced irregular cracks, while the community ate. When the bone was cracked, the shaman went into an altered state. At that point in some cultures he was tied to the pole in order to keep his physical body on the earth plane, while he journeyed to the upper world. In other cultures, he climbed to the top of the tree or pole, where, the community believed, he changed into a bird and flew through the center hole in the sky-tent, to the upper world. Either way, he received enlightenment for the tribe. Whatever the details, his flight from earth to heaven and back with the message, was considered the all-important physical act of connecting heaven and earth. According to Felicitas Goodman's discoveries[4], in many early cultures the whole community went into trance, which could account for the shaman's shape-change.

The major religions, as they transitioned from Shamanism, replaced only the core element of the early ritual, and that in name only—the seeking of divination. That was replaced with the words of their prophets, which are accepted by some Jewish scholars as a form of divination.

The early pagan shamanic religions left us an important legacy, too long ignored—the example of our responsibility to periodically recognize the sacred dimension of the Earth, and its four annual seasons (marked by the Solstices and Equinoxes), and four Moon Phases. This is supported by the discovery we, and many others, have made that there are recognizable energies released at these points in time. They were not only released in the Stone Age, but are still being released in our time. They are not out of date, but are there to teach us something we need to remember about the planet we live on and our purpose and direction within that matrix. This teaching has now expanded into a matrix including the whole universe. In

---

4   *Ecstatic Body Postures*, by Felicitas Goodman

the ancestors' view, we have a choice to recognize Earth, time, and space as divine—or not. Which do we choose?   We believe that an intelligent and purposeful universe of all that is, is the manifestation of the Divine, and has much to teach us through the Moon cycles that can carry us through our evolutionary stages.

The Original Universal Pattern of Ritual

From ancient China we have the most specific early records of ritual, though they are apparently not different from any other location on the planet. Ancient Chinese sources indicate that, in the ritual described above, four basic stages were considered necessary to a correct divination ritual. So precise were the Chinese that they defined those four stages very specifically, perfecting the details over many generations. The pattern for their rituals was— again, why should we be surprised?—the pattern of the four Moon phases, directions, and Solar seasons. This pattern was used with variations in many parts of the world, from early times. We keep mentioning Chinese prehistoric patterns because their prehistoric records go back farther than others, and recent discoveries show that travel between China, Mesopotamia, and surrounding areas was far more extensive in the Neolithic than previously believed; hence the widespread similarities. They were obsessed with recording every possible idea or practice long before writing was invented, and as a result developed pictographic symbols and the early stages of acupuncture and astronomy long before most of the rest of the world. As we describe the ritual patterns below, you will be able to see them hidden in contemporary religious services. The following are instructions later written down to guide the shaman in a proper ritual. We here rewrite them to compare with modern religious services, both Christian and Jewish oriented.

1. A kind of invocation providing a building, mound, or lodge, or otherwise setting apart and designating a sacred space; addressing the spirits or deities; expressing thanks, and stating needs. (Modern: The processional and someone greeting the congregation?)
2. Partaking of communal food of the sacrifice. (Jewish Shabat wine and bread ritual or Christian communion service)
3. Hearing the message of the shaman—the divination or commands of the gods. (The sermon? Reading the Prophets?)

4. Leaving and doing the message of the gods. (Going out to do the commands of God?)

We show below *how* the meanings of the four Moon phases in-form the meanings of the four stages of ritual, or the basic principle behind all "fours". The italicized *names* and *principles* of the stages changed at least four times over many centuries, and their meanings included seasons and elements as well as phases. At times they may have been interchangeable. We have used the ones whose meanings are most recognizable to us. The four stages, and the names and principles are borrowed from Karcher's *The Classic I Ching*, and re-written to emphasize the connection to the Moon Phases. We have quoted Karcher many times throughout our book, because his books contain the clearest, most un-politicized early history (Before the dynasties) of the Chinese people, and customs they brought from prehistoric times. The similarity of their ritual patterns to the Moon phases is our own discovery.

1. NEW MOON Step one, called *Originating*. The principle called *Benevolence*. This was the community gathering, at a moment before creation—the world was beginning, which is always a safe place to be. They had established sacred space. Then they invited First Ancestor, and the ancestral spirits. In inviting First Ancestor they acknowledged that they were now actually *in* the time of the creation of the world, repeating the First Ancestor's original ritual, walking in the steps of First Ancestor. According to Mircea Eliade, this was a worldwide concept. Every ancestor was First Ancestor during ritual, because of "no-time", since sacred space included sacred or no-time. Walking in the footsteps of his own most immediate ancestor (who taught the shaman the ritual) was to walk in the footsteps of Original Ancestor. (See *The Corn Ritual* in Appendix A, where the concept is still alive in SW USA.). The sacrifice was made, blessed, and the animal placed into the cooking pot to cook—an offering to express gratitude to the ancestors and for the creation of the world. According to Eliade, the creation of the world was being re-enacted as though the people were themselves in the original creation time, literally re-experiencing the creation[5]. Sacred time and space was no-time, within which nothing changed, forever. This is what Eliade meant

5   Eliade, *The Sacred and the Profane.*

about sacred or ritual time being no-time. In ritual space all time was just being, not doing, or perhaps all-at-once.

2. (FIRST QUARTER MOON. Step two called *Courtesy*, the principle called *Development*. These were the first activities of the individuals working in the group to create the ritual. It was a gift of *courtesy*, and an honor, to prepare a meal for First Ancestor, and therefore for each other. The development followed a pattern of offerings of gratitude: cooking, offering, and eating of the meat. When the meat had cooked long enough to remove the bones, a flat bone was cast into the fire where heat produced many cracks which could later be "read" by the shaman in an altered state, as a message from the gods. Sometimes they used a tortoise shell if that was the sacrificial animal, but more commonly the scapula bone of a 4-footed domestic animal

At this point the sacrificial cooked meat was offered to the Ancestors and shared among the community. Somewhere in this step the Shaman went into trance. We can imagine a build-up or *development* of intensity, and perhaps a combination of anticipation and fear or awe. Think of the 1st Quarter Moon here, where intensity is building and we are not certain of the outcome. I can visualize this scene as like a big extended family picnic, with scary or awesome and mystical overtones.

3. (FULL MOON Step 3, called *maturing*, the principle called *righteousness*. This is where the shaman returned to the group, "read" the interpretation of the bone, and inscribed the message on the bone using the very earliest pictographic or symbolic markings. Thousands of these inscribed bones have been found in China, dating back to 4,000 BCE. (As at any current indigenous Full Moon ritual, the community receives the enlightenment as a result of contributing to the wholeness of the group).

The shaman's interpretation of the divination (guidance) was called "righteousness", the principle being "maturing". The divination is, itself a teaching of righteousness. Think of the Full Moon (mythically seen as the mature Moon) where we are enlightened about our previous two phases. Think of the later prophets who preached about righteousness. Think about what that means to you in our time. Is there another term for it?

4. (THIRD QUARTER MOON called *Wisdom*, the principle called *grinding*. Have you ever wondered about the ubiquitous statement so often quoted by those who wish to sound wise: "The mills of the Gods grind slowly, but they grind exceeding fine"? I have, and

was surprised at this revelation (to me) that "grinding" relates to wisdom! I learned here that grinding is the last part of the process of harvesting grain. The grain was not ready to eat until it was ground. A Divination was not considered complete until the needed action was done. In this last stage, the people, having received the divination, were instructed to "go do it." The community becomes wise by following the god's instructions, as its hunger can only be appeased by having ground its flour for bread. Grinding into small particles was breaking down the god's statement into the many infinitely small physical acts required to carry out the answer to the stated need of the community—to be filled both physically and spiritually.

These people were masters of metaphor! And this personal action-oriented response to the divination was undoubtedly a primary stimulus to evolving consciousness, and to the later development of writing. Remember this when you meditate at a Moon phase! It is like learning to play a new game. You may understand the rules, but until you actually use them, they will not become yours. Consider all the lists of four that we have included in the previous chapters. They all come down to the 4th Archetype in Chapter 2—the urge for transformation. *Consciousness grows through transformation.* Doing the divination— the ritual, the new game, the rules of the new job, the process your therapist gave you as homework, the theme of the message in the sermon, the intention that came to you in a meditation, or the symbolic messages from the Moon phases— putting these learnings into action will increase your consciousness, guaranteed. The philosophy behind the Moon phases may be deep, but in practice it is humble and homely, as are the practices on any spritual path.

The Moon cycles continue to occur systematically and sequentially through the 12-plus Lunar months, behind generally similar, yet individually different practices, all over the world. Now only rarely is it noted that a number of particular annual Christian or Jewish holidays are on a Full or New Moon, and never why. Here is another lost link between the prehistoric practices and our modern uses of ritual. We, ourselves, have wondered at the loss of interest, and believe that denial of our earth's natural cycles is relevant to the current loss of a world sense of purpose, direction and sense of connection to each other and to the universe.

Our Personal Ritual of Relationship

While we think of the shaman as the only one who went into trance during ritual, Goodman's recent research has shown that in some communities, from at least 30,000 years ago, the whole tribal unit went into trance with the shaman, thus providing him with the psychic support and strength to make his journey to the home of the gods.

While we may not reiterate this ritual in our lives, we may choose to recall in some way the energies of the directions, and find out what was so powerful in them for the ancients. As divination was their purpose, so is ours. We already know it is possible to find out what each phase can show us about the month ahead at any New Moon, given the tools we have now, and will receive in the next chapters. You can meditate on these "readings", interpreting them however they fit into your life, which becomes your own divination and spiritual wisdom. Then notice how many modern metaphysical and religious teachings emphasize that spiritual wisdom is nothing if we do not live it out in our lives. Others might remember the New Testament statement, "By your fruits you shall be known."

In Western Moon work, the exact beginning phase points have been correlated to the 360 degree Zodiac. The degrees have been integrated with the set of 360 *Sabian* Symbols. These symbols have their roots in the divination systems of Sumeria, China, Mongolia, and the Near East and Middle East. Regardless of what you choose to believe about these traditions, they "work". That is, they accurately describe each individual's Moon phases on his/her personal paths to greater consciousness. They are metaphors of which we will become masters, when we act them out in our lives. Beyond that, they contain a mystery we may never understand—how year after year for as many years as we can imagine, past and future, each moon phase and cycle will be accurately described in the lives of every human being! It is so impossible that it is one of those amazements we had to live with before we even reached the amazement.

As we actively noticed and used the positive Moon Phase energies, ourselves, by intentionally tuning in to them, we began to see our destiny patterns more clearly. We imagined our Ancestors doing the same by calling the directions and the spirits at the effective moment. The two primary "moments" of New and Full Moon, plus the other, more personal phases, articulate each month a particular current detail of our lives we might call destiny blended with individual creativity. The whole cycle provides a model for our lives, our unfolding consciousness, and even for our personal rituals. It also gives us back our personal divination ability, the gift we lost for at least a millennium, and a gift to which we are all entitled by virtue of living on Earth in our Solar System. None of these things have any bearing on our religious or personal spiritual beliefs unless we choose to make them so. These are tools originally stimulated by the Moon Phase energies themselves, gifted to us by the first ancestors, and continued by the many cultures in between.

We will occasionally suggest possible ways of doing brief personal or small group rituals appropriate to time and place in part II. However, note here that one's ritual need not include particular outer activities. We do think the intent behind the universal four steps of divination has the most relevance here, if only as a focus of intent for ourselves.

Step 1, we might sit quietly, backs straight, as for meditation, simply intending that this will be a sacred space and time. This would be an ideal point at which to visualize ourselves as a tree, feeling our roots extending deep into the Earth, and our arms and mind extending into the remote spaces of the sky. Or, we could light a candle to focus ourselves in our centers, or make sacred space by lighting 4 candles for the directions, with one in the middle for the Center and recognizing the upper and lower worlds in a contemporary mode, such as the lower world as the unconscious and the upper world as spiritual consciousness.

Step 2 might include remembering things for which we are grateful, saying a special prayer, or thinking about what our immediate needs might be.

Step 3 might be meditating or noting the Moon Phase and what its energy is about, then seeing how it connects us with what is going on in our own lives. This could be done by looking at the signs and Houses, on our personal dials explained in Chapter 7, or reading the degree symbols (to be discussed in Chapter 12) as our divination. Interpreting them in context of our own lives has been a powerful meditation. For those who wish to make their ritual more relevant to a particular religion—who has not at one time or another randomly opened their Bible or other sacred text and, without looking, placed their finger someplace on a page? You know "it works".

Step 4 could be making a decision on where and how to use the information in whatever we do when we return to daily reality.

It is well known that man created mathematics and writing out of knowledge they had of the repetitious Moon cycles, seasons, and star patterns; man needed to create mathematics and writing to record their growing astronomical and other information, so it could grow. We believe some of that early mental growth remains in our DNA with all we have learned since. That natural process may be why our children can learn so much more, and so much more rapidly than we, in contemporary times. Each generation has been building on previous ones. We created and gave our children television, and other electronics to play with and new teaching systems, none of which we had as children. But we created them out of what our parents created for us, and now we complain of the corruption of our children by electronics. The creativity and innovation in every new generation brings change to society even if we don't like it.

We Are Not Alone

In a vast movement toward re-connecting with our universe, a growing number of small contemporary groups gather worldwide for Moon rituals, attempting to bring back the lost alignment with earth and the cosmic energy cycles. Some are directly related to Native American or other indigenous practices; others arise out of more general contemporary and metaphysical sources. One worldwide group called *The New Group of World Servers* operates out of Ojai, CA (See Bibliography), and provides materials for their groups who do synchronized New and Full Moon meditations. All strive to bring back this spiritual connection between us and our world and the Divine.

Moon phases, DNA and Elements

Through the number four, the four of DNA, the four elements expressed through the signs and degrees of the Zodiac, and our immersion in physical manifestation, we are connected both to the monthly Lunar and annual Solar cycles, and to our bodies and DNA.

Our alignment to Earth, Sun, and Moon is the *Old Woman's* gift—re-visioned in modern terms but little different in intent than the ancient ritual. The Moon waxes and wanes. The first half of the cycle, beginning with the New Moon, is about us creating ourselves as individuals. The waning half is about ourselves as part of society—large or small depending on the individual—and our evolving consciousness. To understand and feel the power of the

Moon cycle is to offer its gift to our own physical, mental, emotional being and perhaps change another generation, or through our changed consciousness add to the world's evolution.

It is not possible or desirable for individuals or groups to go back to innocent tribal unity; but we all can and do slip back into a postulated negative survival mindset operating out of fear, greed, anger, and lust. In the name of balance, we can also choose the options, instead, of compassion, generosity, creativity and joy. In this case society itself will reflect our growth, just as it now (in the first decade of 2,000 CE) reflects our long denied history of personal and group negativity. This is how we ultimately will (if we choose) affect the elements of this world that we would like to change—through individually *Being* and *Becoming* together.

We know that the Moon's phases fall over every portion of the planet with their specific positive and healing energies; we know that all people are impacted by those energies, to which they can respond as they choose; and some might choose differently if they knew that every thought they had would influence the world consciousness; at least so our scientists are beginning to tell us.

How important, then, that we receive, enhance, and expand the energies of these phases, releasing the monthly Full Moon insight into the collective consciousness as our second seed   A teacher in a small group many years ago continually repeated to us: every insight, every new way you find to wash dishes or any daily task, consciously and intentionally put it out into the Rain *Cloud of All Knowable Things* where someone else might pick it up as new insight for their particular need. It doesn't matter that we have never seen this cloud, but I am sure beyond all doubt that in the Field it exists or perhaps it is another name for the Field.

Whatever your circumstance—even if you are seemingly "doing nothing"—you can create your ritual and have that bit of personal wisdom. We can offer it as our part in the growth of human consciousness toward wholeness. Those who sow a positive seed will help complete that human destiny.

7
Wheels Within Wheels
The Wheels Go 'Round and 'Round and Where They Stop Nobody Knows

The soul goes round upon a wheel of stars and all things return....
Good and evil go round in a wheel that is one thing and not many.
Do you not realize in your heart, do you not believe behind all your
beliefs, that there is but one reality and we are its shadows; and that
all things are but aspects of one thing; a centre where men melt into
Man and Man into God?

— Gilbert Keith Chesterton

The double wheel in the center of this book is a photograph of your life from birth to death as it is seen from Earth looking up to the stars. It is the interface between you and the Sun-Moon cycles. With this wheel in your hands, the process of following the eight phases will become clear, and life may become more interesting. Make your dial now, if you have not yet done it.

The Game Board

Here is where we get up close and personal with a subject many people try to avoid, which is the technical side of an awesome universe. Trust us that even though astrology seems extremely complicated, this is not a book on astrology, and is no more complicated than you want to make it. It is, as we have repeatedly said, about the dynamics of our relationship to the Moon and the Sun. However, the tools of astrology are based on astronomy, and its most basic original form gives us a necessary language and tool whereby we can apply the cosmic rhythms to real-world dynamics and to our individual selves. They describe energies, as discussed in Chapter 1, which are measurable. We can feel them if we practice using them. We can know them with the Solar Dial and the recommended books. This language and this tool can be viewed as a board game whose rules must be learned in order to play it. Although it is so much more, many web-sites and book sellers list astrology under "games." Yes, it is legitimate even to look at your own life as a game. Consider the Hindu concept of the universe being a roll of God's dice!, and the original famous Hindu Snakes and Ladders game. Serious consideration of this concept (without subscribing to it) has given our personal philosophies a tentative but amazing jolt into a new paradigm. What if we viewed our lives as a game for which the Moon cycles provided the game rules and actions. Without giving up your personal religious or other belief system, just imagine everything you are doing as part of a game, *while you are doing it.*

Before writing, people used the monthly Moon phases and the Sun's annual cycle for guidance of various sorts. They did it the hard way, step by step, counting, observing, etc., with stones and charcoal drawings and hours and years of night sky-watching. If they could do it without writing, we can surely do it with books. Remember the famous 2007 advertisement—"If a caveman could do it..."? But the real cavemen were not stupid—they actually figured out all of this for us.

Originally, protection of the gods and fertility were the compelling factors behind recording the Moon's cycles. Then it was food on the hoof, agriculture, and finally nations and their rulers that were the focus, eclipses being of great political and religious life-and-death significance. In Greece and in ancient Alexandria people began to understand heavenly phenomena in more personal terms. Individuals as well as kings had astrological charts drawn for them. Writers such as Hermes Trismegistus[1] recorded the construction of conception charts, based on Sun-Moon cycles, working backward in time from the natal chart, in order to find the hidden record of spirit coming into the body. Sun was called the world father and moon was called the world mother, of course!

In all this time, the Sun and Moon never lost their primary importance. For most of this time, knowledge of the heavens was only for the initiates, the scientists, or the original shamans. By Grecian times, it was only the well-to-do who could have a horoscope drawn for them, and the street-mongers of personal predictions were for the most part charlatans. As a result European astrology sank into the depths of the Dark Age as a dangerous secret. It would be humorous if not so terrible for the common people, to know that it is widely rumored that many Popes from the very beginning

---

1   A Greek/Egyptian god of multiple origins, under whose name various Greek writers wrote.

either did astrology themselves or had their personal astrologers, as did royalty, while it was forbidden to the people and sometimes punishable by death.

Here, in the Common Era, we are interested in both Western and Eastern astrology because both had common beginnings. After the dark hiatus, in the middle Ages, Orientals and Middle Easterners exchanged massive amounts of information with Western European Astrologers, along with the Arts and general culture. For the most part the huge advance in astrological knowledge still retained much of the early secrecy, for various religious and cultural reasons. Much of its use was transferred to the exclusive Mystery Schools, which then went underground with the advent of the scientific age. In spite of or because of this, the desire to know about the future has possessed people down through all the ages. Astrology provided the most accessible and reliable means of satisfying that desire when practiced by experienced astrologers of high ethical standards (unfortunately all too seldom). The kind of astrology we are discussing here is not prediction, but simple observation and understanding of natural cycles accessible to anyone, from which anyone can extrapolate into the future. Wall Street predicts some market cycles using several well-known astrological cycles.

The Sun-Moon cycle is the basic model for all the other cycles. Because the Zodiac signs cycle is the only one that begins to explain our relationship to the sky and thus our universe; and because it did so very well for all those in pre-history who followed it, we ask our readers to play the astrology game with us and learn more fundamentals like how things are laid out, how they relate to each other, and what they mean. Following the Sun-Moon cycles to the fullest requires the basic technical information contained in this and the following three chapters. In various dark periods of history, and those with misogynistic and male-oriented leaders, people would have died for this information, and often did. You are safe, now, dear reader, to sit down to your desk and seize this simple technique for re-connecting to the universe. It is made even simpler by the rule that everything here is WYSYWYG, and we are only dealing with the Sun and Moon.

Here is the game. Your Solar dial is the map or geography on which the rays of the Moon fall as she scurries continuously across the sky. Her rays are all in code. The numbers of the Houses (inner dial) tell you what people are doing in that particular part of the land. The descriptions of the signs (outer dial) describe the manner in which they do what they do. In this game, the Moon's rays contain messages transmitted as from a satellite, with the phase information, directly to everyone. Like the original Wheel of Fortune, the Moon Cycle is a circle that goes around and around your personal dial, timing all your life events. You can stop it wherever you wish, like taking a photograph of any event, but the Moon never sleeps or stops

It has been said by wiser persons than I that nothing happens without the Moon. What that means is that the Moon moving rapidly through the sky, contacts and aspects all the bodies in our solar system. Every month, she transmits the Sun's messages and urges each of us to act upon them. As she weaves the web of hundreds of aspects to the many other bodies in our system, these contacts do appear from Earth to trigger events in the mundane world. In actuality that is very indirect. The Moon subtle energies and messages plant urges in the minds and emotions of people. The people have free will to interpret those urges and messages in any way they wish, which is mostly instinctual. Often the voices of other persons have greater influence.

The Solar Dial—the Game board

As we have said earlier, the Sun represents spirit, higher Self, purpose, and direction. The Moon in this context represents soul (as our connection to spirit-Sun,) which manifests through our day-to-day activities, and transmits the archetypal meaning with which we invest those activities. In individual charts, Moon describes our habitual responses to life. By following her cycles, we can begin to tune in to the internal movements of the psyche which may indeed be our spirit and soul speaking to us—unless it is ego. As well, we can observe our types of action at the different phases. Such observation is a traditional spiritual practice in which we can rapidly learn better ways of manifesting our experiences. It is true that if we end the day feeling good about the day behind us, chances are that we probably are operating at our highest level. Feelings are our best indicators about how we function in the world.

We call this double wheel the Solar dial. Once you have aligned the first pie-shaped section of the inner dial with your birth sign, it is your Solar chart. The inner dial contains the numbered 12 Houses (areas) of life experience. The outer Dial contains the 12 signs. The dials rotate on each other so that whatever your Sun sign may be, you can match it up with the first house. Nothing can happen in your life that can not be found in one of the Houses. Do that now. Later, we will be putting the Moon's phases in the appropriate Houses according to the months (signs) of the year in which the phases occur. Your Solar dial is what we call "generic" since the world's population (said to be six billion) is roughly divided into 12 groups, of something like forty million people in each sign.

We can see from the dial, however, that as generic as your birth sign may be, there is still much more individualizing information within it than in that one sign. For example, if you aligned your Sun's sign with the first house on the dial, your Solar dial is then set to show the way you express your Sun's purpose through all the other 11 signs as well. For example, if you are a Cancer Sun sign, your second house of resources would be "ruled" by Leo, which might mean, among other things, that you like expensive dramatic clothes, jewelry, home furnishings, etc. A Taurus Sun sign might prefer Gemini resources and love lots of little things like jewelry that was not for effect so much as for a momentary personal attraction.

The activities of the 12 Houses of the chart are characterized by the 12 signs so that your Sun sign, itself, is necessarily affected by the 11 other signs. For purposes of following the Moon cycles, this Solar chart is easy for non-astrologers to use. The advanced astrologer who has usually ignored the Solar chart in favor of the natal chart also may find it quite interesting because it presents twelve facets of your consciousness, will, purpose and direction that are not shown in the natal chart. Of this, more later. For purposes of this book, we will be using the Solar chart only, but will include some information labeled for astrologers about the Rising sign dial, which is a dial based on the Rising sign or moment of birth—day, month, year and time of day.

At this point we refer the Astrologer to the footnote below for a brief comment on the Natal Dial for astrologers.[2]

---

2   Astrologers can use their natal rising sign as the first house on the dial, with the following caution. Natal charts often have intercepted signs and other anomalies, which the Solar dial does not accommodate. There is a traditional chart called the Equal house system which uses these same whole-sign houses all beginning at "0" degrees. It is called a "flat chart" and represents your life as it would be without the influences of environment and other people.

The Symbolic Meaning of the Solar Dial

Briefly, the Solar chart dial is keyed to your birth sign and refers to the development of your self-expression, individuality and consciousness in this life. With it you can observe how you use your will, sense of purpose, and ability to make choices from the core self. Each house in your Solar chart dial refers to an area of your *life expression*. The sign on the outer wheel of the dial characterizes what you need in specific houses, and how you express the things of those houses. At the end of this chapter is a table with sign and houses interpretations that will help you get by until we go into Houses more deeply in Chapter 9. If you are looking for a natal chart, which is keyed to your time of day, a brief outline of natal and solar chart differences is given below, including information on how to use the dial for natal birth charts.

There are many kinds of birth charts, all slightly different, and all work the same way, but they have different symbolic meanings. We are multi-layered human beings, and different charts show subtle differences in ourselves through the different layers. The principles in this book apply equally to whatever chart you use. From this point on, with a few advanced digressions for the astrologer, we will be addressing only the Solar dial and it is up to the reader who wants to use other dials, with the same principles.

First Steps (for Everyone)

We hope this chapter puts the dial together for you in a way that begins to make some sense to you at the personal levels. We are now ready to learn more about how to apply the Moon's phases in our own lives with a closer look at Houses. First note the following statements. You can refer to them whenever you get confused about what's in the dial.

The two Dials in a Capsule
- Houses = areas of life.
- Solar Houses = areas of life expression.
- Natal Houses = areas of life experience.
- Signs = attitudes and needs that define the areas of life.
- Sun = spirit, life, consciousness, vitality, will, purpose, and self-expression.
- Moon = spirituality, soul, focus and manifestation of Sun's purpose; emotions, responses or reactions, and adaptations to life.

GLYPHS

Aries	♈
Taurus	♉
Gemini	♊
Cancer	♋
Leo	♌
Virgo	♍
Libra	♎
Scorpio	♏
Sagittarius	♐
Capricorn	♑
Aquarius	♒
Pisces	♓

We assume you have gathered the basic supplies we recommended earlier. With your new dial, rotate your Sun sign to line it up with houses #1. Place an orange colored sticky-dot in that house to represent your birth Sun. This is your Solar chart. All of the Houses will be tuned to you personally through the Zodiac signs on the outer wheel. Now let's create an example Solar chart for a New Moon. Using your *Celestial Guide*, find the nearest previous New Moon. It will be the date page with a black disk on the right side of the page. What sign is it in? Maynard's book uses the glyphs for the signs and does not write out their names. So here to the left is a list of the signs with their Glyphs. Place a yellow "Sun" and blue "Moon" together in the corresponding houses for the New Moon. These are the "transiting" Sun and Moon we see daily in the sky, together only at New Moon. The New Moon in that house indicates that you are ready to move forward with something new in the affairs of those houses. The sign of the New Moon and its houses needs your attention as a priority this whole month, because New Moon uses those energies for the month's purpose. Keep in mind the positive meanings of the New Moon sign as the overall purpose or intent of the whole month. Then as you go through the phases you will know how to align the Moon's phase activities with the specific archetypal idea and light frequency (qualities) of the Sun's intent.

At this point you can begin seeing how the cycle can work for you. If this seems confusing at first, it will become easier to use these tools as you practice them. Every signs cycle is different in the strength of its impact in your life. Some months spell out the *what-how-where-why* of the month clearly. Others seem uneventful, but some kind of activity, spiritual or psychological, will.

How You Can Use this Information?

Usually the Sun stays in the New Moon sign all month but sometimes it changes. After 12 signs, the Sun repeats its cycle, but at the next level, like a spiral. Thus the thoughts and actions you manifest can reflect increasingly deeper desires, those closer to your soul. While this is not a system for predicting future specific events, at any given time you will know the kind of future activities (houses) that will require attention (Sun), and the attitudes (Zodiac sign) which can most easily move you through your own unfolding process. Most importantly, you will become more aware of your own internal sensitivity to the Yang/Yin cycles, giving and receiving, assertive and receptive, conscious and unconscious, light and dark. These dualities and many others describe the deepest, most fundamental and critical principle of consciousness itself, because duality is the prime necessity for creation. Duality is also a dangerous power because in humans part of it is what we call "the dark side", the shadow which cannot be controlled. But correctly understood and respected our shadow yields up our deepest and most valuable powers. These powers lie waiting to be transformed and retrieved. In following the Moon path you will learn how to balance and manage your own personal duality and manifest with greater accuracy and integrity.

At this point you can begin exploring at least your monthly New Moons on your own.

Your Personal Path of Light

All the rich complexity of the Moon cycles can have the fascination of crossword puzzles, or trying to figure out "whodunit" before you finish the mystery novel. Each month your process of figuring out how to interpret the phases, and what this means to you at different levels, is a powerful meditation which, alone, will change you. Frustrating as it often will be, it pays off with continual small and great insights and self-understanding, not to mention the huge feeling of satisfaction when a really "big one" comes along and you can say, "I've always wondered why…and now I know! It's right here in my wheel!"

Reading and Writing the Houses of Your Natural Self-expression

If you are new to astrology, you are about to discover some important information about yourself. With the Sun aligned to the first house, read the Zodiac description on the outer wheel for the Sun and 1st house. Continue on <u>counterclockwise</u> around the wheel. This whole chart should describe twelve facets of one level of why you are here, as if you never wondered about that! It is a generalized version of your purpose, however, and therefore somewhat abstract so that it can include all the variations that real life gives it. You can "cheat here" and go to the tables in Chapters 10 and 11 to get more detailed descriptions. In Chapter 11 you will get some real detail. . In case you hadn't noticed, the two columns below are a different view of, but identical to, the inner and outer wheels of your dial, except that the interpretations vary. The real difference is that Signs are qualities you have, or ways you express yourself, while houses are things you do or experiences you have.

SIGNS	QUALITIES	HOUSES	AREAS OF LIFE
ARIES	A sense of separate selfhood or identity—self-initiating.	1	Self image. Personal Matters. Beginnings. Personal Image
TAURUS	Self-sufficient—wants productivity with practical results..	2	Personal resources, talents, potentials..
GEMINI	Mental, communicative, flexible, scattered., dualistic.	3	Communication, ideas and mental abilities
CANCER	Protective, nurturing, sensitive, fertile imagination.	4	Home, family, security oriented.
LEO	Proud, generous, the "star" or center of attention.	5	Self-expression, creativity, children, romantic love, drama.
VIRGO	Perfection, detail-oriented, sometimes critical because it needs perfection.	6	Work, Health, Service. Spirit can grow through these three.
LIBRA	Social, artistic, needs harmony and social acceptance.	7	Partnerships, one's audience or clients, social involvement.
SCORPIO	Wants deep psychological involvement. Silent hidden strength.	8	Change , transitions, ego-deaths, joint resources, group involvement.
SAGITTARIUS	Goal-oriented. Mentally expansive, philosophical, crosses boundaries.	9	Travel, publishing, higher education, philosophies, team involvement
CAPRICORN	Achievement-oriented. Boundaries, structure, social responsibility.	10	Achievement, peak experiences, business and career related.
AQUARIUS	Humanity-oriented, non-traditional, innovative, scientific approaches.	11	Life goals, ideals, friends, "the world out there." Foreign countries.
PISCES	Inspiration, transcendence of limitations. The need to lose oneself in something greater.	12	Unfinished business, Karma, limitations, institutions, balancing self with the world.

Table 3. Basic Houses and Signs Compared

At this point, it would be best for non-astrologers to continue exploring only the Solar wheel to begin with. Your tool for this part of Chapter 7 is *Table 3, Houses and signs*, which supplements the Dial meanings. We are not teaching astrology per se, but the fundamental tools of astrology are necessary to following the Moon phases into deeper territories in Part II. As we mentioned above, the next two chapters will fill in the details of using the dials in this chapter. However, we include *Table 3* on the opposing page to give a brief view of the slight differences in reading the Solar and Natal dials.

Understanding those differences is irrelevant to the beginning use of the dials. You can use the interpretations interchangeably, but by keeping in mind that Solar dials are about life expression while Natal dials are about life experience you can later fine-tune your use of them. As to your two dials, one within the other, both Zodiacal and house symbolisms are not just astrological—they are a bank of great archetypes underlying the history of Earth, the history of humankind, and the lives of every human. The 12 segments of either dial represent 12 *archetypal* areas of life expression (Solar chart) and life experience (Natal chart.) Anything you can express or experience will be found in one of the Houses. There are 12 basic ways you can do that, represented by the signs. If you can't figure out how one of the houses relates to your present life, you can look through the next chapters and find other lists of houses meanings. A large houses Wheel in *Appendix F* gives multitudes of meanings to explore.

At this point you need to see how your own Sun sign on your dial *contains* all the other 11 signs! This concept fulfills a spiritual concept or universal goal contained in each sign, which ultimately must include all the other signs (over many lifetimes, of course). You can consider each sign to be a fractal or hologram of the whole Zodiac, if you wish. In this lifetime we must especially integrate to some degree, into our Sun sign, the sign opposite it on the Dial. The Solar dial shows how we get practice in using all the signs, as we follow the phases around the circle. Each houses gives us an experience that must be handled in a way that is characteristic of the sign that rules it. However two different Sun sign people will handle the same Moon cycle signs differently, according to their own Sun sign. It's like having a thin veil of your Sun sign around you, causing the 11 other signs to come to you, or express from you, colored by your Sun sign. For instance, if you are a Leo Sun sign, everything you do will have a veil of the dramatic around it. If it doesn't, there is something blocking that characteristic. Also, an example of how each Sun sign's

Houses are different, suppose you have a Cancer Sun sign. Then your second house would be ruled by Leo, the next sign after Cancer. Your second house, of resources, would be directly influenced by that sense of the dramatic, like, do you make your money in some dramatic way line acting? Or do you love dramatic clothing and jewelry? A Leo Sun person would prefer the practical path to riches described by Virgo.

As you read your dial notice that the signs on the outer wheel give key phrases for the *needs* and *attitudes* of the Houses with which they are aligned. See other chapters for tables with more key words, phrases and sign meanings. Again, there are still more detailed sign descriptions in Maynard's *Celestial Guide*.

Now, beginning with the 1st house of the Solar dial, proceed around the wheel through the twelve Houses, to see what their signs have to say about you in each of the twelve areas of life. Try to verbalize what you see in the first person mode.

It is suggested that you keep a notebook, and write out your own house interpretations, with the idea that you can change and re-write them many times as you go along. As you become more familiar with this process your interpretations will become clearer and more resonant with who you are. *This exercise describes the structure and content of your consciousness in terms of your potential to unfold it.* We encourage you to pick out words and phrases from the various tables throughout the book which feel like you.

Once you have created your astrological "picture" of yourself in this way, most of the hard work will be done. The rest is dependant upon how well you internalized the structure so you can work with the Moon cycles unhampered by the early feelings of confusion some people have when they first look at their lives in an objective way within a new structure. As you become more and more aware of how you are using both positive and negative qualities of the signs in living the experiences of the Houses, your consciousness increases, and you are said to grow in consciousness. At one level, the structure of the Houses represents each 13-Lunar-month year of one's life as a cyclic path unveiled by the changing Moon. In the next chapter we will explore this structure of consciousness more deeply

8

The Twelve Houses of Life
The Structure of Unfolding Consciousness

The cyclic sequence of houses ...refers to twelve basic [Solar] phases in the unfolding of the consciousness of an individual.
—Dane Rudhyar

The use of the will is something available to every human being, but it grows in proportion to one's self-knowledge and self-mastery.
—Liz Greene [1]

And, we might add, the Sun represents our will and consciousness, but the growth stated by Liz Greene comes by annually living our way through the houses.

As we wrote in the previous chapter, Horoscopes contain twelve pie-shaped divisions called houses, which describe all the areas of life experience one can have. The houses are actually categories so designed that anything you do can fit into one of those houses. There is a basic rationale to activities of each area. Like the subheadings of an outline, only those activities which refer to particular houses are in those houses. Once we are born, we have a horoscope, and its houses structure is embedded in the twelve signs of the Zodiac in such a way that each house is ruled by a given sign. The signs are arranged sequentially in order of 1-12, as are the Houses, but as you can see by your own Solar dial, the first sign rarely begins on the first houses, the clock time of birth determining which sign starts off on the first house of a Natal chart and the calendar date determining the Sun's sign in a Solar chart.

Because how we live our lives comes from the nature and breadth of our consciousness, and because everything we do is an opportunity to expand or uplift our consciousness, actually living this

---

1   *The Development of the Personality* by Liz Greene

amazing twelve-fold structure becomes a major part of the activity of building consciousness. The Phases of the Moon move through a horoscope, as described in chapter 1, and help us determine how we live through these houses. By that we mean the Moon highlights the houses-areas of our lives and marks the best time to do their activities.

The Elements of Your Dial

Your game-board dial contains a circle of signs on the outside wheel, and a circle of houses on the inside wheel. The houses in this dial, as you learned in Chapter 7, are aligned with the signs according to your birth sign, with the sign for each house following the previous one in order around the wheel. Here is a companion for the "Dial in a Capsule" of *Chapter 7*.

1. Houses are areas of life, describing in 12 categories all the things we do in a day and a lifetime.
2. The sign aligned with any one of your houses is said to rule the activities of that house—that is, the natural way you approach those specific activities, even unconsciously.
3. The signs of the Zodiac describe attitudes, needs, and characteristics of the houses they rule.
4. Sun and Moon are the two primary fundamental human urges that fill the needs of the signs they rule—Leo and Cancer, respectively.
5. The Sun in any house is the urge to grow and express oneself, or individuality.
6. The Moon in any house is the urge to manifest—something, depending on the sign, house and phase.

Astrologers and some general readers may want to take note of the signs ruled by the Sun and Moon when doing the New and Full Moon phases. You already know that every house is ruled by a sign, and every sign is ruled by a planet, although the Old Woman does not deal with planets in this book. However, Sun rules the sign of Leo and Moon rules the sign of Cancer. Leo and Cancer are especially important at the personal level because they do rule the Cancer and Leo houses, which are affected at every Moon phase; so consider those houses, wherever they are on your dial, as extra-sensitive to the energies during New and Full Moons, even when the phases occupy other houses and signs. In the Cancer house you may be more sensitive to emotional issues during New and Full Moons. In the Leo house you may be more sensitive to individuality issues.

The 12 houses provide the structure within which our consciousness unfolds. Think of houses as you think of a house you live in. Imagine that you own and manage 12 different houses arranged in a circle. In each house you do something different. Every month, throughout a 12-13 month Sun cycle, you focus attention for a month in the one house containing the activities designated by the New Moon for the particular cycle (sign/month). At Full Moon you reach a peak of the activity begun at New Moon. However, you are still managing all the 11 other houses. The houses occupied by the Sun and Moon are like houses being honored by the presence of the King and Queen (your spirit and soul).

What do the Houses Tell Us?

You can see the generic structure of your life on your inner dial. Within these 12 houses are any experiences we can have or imagine. On any horoscope wheel, you can see the structure of a life—any life, anywhere, anytime. On our dials we can see which area of life is being activated by a Moon phase, as shown in the chapter on dials. How we learn the lessons of each house, achieve their goals, or gain self-understanding in each house is described by its sign. Our success is determined by our choices within that structure, the amount of work required to fulfill the activity, and our willingness to do the work. This is what creates consciousness, through what we learn in the process.

How the Moon and Sun Work Together Through the Houses

At each New Moon rebirth, the Old Woman brings into focus the next area of life/house highlighted by the New Moon. Every year the Sun unfolds spirit- or core-self consciousness sequentially through the 12 signs. The Moon (the moon inside of you) manifests this annual journey each month, also through the 12 signs, sequentially unfolding soul-consciousness. Each sequential area or house also defines one Solar step in the planetary unfoldment of consciousness. The Sun, being a star in the galaxy, is leading the way to galactic consciousness—our next step after we master planetary and Solar consciousness. We believe that when the Sun completes its responsibility of growing our personal consciousness at the Solar

System level, it will go on to open up Galactic consciousness. The Mayan Calendar may speak to that process—one which is not necessarily sequential.

To repeat something we have said earlier, whether you are aware of it or not something is going on in all of the houses, at any given time. However, the major focus is on the ones occupied by the Sun and Moon. At all times, except at new Moon, one house is lit by the Moon and another by the Sun. These are the two dynamically interacting areas of consciousness at work dancing the dance between mind and individuality (Sun), with emotion and patterned self (Moon). You can see their effect on your houses/areas of life. The Sun, your individuality/Higher Self, is growing spiritually through the signs, while the Moon, your personal self, is growing through the houses <u>and</u> signs by stimulation from the phases—Moon expresses its relationship to the Sun through manifesting the Sun's message in the house the Moon is in. This is why Moon represents one's spirituality while Sun, itself, represents spirit. The Moon manifests Solar consciousness at the incarnated level, which can never fully manifest the unmanifested. The more Moon (outer self) learns through doing, the more it wants to reconnect with spirit and grow more spirituality.

To repeat the above statementss and further define the sign's activity each month, while the Sun highlights one of the 12 houses and signs, the Moon moves through all 12 <u>plus one more</u>, on its way back to the Sun. The Sun has meanwhile moved to the next sign which accounts for the extra Moon sign as the Moon catches up. Thus, we experience a two-layered process of unfoldment. This multi-layered process is *spirit behind our individuality, growing through the annual Sun cycle, while personal self (soul) is growing through the monthly cycles. Personal self is focusing Sun's purpose through the relevant signs into the* houses/activities occupied *by the Moon.* We are creating our story within this dynamic pattern of wheels within wheels. Even more remarkable, although we may not be aware of these archetypal, micro-macro patterns layering our daily, monthly, yearly lives, we are instinctively following the patterns, anyway, although if not consciously we cannot use our free will as effectively.

Clearly some responses or reactions to life will be more appropriate to unfolding consciousness than others. That is the mystery each of us must unlock for ourselves, because that is the area of our free will. In a nutshell, responses are conscious, and reactions are unconscious, often though not necessarily always negative. New Moon gives us an opportunity to see how we have grown our inner selves.

For example, if we tend to *react* with anxiety or fear of the unknown around the New Moon, we know there is more work and possibly what kind. Most people do best with following their impulses and hunches during New Moon and the waxing phases do best operating consciously during and after Full Moon, using what they already know as the basis of choices and decisions. The reason we qualify free will as we do is that when we react impulsively or emotionally (especially in the waning cycles) we are often still in bondage to old patterns, which then can control our actions and even decisions. Everyone needs to make an effort to operate in both right and left brain related modes, even though each of us is more comfortable in one than another. Those persons born during a waxing Moon phase will be more comfortable with their right brain hunches and intuitions than those born in waning phases. The latter may choose to hold off on decisions until they understand a situation better. This is as it should be, and one could say, "Blessed is the one who knows himself well enough to know which he is."

This is how consciousness unfolds, along with the release of parts of our unconscious, but if we were aware of the process would it unfold any differently? That might depend on what you did with the information. In spite of arguments to the contrary there *is* free will. The option to use it is always in front of us. All persons struggling with outside pressures have the free will to make their own decisions. As has often been said, you may not be able to control the situations in your life, but you have a choice about how you will deal with them. But you can only use free will if you know what that is. Do you deal with issues from your center of individuality, or instinctually, or from your sometimes irrelevant parental patterning? If the last, choices made out of social-parental patterning are not true free will, though we are certainly free to make them. Would you like a way to create better situations in the future? Reread the quote from Liz Greene under the chapter title. She seems to be saying that all will is free will. It is, if you recognize that you have a personal will that is aligned to your personal wants and needs, and are able to infuse that personal will with the intentions of the spirit. As she says, you get better results with a more mature consciousness behind your will. You have more and better choices, which you simply do not see unless you have engaged your higher self.

Our statement of free will in a nutshell is that to the degree that a choice made is free of parental, cultural learned patterns dominating the choice—to that degree it is free will. Thus there seem to be two difinitions of free will. The other, like Liz Greene's, defines all will as free will, and says that our soul has determined how "perfect" or "imperfect" a decision is. The other side thinks that implicit in most decisions are one or more optional choices and that the one you chose could have been different if you had wanted to choose it or if you had had a greater consciousness of a higher option. People will continue to argue this, because actually no one truly knows. So we ourselves like the idea that free will choices are measured by their results and as your consciousness unfolds you will make choices that bring more satisfying results of a more spirit-oriented nature. It seems to be a matter of internal listening (which is best done at New and Crescent phases, and external listening during waning phases, best done at Full and disseminating Moons.

Parental/social patterning, incidentally, is absolutely necessary at the beginning of our lives, and some of it is important for our whole lives. It gives us tools (more or less effective) to live more or less easily within society's structure and shows us ways to deal with the realities of the outside world. But we are individuals; eventually we outgrow the need to follow some of that patterning. That is the conflict of late teen age years until age 28, by which time we need to have separated ourselves from parents, decided who we are as social beings, and worked out our own strategies for living, that we believe are better. This is the real meaning of "the generation gap"—each generation must contribute something beyond the previous one. But if the patterning gets in the way of free will it interferes with operating out of our core selves and making our best contribution.

The Moon Phase Path through the Houses

There are 360 degrees in any circle as in the circle of the Zodiac, with 30 degrees for each of the 12 signs. The same is true for the circle of houses on the Solar Dial. Each signs cycle contains a large amount of sign, house, and degree information to help us use the particular individual energies in the relevant houses, in the service of our own free will and/or spirit-Sun. Through the signs and houses a Moon cycle's eight phases each release a special timing window to which each individual is tuned, in his/her own special way, via his/her own birth and Solar charts.

The meanings of the 12 houses describe the *many applications of consciousness.* The Moon phases time a changing focus through the houses into our lives, as the Moon goes through 13 houses and 13 signs every month. At the end of each cycle the Old Woman dies, but simultaneously is reborn, not only renewing energies but renewing them on a higher level. In time our increasing consciousness requires us to make increasingly higher-level choices, leading to still more consciousness. In Table 4, you can see that the houses themselves are grouped around several basic functions.

NATURE AND FUNCTIONS OF THE HOUSES		
NATURE	HOUSES	FUNCTION
Initiating	1 - 4 – 7 - 10	Beginning Things
Stabilizing	2 – 5 – 8 - 11	Grounding Them
Adapting	3 – 6 – 9 - 12	Adjusting to Reality

Table 4. Nature and Functions of the Types of Houses

There are many levels of individual house meanings. We list as many in the following section as space allows. The table at the end of this chapter shows brief at-a-glance general meanings of the individual houses If you become interested in a fuller spectrum of house meanings (they are nearly limitless), we suggest finding a book just on houses, browsing until you find one which shows you how to figure out houses meanings without a list. For deeper understanding it is helpful to think of Houses as signs functioning in the ways described in the table.

Detailed Meanings of the Houses

Waxing Houses 1-6 are about development of the individuality. They include family and short term personal relationships. Moon Phases each have a different effect in each house throughout the twelve. Refer to previous chapters on how to read each Moon phase in whatever houses it takes place. Read the activity of the houses and think about how the Moon phase and sign affects it. Below are some details of the first six.

In the 1st house everything is personal, about me and how I project that to the world outside myself. It is how I see myself as a separate individual acting upon the world outside of myself.

The 2nd house holds my resources and whatever I have that gives substance to my 1st house self jewelry, clothes, money, talents, independence, self-esteem, body fluids and chemicals, etc. It represents the age of toddlers who run around saying "mine, mine, mine" about everything. This highly important stage helps the toddler to define himself, and hopefully to learn respect for his own things, and those of others. That learning is vital to later self-respect, gained from having initial caregivers respect what is his and requiring him to respect what is theirs.

The 3rd house is my basic relationship to neighbors, siblings, my local environment and how I understand and verbalize it, and what I learn from all this. I am always learning here—language, computer repair, or anything else of more or less practical value. It represents the first experiences outside of home, and the grade school period of life.

The 4th house is the house of the Moon heritage, home, family and one parent. In the Solar wheel it represents Mother, but modern astrologers make you guess which parent in the natal chart by deciding which parent was the most nurturing. It is gestation at many levels, basic foundations or roots to support the rest of your life emotionally. That means your inner self image, and sense of security. Emotional life based on nurturance and need-fulfillment is grounded here, with new beginnings always possible. When you grow up you establish your own home. Since this house is your foundation for life, what you achieve in the 10th (read below) rests upon this house. You will see on your dial that the 10th house is always at the top of the chart, opposite the 4th house.

The 5th house is the house of the Sun's creativity and self-expression, which partly arise out of the re-organization into personal meaning of raw emotions and self-beliefs, generated in the family 4th.. It can be sublime, incomplete, or blocked. This house contains the Heart Chakra and possibility of unselfish love. 4th house love was based on need, and the mother-experience, and must be upgraded to true Heart love with which to approach one's romantic or other love involvements. You learn to play here, as child or adult. Study children to learn from them.

The 6th house is about service and learning to work with others—intra-office relationships: worker-boss, worker-worker, or boss-worker relationships. Since it and the 5th house represent outer-world relationships, beyond family, it is about adjustments to that world. Personality crises occur here, and stress-induced illness, requiring one to learn more about how to adjust to the world outside self. 5th house love becomes spiritual love in the 6th as the inner spirit prepares to emerge through one's service before the step into the

7th house of partnerships. You are also learning here how to find your voice or put your own mark on the work you do—what really distinguishes your work from anyone else's? The 6th house rules health and also therapies. In the 6th house you work to pay your way in this world, and if you are physically unable, you may be assigned to a physical therapist. Even if you can work, but are depressed, have an anxiety disorder, or other mental/emotional problem, you may get a mental health therapist. If you have trouble relating to your partner in the 7th house, you both may end up in a couple's therapist's office. The therapy is a 6th house thing; the therapist becomes a 7th house person because a contract is required. The 6th house contains all kinds of help for people who need to adjust to the world outside them—usually for problems in individualization.

Waning houses 7 -12 are about co-equal relationships beyond family—love and marriage, partners, co-workers, or fellow students. They are co-equal, legalized, and personal relationships, and from houses 10-12 involve the greater Community. Just as the waxing houses refer to developing individuality (*individualization*), the waning houses refer to developing consciousness of the Other (*individuation*).

The 7th house is parallel to the meanings of the Full Moon. It is said to be the most important house in the chart, because relationship is what we are all theoretically here to learn. It is where you marry or become an *item* with someone else and move in, thus partaking together of something personal in the world outside yourself. Or you create something and sell it or exhibit it, or talk about it to a customer or audience. Or you go into business with another. The games played in this house require the beginning of *individuation*, because the dance steps get very complicated and require fast, sure footwork. You need to have all your personal relating skills well learned and established to be successful here. That means having all the abilities of your inner individuality operating together under one command control, and not under various and sundry urges and impulses. Is it strange that 50% or more of marriages end in divorce? And what are we teaching our children in school about relationships?

In this house, *equalitarian relationship* takes you beyond 4th house family relationships, where parents are supposed to model for you how to be in a relationship on your own with a peer. The 6th house gave you some basic skills. Whole books are published regularly on that subject. The critical, ego-bruising fact about your 1st house, your self, is that it is missing qualities that people you relate to in the 7ᵗʰ house will have, and will need to teach you, or mirror for you. Another set of books goes with that one! The sign on the 7ᵗʰ house is opposite the sign on your 1ˢᵗ house, and opposite signs always need each other's qualities to create balance. You can count on your 7ᵗʰ house sign to give you important information about what your partner is supposed to teach you and perhaps your 1ˢᵗ house will tell you something you need to teach him/her. The two houses contain by nature the process of mirroring, allowing partners to balance the relationship by being co-equals. If you look at your relationship as pulling together to create your unique relationship, instead of competing with each other for control, you will get the point.

The 8ᵗʰ house. The minute the 7ᵗʰ house contract was signed, you were through the door of the 8th. This is the wedding night. Here you *merge* into *intimacy,* a place of *committed relationships* which produces *joint resources* at some level (at least theoretically). In the old days, children were considered joint resources. I'm not sure if that is still true in many people's minds.

We cannot begin to discuss the 8ᵗʰ house adequately. It is psychologically deep and complicated. At the simplest level only, it is about your joint bank account, sex, your baby's birth, intimacy, deaths and rebirths, divorce, transitions, small groups, magic, and ritual. However, this is surface only. *Intimacy* in all its forms is the primary issue in much of the 8ᵗʰ house, but also as much in group-relationships as in partnerships. It is as though this house is an either-or. If you don't achieve intimacy or deep psychological involvement, you become separated, as in divorce or breaking the contract. As to deaths, it is more accurately about the *ego* deaths that have to happen in order to be deeply with another. You can't unilaterally control a relationship if you want it to be successful. But it *is* about other people's deaths, and separation in general, which cause deep transitional changes.

Deep psychological involvement here is fraught with sticky, murky, painful encounters in small quarters. The 7ᵗʰ house tells you why, and the 8ᵗʰ shows how you can best handle *the deep stuff* here, such as couple's therapy. Deep stuff also can mean occult or esoteric studies where you learn to work with *energies,* or do *group energy work* of some kind, implying work with other-dimensional beings. *Rituals* and rites of passage operate here, from personal to shamanic, to business rituals in your place of work. Strong personal attachments are here, and when they are broken for one reason or another, the world can fall apart. Detachment is the lesson we can learn from these experiences. You can look at this house as the process of learning how that single drop can retain its individual identity within a cup or a bucket of water. You get to the ocean in the 12th house. I once had a friend who believed her soul was her own, but while at a workshop she was told her soul was a shared one. She cried all the way home on the train and two days thereafter. She had Pisces on her 8th house, the sign of surrender and she had to detach herself from her attachment to her own personal soul. It was not an issue about what soul is or isn't—it was about the attachment and what it meant to her ego.

The 9th house. This is where you *expand* your contacts beyond the current boundaries and gain *wisdom* through sharing. You go to college, take a trip, join an athletic team, learn meditation, publish your book, or join a church. Over a lifetime you are developing your philosophy of life in this house.

While Lawyers, advocates, and prosecutors belong in the 7th house, legalizing belongs in the 9th, and judgment happens in the 10th. House 6, 7, 8, and 9 contain your practices for *individuation* and also the transition into *collectivization* (both of which more later.)

The 10th house. Here begins your practice for *collectivization*, or entrance into full participation in the larger society out there. It represents the highest you can *achieve* in this life, spiritually, through what you do in the outside world. It is both the most worldly, materialistic house and the most spiritual, in terms of possibilities. It is where you can *manage* affairs for others so it has to do with learning the right use of public resources—material, human, and spiritual. This was the main public issue in New Orleans after the 2005 hurricane Katrina. *Responsibility* goes with the 10th house and everyone who was responsible for aspects of rescue, relief, restoration, etc. had a 10th house part in that event. Their *reputations* were tested and some found wanting. Meanwhile someone won the 2006 Winter Olympics Gold Cup, another kind of reputation. The people above were involved with the USA and with the world. It could as well be you crowned president of the National PTA or the local garden club, or a 13-year-old group leader in an 8th grade project.

The 11th house is about your friendship circle, social ideals, organizations, associates from work, or any political, humanitarian, or social/environmental improvement in which you are involved. Are you able to *express yourself and manifest through groups and organizations*, or even a friendly luncheon of the Birthday Group. Activities, organizations and groups, through which you express activism, social improvement and political agendas, belong here. The 10th 11th and 12th houses belong in the *collectivization* department, in "the world out there".

Strangely, ghosts belong here in the 11th. They are the "form" following death. If you start with the 8th house of death and count four houses from that, you arrive at the 11th house. We say, the 11th house is the 4th house from the 8th. The 4th house is called "the end of the matter" in certain kinds of charts. Thus, the 11th house becomes the end of the matter after a death, where the departed becomes a ghost, the form following death. Dreams, both sleeping dreams and those larger "dreams" you have for your life are here, as well.

The 12th house. This last house is about balancing yourself with the world, completing all unfinished business so you can say with heart, "all's right with my world". My grandmother, at the end of her life, speaking out of a kind of distant dream state, or a semi-coma, murmured, "I've paid it all—all the nickels and all the dimes." She had been my greatest role model; I fully understood what she meant and was glad for her.

House 12 contains all things hidden, repressed, unfinished, and karmic—this life or another. Karma is often defined as "good" or "bad". We would say that it just is whatever it is, which is unfinished business and ultimately inescapable. This is also called the house of institutions and limitations such as prisons, hospitals, and handicaps, which we could call final reckoning. If your12th house is activated by a New Moon, you may grieve for a long past, as-yet-unmourned, death, or you may meet someone with whom you had karma, to live out the unfinished business. Or you may take a job in an institution, or be confined to one. At the spiritual end of it you may take up meditation. The ocean mentioned in the 8th hous is that "something greater than yourself" that you can be absorbed by or you can use to transcend with. Or it can be an institution which swallows you up and within which you lose your sense of individuality, such as a prison. Guides, angels, inner teachers are found here, ready to help with these tasks. [Totem and power animals are found in the 8th house.] Table 5, Meanings of the houses, at the end of the chapter, is a quick reference to the houses described in the text above.

As you begin working with the house and sign meaning on your dial, you may find the similarities between houses and signs confusing. If so, please refer to Table 3 in Chapter 7. . There actually is a close relationship between them. You can view the houses as areas of life in which you can learn how to internalize the qualities of the related signs. For example in my Solar Sagittarius dial, my seventh house is ruled by Gemini. I might expect that in my seventh houses I would have opportunities to learn how to understand and use the seventh sign Libra, as well as the ruling sign Gemini, which is part of my nature to begin with. In Table 3, pick any sign, then find its matching numbered house. That house in your dial is where you can learn more about the sign. In any case, it can be said that I will have opportunities to experience a variety of relationsips in that Gemini 7th house.

You will see more of these similarities in the next chapter, so we repeat the point that signs are about needs, attitudes and qualities, while houses are about activities. The signs tell us something about our Beingness, while houses tell us something about our Doing. Chapter 1 gives the four basic Moon phase meanings; for now, use those definitions. Every New Moon will fall in one of your houses. It will indicate that something in this area of your life is beginning. Using the information in this chapter you can see the category of life experiences in which the new cycle is beginning. You will also see the nature of the new activity in that house. All houses can create challenging action. They may require you to balance those challenging energies in order to keep inner or outer harmony. Since the Sun sign of the New Moon essentially controls the nature of the whole cycle, the numerous signs occupied by the Moon through the phases create the challenges. Keep in mind, as we continue, that we do have free will, which is central to everything we are writing about. Houses (what we do) and signs (how we do anything) determine the kind of karma we create and the kind of future we are creating for this life. We did not truly have whole free will until we began finding ourselves as individuals—we operated instinctually. Sometimes our instincts are aligned with our higher Self consciousness, but only to the degree to which we have achieved personal consciousness. We do incur Karma with harmful instinctual actions. If you do not believe in Karma, then just realize that "what goes around comes around" and you will meet it tomorrow and every day after that as long as you live. As we go along, the reader will see how every phase, every cycle, feeds the Moon-follower with consciousness triggering words, ideas, and concepts, and words of advice to suggest new and better ways of dealing with new situations.(See Table 5.)

HOUSE	AREAS OF LIFE EXPERIENCE
1	Self-consciousness/core self/immediate approach to life/ your will to direct yourself and your life/the way you present yourself to the world/your core self/personal attitudes
2	Self-sustainment, self-worth,; personal value;, personal assets; resources of the 1self:: physical, material, emotional, mental and spiritual; substance of t e self (blood, flesh, bones, minerals, chemical); how you make your money; the kind of clothes you wear; money, jewelry; all personal possessions; sensuality,
3	Intellect; communication; learning style; learned ways of making connections with other; mores and customs, siblings; neighbors and neighborhood; grade school part of one's life; blood relatives outside of nuclear family
4	Home; family of origin & family of choice; inner strength and security; foundations; the parent who influenced your inner life; property and non-movable possessions.
5	Creativity & self-expression; children of: body, mind, emotions, spirit; play & recreation; loves; taking risks; the heart center; the nature of your ability to recreate yourself in outer form; your brand of risk-taking and adventuring
6	Work; health; service; discipleship; personality crises & adjustments; learning the difference between perfection and perfecting; rents and renters; how you adapt your creative expression to make it useful and acceptable to others in the above activities.
7	Partnerships: marriage, business, etc.; The Other, such as one's audience, readership, client, or lawyer, doctor, etc.; where the self learns what he-she is missing in the first House—the sign on the cusp shows a quality of self that requires others to bring it out. (Libra 1st House learns independence from Aries partners and Aries first House learns sharing from Libra partners.)

8	Results of relationships: either deeper involvement and deeper intimacy or changes, transitions, separations, physical or ego-deaths (giving up part of yourself when you go more deeply into a relationship or conversely when you let it go); death and rebirth; research; the occult; ritual; sex; taxes; legacies; victimization; surgery; partner's or joint resources; births of your children (which are separations from the body)
9	Expanding consciousness by going beyond boundaries and sharing or gaining wisdom; higher education; travel; religion; philosophy; publishing; sharing wisdom; beliefs; meditation of a thinking kind where the mind is active; team sports; large animals; expectations
10	Career, success, ultimate life achievement; status, public image, recognition—fame or infamy; position in the community; authorities and people in high places; the parent who connected you with the outer world; crown chakra
11	Social process; friends and associates related to career, social life and organizations; dreams, both sleeping and waking; income from career
12	Karma-unfinished business—what you need to release in this lifetime; denied grief and failures; hidden matters; losses and endings; balancing oneself against the world; limitations; faith as opposed to 9th House beliefs; the door to inner guidance and guides; secrets and secret helpers; the ultimate eternal verities: truth, beauty, goodness

Table 5.Activities of the Houses

9
Wheel of the Zodiac
The Forces at Play on the
Whole Field of Space

...astrology is essentially the purest presentation of occult truth in the world... because it deals with those conditioning and governing energies [Zodiac] *and forces which play through and upon the whole field of space and all that is found within that field...*
When this fact is grasped...and the nature of the field of space is correctly understood...
the relationships between individual, planetary, systemic and cosmic entities will be grasped...we shall then begin to live scientifically.
--*Esoteric Astrology* by Alice A Bailey, p.5[1]

History of the signs

The stars of the twelve Constellations of the Zodiac are of course older than man and the Solar system, but until shortly before 500 BC, the Zodiac stars were not configured as we see them in the sky now. They were not originally the familiar 12 constellations, or even entirely made up of the same stars. All we know is that recorded star information began with a few individual stars that rose just before Sun rise (called Heliacal rising) dating back to the Stone Age. When this was measured over certain designated landmarks, such as a mountain, it meant a new season had begun, or it timed such events as the rising of the Nile in Egypt. This is what most of the ancient observatories and stone constructions such as Stonehenge were about, along with the Moon and Sun. The latter two were the main sources of the earliest shamanic belief systems, with these certain few stars as greater seasonal markers and the 360-day year markers. It took 360 days for the Sun to do a heliacal return to a particular star. We always wondered why all the early shamanic societies including Chinese, Babylonian, and Central and South American chose 360

---

1   *Esoteric Astrology* by Alice A. Bailey, Lucis Publishing Company, New York: 1968, 6th printing

days for their year, when clearly it takes 365 days (plus some hours) for the Sun to make its circuit.

An answer is that different sky circles were in use. Our year and seasons, etc. are mostly based on something we call the ecliptic, a circle drawn by the Sun's apparent movement around the Earth. This circle and the twelve tropical signs together provide mirror-image reflections of the 12 constellations far beyond our Solar system, and involved in a different astronomical circle. Eastern cultures still use the constellational approach to astrology and religion, and have a more group-oriented approach to life. We live in the same Solar system and, at least in the West, find the Tropical system more fitting to our individualistic nature (which the authors believe must develop a more universal consciousness to survive).

Many writers, such as Alice Bailey (quoted above), have predicted that when we understand the real meaning of the energies of the universe in which we live we will live scientifically—that is, in conscious harmony and balance with Earth, the Solar system, and the true (sidereal or star-based) zodiac constellations (and the rest of the universe). We believe the Solunar Cycles give us the primary step in "grounding" and clarifying these energies of signs and phases, that demonstrate the larger cosmic energy patterns.

To continue the history discussion, early people universally believed that the passage of the Sun over the same annual Heliacal Rising point of a certain star, 360 days after the previous passage, was more important spiritually, and more accurate than the more obvious 365-plus day cycle. The star-god who marked that passage was more powerful than the Sun, as well as more reliable. However, they also all added the five extra days at the end, recognizing both systems. 365 has no fundamental relation to any mathematical system, but it figured in the agricultural calendars. The number 360 and all of its multiples and divisions, particularly of 10 and 6, eventually formed the basis of modern mathematics. To add a mystical note to that, astronomers tell us that in a few million years our year will have actually shrunk to 360 days! Is this why the complex divination and religious systems of the Chinese and other cultures also later all functioned on this numbering system? Is it perhaps truly a more spiritual system, foretelling the future of Earth? Could mankind become spiritually mature sooner if it built its calendars on a 360-day spiritual year? The contemporary proponents of the Mayan calendar believe so.

Whether or not it is true that the older sidereal system is more spiritual, the Tropical Zodiac is a belt that encircles the path of the Sun as a thought form, mirroring the constellations. It directly channels the constellational energies to Earth via the Sun and Moon, at a more personal or individual level. The *Old Woman* has been trying to align our energies with that flow for eons, and we are still far from that goal. But the sign-energies, whether Tropical or Sidereal, are the major keys to reaching that farther goal, which we hope will become more apparent as we continue. While the Zodiac energies carry the universal evolutionary energies, the *Old Woman* times the cyclic flow as she downloads the energies from the Tropical Zodiac through the Sun to each of us individually and personally.

We know that was a mouthful and a half, so we recap the above in the following way Universal energy flow from the Constellational Zodiac → belt of the Tropical Zodiac → Sun → Moon → Earth → all humans, every month. Meanwhile we also receive these energies annually from the Sun. This is a concept long held by many, and whether or not it is scientifically "true," it contains a number of philosophical truths discovered by individuals over many centuries.

Meanings of the signs

Get out your dial and we will begin digging deeper into the way the signs influence every aspect of your life. Each sign is an archetype which we will live out during our lives, some more significantly than others depending upon our destiny. These archetypes are common to all people, just as the Moon phases hold a common message to everyone on the planet. Even more important is the great single archetype made up of the 12 individual signs. This is the Grand Archetype of Evolution unfolded by the Sun's annual journey. Studying the 2000 year periods of history and perhaps prehistory will offer insight concerning historic periods, to those who are interested

The following traditional list of sign meanings (The bold type is traditional, the rest is our expansion) is actually a pretty clear model for how we progress in consciousness through the structure of the Houses, each of which is ruled by a sign. The following list contains one version of the traditional ideal meanings of the signs, in their positive form

1. Aries "**I am**"—a separate individual.
2. Taurus "**I have**"—the resources I need to support the development of that individuality.

3. Gemini "**I Communicate**"—to connect with people and places in my environment.
4. Cancer "**I need**"—someone to care for and someone to care for me.
5. Leo "**I will**"—express myself with pride, and do what I will in life.
6. Virgo "**I analyze**"—everything, to make it perfect, or to define it.
7. Libra "**I balance**"—myself with others to create equality and harmony.
8. Scorpio "**I desire**"—deeper involvement and self-understanding.
9. Sagittarius "**I aspire**"—to the stars, toward the farthest goals.
10. Capricorn "**I achieve**"—the highest I can be.
11. Aquarius "**I know**"—the spirit within me has universal knowledge.
12. Pisces "**I surrender**" –to that which is greater than myself.

We will go through the signs as we did the Houses. The above key phrases are traditional interpretations, all framed in the positive. We give brief psychological descriptions of the negative use of the signs in the table below and elsewhere. Very important here is to understand that each sign operates at the same four levels as the Houses: physical, emotional, mental, spiritual. If a Moon phase description does not seem to fit where it falls in your dial, imagine to yourself what the activities of the house would look like, seen from each of these levels. For example:

1. In the house of Pisces *I surrender* to events over which I have no control
   physical—an illness I for which I have no cure at this time
   emotional—the joy of a peak experience
   mental—an event with meaning beyond my understanding, but which I accept.
   spiritual—the unknown, or my Higher Power.

2. In the house of Taurus *I have* resources, such as
   physical—money, talents;
   emotional—security, love;
   mental—knowledge, wisdom,
   spiritual—sense of the Divine.

The Elements: Fire, Earth, Air, Water

Each sign belongs to one of four familiar groups called elements—Earth, Air, Fire, Water. There are three signs in each group. Each group operates or functions in the four above ways, affecting the overall behavior of a person in terms of its nature. As you can see in Table 6a, Earth is physical, Air is mental, Fire is spiritual or inspirational, and Water is emotional. You can see the element of any sign in the table. What is really cool here is that if Gemini (air sign = mental activity) rules your 4th house (family), and a New Moon lands there, the issues of the month will likely involve a mental activity concerning family, like important communications, letters, or siblings . Another example is a lunation in Pisces (water sign = emotional) in the 5th house (self expression, creativity, children, romance). The activity will be emotional expressions concerning one or more of those 5th house activities. You can also consider how water and fire affect each other in the physical realm, and translate that into your creative expressions.

You may not want to add this information to your moon work right now, but refer back to it as you move along in familiarity with the basic sign and house interpretations of your moon phases. Juggling both Sun and Moon in eight phases is enough to begin with. But some day when you simply can't figure out why one of the phases is not clear to you, return to table7 and see if it clarifies things.

SIGNS	ELEMENTS	NATURE
Aries, Leo, Sagittarius	FIRE	Inspirational
Taurus, Virgo, Capricorn	EARTH	Practical
Gemini, Libra, Aquarius	AIR	Mental
Cancer, Scorpio, Pisces	WATER	Emotional

Table 6a. The Nature of the Signs

SIGNS	MODALITIES	FUNCTIONS
Aries, Cancer, Libra, Capricorn	INITIATING	Beginning Things
Taurus, Leo, Scorpio, Aquarius	STABILIZING	Grounding Them
Gemini, Virgo, Sagittarius, Pisces	ADAPTING	Adjusting to Reality

Table 6b. The Functions of the Signs

On your dial you can now, as we did in the chapter on Houses, move the inner wheel until the sign on the first house is your Sun-sign. As we explained in Chapter 7, this shows how that you express your life through your birth sign. Each of the Houses from there through 12 also gives you the opportunity to express and experience the other 11 signs. Here is an example of how important this information could be for you. Supposing you have a New Moon in Gemini (adapting) in your 11th house of associations connected to your work. This New Moon has to do with some rule that is being imposed and you are vigorously opposed to it, and want to rebel. This Gemini nature of the whole month to come is telling you the universe and your spirit want you to adapt to it. You will probably have a much more difficult month if you rebel. Now is not the time, but it might come later.

So here are billions of people running around expressing their Sun sign, but throughout the 12 categories of life, expressing those other 11 as a shade or tone of the Sun's color. Then if you reincarnate after this life under a different Sun sign, you will already have had some experience using the energies of the new Sun sign. While in this present life you experience the signs monthly and annually as the unfolding consciousness energy of each sign, sequentially through the overarching archetypal energy of the Zodiac. Humanity unfolded thus through countless millennia to where the Zodiac is now, measured by its position at sunrise each spring equinox. All of us are unfolding our part in this incredible seamless cosmic pattern. The dynamic of unfolding at the human level is managed by the interlocking monthly patterns of the Moon with the annual pattern of the Sun's Zodiac journey through the years. We suspect this magnificently interconnected pattern in which we participate is only a tip of the iceberg in the ocean of space. But it is one we can understand, view in the sky, and sometimes feel. Living within it may be the only opportunity for us to be the witnesses of the cosmic drama unfolding in our Solar system. We are told that *witnessing* is a most important spiritual activity—important not only for our spiritual development but mystically for the drama itself.

Reading the signs You Find on Your Houses

You are like a diamond, with each houses-sign pair representing one of your facets. When you examine a houses that features a Moon phase, combine the quality of the sign with the activity of the house first, making certain that you understand that combination in your own terms. Only then should you add the Moon phase meanings.

The integrity of your expression of each house-sign facet measures your degree of development of that sign. You will not be equally "good" at the matters of all of your houses because of this. You may have problems during some months in relation to this fact. That is neither good nor bad, it simply shows you where your assets and liabilities lie, and suggests work you have yet to do to grow in other areas. This is what evolution of consciousness is about. The eight Moon phases contain the secret of your needed self-work— individually "planned" for each person, and indeed secret, because unless you choose to tell someone, you can let yourself look at the Moon's mirror every month privately with no one to judge. Even you do not need to judge, so be open to the pieces of your dark side as they come up for consideration each month. If you don't see any, you either don't have any this month or you don't want to see them.

In your Aries house you need to feel your separate individuality more than in any other area of your life. In this house you need those things, people, and activities with which you can identify— like having a separate room in your own house. You get ideas here and want to act upon them immediately. All your life you will be defining and developing your identity in this area of your life. The highest purpose here is to push envelopes so you can lead others into new territories (at any level).

In your Taurus house you need tangible results from your Aries ideas to feel productive. You need harmony around you and you dislike sudden changes. Music, art and intellectual activities may go on here. You "build" here, at any of the three levels, and your highest purpose is to bring down spiritual light into what you build in the world. If you are a Taurus Sun, your mission is to bring down the light into everything you do.

In your Gemini house you need to spread out and make connections, communicate, and collect facts. The Gemini houses is the library, the newspaper, the bus line, and all sorts of local gatherings to exchange information (not to be confused with wisdom which is found in the opposite sign of Sagittarius). Most especially, you need to look at and constantly be aware of both sides of issues. You need to be impeccable about your facts here because ultimately you have to choose; otherwise one day you will be on one side and the next day the other side, and sound like two different people. That trait has cost several men the presidency. It confuses others and prevents your turning information into wisdom. Spiritually, your task here is to be precise about facts, and learn to understand duality and paradoxes. The two pillars of Gemini suggest that the wind of truth blows through the center between them, and this is where you should stand, centered on the truth as you know it. You should be able to say to another, "I understand that is your truth, but this is mine.

In your Cancer house, you need to nurture Gemini ideas into being. You manifest through Cancer. Something in your houses of Cancer will indicate the need for which you incarnated at this time, which is based security and comfort. You also need to establish a personal foundation in this house so that you know you belong here, so that you do not retreat into your shell at every critical word. Excessive sensitivity ruins belongingness. Spiritually, your role here is to "keep the candle lit in your window", metaphorically speaking. Whether it is a cup of flour or an understanding shoulder, the people in this area of your life will know you are there for them.

In your Leo house you need to have pride in what you do; so you need to express yourself here in ways that you can feel proud of. In your Leo houses you not only need but want respect, praise, glory, and to be the center of attention. Sun sign Leos express who they actually are by what they create in the outer world as a whole being It is a hard role to play, since if you haven't earned the glory you will eventually be known as an insufferable bore, a wheeler-dealer, or a tyrant. Generosity, willingness to help others, and your own brand of creativity developed to its nicest (without too much fanfare) is your best path. A Leo can be the most reassuring person in the world to turn to when the elevator is falling. Be careful if metaphoric "divine kingship" is offered to you. Pride is necessary here, but in reasonable amounts. Your most spiritual role here is to express your creativity in ways that benefit humanity, while letting your spiritual divinity (which everyone has) radiate, rather than talking about it. Parts of your shadow (those warts we do talk about) will be most noticed by others in your house of Leo(Sun casts shadows!)

In your Virgo house, as you go about your daily work, you "need" perfection, therefore constant analysis and criticism. Perfection is not possible, but perfect-*ing* is. There is a special place for those who keep the process of perfecting going. A Virgo needs very good communication skills in order to keep others from feeling criticized.

You will learn them fast because it hurts you worse than anyone to feel that way. You are a great asset in any group trying to produce something, because you know how parts fit into a whole and can always figure out how to do anything. Your spiritual role here is to polish what you do until it expresses your unique individuality or your inner divinity, which begins its emergence here. In other words, your essence needs to be in everything you do.

In your Libra house you need relationship. It teaches you not to be completely self-absorbed in your Aries houses. You balance yourself with others here. Libra is related to Gemini, in that where Gemini needs awareness of both sides of a question, Libra must balance or weigh them, in order to make decisions. In relationships here, people should be co-equal, or working in harmony. There can be art or music or architecture in this house, and definitely a strong emphasis on partnership. Your spiritual highest is found in something of this houses that reflects "the harmony of the spheres".

In your Scorpio house you need deep psychological involvement and intimacy. It is a fixed sign and intense emotions tend to hang on and turn into long term grudges, bitterness, desires for revenge, etc. Addiction here indicates a need to cultivate detachment. On the other hand you have a gift for getting to the heart of any matter, and seeing truth where others can not. Your spiritual role here is to help others and yourself to clear out the old stuck emotions that keep us all from progressing. Your model is the myth of Hercules who cleaned out the Aegean Stables as one of his tasks on his hero's journey. Your ability to regenerate like the phoenix from the ashes is part of your spiritual purpose.

In your Sagittarius house are your beliefs, aspirations, goals, and your search for the Divine. You want, and usually have, companions on all your journeys from physical to spiritual. At the physical level you are likely to enjoy travel or team sports. At the mental level you like learning, teaching classes, and love conventions and retreats, where you have the broadest opportunities to share your brand of wisdom. Intellectual arrogance and self-aggrandizement are your two biggest pitfalls. The man who sold a refrigerator to an Eskimo was probably a Sagittarius Rising or Sun. Sagittarius' spiritual level holds the search for God in the Hero's Journey. Mountain climbers sometimes have Sagittarius strong in their charts, like Aries. But here mountain climbing is also the metaphor for the search for God.

In your Capricorn house you are meant to be a manager, at the top, even if it is something very small, like managing your own bank account or portfolio, or a department in a place of business.. You are taking your first step into the collective quadrant of the signs Capricorn, Aquarius, and Pisces. You need literally to be right, which can become "righteous". You need to control, and you can be quite rigid about that. As the opposite of emotional Cancer, you control your emotions, sometimes to the point where you appear emotionless You were designed to be objective and detached in this area of your life, but not cold and distant. Avoid being stingy with your caring feelings and emotions. As the first of the three collective signs, Capricorn's control is meant to be that of collective resources such as food, money properties, etc. Righteousness, an ego-state, needs to become" right-use" of social resources. It can be the most materialistic of the signs, yet it is the one where you can be the most spiritual at the same time, a very difficult balancing act.

The Goat-Fish, Capricorn comes up out of the waters as a fish; then it shape-shifts into a mountain goat with momentum upwards that feels separative to some others (like Aries). First you establish yourself in one of society's hierarchies which causes envy, distrust or fear in some others (Cancer); you enter the competitive field (Libra) which threatens others; and finally, you make a name for yourself, which others can perceive as diminishing their place in the world. A well-developed Capricorn will not become emotionally involved in these inevitable reactions from others, knowing it is a lesson for both him/her and those others. Those with a lesser well-developed Capricorn facet will either have problems here, or will find this area plays one of the lesser roles in his/her life. The above information applies most often to the Sun in Capricorn and less emphatically to the other 11 houses.

In your Aquarius house you find your connection to the universe; you need freedom and democratic relationships. You are drawn to people of similar mind in "the world out there", often from other cultures or ways of life, and often as the result of your career. If it is on your second houses, you may have possessions or furnishings, or art works from other cultures If it is on your sixth houses you work with those of other cultures or are involved with technical or scientific expertise; in your fourth houses, you live with them, or follow their lifestyle and home décor. On your ninth you might translate their books, learn a new language, or travel to distant places with foreign characteristics. Here you synthesize the Gemini houses information, which was balanced in the Libra houses. On the

10th, 11th, and 12th Houses, you need to be involved in humanitarian work, though some of that may show up anywhere in your chart.

While Capricorn represents personal or socio-political Managers, Aquarius represents Changers, who break open the dead structures and breathe new spirit into them. Dreams concerning what you want to see happen in your larger view of life stir you to social action here, or perhaps you find unusual people in your social connections of the houses Aquarius rules.

In your Pisces ruled house you can get lost. While Capricorn can be (but often is not) the most spiritual worldly sign, Pisces rules all-encompassing spirituality that has a need to save others. In that context it also rules meditation, mysticism, dreams, oceans and oceanic states. The connection here to cosmic states often implies a magical imagination and a specific kind of artistic creativity. A Pisces Sun radiates peace to others and can get lost in the burdens of those who are attracted to them in order to receive that peace for themselves. On the seventh houses, Pisces attracts partners who need to be saved or rescued from addictions, and sometimes very spiritual partners who will inspire them. I knew such a woman years ago who married four times, all of them alcoholics, three of whom committed suicide. She taught me astrology, and then disappeared out of my life. Another 7th houses Pisces friend married a man who was a sort of self-taught minister and devoted himself to helping others, and they had a good marriage. She devoted herself to him and was inspired by him, while he was helping others. The Virgo Sun with the 7th houses Pisces may attract a Pisces partner with an addiction.

At the most personal levels, in any houses, Pisces rules unfinished business where you need closure for such things as deep grief, abandonment, loss, depression, loneliness, confinements, wrongs that have never been righted. Many such Pisces experiences are karmic, and marriages such as the ones above are quite clearly karmic. Usually they can only be dealt with successfully by giving yourself over to something greater than you, or learning to transcend the situation. The key here is to immerse yourself in the pain, go through it not around, under, or over it, then transcend it. Mark Robertson's[21] key words for Pisces were *turn away from the known past and walk toward an unknown future on faith.*

These Twelve signs describe the experiences we go through at

---

2   Mark Robertson was a well-known astrologer of the '50's and '60's.

many levels, to discover our own way to the ultimate way in Pisces, where we transcend and find closure, peace, and/or final immersion in a great cause, the final Unknown, or God. This sign can help us understand that addicts, in spite of sometimes criminal acts, are looking for the ultimate values of Pisces, just as we are, but are looking in the wrong places.

The Phases through the signs

As you follow the phases through the houses and their signs, begin by reading the brief dial and table descriptions. Only add information when you are ready. This is a text book with enough information to grow on, and not to be swallowed and used all at once This is how we began, and probably how most astrologers began. Most of our readers will never pursue astrology past this book. The thing we love most about the phases is that a few words can open up a situation for any of us and put life in perspective. We also suggest that you won't fully be able to use our sign and houses information until you have completed Chapter 12 on the eight phases. Key words are definitely the place to begin, and then use all the other material as resources if the key words fail to match the situation. Here is our table of key words for signs.

SIGNS	WHAT YOU NEED	HOW YOU CAN BEST HANDLE THINGS
ARIES I am	Needs freedom: to be who he/she is, to have separate space, sense of separate identity, independence. Needs adventures, mountains to climb, to act immediately on new ideas. **Lacks** natural ability to share	Actively: initiates, takes the lead, acts on own ideas. Ability to recoup after disasters; courageous. **Spiritual themes**: channels ideas and acts on them, leads others into new territories. **Healing**: with body work, voice, and self-will
TAURUS I have	Needs tangible results, comforts, beauty, harmony, and intellectual challenges, Hands-on experiences. **Lacks** the native ability to look past the surface of things, ideas, people.	Productively: persistently, artistically, patiently; slow anger, but slow to let it go. **Spiritual themes**: builds in the material world and brings down light into the result. **Healing**: with toning (vibrational) reading inspirational material, art and music therapies

GEMINI I think	Variety, lots of facts, mental stimulation, lots of associations, connections and communication. **Lacks** a naturally larger viewpoint to give facts their meaning.	Communicatively: spreading out in many directions, collecting facts, people, things. Hearing both sides of every discussion and struggling to choose the "right" one. **Spiritual themes**: recognizes dualities and tries to stand in the center point between them. **Healing**: by laying on of hands, bibliotherapy, journaling.
CANCER I feel	Needs security, belonging, to feel nurtured and to nurture, continuity with the past. **Lacks** inherent personal boundaries	Nurturing self and others; imaging ideas, people and things into form, with reverence for the past. **Spiritual themes**: "keeps the candle in the window"—holds and gestates the light within to share with others in need. **Healing**: with "chicken soup" and by visualization
LEO I will	Needs to master something, to have pride in it, to get feedback for efforts. The sun casts a shadow so Leo needs to purify the shadow side to achieve personality-soul-spirit integration. **Lacks** natural group orientation.	Dramatically: puts own stamp on ideas, people, things; shines in the eyes of others when he/she clears away the shadows, otherwise it's a fake. Self-assured, generous. **Spiritual themes**: helping reassuring sharing courage and light with others. **Healing**: by laying on of hands—passing the light; psychodrama
VIRGO I analyze	Needs to work toward perfection while realizing that goal can never be reached; to serve, be useful, defined, and adaptable. **Lacks** natural leadership, trust in own ideas	Analytically and with discrimination: organizing & perfecting techniques; she/he helps others from their viewpoint of what they need, not what she wants. Loves reading, learning, detailed work. **Spiritual themes**: "births the light within through devotional service. **Healing**: natural and alternative healing, herbal.

LIBRA I balance	Needs balance and harmony in relationships, and everyone in the vicinity to be happy and comfortable. Artistically or intellectually inclined. **Lacks** a naturally strong sense of identity.	Equally: always gives the other equal time, mediates to avoid conflict. Loves many but not so deeply until evolved. **Spiritual themes**: balances dualities, develops detachment in order to make good choices and judgments. **Healing** through the arts.
SCORPIO I desiret	Needs deep psychological personal and group involvement, intense alignments, energy focus, depth, discernment, control, intense sensory experiences. **Lacks** the native ability to take things at face value, control, or drop the intensity in let others be in order to relax and enjoy a time out.	Intensely, secretively, silently, courageously. Penetrates defenses, reaches the core truth, seeks total union. Detachment is important. **Spiritual themes**: Cleansing the Aegean Stables to clear channels for group energies. Sometimes shamanically involved. **Healing** through ritual, psychopomp activities, deep psychoanalysis.
SAGIT- TARIUS I understand	Needs to understand life and all its issues to gain and share wisdom, but needs Gemini's details and facts to back it up. Needs goals, expansion, and growth. **Lacks** the native ability to work with many details and facts.	Philosophically: makes broad contacts, shares ideas and games, lets the pains of life increase faith that then universe is basically good. Organizes, but may want to organize you! Voracious reader. **Spiritual themes**: the search for God or Creator, or Light. **Healing** through mind-body work, prayer, believing.
CAPRICORN I manage	Needs respect, structure, a niche in society, competition, power, social belongingness, also social boundaries as opposed to Cancer's personal boundaries. **Lacks** natural warmth and empathy.	Professionally: organizes, is an authority, business manager, but inclined to be conservative. **Spiritual themes**: the revelation of light on the mountain top enables the right-use of social power. **Healing** through conventional AMA methods.

AQUARIUS I know	Needs social action, progress, freedom, group activity, improvement, innovation. wants to bring new life into Capricorn structures, or put a new twist on ancient ideas. **Lacks** concern for the individual.	Scientifically, improves, innovates, and brings ancient wisdom from the past up to date. Humanitarian. **Spiritual themes**: synthesizes the dualities—"We area all one in the Light." "The individual exists for the life of humanity." **Healing** through frequencies and other little-understood techniques.
PISCES I Surrender	Needs to lose self in a greater whole, a oneness with everything including God, a faith that allows one to walk away from the past into the unknown future; inner peace, belief in a vision. **Lacks** attention to details and earthy practicality (head in the clouds, feet in the mud.	Selflessly: on faith alone, imaginatively and artistically. A candidate for world savior, rescues the lost and feeds the hungry, forgetting self. **Spiritual themes**: about connecting with the universe and God while remaining grounded in reality (mother Theresa) Selfless service while taking appropriate care for self. **Healing** by being with God while bringing the other person into that Presence and knowing they are healed.

Table 7. Needs and Expressions of the Signs

In the Next Chapter: A Microscopic Look at the Signs,

The general reader is already aware that the Sun and Moon are always in different signs in all the phases except in the New phase. The Sun and Moon tell us, by the signs they occupy, how one can best approach the signs' house activities at the particular phase. While familiarity with the individual signs may help us understand how the Sun or Moon is operating in the phases, a further deeper look at the signs brings them into a new focus. Each degree of every sign carries a specific quality of action and a specific nature, and these characteristics open up the most fundamental level of understanding just how Sun and Moon will operate and how they will relate to each other. Juggling houses or signs in the phases will be described in detail in Chapter 11, with tables to refer to.

In the next chapter we enter the exciting microscopic world of Zodiac degrees—the sub-archetypes—in a truly microscopic way. A sign is an archetype, but its 30 degrees together describe the sign's archetype. The separate degrees are like the cells of the sign, each being a sub-archetypeThis is our favorite part of doing the Moon phases. It provides us, effortlessly, with astonishing details about each phase, for both Sun and Moon. We have to caution our readers not to allow themselves to be seduced into using this as your one and only technique. Yes, you can see everything about a cell under a microscope, in great detail. However, without the more familiar and larger communities of cells (organs), you would miss the overall medical situation; the same applies to degrees of the Zodiac (30 to each sign) and we need both.

10
Screens of Prophesy
The Zodiac degrees and Their Archetypes

The [Sabian] *symbols are filters through which a meaning pertinent to a situation or problem can be individually and uniquely intuited and experienced.*
They can also serve as a "screen of prophecy" in that they "have a rapport with cosmic order
that gives them potential signature value every moment of their emergence in attention".
—*An Astrological Mandala* by Dane Rudhyar

What are the Degree Symbols?

We have seen how each house on your dial describes an area of your life, and how each sign describes the qualities and needs of its particular house. Now we can re-consider the fact that each sign contains 30 degrees (360 ° divided by 12 signs = 30 degrees). Each degree can describe a different facet of a sign. The 30 degrees of each sign are connected to an image with a meaning, which we have termed sub-archetypes, or archetypal degrees. We will call them symbolic degrees for simplicity. Paradoxically, at the same time, each degree is said to describe each day of the year. As explained earlier, the degrees of the zodiac are stretched out over Earth's annual orbit of 365-1/4 days, so that in fact each degree describes one day plus a tiny fraction of another. Eventually that little bit extra builds up until each one of the five extra days is covered. So again we bring up the subject of fractals. The Zodiac is a unit of spiritual time. Each of the 12 signs is a fractal of the Zodiac. Each of the 30 days of a sign is a fractal of the sign. We recommend you search fractals on the web to get a "feeling" for them. We are surrounded by them, and they are found in all living things. Asparagus is a good example of a plant form. So are many common ferns.

138

The whole circle of 360 degree images together *is* an archetype of the stages of unfolding time and consciousness, so we are calling each individual degree a sub-archetype.

Fortunately for the less mathematically gifted of us, we only have to deal with one day and one degree at a time! For that information, all one needs to do is turn to the desired date of a particular Moon phase in the weekly appointment pages of your *Celestial Guide*. Each of the four phases is shown by a Moon, graphically marked on the correct day of the week, with the correct light/dark proportion. Beside the graphic are two time-zone listings for the degree and minute of the exact phase point—the position of Sun and Moon. That degree is characterized by the nature of the Zodiac sign, and the placement of the degree in that sign. In the ephemeris at the back of your calendar book you can find the degree of the Sun for every day of the year. Some like to meditate daily on the meaning of the day's degree symbol.

There is one problem with Maynard's book, in that it doe not always show you degree of the Sun at the exact phase point, especially if the Sun changes signs in that day between 12 am of that day and 12 am of the next. So you have two options.

One is to make sure that the Sun's degree number is exactly the same as the Moon's degree number at phase point. So if the Moon's Last Quarter phase degree is 24 Leo and the Sun changes from 23 Taurus to 24 Taurus on that day, choose 24 Taurus.

The second option is to visit our website and get the exact degrees on the calendar page. You can get some basic interpretations for each month's phase positions there, as well. If you like you can do without Maynards' calendar book entirely, though I (Virginia) like it so much I use it every day as my appointment book. And who knows—some day there could be a computer breakdown just when you need the information!

The symbolic degrees are descriptions of the degrees of the Zodiac and thus the specific type of energy, or *light frequency* [1] of each day of the year. So consider that on your dial, you can now find any phase, the houses in which the phase occurs, and the meanings

---

1   A term used by some writers to mean the type of energy carried by the Zodiac signs—consciousness (light) energy. It has meaning in relation to the idea of consciousness, and the belief that the higher the consciousness a person achieves, the more light that person carries in h/her being, and possibly the closer to white light. The Moon is a vessel of light, forever filling and emptying out the dark side of the psyche.

of the signs that rule the houses, so you can now add together the following meanings of the current phase as follows:

1. The phase _____
2. Areas of life impacted by the phase (Sun and Moon houses)
    _____
3. The nature of the Zodiac sign energies (Sun and Moon signs)
    _____
4. The Meanings of the degree energies (Sun and Moon degrees)
    _____

We call this gathering your tools. These are the basic factors that you will use for the rest of this book, in every phase. They will provide you with the deeper, fuller, expanded meanings of the eight phases, in an orderly manner. We have found the degrees to be the most challenging, spiritually inspiring, psychologically enlightening, and emotionally satisfying of all four aspects of interpretation.

At this point we suggest you turn to Appendix E which contains the original 360 degree symbols. If the symbolic degree for a New Moon is 26 Virgo, find that degree in Appendix E. *Now, don't read that degree, but do read the following degree,* 27 Virgo. The reason for this was explained earlier in the book. We remember how hard it was to remember this fact when we were first involved with so many other factors. It's that pesky little nothing called the "zero," which caused a historic upheaval in the history of mathematics and permitted every technology (including your computer's language) to be derived from it. We repeat that when you are born you are zero years old. On your first birthday, you are called "one", but from that moment you are working on your second year, which becomes "two" only after you have completed living the second year, and so on.

Archetypes and Symbolic degrees

Archetypes, as we have stated in Chapter 3, are not well understood by anyone, though we have discussed Jung's explanations here, where Jung's definition of them as "thoughts of God" also included that they are principles. Independently, religious philosophers have equated God's thoughts to principles. Principles are defined as primary laws on which all other laws are based. Archetypes are also defined as empty psychic structures (principles) adaptable to an infinite number of externalizations by an infinite number of individuals. In other words, an archetype's form of externalization is dependant upon the life experience of the individual. This is why, contrary to mainstream logic, any one of them could appear to convey a different description to six billion people at once—according to Earth's last population count. An example of this is when we have encountered the same degree symbol several different times in different contexts. In those different situations, we say, "I don't remember that degree saying this at all." So even in our own lives, a degree symbol can convey an entirely different personal meaning in different times and places.

In terms of Zodiac degrees, a symbol (or "form") of the degree carries, via a visual image, an idea or principle—say a butterfly emerging from a cocoon. In this case, the principle is that of transformation. A caterpillar creates a cocoon around itself, into which it disappears for a period of time, at the end of which a moth or similar winged creature emerges. The cocoon implies a process of transformation, of which the variations are endless. The butterfly is the result of that process and implies a new quality of freedom in any life.

If that archetype is being activated in your life, the principle is transformation, and the concept "butterfly" is the form. The actual result in your life is the form your own process takes. This is an important philosophical concept if you are going to use the degree symbols, since every degree has its own symbol. Often a phase degree symbol does not appear to relate to your life until it unfolds in a life process. Suppose that at a New Moon there is a New Moon butterfly symbol, but at this moment your life is the pits. The butterfly suggests that you are in the process of unfolding into a different kind of person with a different kind of life, or a different attitude toward your life, with a freedom (wings) you do not at this moment have. From what you already know of the phases, you can expect some verification of this process by the Full Moon degree. It offers hope because it tells you that the flow of your life is moving toward transformation and is not stuck permanently where it is now. In fact this is what the degrees are all about. The principle, hidden but find-able, is part of 360 principles based on the endless cyclic flow of time, or chi, or energy that is always changing. Some of these principles are much more obvious than others. Many times the month's process has to take place before the end result is seen, as in the case of the butterfly. The original caterpillar could never have imagined he would have wings. Here is where the information about the three levels of life—physical, emotional, and mental-spiritual, will be helpful in terms of the house of your dial in which the degree falls. The actual digging for a personal interpretation of each symbol you find on the Moon path is critical to its value to you personally. What you perceive and actually do with these symbols determines the form they take in your life.

Here is a dramatic example of an archetypal symbol found in the Navajo tribal language. This language has no word in it for *still,* or *motionless,* because the Navajo belief system states that all of creation is continually moving, changing, etc. If you are sitting at rest in your living room, you are still moving infinitesimally so that in a few thousand years you might conceivably move to the opposite side of the room. This makes it possible for the Navajos to talk about things that can't be expressed in any other language in the world. As a result, the US Armed Services in WW 2 hired Navajos to transmit messages in their own language between field commanders and other officials. It was an unbreakable code. The principle of eternal movement is an archetype of immense implications, few of which have ever been pursued.

Historically, a number of writers have discerned through various means, both left and right brained, symbols for each degree of the zodiac. Some appear to be very different from those using the Marc Edmund Jones's Sabian Symbols, which are adapted in the books we have recommended. There is undoubtedly a basic archetype underlying the different images about which many authors have written. If you were to read the dozen or so books containing degree symbols, you might be able to see that basic underlying connection among all of them.

We have chosen for our personal use the Mark Edmund Jones Sabian degree symbols separately re-interpreted by Dane Rudhyar and Diana Roche. You can use either or both sets, or any other set that works for you, but we will be using the Rudhyar and Roche sets in this book. We have found them to be the most applicable for the Moon Path work. They are the most commonly used, and together the two sets provide a wide range of related meanings. In a large set of three volumes[2] Helene and Willem Koppejan did what we have not—they paired the Jones degrees together with those of Charubel—an old and seldom used set—presenting Charubel's symbols as the external degree meanings and Jones' set as the internal or more spiritual descriptions of a person's Sun sign or Rising sign.

2   *The Zodiac Handbook, vol 1,2,3,* by Helene and Willem Kopejan, Elements Books Ltd., 1991

In Appendix F, by permission of Aurora Publishing, we have included the abbreviated set of Marc Edmond Jones' original degree symbols, first published in Jones' *The Sabian Symbols in Astrology,* Subsequently the original abbreviated form was included in *The Astrology of Personality* by Dane Rudhyar. Later Dane Rudhyar revised the symbols for his *An Astrological Mandala.* Our original set is from Aurora Press's reprint of *The Astrology of Personality.* The later Rudhyar version, *An Astrological Mandala,* contains some differences from the original Jones version, and we have often resorted to that original version used here, for more insight into a symbol. The still later Roche degree book, *The Sabian Symbols,* retains the exact images of the original degree-titles, in their original handwriting; but it departs radically from the commentary, usually without destroying the original meaning, but managing to bring the symbolic meanings further down into everyday life. The Rudhyar interpretations and commentaries are full of ancient wisdom, and mystical, alchemical, visionary material, valuable to anyone with a philosophical or spiritual bent who wishes to delve more deeply into the archetypes.

The original symbols are included here partly because they *are* the original form, and partly in order to get readers started quickly using them, without having to immediately invest in new books. They make this book as accessible as possible to any reader who cannot afford or find the more extensive versions.

For the person who wants still deeper or different material, we suggest a recent book, based on a still different set of original degrees, titled *The Inside degrees Developing your Soul Biography Using the Chandra Symbols,* by Ellias Lonsdale.

How the Degree Symbols Stimulate Our Evolution of Consciousness

At this point we wish to offer an example of interpreting degree symbols; we can set the dial to Virgo on the first house, for a Virgo Sun female, and use the degree of 25 Aquarius as an example New Moon position. Please go to Appendix F, or a degree book, and find the degree of 25 Aquarius, which is read as "the 26th degree of Aquarius." With Virgo on the 1st house, we find Aquarius on the 6th house. The initial statement for this degree, in Rudhyar's degree symbols, is *A garage man testing a car's battery with a hydrometer.* The meaning of the image is *Skill in applying knowledge of natural laws to the solution of everyday problems resulting from life in our technological society.*

Aquarius rules scientific and technological activity, so we find our Virgo in a shop containing electronic equipment of some sort. With her sharp eye and mind for details she has probably gained some respect for her abilities to "fix" things that go wrong. Let's say that on the New Moon, something breaks down at work and she is asked to look at the equipment before the repair people are called in. With her natural Virgo common sense, she first runs the self-test program on the equipment, and the test stops in the middle. That gives her a clue so she looks inside, and pokes around, finding a tiny wristwatch screw impeding a tinier moving part.

If this is a New Moon degree, she might expect something new beginning in her (6th house) work situation related to the incident because it seems similar to the degree symbol description. Perhaps she gets a commendation in her file that leads to a pay raise. This is an example of the kind of situation one might experience at a New Moon that seems to key the activity for the coming month. Sometimes nothing actually happens, but you might read the degree symbol and find that in the next few days changes come to your work situation related to using natural laws in solving problems. The details of your situation at the time of the New Moon would provide details unique to you.

How Can I Trust the degree Symbols to Give Me Right Answers?

The primary reason we trust the symbols is that over the last six years of working together, we have never had a failed answer. We haven't always liked the answers, and some were downright alarming, but ultimately we had to admit that the experiences the degrees symbolized were right on the mark as to accuracy, and we learned valuable lessons as a result. Sometimes degrees contain instructions for action, while others contain the meaning of whatever we are experiencing at the moment. We have followed the actions suggested, or we have taken the explanations to heart, and often seen that a seemingly negative explanation has showed us the higher spiritual value of the experience. With all our many words about the Moon phases, we still do not always understand a cycle until after it is over.

We also fully accept that life is an endless series of energy waves, beginning at a low point, rising, cresting, and falling back to the beginning point. Every Moon cycle measures a wave by these eight phases. The I Ching measures waves by 64 Hexagrams, though not in the language of calendar time like the Moon's 29-1/2 days. Nevertheless, the two divination systems are measuring waves of Chi or life energy. With our present technology we can't compare the two sets of waves. The point is that probably no one can "trust" either divination system without (a) a belief system that includes divination, (b) the personal experience to prove the validity of the systems to themselves, or (c) the ability to feel the changing energies. We only invite our readers to try the grand experiment described in this book and see for themselves.

Some may find it harder than others to do this because many people now have not been taught to think symbolically as children. Without that ability they will often miss the point of what a degree symbol is offering. If the reader will follow the system we write about, we will attempt to help him/her re-establish that way of thinking in the process.

That said, Roche's book is much less symbolical than Rudhyar's, so that may be part of some readers' solution.

Why Do Bad Things Happen in Spite of Good Predictions?

There are many answers to this, depending on your belief system, experience, imagination and whether you are an optimist or a pessimist. Our answer comes out of the metaphysical foundations of both East and West where they both meet. The reader is free, of course, to work with whatever answers are appropriate to his/her path. We preface our answer with the general one that our Karma determines some things, and there is an answer from it. But you may not remember the past lives that might have the answer. However you *can* remember what has repeatedly brought you pleasure or pain in this life. These patterns are usually repeats of Karma developed either in this or in a previous lifetime that continue to do so in the present.

Karma is an example of the principle of cause and effect in action. What goes around comes around. This applies today, yesterday, tomorrow, and in past lives if you are open to the concept of reincarnation. However, what is important about Karma here is how we have been conducting our lives in the past of *this* life, which we know about. What we do every day is creating Karma.

Many people find that alarming, and may say, *Oh, my goodness, you mean I caused this?—don't tell me I'm responsible for this—why would I do a thing like this to myself?* What people don't notice at the daily level is scientifically measurable—every action causes a reaction. Sometimes such a confrontation with reality paves the way to a new level of understanding of responsibility for our lives. Once you tentatively accept responsibility for creating your own life, you will begin seeing new levels of power in your life—if you were powerful enough to create this life-impacting situation, you are powerful enough to change it, or perhaps to see it in an entirely different light. That new perception itself changes the situation. You will become aware that words have power, and actions impact others as well as yourself. Both things are contributing to our Karma as we speak.

In that brief time of turnaround in your awareness, your consciousness has already changed to a new level, and you will never be quite the same again. If you can accept this new perception as truth, perhaps you can move to the idea that our destiny or dharma provides us with the experiences that are important to our growth in consciousness. What people call Karmic experiences, with fear or dislike, may be about perceptions; the events happen because our perceptions are blocking more desirable experiences. The events are perhaps intended by the soul to raise our perceptions such that we attract better experiences.

Such experiences happen periodically to everyone in this life, sometimes many times, or perhaps for some the whole of a lifetime. We all know someone whose entire life appears to us to be a disaster. Some people deal with such a lifetime by becoming an addict, depressed, or out of control. Most of us undertake such transformative experiences at least unwillingly, calling them fate, which term we reserve for few experiences. For most of us, there will at least be many months when by reading ahead in the month you can imagine bad experiences and obsess unnecessarily about them, or the fulfillment of our wishes only to find the opposite.

The first necessary act in these cases is to turn beliefs in fate or bad luck, or similar negatives, toward something more positive. Science has recently proven conclusively that the nature of your thoughts determines critical hormones and brain chemicals that in turn control your state of mind and in turn your physical body. Books have been written about anticipating negatives, and one famous saying is that someone who worries about an outcome before it happens dies a thousand times instead of one. Others tell us that what we most fear is what will happen.

Our resort has been to ask, *what is the gift in this experience?* Another answer is to read the fine print before you freak out. Roche's detailed descriptions of some less desired degrees simply bring them down to daily realities. They are *an interruption, temporary loss or delay, upset of plans or turbulence in the smooth flow of things.* It also speaks to the principle of priorities, or first things first, and the need and *power of the universe to sustain itself over the demands of individuals that everything conform to their personal convenience.* Now and then all of us need to learn that our ego-desires and demands are less important than we think and *when their importance to us is too great, they mask the real person inside.* We are spending too much of our consciousness-time on materialities and too little on the inner realities—and missing who we really are in our uniqueness. Life itself keeps on trying to get this message across. The gift we find in our challenges is just this—a new level of our own selves. If this answer sounds too abstract, that is because the gift, like everything about these archetypal degrees, will be seen or understood differently by each person. If you already got the message, you have nothing to fear from these degrees. This is an unfolding process, in which you play a major role. The end of the process is not necessarily a fateful unstoppable event; and it doesn't happen till it happens; and you can't be sure what it is until it does. So the answer here is that if you follow the suggestions for action, and keep the higher truths of the degrees in mind, many times the situation, as you may have first read it into a degree, will change. You might not need the ego-stripping experience if you have been doing your self-work.

Gratitude is suggested by great spiritual leaders, and TV gurus such as Oprah, alike, to *be* the answer to avoiding depression, fear, anxiety, etc. and maintaining hopefulness. A person who is limited by a health issue or financial problem can begin by being thankful for what he/she can still do or have. Just as in winter whose cold and ice crystals and bare trees show us the beauty of the elements which also can cause hardships, we, too, have winters in which our elemental beingness emerges out of a hardship. (You should read Shakespeare's 73rd Sonnet and see his view of the matter!) Lynn Taggart might say that broadcasting gratitude attracts from the field more of what we are grateful for because like attracts like. Likewise broadcasting depression and anxiety invites more of the same.

It is our belief that every challenge is a step in our evolution. Each challenge contains choices and ultimately a gift. It is through these challenges that our unique self emerges, giving us qualities we see in those we admire most. Those people met up with huge challenges and became what you admire now. Would you be great? Then accept the gift and choose to be hopeful and grateful. Just remember that the person who chooses to open up the channels to divination will see things they do not not like, but they will also see things that provide hope. This becomes a personal responsibility which if honored grows one's consciousness.

11

The Four Transitional Phases
Points of Greatest Momentum and Critical Release

The four-fold cross, foundation of both the twelve-fold and the eight-fold divisions of the circle (or of a cycle of time) establishes the points of basic crisis in the relationships between the two polar factors being considered (Sun and Moon). But four more points, bisecting the four quarters, are necessary to mark the positions (or the moments) of greatest momentum and most critical release.
—Dane Rudhyar, *The Lunation Cycle*

Historical Background of the Eight Phases

Documented history sources first show the four Moon phases being divided into eight around 500 BCE. After that they are buried in history, both by astrologers and historians. However, we have found information, from little known Eastern sources, that indicates the eight phases were known in the New Stone Age around 6,000 BCE. These sources will be documented in a following book. This earlier date is entirely new information. It has been overlooked by later writers, most of whom relied only upon previous astrological historians for their conclusions.

As the four major modern religions arose, Astrology, and with it Moon phases, was rejected. The four phases, however, remain in practical use by farmers and fishermen and embedded in the major religions as days reserved for major liturgical calendar celebrations; but understanding of their deeper meaning has been lost to the general masses. They went underground, hidden in mythology and the esoteric sciences—Astrology, Tarot, I Ching, Kabbalah, Alchemy, playing cards—and yes, even Chess—which are full of metaphoric information about the phases.

The Amazing Eight Phases

In the very condensed, technical statement of the initial quotation, Dane Rudhyar tells us the difference between the four basic or action phases and the four transitional phases. Now let's see if we can understand what he has said. The four basic phases are found by making a cross in a circle, each segment encompassing 90^0 of the circle. When you bisect each phase you then have eight phases of 45^0 each. We have called the four by various names, and they represent struggle with the elements of manifestation. What these four phases do not show us is the dynamic nature of the movement through time represented by the cycle as a whole. The transitional phases, according to Rudhyar, show us the points in time where the main phase activity develops the most momentum, and where the release of that energy happens. The simple statement of this is: every transitional phase shows where the major phase energy increases, toward the end of the phase, and then releases the momentum into the next major phase. Better still, it shows the kind of movement by which one quarterly phase transitions to the next.

For Astrologers—the Zodiacal Background Noise of the 8 Phases

We like to see things, so to figure this out for ourselves we did some diagramming to clarify what Rudhyar was saying, and in the process made an interesting discovery. First, we diagrammed the transitional phases in two ways, as shown in Diagram III. We used a circle marked with 360 degrees and with the 12 signs marked every 30 degrees. We first divided the circle into four equal sections then bisected each quarter and

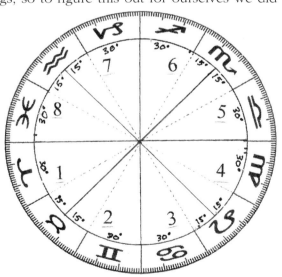

Diagram III. Eight Phases Correlated to the
Twelve Signs.

labeled the eight phases with their names. Please note that each of the eight phases uses up 45 degrees on the circle. This is where we found the first hint of our discovery about the phases. There appeared to be some kind of changing relationship between phases and signs.

Next we drew all the intermediate phase lines in dotted lines. When we looked at the phases, we saw, of course, that each phase encompasses 1-1/2 signs (30^0 + 15^0 = 45^0). We then noticed that each phase covers one whole sign plus one half of another sign. Later, we discovered that we could use this in interpreting the nature of the phases. This sequence of energies operates as a backdrop or background "sound" which is generally not obvious, but can be noticed if we pay attention.

Then we looked at phase one to see how the New Moon energy flows through the whole first phase. Like the sign Aries, it starts with an idea or an instinctual movement, reaching out toward an unknown place.

According to Rudhyar, the energy picks up momentum as time moves the Moon toward the next phase. As the Moon moves into the 15 deg. Taurus area of the New Phase, on its way to the Crescent, the energy intensifies, stabilizes, and the feeling of the idea emerges, but the actual form cannot be released until the Moon enters the Crescent phase, at which time the form energy is released and one becomes aware in a more concrete way (Taurus) of what has begun.

It is possible to analyze each of the eight phases in the same way, simply moving through the phases and signs as you find them on the outer wheel. The exercise may seem like overkill, but much of this information broadens and enriches meaning, and may even help you in a particularly obscure month. We will be referring to the "background noise" of this diagram throughout Part II.

A Path of Transformation

The number eight has come through other channels to mean material or spiritual power, transformation, the next step. In Numerology, the eight is an experienced number which has mastered the ability to manifest (doubled number four). Eight (four doubled) symbolizes infinity as in the horizontal eight—the *Lemniscate* of Tarot, and the *Möbius strip* of mathematics. In astrology, the 8th sign and 8th house are both about transformation.

The original four phases represent action and manifestation in the outer world. The four transitional phases contain possibilities of inner spiritual power, integration, completion, and the mystery of transformation—the last being a part of the very nature of the eighth phase. So we see that the Moon's 8-fold cycle is in fact a path of transformation. How does the Moon's cycle guide us to that transformation?

Each of the original quarterly phases—as shown D. 3—is characterized by one of the Cardinal signs[1], which occupies the beginning 30 degrees of the four major phases. From here on we will be referring to the main four phases as *quarterly* phases.

Each of the four transitional phases is characterized by a fixed or mutable sign and represents the transitional area to be traversed between two quarters. These transitional parts of each quarter represent a time in which possibilities of that quarter-phase are realized

These activities are all about consciousness, so we can say that all eight together represent the cycle of potential interaction between consciousness and outer action. As we go through section II on the individual phases, this will become more clear and personal. So we see the eight phases as carrying the concepts of power and the completion of a cycle of power. For one who fully undertakes the journey, the *lemniscate* is a symbol for the one who has accomplished that journey; and the mystery of infinity in the *Möbius* strip gives us a hint of the great goal of unity to come.

The Eight Phases in Brief

The transitional phases may be agonizing, or they may offer a breathing space, release from tension, a smoother flow if one is willing to take it, and they can bring true transformations to one's life. The key words for the four transitional phases are respectively:

(1) *forming*
(2) *refining*
(3) *distributing*
(4) *releasing*

They are bridges between the cardinal phases. The four transitional phases imply the importance of attitude adaptation,

---

1   Signs have three operational modes called Cardinal, Fixed, and Mutable. The Cardinal signs are Aries, Cancer, Libra and Capricorn: every fourth sign from Aries. These signs are known as initiating in nature, also with the qualities of action and manifestation in the external world.

patience, integrity, method, and sometimes an interlude of letting one door close before another opens; these are all characteristics of the fixed and mutable modalities. All of those characteristics are based in one's consciousness and are fully as important as those of the basic action orientation of the four cardinal phases.

Following are the four transitional phases (or sub-phases), described by key phrases, within the structure of the complete SoLunar cycle. As noted, each sub-phase occupies the second half of a Quarter-Moon's seven days. People who are continually running to "catch up"—to what?—collect the stress underlying many of our ills during the cycle. Taking time to recognize and honor the four transitional energies each month can bring a sense of order into personal chaos. It can allow one to release insistence upon impressing personal time schedules onto the universal order, knowing that all things unfold in their own due time. As one modern author said, "Don't push the river". Here are key words for the eight phases together, with the intermediates italicized:

1) New Seed-intent germinated
2) *Crescent* Forming—project taking shape
3) First Quarter External crisis between self and outer world
4) *Gibbous* Refining-perfecting the project, adapting to outer stresses
5) Full Enlightenment and fulfillment, or realization of meaning
6) *Disseminating* Assimilating-distributing the enlightenment
7) Third Quarter Internal crisis of values between past and future
8) *Balsamic* releasing-letting go of the past

The Eight Phases Together in More Detail

1) <u>New</u> Image of new seed-intent received deep inside. Work from here intuitively or instinctively. Understand with your heart, not your mind—internal unity unfolding.
2) <u>Crescent</u> First conscious awareness of FORM, which begins growing rapidly, while one is letting go of issues or ideas left over from the previous cycle
3) <u>First Quarter </u>Form is established and shape is rapidly defined. Personal-self is asked to build according to his/her own individuality, struggling against outer social/parental patterns. Ego is torn between learned patterns of the past and inner truth or inspiration leading to the future.

4) <u>Gibbous</u> Perfection and completion of seed-intent needs your spiritual essence to shine through it while adapting the work's final shape to the outer, social world.

5) <u>Full</u> light on the face of the moon shows the potential for full consciousness of one's place in the group, society, or the universe, in terms of the current completion of individual intent. With alignment of two opposite areas of life, you can understand the meaning of the New Moon's goal and its contribution to the whole. Possibilities are wholeness vs. separation from the whole, or integration into the whole. Disintegration comes with a negative realization.

6) <u>Disseminating</u> Share the personal meaning realized at full moon. Sharing brings growth as the teacher learns from his/her students. The individual's social and personal values expand and old limiting boundaries are crossed. Emotional bonding through humor, and re-experiencing trust

7) <u>Last Quarter</u> Press into action the new values gained during the Disseminating Phase, which will support the next new phase, while you are being torn between living the old way or living the new. Assess your achievement, and turn toward the new cycle to come.

8) <u>Balsamic</u> Let go of the closing cycle and realign yourself with whatever the New Moon brings. Consider your needs for the future and allow past hurts—physical or emotional— to be healed.

The Eight-Phase SoLunar Path and its Contemporary Value

Why is this basic (4/8) SoLunar cycle so very important to us now? As a culture we are becoming more and more secular, and most of us tend to view the Lunar cycles only as a natural phenomenon. Frankly, then, who cares? We care, we who are writing this, and we hope you come to care as well. Essentially we care because we have discovered that the cycle is about conscious intentional living, and consciousness is the biggest subject on the current philosophical and scientific horizons. Watching the Moon and Sun, our original ancestors began their long journey toward self- and other-consciousness by aligning their lives with the cycles. This is our connection with them through time—a meaningful journey we could share. Mistakenly, people now disdain the Moon's power of connection with our consciousness. Generations ago it was completely internalized, suppressed, and therefore has become invisible to us. Externally it appears to be either the icon of a long dead and buried primitive point of view, or one more object in space without meaning other than scientific or romantic.

What we want to share with our readers is the experience (above and beyond knowledge) that as long as the Sun and Moon together give timing to the oceans, the shell fish, our own lymph, blood, and hormonal systems, and our very behaviors, the SoLunar cycles are relevant to our daily lives and consciousness, our bonding to the Earth, and the alignment of our Higher Self with our everyday self. The mystery is still palpable at the dark of the Moon and the "a-has!" will still ring out at the full Moon. If you watch for the symbols of purpose and meaning, expressed by the signs and Phases, your life may change from a prison of dailiness to an adventure. Pay attention to what is happening within at New and Full Moon, and you will see for yourself.

In the shamanic eras, the Moon cycles were the basis for ritual and ceremony, which brought order into a chaotic world. Is the current one any less chaotic? In today's world, this cycle continues to offer natural lessons leading to balance of head and heart, personality and soul—something desperately needed in our materialistic, stressful, logical, brain-oriented society. We can't stress enough the value of using these very real physical/spiritual cyclic energies to help us move through 3-D time with knowledge of conscious purpose and meaning. We suggest that a few moments at the beginning of each phase would be well spent devoted to looking at our current cycle, noticing the phase energy, and making intent to use the energy as effectively as possible. The power of intent is well known in our society at this point—when it is in lockstep with the current energies it is formidable!

Also, if you look closely, you will find the four and the eight still present in symbolic forms in all the major religions at this time. One tantalizing example, reminiscent of the ancient Pagan New Moon ritual is in the Jewish Kabbalistic tradition where number eight means "the next step"—equivalent to the first day of a new week. In the Temple at Jerusalem (into which several thousand years of symbolism were built) there were eight steps to reach the Holy of Holies, which was entered only once a year, at the beginning of the New Year. The first seven steps were available to the congregation. Only the priest took the eighth step because only he was ritually prepared to enter the inner sanctum. What was in that inner sanctum that was potentially so dangerous (depending on one's point of view)?

In early oral tradition times, the inner sanctum of the Temple contained the Ark of the Covenant, said to be in a box covered with gold leaf[2]. Inside were the carved stones of the Ten Commandments and Aaron's sprouted staff. On the lid of the box were two cherubim facing each other, and the space between held the power of God. It was this space between the cherubim that was said to destroy anyone who came near or touched the Ark. Is it possible that this space was an interstice between dimensions—a kind of creative tension between the cherubim similar to the electrical potential between the plug and receptacle before it is plugged in? And could it be compared to the polarity of the Sun and Moon and the interstice of their alignments, both at New and Full Moon? Whatever the unknown answer, it does remind us that power is destructive and can only be safely handled by one who has prepared him/herself to use it.

Only the Priest could enter with safety, and only after days and nights of purification. Even then, he never knew for sure that he would survive the experience. In that darkness of unknowing, he entered on a special day once a year, and presented the prayers of the Israelites to God. I leave you with the hypothesis that this ritual was based on a mythic memory of a much earlier Pagan Balsamic Moon ritual from long before Judaism became a religion. In that ritual, at the end of the Balsamic, the Moon as goddess is said to have carried the needs of the people to the Sun god to be answered by the Sun within the seed of the new cycle.

*   *   *   *   *   *   *

The Special Importance of the New and Full Moons

Each New Moon brings us all a new, special project for the month. If you want to know where it will take you, look to the Full Moon. If you want to know how to get there, study the First Quarter Moon. And if you want to know the value of the experience, ask the Third Quarter Moon. The other four phases will give you clues and

---

2   There are other theories, including a contemporary one proposed by Tudor Parfitt in his archeological book, *The Lost Ark of the Covenant: Solving the 2,500 Year Old Mystery of the Fabled Biblical Ark.*

added instructions for accomplishing your personal project for the month, but we must always keep the New Moon's message firmly in mind, because it carries the overall purpose of the full cycle. This includes the continuing importance of the house and sign of the New Moon, even though the other phases will be happening in other Houses and signs. The Moon's house and sign will change through the month, and the Sun only strays from the New Moon sign if it begins in the last 14 degrees of that sign. The Sun's position is always where a message from spirit resides. The Moon's positions throughout the month are always where the action is, based on the original intention.

In Eastern philosophy and most divinatory systems, the nature of every beginning foreshadows the outcome of that beginning. In divinatory (I Ching, Tarot, and Astrology etc.) terms, the moment a question is asked, the answer is believed to exist in that moment; whenever anyone begins a project or an activity, the degree (astrology), hexagram (I Ching), or Taro (card) belonging to that point in time is descriptive of the nature, duration, and outcome of the new activity. It is a powerful force in a particular direction, guiding the full period of time until the activity is complete, and ultimately fulfilled. For this reason, the New Moon is the most important of all eight phases, and you will be following its message through all the phases to the end of a cycle. However, the Full Moon is the most important in terms of consciousness and of one's place in the community, local or cosmic.

For instance, the degree symbol of your birth Sun or Rising sign characterizes you throughout your life, though at many different levels. A New Moon project you begin may actually be a 6-month project, which will go through five more New Moons or that many stages or new beginnings of completion, all characterized by their own degree symbol. However, the overall characterization for the total project will always be in the symbol for the first New Moon. Meanwhile every Moon Cycle is complete in itself with some level of a longer activity expressing the law of cyclicity embodied in the Moon's cycle.

The New and Full Moon together have a profound effect upon Individuals and the Collective. Within the cycle the two Moons mark the fundamental two-fold or Yang-Yin structure. Those phases are generally acknowledged or recognized by all people. You cannot fail to notice the darkness of the night sky at New Moon, or the astonishing beauty of a Full Moon. These two phases representing the human journey from individual to relationship speak to even the most technical, intellectual, or materialistic of individuals, often drawing them into the mystical language of the Moon. The effects on social behavior are quite surprising; they lead one to wonder why we never get the point that if something about the Full Moon in particular affects people so strongly why is science not investigating these aspects of Lunation cycles? The answer we always get is "it's a political matter."

These results were discussed recently with a friend, evoking a related response "You said that men have a harder time emotionally at New Moon because their inner nature is not necessarily resonant with their outer, while women's inner and outer natures are the same and therefore resonant. At Full Moon do women have a harder time intellectually than men?"

I couldn't answer that. So we shared some of our experiences. He told me that his male friends found Full Moon energizing. He used to run a restaurant with bar and told me that it is well known in the industry that at New Moon men came in, were quiet, drank some beer or wine, often returned their plates untouched, and frequently complained about the food. At Full Moon, he said, men came in wanting to drink a lot—mostly hard liquor—laugh, socialize, eat a lot and seemingly could care less what the food was like.

I had worked on a mental health team in a hospital detox ward for a year, and saw that it was mostly men who came in through the ER on Full Moon, with injuries caused by excessive drinking, or major emotional reactions that somehow always reached a crisis just at Full Moon. Something tells me that men or women who are out of touch with their feeling side have problems at either lunation. My women friends often comment that it must be a Full Moon because life seems so crazy. Sometimes they are on a crying jag, or else suspiciously too high, avoiding their inner experience, or finally getting some insight into what has been going on. My own male friends, who tend not to frequent bars and restaurants, may want to talk at Full Moon in terms of world affairs or their partners (not themselves!) and perhaps not appear to be outwardly different than at other times. So perhaps one could more accurately say that people tend to act out more or cover their feelings at Full Moon, and to be quieter at New Moon. But there are often hidden emotions behind these two behaviors. Men who are in touch with their inner lives may be more consciously using the energies, somewhat like many women. What psychology might say is that if you act out thoughtlessly at Full Moon, you may be projecting unrecognized emotional problems. If you are depressed or "flat" at New Moon, there is an emptiness that needs filling.

The Old Woman is intimately within each of us, as the mother archetype, and waiting to help us investigate the Moon Phases and find out for ourselves just how they affect us and our friends. Our next short journey is into the mysteries of transformation—what we believe to be the specific purpose of the Moon Path.

The foregoing paragraphs contain a difficult concept. Each month, even if it turns out to feature only part of a larger project, is always a complete stand-alone cycle. You may not even realize it is part of something bigger until later when it is far behind you. There is one possible problem for all readers, with Moon cycles in general. It is that, while there is a promise in every New Moon and thus every beginning, there is a disclaimer in every promise. You only get the fullness of the promise if you are following the spiritual, ethical, or moral guidance that goes with it.

The importance of every New Moon is that they are all potentially significant beginnings, but like seeds they need to be nurtured. Most Lunar months will not be notable for us. However, whenever a New Moon has a close contact with something in our individual horoscopes, the significance of that beginning will raise the impact of the events of that Lunar month for those individuals. Non-astrologers reading this will not know if a lunation contacts something in their charts or not. They, like us, may find it is enlightening and exciting to watch the news when we are due for a New Moon. Events that have impact on large numbers of people will often describe the New Moon. For astrologers, these impactful events are probably contacting something in the US chart.

In either case, it is well to pay attention to New Moons because you never know when a small event may initiate a large one.

How to Find the Transitional Phases in the Sky

The transitional or intermediate four phases are difficult to distinguish in the sky. Also, you will not find them listed in your materials or in an ephemeris. Their monthly positions are available only through astrology software, and some astronomy websites; therefore we are describing them as carefully as we can. Astronomy sites do have pictures of all phases, if you search under that term, and sometimes the degrees. When our site is up and running, we will have the transitional degrees posted once a month.

The Crescent or second phase is thicker than the "first light" or initial "fingernail" Moon but unquestionably not the Half-Moon of the First Quarter, phase. It occurs about 3-1/2 days after the new moon or exactly halfway between New and 1ˢᵗ Quarter. Since the Moon's speed varies from day to day and waxing to waning phases, the number of hours per intermediate phase constantly varies, so the day and degree of each will have to be astronomically derived for this and all transitional phases.

The Gibbous Moon or fourth phase, between First Quarter and Full Moon, occurs about 3-1/2 days after the First Quarter Moon. It is neither half-moon nor full moon. Its odd, unsymmetrical appearance is convex on one half, rather than round, as though someone had just added a bit to the half moon. *Gibbous* is an old English word meaning humpbacked and at this time Moon is carrying an extra load.

The Disseminating Moon or sixth phase, between Full Moon and Last Quarter, is visually identical to the Gibbous except that the light now comes from the left side. It occurs about 3-1/2 days after full moon. Gibbous and Disseminating are sometimes called "Waxing Gibbous and Waning Gibbous."

The Balsamic Moon or eighth phase is visually identical to the Crescent phase except that here, too, the Moon's light is on the opposite side, the left side. Balsamic occurs about 3-1/2 days from the Last Quarter. While the Crescent was just beginning to take form, the Balsamic is form just beginning to dissolve—or the focus on materiality fading. Crescent and Balsamic Moons are sometimes called "Waxing Crescent and Waning Crescent."

At this point, you have what you need to interpret the eight phases as seen visually in the sky, and apply these interpretations to your own life. The only thing that is missing is the degree symbol, for the transitional phases, for which you need the mathematical degrees. In the next section you will learn how to apply the foregoing information to your personal dial, and find the area of life the phase is affecting, and its sign—all of which will which open the door to a world of new ways to understand yourself, your purpose, your relationship to the universe. Do you want to actually step through the Eight Windows in Time?

This completes the first section of the book. You are now ready to look in-depth at the eight phases and expand your Moon phase readings exponentially. See Table 9 showing just how the energies flow between Sun and Moon during each phase. Here is an example of how to use the table. Imagine it is any first quarter Moon.

PHASE	SUN's POSITION	MOON'S POSITION
FIRST QUARTER Challenge	Spiritual or non-egoistic individual desire for the project challenges the outer world with something new, described by house and degree	You may struggle with conflict between Spirit's desire and external physical, material, or social/parental desires. Ideally, you can integrate both creatively. Moon's symbol suggests how,. described by house and degree of Moon's position

Table 8. First Quarter Phase Energy Flow

Using the Phase Energy Flow Table for a 1st Quarter Phase

Sun 16 Gemini-4th house— spirit's message that communication from the core self is important concerning home or family. (Try both the degree symbol and the house-sign meaning.)

Degree— Meaning: mental metamorphosis is needed in this situation to channel physical vitality into concepts through which knowledge can be transferred. (Taken from Roche's degrees.)

Moon 16 Virgo-7th house—Moon's message is about fixing, improving, or refining relationships.

Degree—Degree meaning: an explosion of long-repressed subconscious contents.

One way to interpret this phase is to say that this situation presents you with the instruction to find a new way to deal with your explosive family or home relationships. Struggle will be with others' (and maybe your own) reluctance to change old patterns. You can take the phase energy description here quite literally; you can also play freely with degree and sign interpretations. Knowing that the Sun's message of purpose is directed at the Moon's actions helps to phrase the Sun's message into a recognizeable form.

Bookmark the complete Table 10 below for use in all the phases in Part II of this book.

PHASE	SUN'S MESSAGE, Spirit's Intent— described by houses, signs and degrees	MOON'S RESPONSE, Soul's Task—manifesting Sun's Intent described by houses, signs and degrees
NEW	Plants New Seed-Intent—image, idea, described in the house, sign and degree of the New Moon.	Receive and begin internal process of intentionally gestating the form of the new project, even if it still lies in the unconscious.
CRESCENT	Individual or spiritual nature behind the intent's external form emerge in houses and sign, described by degree.-	New seed's form emerges into consciousness or outer world, according to your Moon's houses and sign, and described by its degree symbol. Meanwhile you must release matters of the past which emerge like weeds, clinging past their time and holding you back.
FIRST QUARTER	Spiritual or pure individual desire for the project challenges the outer world with something new, described by degree	You may struggle with conflict between Spirit's desire and external physical, material, or social/parental desires. Ideally, you can integrate both creatively. Moon's symbol suggests how.
GIBBOUS	Spirit desires the person to complete the project in order to offer it to the outer world in the next phase, described by degree, so spirit can shine through.	Your task is to polish, complete and perfect the project so that it will reflect its inner spirit growing within. Figure out how your Moon degree symbol can let spirit shine through your work.
FULL	Spirit offers insight into broader meanings of the Moon's sign and degree, as it relates to the Sun's sign. It may describe the "second seed"—that which you have to offer to others.	You must make a decision between two opposites—one that integrates both sun and moon house activities in some way. The insight of the Sun/spirit is the integrating factor and the Moon describes how to use it.

DISSEMIN-ATING	Spirit describes to soul a greater meaning behind your insight that wants to be shared.	You share the meaning with others while digesting and integrating the different levels. Listen to others for insights that broaden your own.
LAST QUARTER	Spirit challenges you to leave the past behind, now, and turn toward the future, carrying with you the fruits of the month's experiences.	You struggle between past and future. Do you dare stand up and speak to your inner changes? Can you turn away from old ideas and begin to live out the new ones you have received?
BALSAMIC	Spirit offers you the opportunity to turn completely away from the past and offer yourself to the future? Can you take that step?	Soul wants you to let the past die and be reborn. Call down the Moon, "Call down the creative spirit and summon forth the future". Be willing to risk. Be willing to be healed.

Table 9. the Energy Flow Between Sun and Moon through all the Phases

12
Archetype of Transformation
The SoLunar Cycle as the Living Archetype of Unfolding Human Consciousness

Individuality: that which distinguishes the individual from all other individuals; the unique qualities of the individual.
Individualization The process of developing individuality—the one thing which makes you stand out among all others..
Individuation: Self-realization, the integration of all one's traits in the process of becoming a whole individual.
Collectivization: Individual integration into the larger whole.
—Jungian Concepts Adapted from *The Astrology of Personality*[1] by Dane Rudhyar

Evolving Consciousness

The four phases of the Moon's monthly cycle to the Sun are the bite-sized models for this three-layered eonic growth in consciousness, both in terms of an individual month or life, and in terms of cycles of history. We believe that the pattern of Moon Cycles is the primary expression of the archetype of evolving consciousness. The requirement of an archetype is that it be universal in nature, but capable of infinite forms of expression. We have seen how every individual receives the same message every month, yet the message expressed through every individual is completely different than all others. That archetype is expressed throughout humanity! This may be the same as Rudhyar's 4th archetype of "the urge to transform oneself" because no evolution, personally or humanly speaking, can happen without transformation. That is because many human activities are negative expressions of those archetypes.

Here is the big key, at the center of this book's message, that ultimately underlay our desire to write this book and work on our

---

1   *The Astrology of Personality*, by Dane Rudhyar. Doubleday paperback Edition: 1970, Berkeley, CA.

own lives through the Moon phases. It is the overall message of the Moon Path which is how the phases of the Moon's cycle can actually be the transformational path to human consciousness evolution.

Each month an archetype is being worked out around the planet through the New Moon's message. The more people who work on the positive meaning of the message, the more they increase their consciousness through that process, and the more planetary consciousness increases.

Archetypes are like ideas or patterns or fundamental principles upon which our world is structured. They have no reality in our world until someone acts them out in either a negative or positive manner. The Sun and Moon, themselves, act out—or show us through their regular 8-fold moving relationship—a principle that seems to underlie many lesser patterns. Mythically, that visual, universal principle first becomes real as the primary expression of the archetype of Yang and Yin—Male and Female—and their relationship, the principle behind all life on earth—the male-female principle of reproduction. They also have been represented as a sky-god or father-creator god and the great Mother. As the latter, countless centuries of interpretation of their cycles provide the kind of teaching or guidance one might expect from parents.

We have seen earlier how influential these cycles were in early man's spiritual and intellectual development. We can fantasize that these cycles were the first and most important instruction placed in the sky by the Divine. They are still there, and we know that new expressions of the original archetypes are continually unfolding or changing, and possibly new archetypes are emerging. The Moon is still there, is not outdated, and isn't going anywhere soon, unless it suffers a comet attack. The rhythmic energies of Moon and Sun together are still reaching us, usually outside of our conscious awareness, but as we have said, evolution moves more quickly when we do it consciously. However, it is in and from the unconscious that transformation comes. As science has already discovered, integrating both conscious and unconscious, and left and right brains, improve human functioning immensely.

As we noted in chapter 2 the Personal Unconscious contains facts, details, and experiences that can be made conscious fairly easily. However the PU also contains a metaphorical psychological garbage can where we can, and do, hide and deny all the facts, emotions, and experiences that are just too fearful or painful to accept. The ugliest experiences and emotions are hidden there, and each one is draining away our creativity and power. Transformation, itself, is a totally unconscious process, triggered by something in the Collective Unconscious. In Chapter 4, we described the alchemical process of transformation. Now we need to see where the first hints of need for it are seen, and the steps in initiating it for ourselves.

So what is our first step in transformation and hence increasing consciousness?   We have said several times elsewhere that intentionality is essential to most change. It also comes as a bit of cosmic humor that the most obvious signs we have that change is needed come directly from that dreaded garbage can into our conscious lives!   Just how hidden is it?   Well, like all garbage (whether angelic or demonic) in the Unconscious, it speaks to us in the symbolic language of emotion, knowing we consciously don't want to mess up our orderly minds with emotion. What gets our attention most?

The 3-D world around us will consistently give us clues. Watch for them when you are angry way out of proportion when a car cuts in front of you, when you wake up from a dream frightened or grief-stricken and you don't know why. Anything that triggers a deep, powerful emotion that doesn't reflect the facts in current time is a good clue that you have reached deeply into your personal unconscious and the opportunity for transformation is available. How can you encourage this process?   Breathe deeply and stay in the emotion (but not if you are on the freeway!). Stay with the feeling. Don't label it, don't analyze it, and don't judge it. This may be one of the hardest things you have ever done, but it almost always brings its own reward. Following the Moon phases at this point is like having a pattern or map of the situation. Working with the Moon Phases, being conscious and willing to "transform" activates the left brain and allows some conscious participation in releasing a piece of our repressed Divine or Demonic. Note here that both terms strangely disappear once they become conscious.   Transformation is hard work, so be patient. Remember we are all works in progress.

Evolution at every stage requires transformation; the Moon energies time and enhance the changes of transformation, especially when we can know the phases have messages for us. They help us recognize and understand this all-encompassing process in our personal lives. They also show us how we can intentionally direct our lives into pathways that will take us through the crossings of transformation to a different world that has not yet been created.

We are attempting to do the impossible, but here are some of the related ideas as a beginning. They are sufficient to start one on the path of understanding how the transformational life works, and to offer information on how to write one's own life story without artificial limits. In other words, yes we do have free will when we are conscious. Many of us just go along allowing life to do whatever it wants to us—reacting instead of living it intentionally—and making excuses like *this was fated; I couldn't help it; they made me do it; it wasn't important anyway.* We think some things in our lives indeed are out of our control, or "fated," or destined. But even those things come packaged with multiple options about how we might deal with them. Even the fated things can be handled in various ways. A friend remarked some years ago after a nasty divorce that "It must have been fate, but it was the best thing that ever happened to me. I grew so much through that experience." Having known her both before and after, it was clear to me that she had experienced a transformation.

Another friend went through a similar experience and came out of it a rather bitter person who vowed never to get hooked into a relationship again. It appeared to me that this woman had not had a transformation. In both cases there were options and choices involved that determined the outcomes. So what brings about a transformation? In the first place, it often comes about for people who face life with the expectancy of learning something from all their experiences. Whether we like it or not, it seems that the hard experiences are most likely to bring transformation. We do learn from them. But whether we become bitter or compassionate is also a choice, so looking for the gift in all things is an attitude worth cultivating in the interests of our personal growth.

As we said, transformation itself arises out of deeply hidden feelings that one eventually allows oneself to feel all the way from the conscious level down to the original place in ourselves where we hid them. Transformation is a matter of emotional response to life, instead of reaction, to things in the past that one never resolved. Logical thinking is not necessarily involved in the transformation process itself; but it has a lot to do with intention and one's current level of consciousness. One should be aware that all experience happens step by step and one rarely goes from master of the pencil and wastebasket to master of the computer in one step.

First, we may have an experience that makes us realize that something in our past from which we stuffed the feelings is holding us back. It is limiting us now in our current life, still demanding its due of feeling and emotion. If we couldn't deal with it then, can we do it now? Every month contains information in the phases that trigger such things from our past. They may be, or only seem to be, small matters such as your father is still defining you by having taught you that you are only good when you do things according to the rules; or you taught yourself as a young girl that "My bread always turns out ugly and heavy, just like my mother's bread," Perhaps, if someone suggests some baking hints, you shrug it off with, "well, that's just me. I'm not good at making bread."

Congratulations; you have just received an opportunity this month to release both a piece of poor self image, and a negative emotion around some past memories with your mother, perhaps even a whole cluster of negatives. That's the first step in transformation. Whether we resolve the past by taking the best option for the present, or we do a little therapy on the past when the issue comes up, the answer is always in the phases for us to find.

If this happens around a New or Crescent Moon, it tells you this is the theme for the month. If it happens later, it will be involved with the month's theme, but not the primary issue. The process will be the same, but will not follow the four steps of this Moon cycle. It will follow the natural eight steps in its own time. The following eight phase descriptions show how one person might deal with a transformation theme for the whole month.

The Moon's Eight Steps to Transformation

New Moon. (*A new seed-intent germinates.*) Most New Moons point us toward a new experience that brings some realization at Full Moon, usually small but sometimes life-changing. If this month brings you a recurrent experience that you wish would quit repeating, you can be sure transformation is an open possibility this month. It depends on your readiness to tackle the issue behind this recurrent theme. **The bread lady from three paragraphs above volunteers to work at a bazaar two weeks from now, the job to be specified in a few days**.

Crescent Moon. (*The seed-intent begins to take form.*) Perhaps we must wait for the Crescent Moon, to see that the past is haunting us, because it is distracting us from something we would prefer to do. **Maybe you are the bread person described above. At the Crescent**

Moon you are asked for 2 loaves of bread for the baked-goods table. Once again, you have to face your inadequacy in what you realize are your cooking skills in general. "I can burn water!" You think you will decline, but you can't because these are your friends and you can't let them down. They really need your contribution. You have never thought of asking for help or of getting a book on the subject because the whole process is so distasteful for an unknown reason. You put off doing anything meanwhile, unable to get thoughts of your mother's bread out of your mind. Then your child makes it worse by praising your neighbor's fresh hot bread and butter he just received for a snack.

First Quarter Moon. (*Outer Crisis choice between past and future attitudes.*) You find yourself needing to choose HOW it is you should handle the month's theme. Should you do it the way your social or parental patterns advise, or should you do it the way it will express yourself the best? **The bread lady is in a crisis. Should she decline, or should she get help from her neighbor?** "Declining is letting people down; but asking for help, or displaying my awful baking skills are both too scary—they are embarrassing". Finally she chose the help (which turned out not to be embarrassing) and learned how to make wonderful bread from her neighbor. From her willing neighbor, she discovered the creativity of kneading, and enjoying the smell of the rising dough, then later the look on her child's face as he said, "This just like Mrs. B__'s"!

Gibbous Moon. (*Perfecting your project, making it your own, and the critical point of change for the month.*) If we chose the new way and took the courage to acknowledge the past, breaking through its limiting boundaries, we may have an opportunity here to let a new piece of ourselves shine through. We would have transformed our outer personality in some way, at a conscious level. Since *Gibbous* means "humpbacked" it implies that a burden is on our backs and we are acting in a new way intentionally, that is different from our familiar personality. **For the bread lady, all of the above was true and the burden of the upcoming bake sale contribution was gone. She had a tentative sense of expectation in a (for her) new situation. She discovered a piece of herself she had never had.**

Full Moon. (*Extra effort and hard creative work produce enlightenment or an insight.*) We have worked hard at the Gibbous, and asked a lot of questions. Now, the Full Moon enlightenment (the answer or fulfillment) occurs. From our own depths comes the answer, triggered by an outer or inner experience. **The bread** lady proudly placed her two loaves on the bazaar table and had the pleasure of hearing the first customer exclaim, "Oh, what delicious looking bread. I'll take both." Unused to such praise, our bread lady blushed with embarrassment, wondering afterward why she did that. Then she realized that she had earned it, but had not known how to handle her new feelings. Also that she wondered if her mother would have praised her—probably not and perhaps an issue for next month.

Disseminating Moon. (*Sharing our experience internalizes or integrates it.*) Attempting to integrate this new self-knowledge, we talk to others about it, listening to their comments and their own experiences, some of which have a strange resonance to our own. The more we talk about our experience the more we understand it. **Our bread lady could hardly wait to share her day with Mrs. B___. Other opportunities came up as the bazaar's success was discussed among the workers afterward.As she shared, she became aware of how her feelings about herself and her mother changed in disconcerting ways. She felt more successful, personally, and free of a belief that dominated her life more than she had realized. On the other hand, she experienced a confusing mix of anger, resentment, guilt, and loss concerning her mother.**

Last Quarter Moon. (*Commit to using the new values. Re-orient to the coming cycle.*) With new knowledge come new options, new values, less limitation, and ultimately the responsibility of using these new freedoms. For some this is frightening, as it might be for a wheelchair-bound person who had been healed and now must take on new responsibilities for himself. Perhaps we still have something left from the past issues of this month—either a fear or a last vestige of the old limitation. Let go of this, if you can. If not, it may hang over into the next phase. **Our bread lady is on the verge of a larger transformation than we thought. She may need another New Moon or the healing Balsamic phase to deal with her feelings about her mother. At this point she needs to go with her new insight because she has become more involved with the bazaar group, now that she is not so limited by her low self-esteem.** The Balsamic phase offers healing if one is ready. In fact, it is there where we are most likely to experience transformation, which is healing at any level.

Balsamic Moon: *This is a time for deep thought, surrender to what is, assessment of what we really need, and acceptance of whatever is coming.* However, just at the very beginning, there may be feelings of rebellion, commitment to a new direction, or realization that one's new steps are shaky as yet. Choices are few here. Either let go into the darkness and welcome the new unknown, or hide our feelings and refuse to think about the old business. We are then in the same spot we were in at the previous New Moon. What should our bread lady do? What would you do? The answers are right here.

The Eight Phases and Evolution

By now, it will be clear to the reader how important it can be to pay attention to the messages of the Moon Phases and make an effort, small or large, to be more creative, more transparent, and have greater self-honesty and integrity. Regardless of how few waves a New Moon's project idea may stir up, there is always an opportunity to grow, and that means transformation. Even if, like the bread lady, you don't know about the phases, or are not thinking about them, approaching the universe with these intentional qualities will make you more susceptible to the nudging of your soul and inner self. Having the dates and meanings of the phases is like having a companion beside you in whatever you are doing. With the additional, detailed and specific message resources coming up in Chapters 8-12, you will also have inspirational and informative suggestions, appropriate to the moment.

It is really important here to remember that even though such suggestions will come to you out of books by people you never met, or written in a previous century, you are not in danger of doing everything "by the book" or by someone else's choice. The reason such degree information can work for you at this time and place is because there is a resonance between every calendar date and every particular phase falling upon that date.

Another very important nudge from spirit will come to many readers from their religious and spirituality practices, nature, music, shamanism, or any other connections to the divine. We have not focused in those directions because this book is not specifically about them. It is about the timing behind anyone's source of inspiration of which there are many more than those mentioned. Being open to being in the right place at the right time is not a religion, nor is the Moon necessarily a source of inspiration although some groups gain much inspiration from opening themselves ritually to Moon energies. We, however, do find that the physics and mathematical aspects of the Moon cycle alone are sufficiently awesome to inspire us as they demonstrate the existence of an awesome creator. Discovery of many little-known facts about the solar system have opened up vast and unimaginable mental and spiritual territories that will keep us inspired for years.

The degree symbols belong to those territories. The symbols were originally received at random by a psychic, but years later a mathematical internal structure of great complexity was discovered within it by Dane Rudhyar, at the request of Marc Edmund Jones. After exploring the implications of this structure, including the archetypal information in each of the degrees, it appears that a human brain could not encompass the system let alone construct it.

The Three Stages of Evolution of Consciousness

In this section, on the three levels of evolution, you may be able to discern what level of evolution you are working on, or what levels are being acted out on the national and international stage. When the latter looks discouraging, just remember that one person increasing his/her consciousness increases the total amount out there. Life will be better with increased evolution or expansion of human consciousness, and it takes everyone to bring that about. Let's take a look at what that might be like.

The three words, *individualization, individuation, and collectivization,* are invoked by many writers on the evolution of consciousness and by most Jungian-oriented thinkers. Observable in humanity as a whole, and in individuals, they are at the core of the process the *Old Woman* is undertaking to teach us.

In very simple terms, the unfoldment of consciousness from birth to death in any individual follows the same three-fold pattern that humanity as a whole appears to have followed over thousands, perhaps millions, of years, according to Jungian thought and that of many historians. There are those who see exceptions, and psychology systems which disagree or use different terminology. However, these words offer a generally acceptable base on which to discuss the values and growth of personal and social consciousness.

Dane Rudhyar, a philosopher as well as world-known Astrologer, and the first astrologer to consider man in a modern psycho-spiritual light against the background of history, defines the difference between "primitive humans" and "modern humans". He describes primitive peoples as *selves connected to the universe by means of identification with it and immersion within it.* Their heritage was myth and shamanic magic. At the same time, they lacked a certain conscious awareness of themselves as a separate entity, which is the keynote of individuality. The earlier human's lack had nothing to do with intelligence, but rather the nature of their intelligence and their deep connection with nature and the universe. Their lives were communal, consensus or leader-oriented, and by necessity lived primarily for the survival of the group. It was counter-survival to single oneself out in unilateral action, and apparently rewarded with heavy, often seemingly cruel punishment.

Contemporary individualistic man is immersed in, and identifies with, himself. His heritage is objective awareness, derived from generations of scientific exploration. Conversely, he lacks connection to the objectified universe other than through the narrow lenses of culture, religion, science, etc. Only personal priorities and fears prevent many people from diverging completely from the highly complex legal boundaries required in an individualistic society. An individualist often considers that what he/she wants has nothing to do with what the rest of the world is doing right now. There is egoistic pride in being an individualist as there was non-egoistic pride in being a respected contributing tribe member in early times. Either frame of mind does indeed have something to do with what the rest of the world is doing right now. This issue will be dealt later with in more detail.

Our task as humans is to integrate the two ways of understanding the meaning of life, through new ways of being. We come into this life with both pasts behind us in our genes, our past lives, family rearing, and social patterning. These influences determine how we start this life. However, where we end this life is an open possibility, determined by the five universal much-argued laws—*karma, dharma, fate, destiny*, and whatever *free will* we may have. Contrary to the evidence of the ancients, we can as individuals become masters of our fate, destiny, or karma, even if we can't control them. The ancients were at the mercy of the elements and the movements of the Earth, as well as other undeveloped factors in their lives. We have gained some control over the effects of earth-changes and weather, and have come to believe that happiness will come if we just can control other people and our own bodies and minds, which is neither fully an option nor fully a possibility at this time. The ancients, lacking a strong individualistic ego, found their fulfillment in learning how to live with and accept the dangers of their time through living in harmony with them and participating in finding meaning in all natural events. Meaning is what we lost and now are trying to find.

We are not necessarily evolving in a linear way, either time-wise or linearly with respect to the three stages. Possibly we are talking about evolution in depth. The ancient cultures had wisdom certainly equal to and probably greater than that of which we moderns boast, since much of what we presently call wisdom is only knowledge. Knowledge contributes to wisdom, but does not own it. Modern wisdom includes, *through* knowledge and experience, wider horizons and more permeable walls of limitation. Earlier cultures had intuitive wisdom. Their myths of the world often pointed to or paralleled the more scientific wisdom of our present time. In many cases their deeper truths are still relevant, only stated in more symbolic terms, less pleasing to the committed scientific thinker.

We do not promote either going back to the "Golden Age", or moving forward without the fullness of our remotest past. Our theme here is that the goal of all human life is to achieve some greater level of personal and spiritual consciousness and integration than it has now, or had in the known past. This requires reconnecting with the universe at the conscious level. A major stumbling block for attaining this consciousness is something we have neglected to say much about so far—joy. One of the unexpected rewards of following the Moon Path has been for us an increase in, and understanding of, joy. We are beginning to think that that is the most important reward, one that encompasses everything else.

So let us assume that a major requirement of increasing our consciousness is that it has to include the quality of joy. One who tries this path in the expectation of being happier than they are now, may possibly miss the mark. Joy is a spiritual quality that can be present during any mundane situation, pleasant or painful. It adds a lift to our lives like the buoyancy of a sound boat on the ocean. Happiness is a personal concept that we may chase throughout our lives, believing that joy is impossible without happiness. When Dr. Deepak Chopra tells us unconditionally to follow our bliss, he is speaking of deep inner urgings we have been born with, and which produce joy. Happiness for many people requires material comforts, security, nice relationships, health, etc. In other words, happiness depends upon material things and situations. Joy is a choice which arises in seeing and experiencing our lives from a larger viewpoint of expanded consciousness. If you are looking for happiness in the Moon path, your rational mind will serve you just as well, though it will not necessarily bring you joy *or* happiness. But we can promise you that Moon-watching and reaching for transformation *will* bring joy and probably a lot more happiness as well.

Also, with a stab of humility, we can no longer discount the possibility that far more advanced peoples than we may have existed so long ago that their remains are mostly obliterated and the ones left are rejected by science because of science's limited ability to change paradigms. We may not have just begun our journey in the last 30,000 years. We may have begun many times over, and perhaps this is the last chance. So we must go from the here and now with whatever baggage we bring with us. Wisdom is the outer sign of consciousness. As individuals grow in consciousness, and recognize meaning in, and connection to, the universe, so humanity evolves—slowly over eons.

The larger cosmic patterns of individual human evolvement are lost in the huge expanse of pre-history, but we have found the growth pattern repeated in small enough increments that we can use the pattern to contribute both to our own growth and through that to the whole—*Collectivization*, a much-expanded but parallel goal of the Ancients. And so, behold: the universe provides us with the monthly Moon cycles, in which each month provides us a practice in all three stages of consciousness, a pattern even for our own personal lifetime as it was for the Ancients, at a new level. The Moon and Sun together live out this eight-fold changing archetype in a kind of infinity relative to our lives. It is that forever changing and renewing pattern that is the living archetype manifested in a perfected model. We have seen how we are living this model (less perfectly no doubt) in our total lives, and monthly as well, growing our consciousness in small steps. We have also seen that if we could fully accept that change is fundamental to life itself, we would no longer be so concerned with what will happen this month or the next. The ocean on which our boat is floating could at any moment destroy our boat, but acceptance of change would allow us to enjoy the view as long as it lasts. We are not there yet, but we see that we have managed a few steps in that direction. We never know when the little baby steps we take will suddenly become giant steps. It may depend on how we take responsibility for our unconscious records and their projections.

As we look at the three levels of growing consciousness, we want to be clear that in individuals they are not clear-cut, they overlap, their outer appearances may be misleading, and individual circumstances may completely stifle or mask any or all of them. They are general guidelines only, except to the very observant, and may often be seen only over very long periods of time. We believe that in these early decades of 2,000 CE we are seeing the process increase exponentially in speed. This means we must speed ourselves up.

How We Evolve: *Individualization*

At around three years old, with the emergence of the ego (personal awareness that I am a separate human being), we begin the long path to becoming fully self-aware. We first recognized our own separate individuality through repeated actions, observing their effects on the environment and other people.

If we are really aware of ourselves as individuals, we have achieved *Individualization*—at least some of our actions come from our true inner self and are driven in the interest of that *individuality*. Depending on circumstances such as "nature and nurture", the personality[21] can swing to extreme *individualism* in some cases, such as the artist whose entire life is wound up in making and publicizing his art, which often becomes bizarre and unintelligible to others, as a kind of proof that he is not like anyone else. That individualized person is not yet complete and finds fulfillment only in the one thing that makes him unusual or different. Even that fulfillment is momentary and he continually needs more and more proof from others that he is different.

How We Evolve: *Individuation*

When an individual's motivating center core pulls into itself all the abilities and intentions of the person, so that they are all driven by it, then he/she will have also become *Individuated*. This person sees him/herself as having at least a general purpose in life, within which everything else can fit. She sees meaning in everyday events, is able to connect pieces in the puzzles of life, and considers more options. This person might be called a *strong individual* in the sense that everything he or she does is based on the sum total of her "wisdom". That is, she incorporates her experiences and learning into her total resources for creativity and decision making. Her goal is to be whole and she finds fulfillment in all of living because her life is centered around the integrating sense of purpose and meaning.

---

2   In this context, we are designating the word "personality" to the generic individual who has a name as opposed to the writer's generic and impersonal "one" we are so fond of using, instead of having to struggle with the grammar of a new society when the older "he" is now considered gender-biased or misogynist. As you noticed, we also sometimes use the pronoun "she" to replace the old "he," figuring that turnabout is fair play!

Decisions and manifestation or creation are familiar to all she knows so that small inner conflicts are reduced. She is more conscious than the individualized being.

How We Evolve: *Collectivization*

The process of *Collectivization* overlaps the other two, as the personal goal of living grows from "everything I do is for the good of myself" …to include…"the good of a partner or family"…to then include…"the good of a group". The "good of the group" is a change-point at the beginning of *Collectivization* and ultimately proceeds from a few, to all, actions being directed for the good of everyone in continually enlarging circles (including oneself of course). Early examples of this are loyalty to one's army brigade, the football team, a highly visible volunteer work—often politics, extended family, or one's students. Later examples might be a well-thought-out dedication to creating art with universal qualities, teaching with broad perspectives and thought-provoking depths, balanced activism, honest writing, or some other public or private means of addressing social issues. It seems likely that the men who walked on the Moon, and others who were embedded journalists in the Iraq war, were doing these risky, dangerous tasks as self-named representatives of the human race. Yes it was exciting, but like you and I, they had families and hopes of living out their lives with those families, which for some of them would not happen. Still they were able to integrate personal and family needs with this broader need within themselves. Of course there are many other, known and unknown, collectively oriented individuals.

The Role of the Moon Phases in Evolving Consciousness

Relax! Completion of the foregoing is not expected of anyone in a lifetime, or even a hundred lifetimes. We are embedded in a huge cosmic movement, about the end and beginning of which we can know nothing except what science can tell us of the past, and that is always changing.

Observe the nature of Moon cycles. Although every Moon cycle is different, in terms of its physical relationship to the sky in which it operates, the phases are always the same.

Although all phases in all cycles are the same, they are experienced universally by everyone on earth at the same time (given time zones), fully incorporating their individual differences.

Although the theme of the message is the same in any given cycle, it is experienced universally by every person as a unique message for him/herself only. The assumption is that archetypal information is filtered through individual consciousness, thus becoming unique and individual. The opportunities for individual creative action are there, particularly at that important First Quarter.

Humanity and individuals are living the same energies and receiving the same messages, all at universal and individual levels of understanding. It would seem that, in itself, this is a reminder to stop, look up at the sky, listen, and open up to one's own resonance.

The Incredible Organization of the Universe!

We have presented the theory that the positions and relationships of Sun and Moon, constellations, and other denizens of the sky, are permanently recorded in our brain at birth. All these inner relationships and inter-relationships respond through resonance to the outer sky's actual changing positions throughout our life. Jung has stated that the collective unconscious with all its archetypes and racial memories are also thus recorded in our brain. In researching our earlier chapter on the unconscious and the collective unconscious, it became clear to us that, as we had always believed, there is a working relationship between all these elements.

As astrologers, by following the Moon's cycles against the background of outer sky in our charts, we have learned something about our past, present, and future. We can see the life-patterns of our use of the archetypes and even some traces of the racial memories. This amazing network of inter-relationships of inner and outer person not only has its own language of symbol and imagery (Astrology-inner, Astronomy-outer), but also a way to check our own expression of our personal archetypes, and how they change, consciously or unconsciously. Like other closed systems, this amazing system within and without us contains its own patterns of checks and balances, like a government agency, but far more effective and purposeful.

According to many philosophers, archetypes are meant to be changed in order for society to evolve, which uses the creative aspect of human beings. This is the unexpected "wild card" human aspect, operating in the waning Moon phases. We as individuals are the only beings who can use that aspect productively. If we don't like what we see, we may get pushed by our Higher Selves to do something about it. Alone we can do little, but others will be getting the same messages as we, and together we will bring about change, the ringing theme of the 2008 US Presidential Candidacy.

It is through the Moon phases that we connect with selective, sequential pieces of this enormous system (packed inside more efficiently and more compactly than the most sophisticated technology known to man, but externally filling the whole universe! We never get into more of it than we can handle, nor are we capable of touching what we are not ready for. But as a whole, we are connected to the farthest galaxies, and those who are listening will connect to surprising messages through the Moon phases. Astrologers reading this will understand when we say this, that the eight Moon phase points in our birth charts will often have fixed stars, asteroids, comets, and galaxies near enough to them to get a new message across. These messages encourage us to live truthfully to our own creative Selves. Do something different!

Closing Part I

We have described a few of the emotional conflicts to which we all are subject. There are many more, and many variations on these two. Since we can not make this a book on psychology, we leave as examples the above projections and misperceptions of ourselves and others. These are the basic kinds of growth lessons we all are here to learn, in some form. There is no way that these can be anything but hard and long in the process. Tiny steps are all one can expect until one is almost to the resolution. That is why the Moon path is so helpful. We can observe and feel successful about the small changes in ourselves. However, all we can put in this book amounts to a sort of cookbook psychology, and there will be times when we are on our own, alone with the Moon and what she can tell us. We have to trust our own guiding spirit to hear the message. It is our job to do what we see and know to be true and right for us, to the best of our abilities, and let the rest happen.

You probably already know that when you become aware of the need to change, you can begin by changing your actions related to that, a little at a time. That is a pure act of will to begin with. You may believe it is right, but it certainly doesn't feel right. Eventually, you will be able to say, "I really know this is right", and later, as you keep doing the right thing, there will come a sudden feeling that it *is* right. First you realize after the fact that you reacted the old way.

Then you catch yourself in the middle of the old reactions. Then you catch yourself before the fact. At that point you are not far from transformation. As you go through the chapters on the Moon phases, you will find many reminders and helps to keep you moving, for every month of the year. The foregoing are some markers to look for, to see if you are making progress. This may be a spiritual path, but all spiritual attainment manifests only in relation to mental, emotional, physical and actional progress.

* * *

Part I is finished and we are ready to part the curtains of the Eight Windows in Time.

In Part II we open the final secrets of the *Old Woman*, and offer them to any and all who come. Step by step, we will gradually explore inner depths of the phases, information that for millennia has been so hidden in our very bodies that we could not see it by reason of our ages-long divorcement from our bodies. Bear with the process as we prepare to look at the fullness of the eight phases in their greater detail.

May we all live a thousand and eighty months and at the end of our lives may we be as wise as the Old Woman.

YOUR SOLAR DIAL

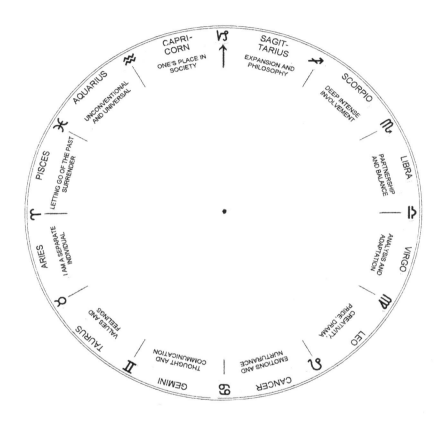

Diagram IVa. Solar Dial Wheel 1.
See Solar Dial Wheel 2 for instructions.

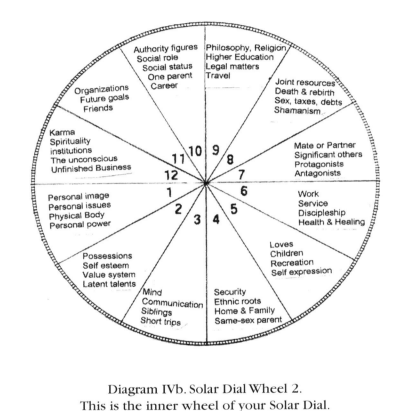

Diagram IVb. Solar Dial Wheel 2.
This is the inner wheel of your Solar Dial.

1. Drections: Copy wheel 1 and Wheel 2 onto card stock and cut out the wheel.s.
2. Center the small wheel exactly within the larger wheel.
3. From the front of the dial, stick a straigaht pin through the two centers and bend pin closely against the back of the big wheel.
4. Tape the bent pin tightly in place. The smaller wheel should rotate against the larger one.

Part II
Windows in Time
The Archetype of All Cycles of Relationship

The Cycle of the phases of the moon becomes thus legitimately the archetype of all cycles of relationship. But it does not reveal its basic meaning unless it is made clear that what the lunation cycle measures is not changes in the moon herself, but changes in the soli--lunar relationship. The phases of the moon tell us nothing about the moon, itself, or the position of the moon in the sky. They refer only to the state of relationship between the sun and the moon

Spirit operates creatively only where relatedness is given a basic significance as a dynamic factor having a cyclic rhythm of its own; and as spiritual evolution in man is polarized by the need for total consciousness in selfhood, it follows that to live spiritually is to live in the consciousness of relationship.

—Dane Rudhyar, *The Lunation Cycle*

We have earlier mentioned that for the ancients there were two kinds of time, sacred time and profane time. Sacred time was (is) no-time—that in which one participates within the context of the Divine— in unity expressed as *Being* (ritual, divination, celebration, meditation, mindfulness). All the rest was (is) profane time, which meant, in that time something entirely different than the current dictionary meaning. What Mircea Eliade calls *Becoming* means linear time in which we are doing the ordinary work of daily life within the context of community. *Sacred* and *Profane* times are, respectively, the Ground of our *Being* and the Ground of our *Becoming*. The nature of our *Being* depends upon our *Becoming*, just as our *Becoming* depends upon our *Being*. That can only happen when Spirit and soul, soul and body, body and mind, person and other, grow through reciprocity—giving and receiving—possible only where two or more persons, two or more parts of ourselves, or self and the Divine, are in relationship. Among other possibilities, it may be the "environment" within which we "do the divination" as discussed in Chapter 6.

So, one can see that the Moon's cycle can be both the archetype of evolving consciousness and the archetype of cycles of relationship, since it is only through the operation of opposites and therefore of relationships that consciousness can evolve.

13
Eight Windows
A Time for Being and a Time for Doing

With Sun and Moon to guide me
And Earth to sustain me,
I fly with the winds and tides of the present moment,
Free to become one with the whole.
— *Seagull* VLM

Sacred and Profane Time: Why We Call the Phases Windows in Time

Now that we have a bird's eye view of how the eight Moon phases work, it is time to look into their deeper significance. Our lives are aligned with the Moon cycles in a mysterious and fundamental way. The Ancients believed that when they were involved in ritual, time did not exist—it was no-time, perhaps like the interstice expanded. They were in what some of us would call an alternate reality, or more precisely, an "Interstice"[1]. Eliade calls it sacred time. They lived their ordinary lives of what Eliade later unfortunately called "profane" time, simply *doing*—its only purpose being to live according to the gods' revealed commands till the next ritual. Being with the gods was apparently their purpose for both being and doing. This has changed over the time since, in various ways depending upon the time or the culture. We found that the dictionary defines "profane" as "irreverent, unholy, irreverent toward holy things, blasphemous"

---

1   Interstice. In modern terminology, a space-between. Some writers are now using "Interstice" to imply a mystical, no-time point of crossing from one reality or dimension to another. Science fictions describes experiences in which someone enters a kind of dreamspace in which a period of time seems to elapse; but when they return to normal space, no time at all has elapsed. We use it here to designate the time between an Old Moon and a New Moon, a space of time which does not technically exist. When the Moon reaches the Sun, one moment it is old and the next it is new. That no-space, no-time, moment is for us a very mystical, magical point in which the old energies of Balsamic Moon are suddenly the New Moon energies of rebirth.

and so on (Webster). Our modern definition is rather ugly and judgmental, and we wonder what changed in people's minds to cause that change. In Eliade's work, however, he describes the ancients' non-ritual/non-sacred time as more likely "god-less", or unconnected to the god-space— as they did the five extra days at the end of their 360-day sacred year, except those were dangerous simply because they had no gods to rule those days and protect the people. Regular *doing*-time or profane time was ruled by gods who protected them. The difference between them and us is one of judgmentalism. We judge their concept of *doing*-time as profane in the modern sense, because it does not agree with our own current meaning, which is not news to anyone. We also take into account that the words, *sacred* and *profane*, did not exist in the Stone Age. They were used by a writer of our recent time, whose understanding of their meaning has changed since he wrote. Non-sacred time in our view was and still is time spent in manifesting spirit's intentions in spirit's creation. In sacred time we refill our spiritual cups and renew our intentions.

As we struggle to keep the basic truths of the Ancients' legacy, we are bringing those truths into our own time after millennia of change and transformation. The sacredness and mystery of the interstice are still with us because the moon's cycles are still here and the basic need to make connection to the beyond. However, some people think now that all time is sacred, at least if we choose to make it so. Where the Old Ones spoke of *Being* and *Doing* (of which only the former appears to have had meaning for them), we see *Being* and *Becoming*, as two inseparable sides of the same thing, the former being Yin in nature, the latter being Yang in nature. Each has a meaning springing from the other. We keep the Interstice as that mystical crossing between Old Moon and New Moon—that sacred, no-time instant when the Old Moon dies but at the same time is now miraculously reborn. Meditators often say that when they meditate deeply enough they experience a period of no-time, in which they feel renewed, healed, or received back into relationship with the Divine.

On our Moon Path we find a similar possibility. According to astronomy, each phase of the Moon is a crossing at an Interstice during which (though there is no duration) the energies change in a way that reach out and connect each of our lives with a different frequency. They seem so much like windows in time. As long as we remain on this side of the window we may see the flowers on the other side, but we cannot smell or pick them. But just as we pass through, we are welcomed by the flowers' scent. In a sense we then have a divination or message about the nature of the next few days or month. That message as you will remember from Section I is defined for us in one way by one of the Sabian Symbols. When we resonate to a particular symbol at a particular phase, we have momentarily stepped through the window—we already knew what that symbol was about.

Another way of describing these windows is that sequentially each phase opens a window with an increasing or decreasing amount of light on the Moon—an area of our consciousness is increasing with either one. In the Hebrew alphabet the fifth letter is *H-e-h*. It means window in Hebrew.   Pronounced "hay", and correlating to our English letter "E", *Heh* means "connection with"— or "window to"— (the Divine). Stan Tenen, in his book *First Hand* (see Bib.) explains as follows:

> H-E-H is the Interface archetype. Heh brings mind and matter, flame and vessel, wave & particle together; it is an abbreviation for *"HaShem"*, meaning *The Name*, a stand-in phrase for G-d. *Heh* is the interface that provides a Framework for Connection. That is why *Heh* means Window…it window-frames, and connects, the center and the equator…of the APPLE of Continuous Creation. [Yitzchak Ginsberg interprets this letter as *behold-revelation*.]

The letters of the Hebrew Alphabet each have an exoteric meaning from ancient sources going back to the Egyptian Proto-Sinaitic hieroglyphics, where its earliest forms emerged with the world-wide primal shamanic religion, as pictographic type symbols. So there may be a significance that the 5th phase is the Full Moon, and the one in which we receive enlightenment when the window is fully opened.

Ritual and Sacred Time

In an earlier chapter, we wrote that the structure of Stone Age ritual is strangely parallel to the structure of the fourfold Moon cycle, and that, in fact, we believe it to be originally so intended, along with the four seasons, the four directions, and other "fours". The Ancients believed that ritual itself created a space of no-time, of

Being, between their recurring periods of *Doing*. Thus early ritual brings us another picture of the Moon Phases and the earliest understandings of the phases. While we were exploring our own experiences with the life-renewing Interstices of the Moon Cycle, alternating with periods of living the phases, we were repeating the ritual of the Ancestors (Chapter 6). No wonder we felt so close to these ancient beings. We had opened their early Windows in Time. And, in fact, we were (and are) attempting to live the whole cycle as a ritual, creating *Beingness* in our Becoming, or perhaps a kind of mindfulness. Now the reader can see that each of the four phases begins and ends with an interstice—in modern terms, the four basic phases could be termed the steps of an actual cosmic or universal ritual. It seems to be a natural order, inherited from the beginning, with the archetype of the human urge to transform. To repeat the ritual steps from Chapter 6:

> Step one *"Originating"*—New Phase
> Step two *"Developing"*—1st Quarter
> Step three *"Maturing"*—Full
> Step four *"Wisdom"*—3rd Quarter

These keywords were translated by Karcher directly from the writings of early Chinese historians. The historians wrote from still earlier sources, closer to the people, more intuitive, now lost to us but stored in custom, myth, and recently unearthed bone pictographic inscriptions. They knew these words as universal principles. We have found these principles in similar sources around the world so we accept that these four steps represent all kinds of growth cycles. The point where one stage merges into another has, however, never been articulated. Those points vary according to the nature of any cycle, and may never be defined; but, for Moon Cycles, they are exact and verifiable in our time, no longer a simple guess or belief. When Eliade states that the Moon's phases *are* the archetype of *Being* and *Becoming*, the very structure of life can be revealed through the Moon's phases.

To follow the wisdom of any guiding principle is to grow both in daily *Becoming* and in spiritual *Being*. These patterns of the ancestors are still with us, and we can carry the sacred times of *Being* into our daily *Becoming*. We, like the Moon, can become vessels of light as we read the divination for each phase and consciously practice its principles. This is the concept with which we began the Old Woman's book, even before we learned about the ritual principles.

We will leave the readers to consider these interesting parallels as they work their way through the phases themselves, gaining the wisdom through doing the work. Under no circumstances do we want to leave an impression with the reader that we must submit to some written body of statements telling us what to do every day. Archetypal statements do not work that way, as we stated earlier. Principles are what we live by, chosen by each of us. It is already obvious that six billion people instinctually following (or resisting) a given archetypal statement belonging to a specific Moon phase, do not look alike and are not doing what anyone else is doing.

Being While Becoming

For us, the Sacred has always involved elements of will and intent, as in the power of intention in ritual. One may not fully accept or believe the efficacy of a ritual, but sometimes the intent to participate affects the outcome. We suggest that in following the Moon phases as spiritual intent we are finding a key to living in conscious oneness or *Being* while busy doing the *Becoming*. Along this line of thought ideas like the Buddhists'—that chopping the wood and carrying the water is sacred along with everything else— carry the ring of truth. Even the Buddhists struggle with it, but in time both they and we find longer, more frequent times in which we feel we are truly experiencing the sacred, or *Beingness*, in our daily lives. We are not saying that the Sun and Moon are sacred in themselves, but that they are living archetypes which convey to us a continual stream of guidance from the universe through their, and our, very participation in the cosmic structure.

An interesting fact which some readers will appreciate is the concept of "practicing the Presence" as described by an early Christian saint, Brother Lawrence, in a small book by that name; and another, anonymous, writer who wrote "The Way of the Pilgrim." Our concept is no different. The Old Woman merely shows us some of the principles that one can find hidden in such practices. Which is to say that Moon practice is a nonspecific archetype of embracing the sacred within the mundane.

What We Learn from the Moon cycles

Every New Moon is a new step in our lives, from birth to death. They each fall in a specific area of our own birth chart for that particular step. In the larger picture, all the New Moons in our lives sequentially trace the path of destiny we were meant to fulfill. If you follow the cycles, you will see that each New Moon brings a timely and relevant new image to incorporate into your life during that month, through the psychological/spiritual processes connected with each phase, and ending with a new piece of wisdom fully installed in your structure of consciousness. You will also understand how the whole of humanity is intended to grow with these same images. <u>One image, one Organism, and a path to lead us all back to unity/ wholeness</u>. How could we not know we are one with humanity, moving toward a common goal?

Early men and women recognized different ideations for the Moon phases than those we will be following with the degree symbols. The ancient images of Pagan gods and goddesses with their emotionally potent power impacted in different ways, appropriate to the cultures and evolution of the millennia of our ancestors. We believe the Moon phase energies/ideations stimulated the brain activity that developed the frontal lobes, the part of the brain that recognizes time, sequentiality, and logic. The Stone Age images surrounding the Moon probably embodied the same collective projections time-appropriate myths, rituals, mores, taboos, and mating customs. We think that what the Moon cycles can teach us in our time has more to do with our current emotional and social evolvement, based on an urgent need to work with relationships of all kinds. Therefore we use the contemporary images provided for us by Mark Edmund Jones (ibid.)

An initial and primary lesson that the Moon cycles teach us, and probably taught the earliest of man was the concept of giving and receiving, the ancient Hebrew version of the Yang/Yin duality[2]. Giving and receiving by the community, to and from the gods in ritual, and between individuals and the tribe in daily life—ultimately were the greatest dynamic of the early fourfold principle. It has allowed humans to survive and develop. This dynamic is *Relationship 101*. First, in pairs and families, it later became necessary for humans to have extended families or tribes for protection and subsistence. So giving and receiving extended beyond two humans and became the dynamics of relationship between individual and collective. It was experienced time after time in the early tribal rituals. Now, in recorded history we have relationships between nations. We

---

2   Still a primary teaching in biblical, Kabbalistic, and contemporary Judaism

experience a lesson in this dynamic every Full Moon. On the round of cycles of this millennium, however, we are learning to become conscious simultaneously in the personal, social, and universal levels.

Bringing Earth Back into its Relationship with Sun and Moon

Since the beginning, the Sun-Moon cycle—faithful clock of time—has consistently not only divided and marked time, but regularly released subtle energies that stimulated growth-producing impulses toward plant, animal, human, and collective growth. The precessional periods of 2,160 years have marked the spiritual character of historic and prehistoric cultural periods of that length. Within the precessional epochs, the yearly thirteen Moon cycles mark the spiritual character of single years and months.

It is high time for us to retrieve the universal cycles back into our lives, as we grope collectively, with pain and struggle, toward a future seen in multiple and mostly negative ways—all as the outcome of current physical, cultural, religious, political, social, and individual imbalances. A negative future will surely fulfill itself if we do not as a whole change rapidly. The mysteries of alchemical transformation, long hiding behind walls of secrecy, meant only for the few, are now necessary for everyone.

As of this chapter's writing (July, 2008), our planetary salvation appears at a critical crossroads. We are being told the desperate nature of our environment, and for the most part the information is ignored. The solution is spiritual. The vast number of leaders and media CEOs must become conscious of the Yin-Yang balance in environment and the principles of relationship. They must evolve out of their ego focus from "I" to "we" before they are willing or able to see the true state of affairs. We suspect that the Moon phase path will never become conscious for anyone until that transition occurs. Until then, people submerged in ego consciousness have an ego voice within that out-shouts the unconscious knowing imprisoned behind that present voice. The pendulum has swung hopefully to its extreme in favor of ego, and will soon begin its swing in the opposite direction.

"The Mysteries" of the Moon Path have always been instinctually available to everyone, but now they must be consciously followed. It is our belief and working knowledge that every challenge of our lives is a practical spiritual lesson, the "secrets" of which can be found in the symbolic degrees of the Moon phases. We have seen that the degrees taken as a whole contain the basic principles of all change, whatever that might be. If every experience is seen as a learning, and we are all mirrors of each other, we certainly are not lacking in teachers! If we do not see the teachers crowding around us, it is our choice, conscious or unconscious, and we are the losers.

The Path of Giving and Receiving

In the Kabbalistic context of basic duality, giving means any Yang, outward-moving, sharing or inclusive type of action—be it physical, emotional, mental, spiritual— toward a person or persons. In Kabbalistic philosophy one has to do the Yang thing unselfishly. To act out or speak an idea, to make or prepare something that others will hear or use, to paint a picture, say a prayer for someone, fix a car, pay your bills, and so on, must be done without self-interest. Receiving or Yin means one must allow all life to come to and into us at any level, such as allowing the phone company to send us its bill, and "allowing" what we don't like as well as what we want as long as it works to the good of all involved. In that latter *allowing*, you agree to follow selflessly the repeating rhythm of Yin. Giving and receiving at all levels provide the basic substance of *Becoming*. Below are several different types of actions associated with Yang and Yin.

YANG	YIN	YANG	YIN
Do	Be	Throw	Catch
Aggressive	Submissive	Give	Receive
Attack	Withdraw	Active	Passive
Argue	Placate	Assertive	Receptive
Sun	Moon	Masculine	Feminine
Speak	Listen	Out	In

YANG	Aries	Gemini	Leo	Libra	Sagittarius	Aquarius
YIN	Taurus	Cancer	Virgo	Scorpio	Capricorn	Pisces

Table 10. Yin and Yang of the Signs

Above are the Yang and Yin qualities of the signs. The signs of Sun and Moon at their sign phase-points will be the strongest indication of which quality is dominant in that phase; however, the "background noise" of the generic 8-phase vs. 12-sign arrangement will sometimes reveal a secondary sub-level of opposite action. Each of the three-day phases of the 8-fold Moon cycle presents us with a Window in Time, with specific Yang or Yin energies that give us just so much—not too much, not too little—time in which to unfold our dance with duality (= Yang-Yin), in steps that are never too big or too little, but only what we are ready to make them. A divination is contained in the degree of each phase. We can choose to ignore these windows, but life moves on anyway, only so much more magnificently when we use the energies consciously. The ancient Chinese called it stepping into the Great River, the Buddhists call it following the Tao, Jews call it *Halachah* (The Way), and Christians call it The Way, The Truth, and the Life. Some people instinctually follow the Moon energies and call it nothing at all. They may not need to know about these Windows in Time because they are already attuned to them by another or no name. However, they might miss some of the fun by not being consciously tuned in to their guidance system.

We are sharing our discoveries of the Moon path because there are so many who are not aware that they can feel the changing moon's energies, sense their own struggles between soul and spirit, or even body and mind. They need and want a way to live that they can understand, as whole beings—body, mind, and soul—objectively as well as subjectively—a path with observable markers, invisible matching energies, and guidance when life is chaotic, even a hint of what is to come. We add that the earlier description of ego-centered persons who can't yet move out of their limited consciousness into the Moon path consciousness does not apply to the above description. Many people have an instinctual guidance system and an already evolved ego that has balanced itself with a greater consciousness, which works very well for them.

Now we begin looking through the eight Windows in Time to see the particular energies in their fuller and more specific nature.

14
New Phase: Lost in the Light
A Time for Being in the Heart

...a time of allowing the external self
to be spiritually welcomed back into its intuition.
—Blaschke, *Astrology, A Language of Life, Volume II.*

May [the new month] *come upon us and...the entire whole world for*
good. May the Holy One renew it for us..., for life and for peace, for
gladness and joy, for deliverance and for consolation...
—Excerpted from an ancient Hebrew Blessing for the New Month

<u>What</u> is Beginning?

The "What" of the New Moon is simply its statement that
something new is beginning. The general concept of "beginning" and
"renewal" are the primary meanings—the end of an old cycle and
the beginning of a new one. But the unusual reverence with which
it has been welcomed since the Stone Age comes from the notion (?)
that all things are renewed along with the Moon. After working with
the Moon phases for a year or so, you may question whether this
was just a "notion," but rather an intuitive knowledge of the human
organism springing from the cellular levels of the unconscious body-
mind. A deep connection to New Moons gained over time can bring
a feeling of being linked to the ancestral and distinctively human
Lunation experience.

At this first of the eight windows, Sun, representing spirit,
purpose, fire, basic will and drive, imparts to the Moon the initial
impetus and intention for the month. Moon represents soul, water,
emotion, receptivity and focusing of the message through whatever
challenges the month brings. As the Sun initially meets and merges
with the Moon, the archetypal image of the seed-idea is conceived.
This functions within us as a deeply felt impulse, always speaking
as the archetype of transformation, although as yet it has no actual
or rational form. This cosmic mating symbolizes for mankind the
personal rebirth of the individual, a new beginning and a new

purpose for the month. The degree symbol for that moment gives you a word-picture or metaphor for the month ahead.

The ancient Chinese shamans made more of an issue than Western astrology of the fact that both Balsamic and New Moons are mostly in darkness. Their geography—dark cold winters, treacherous mountains, deep shadowed valleys and raging rivers in spring when the snow melted—suggested images of dangerous places, falling from great heights into rocky canyons and rushing rivers, and mountains blocking every which way one looked. This translates into metaphors about blocking old cycle content from intruding into a new cycle, trying to get to the other side of the blocking mountain, resisting the dangers, which were, after all, a natural part of all ending cycles. Winter was the end of the year, or "the dark of the Sun", and therefore a metaphor for the dark of the Moon. It evoked fearful possibilities and the Chinese philosophers counseled the wisdom of letting go into free fall, so to speak, going with the flow, falling to the bottom of the canyon. This is a metaphor for reaching the end of the cycle with continued concerns about it. It may well apply to you if you are resisting letting go or releasing something in the Balsamic. It will be harder to deal with in the New Moon. Unconscious material, even from childhood, often comes to the surface, and can appear to block your way. Could this imagery be the beginning of Chinese philosophy about the *Tao* which tells us, "Let it be, allow yourself to accept the past as it is and leave it behind?" Taoists believed that only the transformation we Westerners know as "The Rose"[1]— suddenly, miraculously, coming back to life in spring—would get us past the mountain range. We have found more truth in some of these metaphors than we expected.

Moon's constantly changing position through the signs and houses throughout the month shows where, at any time, we need to ground the message into reality. New Moon's message lasts the whole month and is the overall guiding purpose.

By now you have your wheel out and you have found the area of your life highlighted by the current or most recent New Moon. What sign is it in? This wonder-full meeting of Sun and Moon has a message for you about the theme of the new month. Look at the

---

1   Song, "The Rose," written by Amanda McBroom and sung in the movie of that name by Bette Midler, 1979. Lyrics are about the life cycle of the rose, which seemingly dies in winter, but blooms miraculously at return of spring.

house of the New Moon, the sign, and the Sabian degree symbol[2], and spend a few minutes thinking about their meaning. Symbols need a "loose" focus of attention, one not bound to a single literal understanding. Some degrees are harder to understand in personal terms than others, but Roche's interpretations are generally easier with that than Rudhyar's. Also, we have discovered that negative sounding symbols are only truly negative in outer action when we ourselves are negative. Unpleasant maybe, but they are principles and not actual images of what is going to happen to you. Looking behind the image to the principle can be the way you need to see the purpose or meaning of your experience. Sometimes it also helps you accept a higher level of good in a truly tough situation. Sometimes we simply do not feel ready for the next step up on the ladder of evolution. Perhaps we create the positive or negative expression of the symbol by our willingness or non-willingness to accept reality and the hidden meaning behind it. As one nine-year-old said, after a hard day at school, "I don't want my character improved any more!"

The Nature of New Moon Energies

Many writers describe this as a period of instinctive, youthful, essentially unconscious and irrepressible activity. However, the other side of that is that what consciousness there *is* is essentially subjective, with a tendency not to distinguish accurately between inner wishes, dreams or feelings, and the actual realities of the external world. We have hunches, feelings, deep strong urges, and ideas that may be seen by next week to be unrealistic, and therefore needing grounding. There is this feeling of urgent activity within, without a sense of where to express it or why.

Our experience suggests that the more common description of a "bursting-forth" of action actually begins after first light as we approach the Crescent phase. We find for ourselves that in most months the outward-directed forward movement comes at the end of the new phase and is more characteristic of the Crescent, which announces, "Here I am!—what you have been waiting for!". At *first light*, we get the first glimpse of the form this month's seed idea will take, which is a day or two before the Crescent. Anyone who has seen the suddenly exploding division of cells in a Petrie dish will

---

2   Note Appendix E containing the original Mark Edmond Jones 360 degree symbols for a brief version of the symbol.

recognize the feeling of the end of the New and beginning of the Crescent Moon phase—how different from the quieter movement of the initial few cells following conception. The beginning is an inner movement only, and sometimes very outwardly quiet, inviting meditation or listening; other times it is an inward expectancy or the undirected urgency, even a moving forward without thinking beforehand, youthful and inspired by…what?

It is difficult in contemporary western culture to be still and wait, which is exactly what we suggest training oneself to do. Also, our personal experience of the phases as westerners is blended with early Eastern shamanic descriptions, which emphasize the continuing darkness from Balsamic through the first part of the New Moon phase, with its sense of forward movement being blocked. You may decide differently, so watch your activity and mental state during this new moon. You may find that an urge for constant activity covers up the deeper need to be quiet inside. In our society, there is a false need to fill silence or spaces of not-doing. Balsamic-New Moon darkness is often the signal to get very busy doing something, anything, to avoid looking too deeply into one's dreams, images, fears or dissatisfactions. Drink more coffee, get busy on small tasks at hand, talk on the phone, and watch T-V. Some may even blindly tackle the beginning of a large task, the full scope of which is not yet clear, and which has not yet been well grounded. Surely busy hands are better than feeling guilty of laziness or wasting time! In fact, however, feelings should be allowed to rule here—feelings, the domain of the soul, are where we need to be right now. Through our feelings we may connect with the soul. Listen to feelings, hunches, fleeting ideas, and don't miss the moments of inner connectedness.

We think there is also a need to honor the sacred character of beginning and what it means, for our consciousness and for the organic aspect of our body-brain. This is a kind of holy darkness-- silence and lack of clarity about what is beginning, like human conception, where the initial expansion of a few undifferentiated cells may be felt by the intuitive mother as an inner excitement and expectation. One can sometimes actually feel the speeding up of body processes. Then again, one may feel a physical inertia that pervades the mind as well, or simply be "at loose ends" with energy on hold. There is a definite organic element at New Moon carried over briefly from the catabolic processes of declining Yang energy mentioned earlier.

In other months, one may also feel the strong unformed desire energy of something that still exists from the last phase of the previous cycle. Or, perhaps one feels a powerful urge to do something that seems out of context with one's surroundings, and there is fear it will not be accepted by others. One may feel blocked, echoing the ancient shamanic mountain of the past to which we are still clinging and which appears to be blocking our fuller entrance into the new phase. There are times when the mountain blocking is almost palpable. If that happens to you, you may later recognize it as merely the boundary between the old and new moons. Perhaps a task that began in the previous phase has not been completed and one is feeling pressured to get on with it, not recognizing that one phase of that task needed closing in order to make room for a new way of finishing it. In any case, the Yang and Yin energies have cancelled each other out and the new Yang energies are just awakening during these three days. If this New Moon is about finishing or continuing a previous task, it signals a new start, direction, or way of perceiving it. Wait long enough to see how the new idea will change and improve the outcome.

In specific terms, what is beginning is something both brand new and unexpected, or something from the previous cycle couched in terms of a new purpose. Something in that cycle may have left us feeling unfinished. We projected it ahead of ourselves as an image or feeling of something bright we didn't get to finish, or as something dark we turned away from. Then it comes up in some unexpected way.

Elements of security or insecurity accompany this new beginning. The *project*-ion is the current month's "project". This kind of projection is not the kind where you project something unconscious onto someone else. It is a conscious projecting outward of a desire or goal, which one may find mirrored by the degree symbol.

When the reader has played with the Moon phases for a while, he or she may discover that the feeling experience of New Moon is described by the sign in which the Sun-Moon falls. Metaphysical teachings speak of *The Observer*, or *The Witness*, a part of each of us related to the High Self, sometimes called *the eye of the soul*, and which observes us and helps us see ourselves objectively. It is a valuable aspect on a spiritual path. It encourages us to watch how our experience expresses the signs, houses, and degrees that are active for the month.

The Deeper Meaning of New Moon—the Unity experience

Given the endless list of individual experiences of a New Moon, at the beginning of each Lunar month, the common experience is a physical, emotional, or mental renewal of energies and an opportunity to focus around an initially formless new intent or goal. Occasionally, as soul and spirit join, we can open to an ultimate New Moon in which our conscious self becomes momentarily one with our own Higher Self. These are mystical moments called "unity experiences" in which all the parts of our being are resonating as one tone or frequency. They parallel similar experiences in those uncommon human relationships when momentarily the two parties experience the bliss of oneness. Such experiences are never forgotten, and for the rest of one's life, the knowledge of unity is never lost.

The first word one can say about the New Moon is "Unity". Perhaps we can hear its whispered shout deep inside, even while we cannot see it. Our own spirit and soul are in total unity at New Moon, and we are in a unity with humanity. If we are fully to participate in that cosmic focus of purpose and intent, we must at least hold ourselves to a conscious intent to be so aligned. Every cycle opens a new experience that can increase our consciousness of that unity. Essentially this is a personality experience—a moment when we directly experience and participate in that unity of the soul-spirit, Moon-Sun. To get an image of our personality's relationship to the New Moon we suggest you return to Diagram II. (Chapter 1.) It is a sort of map by which the movements of the inner and outer selves (soul and personality), in relation to the spirit, can be tracked through the month. It is a piece of western metaphysics which has circulated here and there, and whose source has been lost, but we have found invaluable.

As you can see, at New Moon the personality or outer self appears at its farthest from the Moon. Emotionally, and energy-wise, the Moon is our connection to the soul, as the Sun is our connection to spirit. Just now, the soul is far away communing with spirit which is passing to the soul the new seed impulse for the month. At the point of the Interstice, the Sun and Moon occupy a single degree of the Zodiac. Earth is aligned with that unity, so it becomes up to the individual representing Earth to be that alignment. If one can do that, the distance becomes a mystical nothing. The three are one. This diagram visually shows the need for inner quiet. The outer personality consciousness is not in a mood for meditation. It simply is not able to reach the realms of spirit. But the soul can; and the personality self can reach the soul if it is quiet enough. If that happens, then the description of unity consciousness in Chapter Three can happen. If it doesn't happen—ah well then, you can simply be aware, in an attitude of acceptance, that somewhere in the great "out there/in here" your soul is receiving a new idea. You can intentionally be lost in the light at deeper levels, and you…will…be….

The Moon (soul) is the representative and doer of the Sun's (spirit's) purpose. The actual new energy that many of us feel in our emotions, bodies or minds is a new influx of creative Sun energies which Moon will use to embody the purpose. It is this constant renewal that gives us the energy, even the passion, to begin again, to finish, to overcome. So here in this incredibly intimate meeting within ourselves we are spirit, soul, and body in a timeless embrace to mark our internal commitment to ourselves and each other. It is our responsibility to ourselves that we commit to carrying onward the creative river of our unique work in this incarnation. This is a monthly commitment to live all of our life the best we can. If we have made such a commitment about the whole of our life, how much more powerful that commitment will be if we renew that commitment each month! The Sun in our birth chart gives clues to the purpose of our life; the Sun each month gives us a piece of that purpose. "This is my life and I intend to make it the best life I can." That can happen if we honor the interstice of the New Moon.

The History of the New Moon

Clearly, early peoples had no way of knowing the New Moon's beginning other than by intuition. Early societies other than China all counted the new moon from the "first light", the pre-Crescent fingernail sliver first seen a few hours after the actual new moon.

From early shamanic times, worldwide, the sighting of that beautiful thin edge of moon was celebrated with great reverence as the gift of renewal of life. Early religions carried the belief into newer practices and cultures, but always as the celebration of new life. Maimonides, a famous Hellenistic Jewish philosopher and physician to Egypt's Pharaoh, must have had a special feeling about the healing possibilities of new moons, because he wrote that *the renewing moments of the year, they are the renewals of the moon.*

In all times, women have kept the knowledge of New Moon,

which has become known as the *women's mysteries*. In early
China, the women knew that actual New Moon happened in the
darkness, but also that it occurred somewhat earlier than first light.
They meditated together at dark of moon for several days to receive
intuitively the exact moment of new moon. Immediately they
informed the male shamans of the community, who made ritual in
honor of new life and new purpose beginning again, and to appeal
to heavenly protection for whatever new beginnings were present in
the community.

Recently, small groups (often women only, but also increasingly
mixed groups) such as shamanic and Wiccan groups celebrating New
Moon are on the increase. While Christians do not celebrate the New
Moon directly, some of their most important liturgical celebrations are
based on New Moon. It still marks the beginnings of the months in
Jewish, Muslim, Hindu, Buddhist and Chinese calendars. It is almost
unimaginable that in North America we find mass unawareness of
New Moons. New Moon belongs to humanity. Since the earliest ritual
beginnings of man, the New Moon has offered us hope in every time
and culture, and has been addressed by ritual incorporated into the
life of the community

Before the computerization of astronomical events such as
Lunations, no one had a way of determining the exact lunation, so
everyone except the Chinese used the first visible thin crescent as
the official New Moon. We can use the technology and follow the
exact New Moon times. But we suggest you try to find the first light
yourself, as well. It will appear about a day after the actual New
Moon, low on the horizon between Moon set and Sun set, which are
usually listed in the newspapers. It is the thinnest crescent you can
see in the sky, the time of which varies from place to place and from
one viewer to the next, due to local conditions.

The Myth of the Moon and Sun

In Neolithic and Pagan times mythology became the carrier or
instructor of Moon wisdom, and our primary way of tracing early
beliefs. We offer the reader just three of the themes we found during
many hours of reading and study. One of the most important myths is
that of Thoth. Thoth (under various traceable names) was a primary
and very early Egyptian Moon god who created four more gods called
the Ogdoad, which he then split into four pairs, who then created
a mound out of which the creation came. The Ogdoad persisted
into Greek thought, where it was associated with the eight phases.

Unfortunately, many myths apparently belonging to Moon beliefs are not labeled as Moon phase stories, since writing was not available. In this fortunate case, the Greeks had some kind of information that caused them to label the Ogdoad for what it undoubtedly was. We found many archeological, graphic and pictographic clues that tantalized but which we did not use in this book since they could not be verified. The later traces of eight phases in divinitory systems and in Greek and Chinese philosophy all parallel the meanings flowing from the meanings of the 8-fold Ogdoad to an uncanny and originally unexpected degree of accuracy.

One of the oldest planet-wide themes was that of Sun and Moon being the world mother and father.

Fragments of an ancient myth (the source of which we were unable to trace) of the Balsamic Moon (last phase before New Moon) speak of the antechamber of Spirit where the Soul waits in silence to present, to the Sun, humanity's need for a new answer, a new beginning, a new purpose. At the exact conjunction of Sun and Moon behind the curtain of darkness, the Moon, representing all humanity, allows herself to be consumed by the greater light and consciousness of spirit. In this consummation she receives the New Moon seed-impulse which is the answer. Out of that answer will be created something that can, at the Full Moon, be offered to a larger community as partial answer to humanity's greater need.

This myth is referred to by Dane Rudhyar in his book, "The Lunar Cycle" which book unveiled to the contemporary world, the lost significance of the Moon and its eight phases.

We remind you here that humanity's need breaks down to each individual's need, but it is even more important to remember that our personal needs are somehow unified at New Moon with those of everyone. As you go through the month you are in, see if you can see how its events are the answer to a need of your own from the previous month. At the same time see if you can trace the same process for your country or another person.

The Interstice—Space-Between the Old and the New.

The dictionary meaning of *interstice* is a space between two things. It can also mean the space between realities or dimensions. To pass in meditation to another level of consciousness or alternate reality is likened to going through an interstice. Moses was allowed to see something other-worldly when he looked through a cleft in a rock and saw God passing back and forth. Perhaps that was a way of describing a vision he had while in an altered state, the cleft in the rock being an interstice of sorts.

People who found the previous Balsamic hard to release or difficult to deal with, and find it still hanging around in their mood or emotions after crossing the interstice, have brought some of the past into the new phase. It will have to be dealt with and may take up energy needed for the challenges of a new cycle, particularly in the Crescent phase coming up next.

The early Chinese considered the moment of New Moon to be a point where both Yang and Yin stopped and began again, Yang now ready to begin moving ahead. This was a mystical interstice because it involved no-time. We understand that in Eastern thought the (interstice) of the New Moon moment, in which neither Yin nor Yang "move," is a powerful moment of potency and potentiality, even though hidden in stillness and dark. When does the Moon exactly conjunct the Sun? When does a ball, tossed into the air, stop going up and begin coming down? The Moon is approaching an exact conjunction to the Sun one instant, and in the same instant it is leaving the conjunction. Both Yin and Yang of the old cycle are dying and the next instant the new Yang and Yin have already begun. If you want to meditate on that exact moment, note that your Cosmic Guide book lists the time as well as date of every lunation. If you meditate for five minutes (2 ½ minutes before to 2 ½ minutes after) you will be sure to experience that interstice.

The New Moon interstice, like the mystical space between drumbeats or thoughts, is like the goal of meditation and drumming "journeys". This interstice is charged with the spiritual potential to manifest or co-create something entirely new. Whatever that is, it will in some sense fill the need evoked by the changes of the past cycle, if we are willing to be so-aligned with divine potential. The task of the previous and final phase was to willingly prepare ourselves to leave the old behind and accept the new.

We do not yet fully know our own power in relation to this Interstice, or how to use it, but nature herself gives us a clue. The fact that the New Moon is not seen in the sky because it is visually lost in the rays of the rising Sun is a powerful image of our soul being momentarily lost in a greater spirit. Like a candle being lit,

Sun's rays over-ride the Moon's light as they both rise at the same time[3].

There are two possible but differing moments of acceptance here, one on the Balsamic side, and one on the New Moon side. At the very end of the cycle letting go into the dark or unknown—at the very beginning of the next letting go into the light or the future--allowing ourselves to be absorbed by the spirit's new intent for us. Both are conscious, intentional mental/emotional actions. We do not have to accept the darkness, the mystery, the creative chaos, the situation of the moment. We do not have to accept and be absorbed by spirit's new intent. We can refuse both with our personal ego consciousness. We can't imagine what might happen if we did that, except that life does seem much harder when we resist what it brings. Going with the tides is certainly easier if you are in a rowboat.

It has been said that the darkness of late Balsamic and New Moon represents the collective unconscious in which personal unconscious is involved. This is another reason for the difficulty of pulling our feet out of the entanglements of the previous cycle at new phase. So we suggest that when some hours later we see the paper-thin fingernail Moon, *it is time to refocus to the present* and forward movement. Now we can see that something inside us—the hint of a piece of our own evolution—emerge from our own unconscious. The new and the personal are born out of the past and the collective.

In personal terms, we as individual souls are meant to be lost (totally receptive and open to) in the light of our own spirit; parallel-wise, the soul of humanity is meant to be lost in the light of the God-spirit, to which we see it often is highly resistant, and which explains its constant travails and struggles. This is why the Eastern idea of going with the flow, or letting oneself "fall" rather than resist, is so important. Only complete letting go into one's darkness can prepare one to be lost in the light, to be fully receptive to the new month, to be able to say, "I fully accept whatever the new month brings". If one is fearful of the coming month because the Balsamic

---

3   What we did not explain earlier is that from Full Moon to New Moon, the Moon rises and sets progressively lower in the sky. At New Moon, the Moon rises with the Sun, just over the horizon for the moment of her union with the Sun, and then sets again. In a day or two, we see the Moon rising again, remaining in the sky a few more minutes each night thereafter, until at full Moon she reaches her zenith (highest point in the sky), exactly opposite the Sun, then begins her waning path back to the end of the cycle. It is very complex, because the plane of the Earth's orbit around the Sun is at one angle, and the plane of the Moon's orbit around the Earth is at a different angle.

situation was fearful, then one needs to say, "It is OK to be fearful" and simply fall into the fear to its very bottom. (To be unable to do this is a Balsamic problem and the Balsamic chapter will address that.) At the moment of Sun-Moon conjunction, one is suddenly in the new month, past the mountains, gorges, torrents, and so forth. Looking back, we can see that the mountain was not a barrier, but the boundary, between the old and the new.

The ancient rituals to invoke the Moon power are lost, and in any case would not be appropriate in our time. We cannot see the Interstice, any more than we can see the momentary cleft between heaven and earth left behind by a lightning flash, the closing of which brings the clap of thunder. But we do know that the Interstice, a function of no-time, marks the germination of a new energy, a new intent, a breaking through the softened seed-shell of the just-now-Sun-charged germ in the old seed. This sounds much like some scientific suggestions that lightning's power-filled electrical discharge may be helpful for growth and fertility of crops, and perhaps played a role in the transition between chemical elements and living cells during the early days of Earth itself. Many cultures celebrated the creation of their new year on a New Moon, reenacting the belief that they returned to the original creation in doing so (which was a part of the concept that no-time existed during rituals). That resembles a Kabbalistic belief remaining from the past in the Jewish High Holy Days, beginning on Rosh Hashanah, the celebration of the creation of the world, the "opening of the gates of Creation" as though it is happening in the present, and asking the celebrants to separate from material life and connect with their essence.[4]

There is power in an Interstice, as there is power in blessing things. So bless the New Beginning that has just begun its journey—for you, and for others.

Living the New Moon

We do not need to isolate ourselves and spend all our time in meditation and introversion. We may really have much external work to do of a general nature. As mentioned previously, we have twelve houses— twelve areas of life experience—eleven besides the

---

4   In early practices, there were several New Years. Spring was the new year of plant life and renewal , which remains today in Jewish and Christian rituals of Passover and Easter. Near the winter equinox we find festivals of light and the hope that spring will finally return. Midsummer brings harvest rituals mostly remaining in Pagan religions.

New Moon house, active in some way all the time; and we must fulfill their needs for our attention. Simply, do the Buddhist things— chop the wood, carry the water, *and keep a corner of your attention focused on the bend in the road to see what comes around it.*

Trust is an issue in the Balsamic and New Moons. New Moon requires a different kind of trust than the old or Balsamic moon, which, being the most conscious of the eight, may partake of such feelings as hope, despair, or rebellion—the fear of change—or not-change as the case may be. Trust at the Balsamic is in something beyond oneself, while New Moon trust is in one's self, knowing (someplace inside) that something momentous is happening. Remember, the first half of the cycle is for building the individuality. We are in soul country here, with access to unity as expanded as the universe, offering us a new opportunity for increasing our sense of self or Self.

Cultural, social, political, and yet very personal, each New Moon sets in motion the next learning curve on the spiral of growing human consciousness. Mythologically the Moon weaves the web of human destiny that connects every individual to the collectivity through the continuity of its threads. As each of us carries out our own facet of the message, our individual spark contributes to the evolution of the whole.

What if there is an Eclipse?

Every six months, the New Moon is an Eclipse, either two weeks before or two weeks after a Full Moon Eclipse. A Solar (Sun) Eclipse is always a New Moon. A Lunar (Moon) Eclipse is always a Full Moon. For the Ancients, the Solar eclipses provided the archetype of death and rebirth. In early times, the black disk of the Sun-eclipsing Moon at New Moon was also seen as a "hole" or opening in the upper world through which spirit could come into this middle world of 3-D. For a full explanation of eclipses please see Appendices C and D. We will give here a simplified interpretation of both Solar and Lunar eclipses for personal use. The appendices are for those who want to know more about eclipses.

The New Moon (Solar) Eclipse The light of the Sun will be partially or totally blocked by the body of the Moon, which is aligned exactly between Earth and Sun, so that the body of the Moon blocks out the light of the Sun. At the simplest level, this means that everything about this New Moon will be more intense. At the next level of understanding, the house that holds this New Moon tells you where in your life you need to *change your direction*. The Sun, representing spirit, always gives us direction at any phase, but at an ordinary New Moon, spirit offers direction for the whole month. Imagine you are captain of a ship and responsible for keeping on course. None of us is perfect or we wouldn't be here, as you have often heard. We often get off course in an area of our life, and a *Solar Eclipse* offers us the opportunity to make a course correction. One example of this is when we become so involved outside the home that we neglect our family life, or health. If that happened to you, you might find a Solar eclipse happening in your fourth house of the home or your sixth house of health.

One might say that the Moon (the past, unfinished business, etc.), by blocking the Sun (future, direction), requires us to change direction. Others say, the past changes the future, or rights a wrong, or reestablishes the balance.

The Full Moon (Lunar) eclipse. The reflected light of the Moon is blocked by the shadow from the Earth exactly between Sun and Moon. As Sun represents spirit, Moon represents *how we do things* in the process of soul manifesting Spirit's directions to us. So the message in the house of the Moon at a Lunar Eclipse is that *we need to change how we are doing things in this area of our life*. We use the following brief formula for all eclipses:

Key phrase for a New Moon (Solar) eclipse = the need for a change of direction in the house of the eclipsed Sun.

Key phrase for a Full Moon (Lunar) eclipse) = the need to change how we are doing things in the house of the eclipsed Moon.

We use all of our regular methods of interpreting our New and Full Moons, but add the above, giving it the greatest weight in the complete interpretation.

What Can I learn with this Chapter's Information?

What we can learn is the gift of astrology, but of course you don't need to be an astrologer to gain this information. The New Moon always contains three pieces of astrological information from which you can find literally pages of information valuable to your path. The New Moon is in a particular sign, and a particular house, of your Solar wheel, and on a particular degree of the Zodiac. The degree is found in your date book along with the sign. You can see in your own wheel the area of your life highlighted each month, and the nature of the life activity. The detailed description of the degree is in your Sabian Degree books. The other seven phases in a cycle offer six pieces of information because the Sun and Moon are always in separate houses except at New Moon.

Getting the most out of the three to six steps in the process will be easy for those who often think in terms of symbolism. As we have mentioned elsewhere, this will take some effort for those who don't. Symbolic thinking has a major connection to the ability of a person to access and use the right-brain. Society and its schools do not teach us about our own brains and how the two halves function. Several months to a year of Moon practice will change this if you are not naturally right-brained to begin with; so if this is not easy for you, it will become easier as you go along. The reward is that you will have built new neural pathways, and found more ways to use your brain. Of course the opposite follows if you are not naturally left-brained. In that case the multiplicity of factual details required in the later stages of Moon work will require some new neural pathways as well. Either way, if you are aging and *sage-ing*, the Moon path is good for keeping your brain young.

Listen to the Voices of the Elders

The Egyptians and Buddhists each had eight markers of wisdom. We do not know if the Buddhist list came out of some early connection to the Moon Cycles, but we have chosen to include them for their remarkable wisdom that truly fits and expands the meaning of each phase. This list, like so many "eights" all over the world, is so related in meaning to the eight phases that we expect there is an underlying principle in the number eight that tends to show up in such lists. And, in fact, in Greek philosophy and modern numerology, the first 10 numbers had specific meanings wherever they might be found.

The Egyptian Guardians of the eight windows of the phases are adapted from the work of Mark Robertson, who did the research. You can find his complete descriptions in a little book called *The Past in Your Astrological Birth Chart and Reincarnation*. He introduced them in reference to the Moon phase under which one is born and which governs one's personality throughout life. We find them equally helpful at the monthly level as iconic reminders.

The Buddhist list contains four attachments and four aversions, supposedly the most important elements in human growth, and vaguely reminiscent of the Catholic lists of cardinal and venial sins. Buddhism however has nothing to do with sin, as you probably know, and the aversions and attachments are simply common issues among all of us, which need to be gradually left behind as we grow.

They *will* be triggered for everyone throughout the year in one or another of the phases. The house and sign of each cycle at New Moon will be your personal area of life where that attachment or aversion might be an issue for you. You can use the eight attachments and/or eight guardians for each phase of any cycle. We will list the specific information at the end of each of the phase chapters.

The First of the Buddhist Eight-Fold Path Attachments: *Fame*. People with Leo-Sun star-like dramatic abilities are especially addicted to fame, but anyone can be, because everyone has Leo somewhere in their chart. Look at the house in your dial ruled by Leo. Wouldn't you like a little fame here, a little appreciation, admiration or esteem? That's OK. Just don't be addicted to it like some people you know! Interestingly, *notoriety* (the Full Moon's aversion) might result from misused fame.

The Egyptian Guardian of the New Phase *Amen-Ra,* the Sun. This Guardian represents the reproductive forces of life, and the form of your intent to be manifested during this cycle. Ra the Sun is the incarnating force. Suns and other stars are said to be great spiritual beings. If you like that thought, our Sun can be your guardian during this phase, lighting your path.

"Reading" the New Moon into Our Dials

This segment of the Part II chapters is where practical, hands-on information can help that feeling of cluelessness or being blocked. It can be a productive exercise, and at least set the positive patterns into your unconscious ahead of time.

First you collect your information and your tools, and fill in the blanks in the form below. Then follow the easy steps labeled in bold letters. We suggest you write out the information from the form in your journal, as you follow the steps of the process. Then "play" with them, making sentences or paragraphs, putting them together.

Tables found elsewhere in the book , including tables of signs and houses, will help clarify the interpretation of the New and Full Moons. Bookmark them for quick reference.

Most important is the Sun-Moon Phase Energies table(Table 9, Chap 11) which may be applied to signs in any phase. All of the tables will help you "read" the sign, house, Degrees and Phases all together—a confusing job however you look at it. That is a spiritual as well as mental practice and struggling with it will bring skill down the line, and help you internalize the information. It is interesting to note that in our time, the spiritual goal of humanity is to bring head and heart together, and the Moon path is one way to work at this. Both mind and heart are necessary for objectivity, understanding, and integration of the life of spirit and personality.

We now ask the following questions. Please open your journal to answer the questions.

1. In what area (house) is my New Moon intent beginning at this New Moon? the _____.
    Mark the house with a blue and yellow dot
2. What is the nature (sign) of this new beginning? _____.
    Copy the information from the table below into your journal
3. What is the New Moon's Zodiac Degree?_____

The Process

The first time you look at the above, it may seem very detached from your personal life. Right; so here is the nitty-gritty side of this cosmic process. We refer you to the chapter on signs for detailed information about them.

Following the steps in the process below for each phase will show you how to change your life by how you think, speak, and act, especially in critical situations. These tools will help you create your own personal blueprint for evolving consciousness.

The tools. Your tools are the following:

A Solar dial

The houses

The signs

The degree symbols

Maynard's Cosmic Guide

The example chart. We will use an example Solar chart of "Ed", a fictitious client with a first house *Scorpio* Sun sign. Set Ed's wheel now to that coordinate, and your second dial to your own Sun sign, so you can follow as we go through all eight of the phases, one chapter at a time.

In Ed's example, his employer has just eliminated some positions and otherwise cut back on spending. There is a newly created position open which will consolidate the surviving jobs. Ed's current job is personally limiting, insecure, and not even full time though he feels he could contribute much more to the company if he were full time. Frustrated, he is anxious about how this cutback may affect his job, but feels confident that he not only fully qualifies for the job he has, but that he would qualify for this higher level position in the same company. Everyone in the office agrees he would be perfect for the job. He eagerly enters the two weeks until Full Moon time, believing that after a tense few days, he will be given the new position, or at least more security in the job he has. We will suggest that he has access to all the information you the reader have, but in most cases, we will not suggest his moves, decisions, etc. We are using a cycle containing two eclipses, right at the beginning of the great economy drop of the Fall of 2,008.

At this point in the story, we start with a Solar (New Moon) eclipse that took place on August 1ˢᵗ, 2008 at 9 degrees of *Leo*. The 10ᵗʰ degree of Leo falls in Ed's 10ᵗʰ house. Please remember that a Solar eclipse is read just as a regular New Moon, with the exception that it also signals a change of course or direction in the house of the eclipse.

The House. This Lunar eclipse happened in *Leo*, so put your blue and yellow dots in Ed's 10ᵗʰ house which is aligned with *Leo* in his Solar chart. These two dots represent his spirit and soul meeting as in Ill I (first chapter), giving him the first key to the purpose of this month's cycle. This house of career will be highlighted for the whole of the Lunar month. He needs to pay attention to this part of his life as something new is beginning here, which as an eclipse also marks a change in his career <u>direction.</u>

The Sign. *Leo* is the second key. The sign on the New Moon house tells you something about the energies operating here. Find the table of sign descriptions in Chapter 9, and see how that describes Ed's career and his possibilities for achievement in this life. *Leo* likes drama and being a leader or the center of attention here. Career should be a field which allows Ed to be creative at work and contains opportunities for self-expression. He relates well to his co-workers as individuals, but *Leos* need to learn how to operate in groups in order to fulfill the sign. Since this is also an eclipse, we can say that the current situation clearly promises Ed a change of direction (or course correction) for his career. Something from the past (Moon) is blocking what he thought was his direction into the future. WHAT is beginning is a new seed-idea about that new direction.

The Degrees. Now find 9 degrees (the <u>10ᵗʰ</u> degree) of *Leo* in one of your degree books or in Appendix F in this book. Rudhyar's theme for this degree is *the exalted feeling that rises within the soul of the individual who has successfully passed through the long night which has tested his strength and his faith.* We might guess from this that Ed's career area has experienced a protracted period of frustration, difficulty, or perhaps being without a job. But this is going to change. Of course, at this point, the precise details are usually not available. Were you able to place this New Moon in your memories? If so, were you frustrated or ending a difficult period of time in the *Leo* area of your chart? Did you experience a change in direction there? There is a possibility, with this degree, that Ed may have begun this day with an unexpected release of anxiety over career issues, and either a sense of relief for no known reason, or possibly a piece of hopeful information has come to him.

The Phase Dynamics. The house, sign and degree answer the question of WHAT is beginning, and describe the overarching purpose and meaning of the whole cycle. This is the only phase wherein there is no distance between Sun and Moon, so the energies simply "are"— the essence of being. Even though the Moon begins immediately to move away from the Sun, that powerful initial message of "being"remains, only gradually dissipating throughout the following three days.

Table 10 encapsulates the personal phase dynamics between Sun and Moon. Table 11 below describes the transpersonal energy of each sign as it operates at any given New Moon.

ZODIAC	KIND OF NEW MOON ENERGY	FUNCTION OF THE NEW MOON SEED-IDEA
Aries	The impulse to begin something new.	Birth of an idea at the mental level with the urge to begin it immediately
Taurus	Illuminating, bringing light or spirit into the physical	To enlighten you about your desires
Gemini	Relating to, connecting with, people, ideas, things	Being the "3rd factor" (connection) between others or between ideas or things
Cancer	Manifesting, birthing values	nurturing the seeds of your ideas or children into physical reality
Leo	Sensitizing yourself to what is beyond your ego—the group, society, humanity	Immortalizes selfhood— moves you away from self-centeredness toward inclusiveness
Virgo	Nurturing the Higher Self in everything you do	Growing toward selfless or sacrificial service
Libra	Two things (or ideas or people) being weighed in the balance	The process of making choices
Scorpio	The battlefield (testing)of desires and addictions	(A) Purifies by fire. (B) channels energy through self to others

Sagittarius	Self directing, living one's ideals, ("searching for God"), "climbing the mountain"	Growth, expansion, reaching ever expanding goals
Capricorn	Culminating, "reaching the top of the mountain. The highest you can achieve. Position in the social structure.	Initiation, peak experience, bringing new responsibilities. The right use of resources, people
Aquarius	Knowing yourself as part of the human race	Scientific service: service geared to be most effective for the group.
Pisces	Absorbing (into a greater whole) without artificial boundaries	Restores and redeems, by renunciation of all barriers to what is and what can be.

Table 11. Transpersonal New Moon Energies adapted from Arcana Materials (see Bib.)

15

Crescent Phase: The Mother of Form Arises
The Initial Intent Begins to Take Form

When we come to the complete fragmentation and entombment in matter, to the rock bottom, we cannot depend on any outside thing to lift us up We must do it ourselves, and in that act, we are reborn.
—Arthur M Young,
The Reflexive Universe: Evolution of Consciousness

Phase 2—the Transition between Seed and Plant, Intent and Substance

This is the first of the transitional phases, occurring 3-1/2 days after New Moon Unless you have access to a detailed on-line ephemeris that we do not know about, or a software program which calculates the Moon's phases, you will probably not be able to do the degree symbols for the Sun and Moon of this phase. Sometime in the year of publication, our website will publish this information monthly for our readers. Later in this chapter we offer a rough calculation method that will give you the signs and houses, but not the degrees. Remember that the four main 90-degree phases are critical turning points of the cycle, guaranteeing manifestation. What is manifested is up to us as individuals and has a great deal to do with how we internalize the main four during the transitional stages.

The quotation above tells us the nature of manifestation. As long as a thing is still in the intent or idea stage, we can make whatever changes we choose. When the idea begins to incarnate or draw substance to itself in a form, it consists of pieces and parts and the over-all die is cast, so to speak. The rest is up to us. This does not imply that the Divine cannot "lift us up", but that the idea comes from the Divine and it is our nature as humans to "co-create" the idea by bringing it down into matter. This is how our universe works and this is the transition. The next phase needs a manifested idea to work with.

The Crescent Brings the Unfinished Past with the New Form

Just before the Crescent moment, two little generic leaves had burst through the soil and you began to feel an urge to move forward on something specific related to the house of the New Moon. The night sky was clean and Moon had reappeared in the most elegant fingernail sliver of her own new form.

Then, with the Crescent moment, heaven opens, spring pours down in torrents, lightning flashes, thunder sends us scattering and shouting. The recently sprouted seed hears "Hurry up!" and its true leaves begin to unfold, letting us see the form or variety of the plant—the form of our new project or intention.

It may also bring things from before this cycle began—things from the past that haunt you and pull you back. "Can't I fix that before I go on?" "I really can't go on with this hanging over me." Like seaweed clinging around our ankles as we wade back onto the sandy beach, unfinished business has a way of sucking our energy and keeping half of us facing backward like the two-faced God Janus. "Why didn't I take care of this during the quiet Balsamic phase when I had time?" Image this situation as the seed, at New Moon underground where it is unseen. The past it carries with it is first seen at Crescent because this is when the true plant first appears above ground. It seems as though once we start moving we can feel the past trying to pull us back. Or else it is like that annoying fly that keeps you swatting when you need to focus on the pudding so it won't boil. Of course, this bit of the past may be so small you don't notice it at all some months, but some will be quite noticeable.

We are at a critical repolarization point (a word you will read many times through this book.) Repolarization means you have to choose one direction or intent or belief over another. The energies are moving forward with increasing speed at this point, and guess what— if you do not follow them you will have the same problem next month on the Crescent Moon. Stay oriented toward the future at this point and if you really can fix things from the past, do it on the side so to speak. If by chance you are lucky, your new purposeful actions will automatically fix the unfinished business anyway. But even in that case, the past problem can not be resolved using the past attitudes or the old ways. Forward face!

Developing the Form of the Intent

Up to this point, you have conceived an urge to begin something in an area of your life, and now you are beginning to define and create a form for it. Sometimes it almost seems as if it takes form of itself. If it is beautiful, accept that it comes from inside you and take pleasure from a moment of joy. If it seems ugly, frightening, or otherwise uncomfortable, accept that your shadow side is taking an opportunity to be brought forth and integrated into your consciousness, thereby making you ultimately more whole. Shadow-things release some of your hidden power when integrated; and remember that what you see outside yourself is a mirror and often a gift of the Moon. The meaning will be found at the Full Moon and at the last quarter..

For now, give over to spirit the shaping of your task, if that fits your path. Or— find a way to allow your task to be what it is and work with it. The Sun has moved away from its New Moon position and is giving you an update on its initial message. It. will tell you spirit's purpose for the next step, and how it wants you to create. The Moon's degree, house, and sign (now 45 degrees away from the New Moon's single house) will tell you something about the form and how you can create it. Your job is to fit spirit and form together. The 45 degrees marking the Crescent phase are considered to be a difficult or struggling aspect, in the sense of a baby being born, but two days later it can resolve into creative harmony, where the newborn baby adapts to its mother from the outside world.

For Astrologers

In the phase-sign diagram (Chapter 12) the new phase began at 00 degrees Aries and ended on 15 degrees of Taurus. Crescent begins with 16th degree of Taurus and ends with 30 degrees Gemini. The characteristics of these signs operate in a hidden manner behind the actual signs of the phases. Consider them as undertones or background music, while this background music is a little like a CD playing the sound of birds when you are in the middle of winter, or water running when you are in the midst of summer and wishing it would rain. This background element, however, has its own reality and is part of the timing aspect of phases. We will bring this element up frequently in Part II, where the general reader may wish to use it, as well, but it is not necessary and not recommended until the reader is comfortable with managing the basic houses, signs and degrees of the lunations. Be aware that the phase only starts out as Taurus so that if you are a day into the phase, the energies change to Gemini. All phases with two signs operate in the same way.

Spreading Your Branches

This period is like the first draft of a poem—raw, direct, powerful, moving, but rough and incomplete. Let yourself flow with what comes from inside, and "edit" it later. In the plant metaphor, the first two little New Moon generic leaves are growing rapidly on fragile stems. The definitive second set now arrives, shouting "I'm here!", defining its identity (variety), but a driving rain or a strong wind, or someone's boot could so easily destroy it. Protect this fragile beginning. The first day is time for *making* time, to let your idea or plan grow and multiply as much as possible, even if it does feel fragile. The next two days are about reaching out and making connections—growing whole branches of leaves, collecting information or more ideas from books or people, the web, or your creativity, getting assistance, organizing. As leaves nourish the plant with Sunlight, you are nourished in some way by the connections to people and information.

The Crescent finishes with some possible opportunities revealed by these new connections. You have collected all the ideas or information, parts and pieces. It will soon be time to digest the information (knowledge or feelings), and complete the basic form during the 1st Quarter. The creative individual, or spiritual nature, in-forms the new intent as its external form emerges in the Crescent Moon's house and sign, described by degree.

By the end of this phase, the intent or plant will have outgrown its initial root system and must slow its reaching out in favor of building better foundations and stronger stems. If you are cleaning house, you can pull everything out of the cupboards, throw things away, make as much mess as you need to—until the end of this phase.

Problems One May Encounter

As I have read this over, I am struck with the image of a baby being born—kicking and screaming as if it has been forced to face the prime insult—the hard, cold world outside a womb it clearly would have been quite happy to remain in, if it weren't' so crowded.

There are problems that are peculiar to the Crescent Moon, and which parallel the birth of the plant, the idea, the baby. The problems may be with the environment itself, or with a fixation on the past. We have a completely new lesson to learn each and every month of our lives (even though we often wail, "I've been here before and I don't need this anymore") The Christian Gospel's parable about the seed cast on different kinds of soil is very apt and very realistic. Nothing, including a baby, often has the opportunity to be born in ideal circumstances We all have unfinished business from the previous cycle; and mental physical, emotional or spiritual environments often provide less than ideal ground for seeds to flourish in. This is a vulnerable moment for a new month. We often long for encouragement and support from others because we are used to "knowing what we are doing" and since we probably don't at this moment, we think praise from someone else will let us know we are "doing it right."

Another type of problem may be the fact that the month's seed-image is objectified at Crescent phase and what was only in your conscious or unconscious mind may now appear strange or alien to your previous concepts or to those of others. Some antagonism may be felt. Check to see if your way of objectifying this purpose is realistic, but otherwise consider continuing because this is your project, no one else's at this point. Logic is not yet an issue but creativity is.

Basically, if we are emotionally free and living in the moment, this should be a stimulating period of activity, but unfortunately few of us are free—of lingering doubts, fears, regrets and self-esteem issues. This will change in time after following the Moon path with integrity for several years. It is happening for us.

For the Astrologer

You can guess at the house and sign of Sun and Moon at Crescent, or any transitional Phase, using the following information. There are approximately 3-1/2 days (84 hours) between every previous cardinal phase and the next transitional phase. The Sun moves one degree every 24 hours and 3-1/2 degrees in 84 hours The Moon moves approximately 1 degree per every 2 hours, 12 degrees in24 hours, and 42 degrees in 3-1/2 days. If you can read the ephemeris, add the above amount to the position of the Sun. The Moon will always be 45 degrees ahead of the Sun at any transitional phase. These are very approximate, which is why each position in any phase must be individually calculated using astronomical mathematics, which this is not. Most readers may not be aware of this, but neither the Sun nor the Moon moves at exactly the same speed from day to day and month to month.

Listen to the Voices of the Elders.

The Eight-Fold Path of Attachment, *Praise.* This attachment goes with the second phase of the Moon, a time when our project is fragile and we may be also. Praise is good for the self-esteem and certainly should be desired for something well done. However, doing things *in order to* receive praise is an addiction or attachment which could raise its head here, interfering with a true sense of guidance and purpose. It could also refer to the leftovers from the last cycle. Neither praise nor blame is called for here since you probably haven't done anything to earn either one. If you are addicted, either praise or blame from someone can prematurely fix with a label the vulnerable new creative movement, shutting down the right brain, which is primarily operative at this point. Don't ask for praise; don't loudly announce what you are doing, if you think you might not like the answer..

Egyptian Guardian of the Crescent Phase *Khensu,* the Moon. The Guardian of the Crescent phase represents the form or vehicle of the idea that you are manifesting in the house of the crescent Moon–that which the spirit must now take over. You can trust your instincts here, or your guidance, or higher self. Remember, the Sun is the spirit that gives the Crescent Moon a message. That message is about how spirit wants to work together with you (Moon).

"Reading" the Crescent Moon into Your Own Dial.

Set up your wheel and gather the information for the blanks below. We will be using the actual Crescent Moon degrees for the interpretation of "Ed's" chart. If you do have access to accurate transitional phase degree information, by all means use it and the degree information books. However, If you are following along using your own chart for the same dates, you will be using the degrees and signs discussed herein.

1) The Sun sign of the Crescent Moon phase_____

   house_____, and Degree if possible

   _____

2) The Crescent Moon's sign_____
   _____ house_____, and Degree if
   possible_____

3) Place two different-colored sticky-dots on the two houses of
   the signs above It will be helpful to use the same two colors
   each month, such as yellow for the Sun and blue for the
   Moon Note the activities of the Sun's house, using our sign
   and houses table.

4) Use Table 9 (p. 162) to see how the energy flows between
   the Sun's house and the Moon's house.

5) Using table 9, describe how and where the information/
   energy flows in your life at this Crescent Moon phase.

6) Sun's message: In the Sun's house, spirit is bringing me a
   message about the form of this month's intent._____
   _____

7) Moon's Response: In the Moon's house I am looking for a
   clue to the actual outer nature of my New Moon project.

The Process—Putting it Together

"Ed's" example chart. In Ed's chart, the New Moon Sun was
eclipsed at 9 Leo in Ed's 10th house of career. The Sun of this Crescent
phase is now at 12 *Leo*, still in the 10th house; the Moon is at 27
Virgo, his 11th house.

The Houses. In Ed's example, the New Moon in the 10th house
of career indicated this whole cycle would be about a career change
as described in the previous chapter. The Sun of the Crescent is
offering guidance or purpose from the career house to the Moon in
the 11th house of major life goals, social relationships, and associates
connected to career. Moon is form-building in the 11th which might
indicate that Ed is building a base of relationships to support and
bring new values into his career .He hopes this 11th house emphasis
will contribute to the change coming in his career.

You have put a yellow dot in your own *Leo* house and a blue
dot in your Virgo house, and of course your houses will probably be
different from Ed's two. These two dots represent spirit-Sun (yellow)
and Moon-soul (blue), separating, as in Ill I (first chapter), giving
Ed's or your own chart the second key to the purpose of this month's
cycle. Moon is separating from Sun, making it possible to "see" the
beginning form of the new seed-intent, described by the activities of
this *Virgo* area of life.

The Signs. Ed's 10th house *Leo* represents self-expression and creativity, and he loves self-expression and drama at work. A higher expression of *Leo* here can be creative leadership, the ability to encourage employees, well-earned pride in a job well done, and respect for others. A negative expression might include being arrogant, a "wheeler-dealer", needing to be the center of attention, all show and no substance, etc. What might *Leo* sound like in your *Leo* house?

The *Virgo* Moon describes the nature of Ed's unfolding seed intent. 11th house V*irgo* friends or associates can define and refine the 10th house *Leo* expression, which *Leo* often needs from *Virgo*. His seed intent takes its first form from the nature of this 11th house, suggesting that part of the promised career change is about social connections of some sort. Perhaps it is a group of clients, or of contacts for networking. Building the first form for major change (eclipse) in the 10th is to use *Virgo's* 11th house abilities in practical application of creative career endeavors. The *Leo* career change will initially be manifested in the 11th house which equates to the 11th sign, *Aquarius* (technology, innovation, humanitarian.) This will help Ed develop skills in the group-oriented side of the very individual-oriented *Leo* sign. One could read this house as suggesting that Ed project his best side to people who might be future clients, or people he knows in other departments or careers who might help him get a good position.

The picture is positive if he uses all his signs and houses at the highest level to get all the benefits. However, since we do not have a complete chart, we don't know how he as been using his talents or how he will use them after the eclipse. In a negative scenario, he could have been flaking off at work, counting on his charm to carry him through, and may lose his job due to criticism (*Virgo*) from his office buddies.

The Degrees. In Ed's example, the Sun was at 12 *Leo* (read 13th Leo) and the Crescent Moon at 27 *Virgo* (read 28th Virgo.) Throughout the cycle, we can see how the slowly moving Sun degrees provide up-dated messages that operate out of the original New Moon message. The Moon degrees provide up-dated information on building varying aspects of the month's intent.

The Crescent Moon degree in the career associates 11th house offers *the sheer power of personality in times that call for decision.* This is a powerful energy which can bring impactful results in either negative or positive directions. Ed should focus all of the most positive qualities of his personality in his career issues at this time, realizing and projecting *who he is* in the 11th house at the core level, rather than who he fantasizes he is, or wants to be (a pattern of negative Leos).

The Moon degree also carries the keywords, *the power of the will,* and also suggests a possible "take-over" of power by someone else . Very clearly, Ed must either exert will power here, or watch out for someone in the house of associates and contacts related to the company who does some kind of takeover which may not be beneficial to Ed, but which will be out of his hands (read the entire 28th degree Virgo.) We can use this degree to describe the form the cycle takes. Not everything in a degree commentary will apply to everyone. We recommend picking out what applies to your life right now and using that to describe the form your Crescent Moon is taking.

The Rudhyar theme for Ed's Crescent Sun degree (read 13th *Leo*) is *The quieted mind's recollections of crises and joys long past.* We can read this as the purpose or meaning behind the Moon's action; it is about being able to use the wisdom of past experience in current situations, in this case in the career arena.

Since this follows an eclipse signaling major change in direction of career, it implies that a decision is required or a change in his patterns of behavior early on when the form is being created. He is cautioned by spirit, from the 10th house, to draw on his past experience to make this change (as opposed to relying on hunches and uninformed ego-opinions.) Apply these interpretations to your dial to see if you can tell what the form of your Crescent Moon was about.

16

First Quarter Phase: Outer Crisis in Consciousness
Establishing the New Moon's Intent in the Outer World

This reaching out in the first Quarter Moon occurs as the personality delights in clearing the landscape of old structures so new forms can come to life under the Gibbous Moon
--Marc Robertson, *Time Out of Mind*

Phase 3—the <u>HOW</u> of It

This is the phase that answers the question of how we will go about building new foundations for the New Moon intent. Dr. Wayne Dyer in a PBS televised lecture gave a pointed answer to this question with the story of a young man who asked Mozart to teach him how to write symphonies. Mozart replied, "Go home and practice writing etudes for a few years." The man, a bit miffed, complained, "But you were writing symphonies at age five—who taught you?" Mozart replied, "No one. The symphonies came to *me*."

That is a hard answer, but the truthful one. Inspiration (the How) comes to you from your Higher Self; you can't ask someone else for it or how to get it. However, we often get our inspiration tickled by reading the Sun's degree symbol for this quarter. It presents an image or idea that resonates deeply enough to trigger our own intuitive answer. The other and best way it comes is by being so in touch with our inner true selves that the answer is obvious. We know this is not always true for everyone, which is why we encourage you to check out the Sun's symbolic degree. Just the act of meditating on the symbol can open up your own personal store of intuition.

The Sun offers suggestions from spirit, the Moon offers the methods we actually use or refuse. The Sun most likely will be the voice of our own inner core while the Moon will contain the instinctive knowledge of manifestation. Moon also contains whatever learned patterns may be blocking that core-self from breaking through the walls of the world outside ourselves with our ideas or structures. The world outside may be others or society or it may be the old patterns themselves which have been internalized from the world outside: "I can't do this because......, etc." Remember, the learned patterns are ways of manifesting that we may or may not have outgrown. The limitations of childhood do not belong in adulthood.

Each generation uses its creativity in new ways (we hope) in order to improve the system beyond what our parents created. This is part of the plan for evolution: each generation must outgrow some of the parents' cultural patterns and create new ones that their own children will later hopefully outgrow. It is easy to see how the seeds of *evolution* and *r-evolution* grow from the same roots. If yours is one of the latter, you will see it at the Last Quarter Moon. It seems in our view that this First Quarter phase gives us the greatest opportunity for us to do either, whether we are young adults or old adults.

If the plant does not start a strong root and stem system at this point the branches will over-weigh it and it will simply fall over.. The Mozart answer reveals that too much reaching out to others (branches) after the close of the Crescent phase leaves one disconnected from one's center from which the core nourishment and creativity comes.

The ultimate result of these conflicting factors often creates a crisis in the Moon's house. Remember, *it is through crisis that we develop our identity*. Each month we have this opportunity to define our identity a little more. When the outer self, patterned by family and society, allows this still fragile inner self to use its muscles and become strong, then one is ready. The answer to the question "How" will come to you. In any case, the "crisis" is more often than not an exhilarating one if you are working from your Higher Self.

The Importance of Action to Build Foundations

Do you remember from the chapter on Ritual, where the last step of ritual was to leave the gathering and go do the wisdom of the spirits' message? This is like that—the New Moon was the message, and now you have to bring it into manifestation. The actual foundation and outer structure (roots and stems) are to be built now.

The soul is ready to activate the new project, to challenge it with crisis. We are ready to *activate* something. In other words, as we said, it is not enough to get the message. You have to make that phone call that will be "putting your money where your mouth is." Blaschke calls it decisive action taken by the soul to manifest concretely what is within the Self. It is you taking a first step in breaking from the past by paying attention to what your inner core says versus what your habits and patterns tell you. This is new business, even if it is something so minor you would ordinarily not give it a second thought, just moving ahead automatically. Often, though, you know that someone is not going to react well to your taking a new kind of action instead of doing what you've always done, and which others expect. Naturally there will also be some inner conflict when you override your "expected" ways of acting. The reader is here again reminded that a "project" is not always in 3-D. You may be studying for a test, working out a relationship problem, dealing with a health issue, involved with an office problem, or doing a "a make-over" with diet or exercise—or whatever you are doing at this time of the Lunar month. But your actions now will affect others, so be sure that the actions are what your whole self wants. Your purpose here is not to please others unless that is what the month's theme is about. But you walk a fine line because you actually need for others to accept the project once the field is cleared.

The Moon path tells us that *whatever is set during this period keeps on developing, for better or for worse.* It is irreversible. Negative use of this phase's energy comes from *mental hesitancy or a confusion of values, both of which sap the power to act or build.* This phase contains, with its increased activity, stresses and strains, your most creative energies; therefore the decisions made here are of prime importance for what is to come. The instructions on how to complete a new project are based in your own core. You want to be centered and grounded so that your intent becomes a worthy product to fulfill yourself or to offer society as a "second seed".

Establish is a key word for this phase and for building foundations. Mentally establish that centeredness each morning of the First Quarter. Even if you feel that what you are doing is of little significance, take this part seriously. Every month is an opportunity, however small, to increase your consciousness. The Sabian Symbols will be remarkably helpful to you in this phase, because they help to sort out which thoughts or feelings belong to the patterned self (Moon degree) and which are from one's center (Sun degree). The Moon's position by house and sign may remind us of something we were taught that is appropriate, or not, in the present situation. The Moon is the Doer, its house is where we are working at the month's theme, and the first thoughts may be, "I learned how to do it this way". We may have to balance that against the Sun's position which reminds us that we are doing something completely new (to ourselves), and the approach or technique also needs to be new. However, just as often as not, what you learned and what you feel from your center that you need or want to do, will agree and you can be grateful your parents or society taught you a skill you can now use.

Another, simpler way to view the first Quarter is to say that *the Moon is what you are manifesting, while the Sun is the purpose or meaning behind it.*

You meet the source of your inspiration, your inner being, the moment you encounter inner/outer conflict or patterned social barriers and recognize them as such, while not allowing yourself to *identify* with them—in other words, you are "staying with your self". You are not your habitual patterns. Most early patterns had a useful purpose at one time, and many are good for a lifetime, but you need to know which are which.

Meet the Family

Moon is exactly half light, half dark—half masculine thrusting energy and half feminine receptive energy—half logical mind and half feelings; it is the perfect balance for creativity and inspiration, in active pairing with action. As my son would say irreverently, "Time to kick ass!" or, as the Bible would say, "faith without works is dead." On diagram (I) the Moon (soul) has moved halfway down the path from Spirit to Personality. This is the challenge point. Moon's shadow represents every stored memory from birth to now. All the things we have been taught in school, home, society are there. Sometimes specific ones will be triggered by, and confront, our own new action ideas. How will we handle this? Which technique for action will we choose—the one from our inner source of inspiration or the one we learned so long ago?

Imagine the family gathered outside the front door as you approach to tell them that you are doing exactly the thing they always said you couldn't do. This is a perennially new situation where decision and action are required, and what we have been taught regarding this month's purpose may no longer be useful, at least in its present form. However, at this point we need to be discriminating enough to see and use appropriate past learning that will be helpful, since often the teachings of the elders are the door to society's acceptance.

This is meant to be a cooperative venture, not a rebellion, though if that is your path the term may be valid for you.

There is, however, another kind of situation requiring what appears to be an opposite kind of action. If one is working on a highly spiritual or "way out" artistic project, one needs to become extremely aware of what others might think, need, or accept from you. If you want your brand of Spirituality to be presented to others then it must be at their level, in forms they can immediately connect with where they are now.

But where are we in this phase, right now? Have we learned that it is not OK to succeed, not OK to do something new, not OK to follow our own creativity, not OK to question what we have learned? Do we then turn away from past fears, doubts, or other emotional signals triggered from outside ourselves? If someone says, "you can't do it that way, because 'they' won't like it", "it's never been done", "it's too much for you" or some other standard objection, will you break through the doubts and continue something you feel deeply you can or must do? And what if you don't succeed completely? You will learn something very valuable from the experience. Naturally you want to check the validity of others' logic, but do it objectively. Explore alternatives for enhancing your creativity, but essentially, follow your creative instincts and your own feelings. Or, rather, give each equal time.

Dealing with the Family

The western concept of "clearing the field and breaking through barriers" or outer resistances so often is one of "so just do it!" That often sounds pushy or obnoxious, even though it gets the job done. We think the Eastern way may sound more appropriate in some situations. Karcher in his *I Ching* suggests an alternative as subtle penetration of hard ground, by the roots and trunk of a tree, as a classic generic description of the way to get something important done in a resistant situation. As usual, we have found the oriental way of doing conflictive things is subtler and more diplomatic than the ways of the West. The *I Ching* is full of simple, earthy nuggets about how to live life. "Subtle Penetration" is a sweeter way to break through barriers, clear the ground and establish our territory, although not always possible in some cases.

An old friend, (who was actually born under a 1st Quarter Moon) taught in the government nursery schools during the 2nd World War. Interestingly she was a lifetime follower of Krishnamurti, practicing

Hindu Buddhism. The following scenario occurred as she was having a progressed 1st Quarter Moon. She saw some out-dated authoritarian practices in the team teaching system and knew how they could be improved. However she was not well accepted by the others, as being too young, progressive and free in her manner for their style, which they did not see as needing change. Using Krishnamurti's teachings, she subtly began in tiny ways to change what she did in her own classroom, quietly sharing the results with the others, who sometimes unsuspectingly incorporated them in their classrooms. She was terrified at first, and nearly lost her job, but the others finally admitted her ideas into their own teaching. Later, she became the lead teacher in that unit.

The Importance of Cause and Effect

The Ancients learned from cause and effect. It was all they had to work with if their lives were as we imagine. From their environment they learned to understand and manipulate numbers, language, letters, words, as well as to plant and harvest, and one of the effects of these expansions was the evolution of consciousness. We still do, individually, learn this way. Our parents may tell us that touching the stove is dangerous and it will hurt; but this author vividly remembers, at age three in a home with a wood stove, deliberately touching the stove to see if her parents "were right".

Consciousness is still built on the foundations of dealing with the cause and effect of real life in the here and now. The child touching the stove took a step in finding her identity. No matter how small, there will most likely be an inner or outer conflict at this point in the month. How we deal with it both comes from, and leads to, who we are. The person who has always reacted angrily in certain situations, but who gives instead a soft answer for the first time, creates immediate new neurons in her brain, and sees herself in a new light afterwards. We mention such things as identity here, because the waxing phases are all about developing our individuality. Cause and effect on the waning side of the cycle may have different implications. This 1st Quarter phase is specifically about building identity, and learning from cause and effect resulting from trying new things or ways of thinking.

This phase represents outer crisis because demands—in terms of Yang and Yin, creative imagination and logical thinking—are in equal balance here. They are usually assumed to be mutually exclusive, which often produces a tug-of-war between the polarities. It is the focal point of cause and effect in the Moon's cycle. The cause and effect process is activated whenever you act on a decision. Here you weigh your sense of individuality against your socio-parental mind-set, your right and left brain involvement. The Moon didn't invent this—it is the nature of a human within a historic cultural context. The stakes are high because identity is forged in this phase. Causes are set in motion whose effects can not be changed later. Courage is sometimes needed here. Not moving ahead in your truest direction has the effect of not breaking through old barriers, not establishing your territory, not developing the bio-psychic muscle to reap the benefits of the Full Moon, and that mythical reaching for the Sun.

The issue of cause and effect arises out of the absolute need for action at this point. Zodiac signs are so arranged (not by us!) that at every quarter-cycle they are at what we call cross-purposes, or as described earlier at 90 degree angles to each other.. We are the ones with the polarity patterns. The demands of the first and third quarter-phases are not so much about integration of opposites (also polarities) as about resolution of conflict. With personal divisions of heart and mind or individuality and social patterning, we approach the 1st Quarter's so-called problems with "divided minds" which can prevent us from making the decisions on action to deal with the problems. If we do not take action, the foundation of the cycle's manifestation is never built, and our evolutionary growth cannot happen.

Below we have a table of Zodiac signs. We suggest that you start with a sign and compare every fourth sign from it. The process will only need to be repeated twice more and all the signs will be covered. Consider the meanings of the signs and ask yourself how you would resolve the qualities so they could work together. For each phase's Sun sign, the fourth sequential Moon's sign will need conflict resolution, while the 6th or opposite sign from your beginning sign will require integration of opposites. Note that in this system, we start the count with the first sign and include it as well with the fourth sign, like this: (1)-Aries, (2)-Taurus, (3)-Gemini, (4)-Cancer. The next pairing begins with Taurus, and the last begins with Gemini.

One way of looking at this task is to consider your hard-won values and apply them. As we commented in an earlier chapter, and an earlier paragraph above, the most powerful thing one can do is to act according to our higher values in a situation where we have learned to go with our lesser feelings and increase the conflict.

Have you ever observed how a person going the extra mile or doing a random act of kindness, etc. achieves a positive effect out of a negative causal situation?

Completing the Root System

The task here is to complete the root system and strengthen the trunk of the tree or stem of the Sunflower (or the Moonflower if it is an inner or mystical project). The trunk or stem represents the identity, which enfolds the core self. Once you have acted, take responsibility for your actions. Dare we say, "Strengthen your backbone"? Be sure your projected idea is based upon solid facts, substance, emotional satisfaction, etc. Do the homework if you haven't already done so, and enter an exhilarating moment of expansion and *break-through*, the true creative essence of this phase. Jupiter the principle of growth and optimism is on your side, since it rules the First Quarter Phase. Like bungee-jumping, it can be a heady experience.

We are serious when we add here that the above paragraph applies even to unpleasant life-tasks, such as legal suits, someone's final illness, filing bankruptcy, losing a job, and so forth. We have found that our ability to accept these difficult experiences and our emotional reactions to them as adventures in consciousness has grown measurably during the recent years. It is clear to us that the Moon practice has played a large role.

And here is another point. We are reminded again of those ghosts of the past. They may be hidden in the parent-tapes you are hearing. If you want the illumination promised by the Full Moon, you must finish clearing the *ground* your tree is growing *in* of its remaining unfinished business from the past. You may have current shadow issues to take care of—an allergy to the problem of needing to do something others wish you wouldn't. That means separating your identity appropriately from the matrix out of which it emerges. At the entrance to the next phase, you will pass the Last Chance Tavern where you could be stuck if you do not complete the reorientation that rears its head in this First Quarter-phase of the cycle—and just when you think you have finished with that, it hits you again at 3ʳᵈ Quarter phase with more recent dingbats. This is the eternal nature of the Moon, and of you.

I am fascinated by the image or degree symbol for 1 Cancer, the analog to the first Quarter Moon, found in Chapter 11, Diagram

III. The image is of sailors taking down the ship's flag and hoisting another showing a change in alegiance.

If you can, treat this phase as if you were climbing Mt. Everest—a challenge offering an exhilarating and rewarding achievement, hard and painful though every step may sometimes be (according to successful achievers of such challenges). You might emagine taking a new flag to replace an older one that is no longer relevant.

Listen to the Voices of the Elders

The Eight-Fold Path of Attachment: *Pleasure*. A perfectly nice word reveals the weak spot in this phase. It is attachment that spoils it. Pleasure is good, and to be desired. Attachment to it or anything else is addiction, and it will cloud our judgment and put us to sleep at the wheel. A fully involved creative person, by nature, will derive his/her pleasure from the exciting challenge of the 1st Quarter. An ambivalent, fearful, or angry person may use familiar pleasures as a distraction or avoidance. Addictions help us avoid hard work, chances taken for our ideas, criticism, or loss of popularity or love. This is shadow work.

The Egyptian Guardian of the 1ST Quarter Phase: Maat, the planet *Jupiter*, is the representative of growth and expansion. First Quarter is the phase of the most active external growth in the cycle. In ancient Egypt, Jupiter/Maat represented reality, the right way, action through the vehicle. Growth is the result of following "the right way" and acting, not just thinking about it. The issue could be: whose vision of the right way are you following?

The most effort of the cycle is needed in this phase, and that means hard work. This is not the moment to take a time out at the beach or in bed with a novel. Eat some chocolate and keep your sleeves rolled up. Take pleasure in the action itself.

"Reading" the 1st Quarter Moon into Your Own Chart Wheel

Collect the information listed below and find your own way of putting it together that makes sense to you.

1. Mark the two houses on your dial with the stickydots_____
2. The 1st Quarter Sun's sign_____
    House Position_____

3. The 1st Quarter Moon's sign_____
   House position_____
4. Activities of the Sun's house, using our houses keyword tables _____
5. Activities of the Moon's house_____
6. Nature (sign) of the Sun's activity_____
7. Nature (sign) of the Moon's activity_____
8. Sun's Message (degree symbol)_____
9. Moon's Response (degree symbol)_____

The Process

Ed's Chart. This phase is about challenge. Ed's Higher Self or Spirit (Sun) is challenging his incarnated personality (Moon) to make a decision about doing things according to his core self. Using the positive Sun-sign and Moon-sign energies in their houses will help that happen. If he doesn't understand what is happening right now, he can simply ask the Sun what the purpose is behind what he is doing in the Moon's house.

The Houses. The Sun's house and the Moon's house are in a challenging (90 degree) relationship to each other. In Ed's chart, Sun was at 16 *Leo* and the 1st Quarter Moon was at 16 *Scorpio*. 1st Quarter Moons are about grounding or building foundations for the New Moon seed-intent. The Sun's message can be thought of as his purpose, and the Moon's position may or may not represent the argument: "I've always done it this way and it worked, so it is good enough for me now." On the other hand, you are already connected to your core self and are simply faced with something that you question your ability to do—you went to climb a hill with your friend and it turned out to be a small mountain. In that case, the Sun may be telling you to try it, anyway. Deciding to climb it to prove your invincibility, however, is not a reason to think you are engaging with your Higher Self here. Moon needs to use common sense and find a way for you to deal with this situation that challenges you, but not past reason. Read the degree symbols to see how we reached this conclusion.

In Ed's example, the Sun of the 1st Quarter Moon is now still in the 10th house. The Moon is in *Scorpio*, having moved into his 1st house of self, personal matters, new experiences. Here action (Moon) is speeding up, intensity has been building. Ed is already going full bore ahead on whatever he is doing, which we think started in the 11th house. He may have been busy connecting with others in the company or some of his own friends, or possible clients should he end up with a job.

At Crescent phase the Sun's guidance from the career house offered suggestions about the Crescent Moon's 11th house form-building . Now the scene changes to the 1st house. Ed's career area Sun has new instructions about how to ground his job-change through personal action (Moon). The signs and degree symbols below will contain the specific instructions.

You have put a blue dot in your own *Leo* house and a yellow dot in your *Scorpio* house, and of course your houses will probably be different from Ed's two. What information do they have for you?

The Signs. Here, the Scorpio Moon shows Ed in his element (he has natal Scorpio Sun in the first house driving his will power (remember that one?) and all the Scorpio tenacity and willingness to fight for what he wants to get. Ed's 10th house *Leo* Sun continues to offer guidance from Higher Self about doing the "personal" career thing in his 1st house—with pride and self-assurance. Since Ed's birth Sun is in this house, the Moon's position here is particularly significant. It may represent a significant piece of his life purpose. His personal abilities and very consciousness are at stake as he builds the foundations of his original project. The Moon here in the natal Sun's house shows that what he is manifesting is part of his overall life destiny, and that the Solar eclipse is trying to get him on that path. He may be inclined to follow the Higher Self; but Moon does contain social-parental personal patterns of action which may be different than what spirit suggests. The sign *Scorpio* describes the nature of this stage of the project. Using the sign table below, we see that the following qualities and characteristics may apply: *Scorpio* channels energy through self to others, and any desires and addictions will be tested. In really important situations purification by fire may describe the latter. Since *Leo* is highlighted, we might imagine that pride, desire for praise and acclaim, making dramatic impressions on people, could be addictive for him. The natal first house occupied by the transiting Moon here increases the importance of "doing this phase well" and playing down the drama. It is like two Scorpio statements augmenting each other.

The process might be stated as follows: Ed needs to be realistic in completing his project, and not allow personal needs and wishes for Scorpio control (an extreme of Scorpio in some people) to dominate.

Instead, when involved with groups, he should allow himself to be a channel for their ideas or energies rather than to push his own. Only the degree symbols will give us the details.

The Degrees. Ed's Sun degree of 16 *Leo* (read 17ᵗʰ degree) brings him spirit's update, about *the feeling of togetherness which unites men and women in their dedication to a collective ideal*. He needs that perhaps new attitude with which to approach building foundations for the project and breaking through social barriers that may challenge him.

Ed's Moon degree of 16 *Scorpio* tells him he should *have total reliance upon the dictates of the God-within*, a fitting degree for the 1st house. This degree falling into the 1ˢᵗ house of the self gives Ed's personality a strongly individualistic tone, which would need some adjustment to work with the Leo Crescent Sun's degree of togetherness and the collective ideal. Since the Sun degree speaks from the career house, we might see this togetherness statement as a job expanding into new territories, literally or symbolically. There could be many more employees, a more complex infrastructure, or a need for Ed to motivate employees to dedication to some high goal. This could be a major learning experience for an individualistic *Leo*. As we have earlier commented concerning opposites, one could read this as Ed being asked to align himself with the group and through that powerful alignment receive from within the way to align strong self-reliance with group oneness, as appropriate leadership

Meanwhile Ed's Moon may actually be focused upon the *Scorpio* tendency of "I trust my own gut-level and I think it should be done my way." On the other side of it, *Scorpio* owns an interesting key phrase of "I need to understand myself." This phrase applies to any *Scorpio* Sun, Moon, OR Rising sign. Quite unexpectedly Ed may therefore be aware of this need and be drawn to explore some depths of his *Scorpio* personality. It could be an interesting journey because *Scorpio* is a fixed sign, stubborn, disliking change yet fascinated by it. Scorpio is, indeed, the sign of change and letting go of ego-oriented patterns. Transiting Moon there can be hooked into the Scorpio message and make some needed changes. Ed may therefore finish this month with a more inclusive way of looking at people, his career, and his own personal self.

A final note. If you think deeply about the degree symbols and the signs they characterize, you will see an amazing internal consistency among the sign and degree symbols as they might be read in your own chart as well as Ed's. We found the same consistencies in our own charts, even though our situations were vastly different, as neither of us is out looking for a job or a career change, and the Sun and Moon were both in different signs and houses—different from Ed's and different in each other's charts. We think your readings will be equally internally consistent. Start with the degree messages in which transiting Sun here is telling you that, while Moon needs you to trust your deepest self in the *Scorpio* house, you must do that in the context of a larger picture that includes building togetherness in your *Leo* house.

Because the first quarter Moon tends to stir up negative emotions, we add below T. 16, with some of the negative uses of the signs.

SIGNS	POSITIVE USES	NEGATIVE USES
ARIES	Assertive, act on own ideas, help those who would follow one into new territories	Pushiness, arrogance, inability to listen to others' ideas. Forging ahead while leaving the mess behind for someone else to clean up. Impatient, careless of risks.
TAURUS	Build. Put Aries ideas into form. Enrich, produce results through practical effort. Nurture the senses with beauty.	Physical and material excesses, stinginess. Passive in the face of others' needs. Rigidly unchangeable to the point of "stuck-ness"
GEMINI	Spread out, "get the facts", make contacts, collect facts, understand both sides, relate opposites.	Scattered, shallow, or talking too much. Constant switching from one thing or idea to another.

CANCER	Nurtures things people and ideas into being. Finds and protects security and belongingness, expresses deepest values when it feels secure.	Clinging, possessive, sentimental, wants to be taken care of. Uses "the silent treatment"
LEO	With self-assurance, I put my mark on ideas, things, or persons	Avoid casting shadows or demanding to be the center
VIRGO	I ask questions, figure things out, sift information, organize details, and eliminate non-essentials. I am helpful and give others what they need	Requiring perfection, while resisting criticism from, others. Micromanaging in a work situation.
LIBRA	I coordinate & relate to, people or artistic elements. I cooperate and beautify. I am objective	It is good to see both sides but avoid indecision, and never making up your mind
SCORPIO	Focus intensity, gain self-control through self-understanding	Avoid holding on to negative emotions. Being controlling
SAGITTARIUS	I broaden contacts, search for significance, share ideas. I follow a star beyond ego-boundaries.	Avoid arrogance and inflated expectations
CAPRICORN	I am response-"able", for right-use of social power. I have something worth selling here in this House.	Avoid rigidity, stinginess, coldness, self-righteousness, self-limitation

AQUARI-US	I break up limiting personal or social patterns. I innovate, expect a miracle, I am Intuitive	Ignore individual needs, not compassionate toward others
PISCES	Project your dream into the future and walk toward it. Leave the past behind. Dissolve ego-boundaries by loving the rejected in self and others	Avoid glamour, denial, don't confuse others.

Table 12. Negative and Positive Uses of the Signs

17
Gibbous Phase:
The Spiritual Apprentice
Perfecting the Form with the Magical Firebird

*Eastern [US] Native Americans called fire 'our Grandfather Fire',
and believed its smoke carried the words of prayers up to the
supreme deity.*
—Funk and Wagnall's *Standard Dictionary of
Folklore, Mythology, and Legend*

Phase 4—Transition from Individual to Social Consciousness

Gibbous begins with the second half of Leo background energy and finishes with the full Earth sign of Virgo. Western Astrology assigns Earth to the Gibbous phase and generally says nothing about fire except to mention that spirituality is born here. Fire is spirit and we bring some bit of spirit to birth in the process of perfecting what we are finishing here.. However, surprisingly Kabbalistic Astrology states that all the signs (here Virgo Earth) have an inner element different than its obvious external element— here Earth always nurtures fire inside. So in this roundabout way we see how Eastern and Middle Eastern roots of the sign meanings help us understand modern Western signs at a deeper level. As you read on, note that we naturally call forth our personal spiritual powers as we move away from the greater spirit of New Moon to our own autonomy at the Full Moon.

We are moving from the power of our own creative source (1st Quarter Moon) toward the power of alliance (Full Moon). Entering the Full phase directly from the 1st Quarter without the Gibbous energies would be like going onstage naked. That is how you could actually feel at Full Moon if you did not have the wisdom of Gibbous

Moon to prepare you. "Oh, my goodness, I'm not ready for this!!!" Of course you might feel that way anyway if stage fright is your thing. But this transitional phase energy supports some adjustments that are needed between the third and fifth Moons, plus the practical application of one's deepest creativity. All four transitional phases assist us in integrating the material and spiritual sides of our actions (waxing) and ideas (waning). In the Gibbous, our effectiveness is supported by our doing our part. It "dresses" us for our personal act in the outside world. In the Gibbous phase we can find some spiritual essence coming through from the inside to help us find our voice or make our mark. There is also a sense, in looking at a Gibbous Moon, of something being unbalanced. The moon on our book cover is a Gibbous Moon, which accounts for its strange shape. Perhaps the following can explain.

The Touch of the Divine

Mythically, Gibbous stands between *overcoming, in a struggle between the external forces* of 1st Quarter Moon) *and the illumination* of the Full Moon. In terms of a lifetime, the Gibbous *search for illumination* often requires one to travel through a dark night of the soul, or cross a dark river or a desert. Such experiences can draw us into the religious or the spiritual, through which we realign ourselves with our life purpose or a search for spirit ready for rebirth. The transiting Moon phases of this book often reflect such past experiences or prepare us for future ones. Sometimes they present us instead with a true sense of the spiritual behind what we are doing.

The Gibbous Moon is *convex*. Not yet fully round, the perfect half-Moon becomes convex on the right or light side soon after the 1st Quarter when the sides become asymmetrical with the light half becoming convex or bulging, and the left half becoming concave.. There is a mystery, an unanswered question. Maybe a task is not finished, but in our shortsightedness we think that it is complete. There also may be a certain freedom that has not existed earlier in the cycle, suggested by the non-symmetry with its indeterminate possibilities. This time just before the Full Moon is traditionally said to be one of the most spiritual of the phases because it is nearly "full of light". Your spirit has co-created and embodied a form. The spirit itself is not yet seen, but it radiates outward from the person or his/her project, a possibility that only happens if the person at some level chooses that option. By Full Moon the form created by an individual has to some degree been perfected. The inner radiance becomes the full reflected light of spirit, demonstrating the integration of spirit and matter. Your Moon-personal-self is reflecting all of spirit's light that it can hold at that point in time. Hopefully, it has become worthy of contribution to the collective. But until the Full Moon, the contribution is not perfect, not complete. Something is missing—the shape is neither a perfect half circle nor a perfect full circle. What is it? Each of three nights it is something different.

We wonder: as children we have all held a convex piece of glass over a piece of paper and focused the Sun's light through it to make the paper catch fire. Did the ancients have access to this trick? Did they find convex pieces of crystal with which magically to create fire? We know that they revered fire and feared it. Lightning was the ultimate symbol of spirit. This divine form of fire (as opposed to the kind controlled by humans), was known to hit trees and people. If people survived, they and even their families belonged to spirit and could become shamans. Whatever was left of the tree carried the mark of the divine. A drum or tool or pipe made of such a tree had magical properties.

Kabbalah contains the Tree of Life, originally the World Tree in early cultures. It is made up of 10 or 11 spheres representing qualities of the Divine, and the pattern of their descent into matter. If you start from the top and draw a zig-zag line all the way down to the bottom, you have the image of *the lightning flash* at the human level. Your idea traveled that path to materialize, bringing with it the Divine Fire.

Our creativity and inspiration are outward manifestations of the Divine Fire, of which lightning became, early on, the symbol. Our creative activity is considered to begin in the upper or subtle realms and descend like a lightning flash, in a zigzag manner, from energies to forms to energies and so on, through a series of subtle planes beginning at the most subtle in the upper realms, and becoming more solid as it descends toward the physical realm. Anyone familiar with the Tree of Life, has seen that as a Kabbalistic pattern. It is very ancient, indeed, and we might wonder how the early shamanic peoples knew this pattern so well that it continues to be a spiritual truth today. In the days before religion it showed up as the gods' energies coming down and possessing the shaman's mind or body. In the middle ages, the pattern began to take the form of The Tree of Life as Kabbalah sees it today, with the creative energies originating in God and coming down to a human in a lightning flash through the Tree of Life.

Because spiritual energy is considered to be like a subtle form of electricity, there must be a receptive point at the bottom to attract this Divine fire into your activity. Initially intending your New Moon's seed-project to be an offering to the world could guarantee that what you do or create this month radiates the Fire. We make an intent at New Moon that whatever form the intent will take, it will be our Full Moon offering. This is what the Eight Windows are about—giving and receiving at all levels. In case we have not said this clearly in earlier chapters, your New Moon project can be anything at all—anything. It can be your desire to make a relationship better, to make time for some painting or woodworking, or compose a letter about a critical issue currently being dealt with. Or maybe you are practicing a new technique and learning how to apply it to something. New Moon projects can be inner or outer. You will find out for sure by the end of this Moon phase.

Gibbous and the Divine Fire

Western astrology speaks of the Gibbous as the first point in the cycle where the spirit must be activated. Spirit is strong in fire signs. If you look at the 12/8 division of the Zodiac/Phase circles (Chapter on the Eight phases) you will note that the last half of the sign resonates to the first third of the Gibbous phase. *Leo* is the personal fire of the individual's creativity—the development of individual consciousness. However, the larger third of Gibbous energy resonates to the whole sign of Virgo. Leo is "behind" Virgo and is therefore not directly observed in our monthly journey, though it is a most important aspect of this phase. In Western religious terminology, the Leo energy here is called "the birth of the spirit within."

As we have done earlier in this book we share the expanded richness of the phase by including its meanings from other times and cultures. Our favorite is the Gibbous image of the Firebird, with its visual impact, and depth of spiritual meaning. This magical firebird has feathers with magical powers, a very ancient religious symbol that may have operated as a totem spirit to those on vision journeys, or in healing rituals.

The Ancient Chinese associated the Gibbous phase with Autumn, together with the Firebird as representing spiritual radiance. They believed that radiance was the power of consciousness. They recognized that radiance is not the fire, but the emanation of the fire. Someone in our time who is "radiant" is emanating something invisible; we want to ask the person what is the source or cause of this radiance. So it is with the radiance of your friend, or your spirit within. When Moses came down from the mountain his face radiated so powerfully that people covered their eyes in a kind of fear or awe.

At the mundane level the Chinese ancestors associated the Gibbous phase with the fire of the harvest communal gathering indicating spirit is nearby. They counseled that people should deal with the awesome power of spirit by spreading light and warmth, themselves. This is consistent with all early beliefs, that one could find safety in imitating the gods, a sort of befriending—sometimes called sympathetic magic in our time. This they believed would release transformative energy. It is quite astonishing that these ideas from so long ago and far away could match our own; but then, we are finding so many underlying similarities among cultures. We should not be surprised, either, that they are as bright and new as today's new book fresh off the press.

How Do We Make Spirit Emanate from Us?

The spiritual aspect of the Gibbous is the most significant part of this colorful phase, and one is right to ask, "But how do we make it happen?" The magical thing about spirit anywhere is that you never have to "make it do anything." You just "allow" it. The interesting paradox is that after all, the September *Virgo* thing is in its own way the most important. If you do the earthy *Virgo* sorts of things, spirit will radiate in exactly the right way at the right time. It is practically guaranteed that, if you truly do your best at even one of them, spirit will activate itself here. The mystery is that you never know ahead of time what or how that will express. And it is probably not going to happen if you do the work *in order* to have the spiritual experience.

For Westerners, we need to begin with the earth, because that is where we are most focused. Our contemporary society is obsessed with the *substance* and the *products* of the earth. That sounds like a fairly simple, clear cut, well-defined earth moment, if one skims the top; but that really means *ego*. This means looking at the other side of the Gibbous. Leo, the initial half-sign, also represents the ego, which initially covers the spirit and which the Virgo part of the Gibbous work will purify. This is the last place anyone wants to start. First, here are some detailed basic spiritual requirements, which are only gained through purity of attitude toward the mundane tasks, as well as the envisioned creative success—purity being a Leo keyword.

Ego boundaries—in preparation for relationships at the Full Moon. They protect you from intrusive moves by others and others from the same by you, but without negativity such as arrogance or excessive individualism.

Personality Crisis which deals with who we are, versus the 1ˢᵗ Quarter phase of outer world crisis. An increased sense of identity gained in the 1ˢᵗ Quarter may initially make us too sensitive to criticism, or too willing to criticize.

Personality transformation—in this phase, we turn from individual toward social consciousness (Full Moon phase, *Libra*-related). A clear look at our polishing of the project, now, will help us see where it fits in the larger realm of the world outside ourselves.

Here in Gibbous we must complete or establish the piece of identity we found in the 1ˢᵗ Quarter phase. We need it to *make our mark* on the month's project, which requires knowing who we are in terms of that creation. Boundaries may feel limiting, but they are needed to define us or the project. It's all about knowing ourselves as spiritual as well as physical beings, which provides the channel through which spirit can move out in radiance.

In many places we can find information about the basic tasks of work, health, service in all their meanings. These are much written-about categories in which the above personality changes take place. Many people born under the Gibbous phase feel they carry the burdens of the world (humpbacked Moon-form). They may be drawn to do service-oriented work such as allopathic or naturopathic medicine, human services, etc., which are ideal ways to deal with this phase. These activities can represent the life work of those born under the Gibbous. But we deal with the 4ᵗʰ phase every month, so we might find a doctor visit, the discovery of a helpful herbal, the need to analyze a problem or event, or to fine tune our car, these being part of bringing the form of some New Moon intent to completion. If one is fixing the neighbors' car to help them out, the spiritual value might be stepped up a notch.

The Task of Purification

Western astrology refers to another task— purification—though we also find it in several other phases. Gibbous purification may be of the ego, or of a physical nature, like detoxification, a sweat lodge, a diet-exercise regimen, depending on what the New Moon's project is. Why are you doing it? To rid yourself of toxins, negative emotions, or fat? Exercise, required to eliminate fat, is the fire that burns the fat, while the liberated fat and toxins carry away the negative emotions or memories stored in the cells. There are also purifications to be found in psychotherapeutic work. Someone who performs and is working on a project conceived at the New Moon may need to purify his/her psyche in order to sharpen the integrity of singing or acting skills during a performance in the Full Moon. Most importantly, purification is required to tame the ego's emphasis on self, or as the teachers say, increase humility. The aspects of service and healing here offer opportunities to purify the ego at the same time as the body.[1]

Referring to the 8-fold Path below, we could say that the specific purification for the Gibbous is from the attachment to GAIN. One only needs to look at the political process of the first decade of the 21st century. We the authors are experiencing it firsthand in the market plummet of September/October, 2008; enough said. If you are struggling this month with a conflict of interest involving gain versus possible loss, as opposed to service without expectation of compensation, this month may offer the opportunity to transform your personality through sacrifice of a golden calf, or a cash cow, however small. In the bible a big fire was required and the gold was a highly questionable sacrifice (Ex.:32), followed by a greater one which we leave to the reader to decide about. Did the women who contributed their jewelry realize what they were really doing? The "gain" simile shows up in the 6th house mirroring of the sign Virgo. The 6th house is about work as recompense for the privilege of being here. We experience it in real time as our employment, for which we appropriately expect reasonable remuneration. This, however, becomes generalized into a similar but sometimes less appropriate expectation for any service. Therein lies a dark path. It is too easy to ask at Gibbous, "What am I going to get out of this?"

The 6th house work theme may also underlie the original name, itself. Gibbous means "hump" from the Latin, which inspired many people to call the Gibbous phase the "humpbacked" Moon. One

---

1   Various forms of detoxification of the body remove toxins from the cells. Many people believe that negative thoughts and experiences create toxins or memories in the cells and physical detoxification will carry away the memories as well as physical or psychological toxins at the same time

might image someone whose back was bent from years of heavy, perhaps sacrificial work.

Day to Day Life in the Energy of the Gibbous

Clearly we want to follow the Firebird to see where it leads us. No matter where we look, fire is a bird, is the spirit. It seems to emerge when the heavy covering of material greed and substance is burned away, which reminds us of the phoenix which is mythically related. This firebird always returns us to the individual emphasis of *Leo* in beauty, riches, and display, or one's spiritual radiance. We have a choice at this phase, we can live from our truest spiritual center or from our ego center. If we experience purification, our firebird turns into the phoenix and rises from the ashes. For anyone to whom this has happened, the answer to the Gibbous question is "It was a gift." But of course, it wouldn't have happened if you had actually asked the question—perhaps unconsciously— "What am I going to get out of this?"

In many myths, East and West, fire was hidden inside the earth. Remember we said that in Kabbalistic Astrology the element Earth always contains fire at its core. Gibbous phase of course represents the emerging spirituality (fire,) hidden inside the person made of dense earthy elements. Through the efforts at perfection (*Virgo* trait) of the newly formed creative (*Leo*) product or intent, you are purified, by the power of the spiritual fire or spirit, from the inside. *This is the goal of the Western disciple, or one who sits at the feet of a master to learn,* which requires humility. Your truest goal is that your spirit (true individuality) will shine through every act or word. Once each cycle this energy is available to support and help the spiritual incarnation of the month's intent, during the Gibbous. Our mark is not our beauty, but our spirit; our voice is not our physical voice alone, but it might be heard as spirit, filling the hearts of others. Spiritual voice here can mean art, music, acts of compassion, healing words, and simple spontaneous services to others.

Some writers describe Gibbous as a time to be analytical, critical, and practical, because of its association with the 6th house and Virgo. And surely, the Virgo obsession with perfection wants to correct the imperfect or unsymmetrical (humpback?). However Virgo would miss the little understood but most significant and deepest meaning of the Gibbous Moon, which is its potential to reveal the new radiation of your inner spirit emerging during the last few days before full Moon. While the period of greatest creativity came during the 1st Quarter phase, the period of greatest spiritual work may be in the Gibbous.

Polishing the Crystal.

On the mundane level, ask yourself, "What am I trying to accomplish at this time, in what house and what sign? If you have been doing the work suggested by each previous phase, you have most of the work done at this point. But probably you have not fully refined your work (mental, material, and emotional) sufficiently so as to reveal its deepest essence. Are you saying, thinking, feeling, its deepest truth? Are you painting the greatest beauty still locked inside the form you have been building? If you sense a spirit at work beneath the surface since New Moon, can you manifest that spirit now? Will polishing reveal a lasting inner radiance? Only you know at this moment. But this is the potential of Gibbous Moon. As your grandmother warned you, every water-spot on a crystal goblet gets in the way of its message of beauty. So get busy and analyze, assess, and polish, but all the while be fully in touch with your soul essence which wants to be embodied here, along with spirit, in the next phase. If you are so minded, ask spirit to polish through you.

The Railroad Crossing

Mark Robertson used to say of the Gibbous Moon: *Stop, look, and listen.* We need to do that because the Gibbous begins at the cyclic point of greatest forward motion (end of 1st Quarter Moon phase) and the railroad stop bell clangs and the stop-guards go down. Yin-Consciousness is increasing, and headlong Yang-creative, instinctual action is no longer the most needed element. We need to:

Stop rapid expansion,

Look at what we are doing, and

Listen for guidance. We then add "*where*" to those three words as we consider our project's original New Moon purpose: *where will I and it fit into a Full Moon's larger context?* Then we will see where we need finishing, perfecting, etc.

Living the Gibbous

During the three days of Gibbous Moon, one refines the form of a wood carving by sanding or carefully shaving off all extraneous material, and then polishing. There is a sense of loving in the polishing. We see the beauty in it as we refine and polish, and begin to wonder if it is "good enough". What will it look like in three or two more days? Will others like it? The fact that it catches the light and reflects it back as a softly shining object, like the Moon, attests to the inner spirit. And such shining resulting from your work resonates deeply inside, as you feel your own spirit rising to give form to the spirit in the carving. Incidentally, this is why different people who view the same work of art of another person (or hear their words, or sense their emotion) can resonate in their own being, even if they interpret it entirely differently from others. Their spirit, which is always in the Oneness dimension, resonates to yours, which is also in that dimension; and spirit is universal.

But this is metaphor. Does it work the same way if you have been trying to heal an old wound, plan a schedule, restore a broken relationship, sew a dress, repair a washing machine, or create a more pleasant environment by adding color or playing music? Can you feel and welcome your inner magical firebird? Answering that question is part of the process itself. You may need to re-clarify your goals here and to realize that what seemed like a very mundane task can contribute some value or meaning to another person, to society, or to life. In so doing, you will have allowed your inner spirit to work through your now objectified New Moon intent. Even if you do not see it, at Full Moon others may see a kind of radiance emanate from you or your action or object. Have you ever looked at someone and said, "You look radiant!"? That person may look back at you, puzzled, and say, "Do I? Really?" But the rest of her day may be different.

During these three days, polish, edit, perfect, whatever the task may be. There is a deliberate quality to the energies at this time as you analyze what you are doing, or discriminate as you complete details. You may wonder where this fits into some larger scheme of things. There is a sense that here is where you learn a skill better, practice a technique, analyze, repair, and heal. The healings have always been important. Characteristic of these are the many outpourings of service through the last few thousand years, such as the service provided by monasteries and convents where whole religious communities devoted their service to caring for the sick. Government organizations now offering such services proliferate, not to mention grassroots organizations begun by individuals or small groups.

Once when I was working with a group of chronic mentally ill persons, I took a week's vacation at the ocean, staying alone in a borrowed condo by the shore. I had a terrible cold, and the weather was cold, wet and blustery. I would go out in the morning to find the raging ocean had left many shells, which I collected in a bag. The rest of each day, I spent long periods polishing these shells to a high sheen with a piece of paraffin. I listened to music and thought about each of the individuals in my group and how I would give a shell to each one because the shells represented a wider horizon than their current mental/emotional boundaries allowed. When they were done I was shocked to discover that my cold was gone! I don't know if I was in the Gibbous phase, but it doesn't matter, because this experience describes the Gibbous potential quite well.

For Astrologers. It is important to note that the *Virgo* undertone of healing at the Gibbous Moon is specific and involves a technique such as herbal remedies, massage—or something we must do, know, eat, or practice. There is a different kind of healing in the final, or Balsamic, Moon phase—one into which we must let go in trust, and for which there is nothing anyone can do except to passively receive. The Balsamic healing of the 8th phase is related to *Pisces*, the sign opposite *Virgo*. The Gibbous healing of the 4th phase is related to *Virgo*, the two signs being opposites on the Zodiac and the phase-sign wheels.

Impeccability

Criticism arises from analysis, and is billed high on the list for *Virgo* and so also in the Gibbous. Are we metaphorically trying to "fix" the awkward shape of the Moon? Or are we criticizing another? Or are we being over-critical of ourselves and too sensitive to the criticism of others? A good friend had two small children, one was a *Leo* and one was a *Virgo*. The irrepressible *Leo* expressed all over the place, while his older *Virgo* Sister followed him around criticizing (when asked by an irate mother just who did he think he was, he responded, "I'm me!") a true Leo response!) In our own charts, we can say, Leo creates and Virgo criticizes, as long as we use those words in a positive way. Struggling for impeccability is the intent of this phase, but there is a fine line between that and micro-managing or criticizing.

Also here may be struggles of various kinds. What happened when you passed the "Last Chance Tavern"? If you were still hung up in issues from the previous month, you had one last chance to dump them. Impeccability has little patience with sloppy cleanup jobs. Saturn is ruler here—demanding but fair, offering exact reward for exact effort. Saturn's purpose is to clarify and establish boundaries to all forms. Your skin is a boundary, ruled by Saturn. Your psychic "skin" may be too "thin" and Saturn helps you toughen it up here, in order not to take everything personally. Here at Gibbous Moon, without Saturn there would be no definitive form with any lasting value. The greatest artists produced the most definitive works and they lasted the longest in the public consciousness. (They probably received the most criticism as well!) Remember that Full Moon is the most emotional time of the month, so it is well now, at Gibbous, to tighten up your personal emotional boundaries lest you get caught off guard and have a tantrum or a melt-down over a small issue tomorrow or the next day.

The most important boundary definition made here is the boundary between one individual and another. Full Moon is about being both a fully defined separate individual as a part of the collective along with all other individuals. You will find at the Last Quarter phase that you need boundaries between you and the collective. This is the deeper theme of all Moon cycles. When you feel satisfied that your project is fully polished and that it clearly speaks some inner truth for you, then you have added a further definition to your individuality and are therefore prepared to contribute it to the collective. If you have purified your ego from expectations of GAIN, praise, remuneration, or fear that none of these things can possibly happen, then you may be protected from disappointments. They may happen, but you can stand above them, or accept the legitimate ones.

The perfected state that characterizes the goal is exemplified in such things as crystals, shapes, structures, boundaries; all are ruled by Saturn the Guardian of this phase. Take a piece of wisdom from the crystals: no crystal is perfect. It is what it is. (But they are often valued for their "imperfections" or individualities). Have you noticed that some handicapped people are outstanding because of the creative ways they have found to overcome their limitations? They become a model for others in a metaphorical Full Moon situation, which means that their hard work to perfect their potentials is their offering to the collective. Boundaries and limitations are key here, because they define the kind of crystal, structure or other offering. Most of us either have too many, too few, too weak, or too strong boundaries. The full phase will require adequate, moderate boundaries because other individuals are going to be involved. You can test yourself out now by observing your own reactions if you are criticized! Criticism is part of Gibbous time. Your own, for sure, in order to refine the form, but if someone sees what you are doing at this point, it will likely elicit a reaction. What do you do when people "get in your face", or turn their backs? The world out there is full of such widespread boundary problems, and there are no playground supervisors to help out. It seems you are really perfecting yourself here. This is the time you want to make an attempt to keep your cool if what you have to offer here, or in the full phase, doesn't seem to measure up in yours or someone else's eyes. Personal questions or unexpected praises can also be scary for some who do not yet feel strong in their own personality "structure". These are boundary issues. As much as possible prepare for them in this particular area of your life. Important personal growth is happening here and intent stretches a long way.

This is the last 3 days you will truly have control over your creation or project, or piece of a project. (We hope you understand that projects are never just one month long, and you are usually dealing with parts of projects.) If you hope to offer something that will benefit others in some way, be ready to share control. Sometimes that looks like this: you have a really good idea during a meeting, and you share it. Later, someone else claims it. Or, you wrote a book and now that it is published, you discover that others are using it as part of their own work, which you don't agree with. Sometimes this is a genuine legal issue, but mostly there is no wrong intended and you have probably done the same thing yourself at some time.

Listen to the Voices of the Elders

The Egyptian Guardian of Phase Four: *Khenmu*, the planet Saturn, called "The Molder". Think of your task as that of a sculptor or a potter. You are finishing and perfecting the object as a work of art, at the same time forming it to function or conform to the purpose for which you are making it. To make a work of art out of the daily activities of our lives is to learn that the art of life itself is a spiritual life, which one does for no expectation of gain.

The 8-Fold Path Attachment: *Gain*. This is the last attachment on this path (at Full Moon we will begin the four aversions). To some extent all of us have gain in mind whenever we do most anything. For some, the gain is the entire reason for doing at all. What do we wish to gain from this life-labor, and particularly at this phase?

Energy must flow in both directions or it will become blocked. Some times, but not always, it is as spiritually appropriate to expect a fair gain from the energy put out as it is spiritually deadening to do the work only for the gain, especially when an agreement on both sides is involved. Most of us are on one side or the other of the middle. This is another small but very important lesson we can learn more about if we choose. If we are too attached to the gain, perhaps there is an attitude behind it that came from someone in our past. It is not legitimate to expect gain if we are making a gift, or performing a service of love that is not related to any arrangement. It is not legitimate to refuse gain simply because our self-esteem is not high enough to expect anything. The ultimate gain is then not external. It is the acquisition of more of ourselves via our own spirit.

We need to pause here, at the end of the first half of the cycle, and comment on a key point we have not mentioned. We have now gone through the energies of individualization, covering four aspects of that process. Perhaps the reader has not noticed how each phase offers measuring devices by which one can assess where one is in the process, and what needs working on in their own life. We have used them and they are valuable guides to more personal objectivity.

Locating the Gibbous Moon on Your Own Chart Wheel

Again, we refer you to the Crescent Moon Chapter for the rough calculation of transitional phase positions for Sun and Moon. Briefly: find the Sun by adding 84 hours' movement from the previous, 1ˢᵗ Q phase position. Place Moon 135 degrees ahead of the Sun position. Degrees will not be exact; they can only be accurate if the Sun is first mathematically calculated. Gibbous Moon is always exactly 135 degrees ahead of the Sun which, of course, is not exact without calculation.

If you are using a journal, you have enough practice that you can gather and arrange the following requested information in your own manner in the journal.

1. The Gibbous phase Sun's sign (yellow dot) _____.

2. The Gibbous phase Moon's sign (blue dot) _____.

3. Note the activities of the Sun's house_____.

4. Note the activities of the Moon's house _____.

The Process—Putting it Together

<u>Ed's Example Chart.</u> The Gibbous Moon phase in Ed's Moon cycle began on August 12, 2008. Sun was at 20 Leo in his 10th house and Moon was at 5 Capricorn in Ed's 3rd house.

<u>The Houses</u>. Moon tells us that the completion of his New Moon intent regarding career change was to be done in his 3rd house of communication, with official "advice" from Sun in the career house. Moon's third house is five houses away from the Sun's career house, as well as five signs away. This intensifies the fifth phase, fifth sign Virgo quality with its humpbacked shape and suggestion of hard work. There is also indeterminacy about these three days. Is this good enough? What will "they" think about it? Most of all this phase asks the question, "Where does it fit in the world "out there"? Or "Where do I fit out there"?

<u>The Signs</u>. Moon in *Capricorn* wants structure, definition, and above all conventionally acceptable form. If Ed is working on a résumé or a lengthy response to a potential employer, or to his current employer, it needs to be carefully constructed. Whatever form the communication takes, it must not be showy or flashy or unsubstantiated. Capricorn is often uncomfortable with *Leo*, the Sun's position. Something in the *Capricorn* 3rd house may feel limiting or constricting to either the employer or to Ed's *Leo* side. This is not the time to rebel. *Leo needs to feel pride, and Capricorn honors or rewards careful work.*

Work any two signs together this way to make your way easier. What in each sign needs something that belongs to the other?. In ordinary life, with ordinary people, certain signs are traditionally at odds with others. However, people who use the highest energies of signs often say the energies are challenging, but not negative. Using the highest expression of signs makes them compatible and more effective. You *will* be working two signs together all through the month, every month, and you can find in every sign a quality that works well with any other sign, just as with Capricorn and Leo in this month's Gibbous Moon.

Sun in Leo in the 10th house sends spirit's message that here is where Leo can be an authority and it will support moon's creative expression in a perhaps conventional structure through communication

<u>The Degrees</u>. In this example, the Sun was at 20 *Leo* and the Moon at 5 Capricorn (August 12, 2008). The theme for the Sun degree (read 21 *Leo*) is: *A carrier pigeon fulfilling its mission: spirituality, in*

terms of training for service to mankind. Dare we ask: has Ed put his written statement into the mailbox? This is one of those exceptional images that fit so closely to a situation that "we can't believe it". We don't know, but it is certainly suggestive, and such degrees have been that close for us occasionally. The second half of the statement could suggest to Ed that he needs to look at his Gibbous task as "a spiritual step" toward some kind of human services.

The Moon's theme (read 6 *Capricorn*) in the 3rd house offers: *Ten Logs lie under an archway leading to darker woods—the need to complete any undertaking before seeking entrance to whatever is to be found beyond.* This degree is about the hidden opportunities in every situation. You will want to read Roche's full description of this degree. It seems to tell Ed that he "has everything he needs to succeed in life" and if he is worried he needs to look deeper to find his answers. But, in any case, he needs to complete something here before he launches himself into a new career situation.

Apply these interpretations to your own Solar dial to see if you can interpret your Gibbous phase.

18
Full Moon Phase—
Seeds of the Moonflower
"Us" and "Them"?

Pierced by a dart of light a butterfly is made perfect. The symbolical death that is initiation into spiritual reality and wisdom. Sudden awakening. Craving for inner light.
—LIBRA 1° Marc Edmund Jones
The Sabian Symbols

The earth brought forth vegetation:
seed-bearing plants of every kind,
fruit trees of every kind
bearing fruit with the seed in it.
—Genesis 1:12

Illustration 1. Harvest Moon. **Credit::Wikipedia.**

Whereto Did this Cycle Lead?

This is the longest chapter in the book, because it is the most important. When we began our journey, we resisted that possibility, and we are certain that many of our readers will struggle their way through it without initially understanding why all the words. It was only as we journeyed, wrote, re-wrote, examined the degrees and signs, and discussed for endless hours, that we reluctantly agreed that this was the most important of all the phases. Again and again, we questioned the greatest authoritative statements that that was so. In the end, we realized the truth of the Full Moon phase in our own lives. Relationship is the most fundamental truth of the human spirit, in infinite ways that can never be included within the covers of any book. I have lived alone for 40 years and never been outside of numerous of the infinite kinds of relationship. We will try to communicate in words what we have learned about Full Moon and relationship.

The Full Moon is very much both about duality and unity, about relationships and the field of harvest. Now physics has introduced to us something else called "The Field." Lynne McTaggart describes it in her book of that name[1]. She tells us that according to Einstein the field is the only reality and that we are embedded within it. Therefore there is no "me or not-me." This field is a source of intelligence that acts as a sort of dynamic blueprint guiding all life processes— mental, emotional and physical. It apparently includes not only the imperfections we all carry with us, but their perfect blueprints, so therefore it is a force to which we can turn for restoring health, substance, and life itself, as was the harvest field of the early planters for whom the field was a holy and joint creation— they planted and tended the seeds, while the gods completed the harvest. Many great writers have written about the harvest field and its metaphors. We believe that we are learning how to tend this universal field of everything as we work and live with others, and we are continuously trying to remember that if the field-concept is true, we are all of a piece, and we can no longer act as though there are "us" and "them", with whom we compete for a finite amount of the universe's substance. Full Moon in that kind of universe carries the true harvest energy—one where coming together with others can allow us to tap the harvest for which we have worked the previous two weeks.

Seldom expressed, this new beginning involves a sacrifice— giving up part of our total individuality in order to be unified with the Other—an ego-death. We will look at some of the implications.

Relationship, the primary mirror of personal consciousness, often presents a split between our mind and feelings. But the moment of

---

1   *The Field*, by Lynne McTaggart. HarperCollins 2002.

Sun and Moon's greatest distance from one another offers unity and creative conception. It produces the seed for the next cycle, which is the root of progress in humanity. This seed of the next cycle is formed in the flower (Full Moon), warmed and nourished by the Sun—the emissary of He Who Created All Things. One can read about this mystical seed in an ancient Chinese manuscript called The Secret of the Golden Flower (see Bib.)

All New Moons lead to a Full Moon; all individual efforts lead to relationship, either within one's own structure of personality, selfhood, soul and spirit, or within the structure of all relationships outside the self such as personal, social, collective, universal, and cosmic. In your humble dial, and with your degree books, you can enter the meanings of those relationships each month, as you see where your waxing Moon efforts have led you. The house of the Moon will tell you the area of your life where you can reap the harvest, and the house of the Sun will tell you the purpose and meaning behind this culmination, which has nourished the crop.

Unity in Separateness (Polarity)

Full Moon is a model for the creativity and abundance resulting from polarity, throughout the universe. It is a model for us in our personal and internal relationships, in the sense that through those relationships we can produce something that goes beyond ourselves, just as the physical coupling of any two people can produce a child, or a book, or a song. And yet, within the Field we are indivisible, a quality boldly claimed for Americans, by the U.S. Pledge of Allegiance. Perhaps duality is a perception to be found at the outer edge of the universe, with the Field midway between outer appearances and inner reality. The Aries 14 Sabian Symbol (Dane Rudhyar), representing Full Moons in general, discusses polarity in terms of human relationships. It presents this clear observation that while polarity is supposed to lead to unity and thus to a seed, modern individuals do not understand the meaning of this. He says, we have become so individualized that we can't find other individuals enough like ourselves to polarize with and therefore consciously create! Is this a fateful truth, or is it possible to overcome this extreme duality perception?

Here, at Full Moon, we need to find a way to re-align our inner and outer needs so that they each fulfill the other; or, in a personal relationship, we need to come together with the other when we are most clear in our separateness, hopefully to find a point of unity. Those are our possible individual tasks. The urge for both separateness and oneness is at its peak in the 5th phase. From the moment of Full Moon, the Moon in its waning phases is always hurrying back to Sun where the two can be re-unified, again modeling the relationship aspect of consciousness. That is a different kind of unity—one that never separated into polarities. Full Moon polarity brings experiences of the unity of wholeness.

Once achieved, the unity of the polarities of Masculine and Feminine, mind and emotion, on the waning side of Full Moon, can start to see their unified individual polarities reach for unity within a greater perspective. They are always attempting to "return" to each other, to find unity, though society's patterns seem forever determined to prevent that. On the waxing, or individualizing side of the cycle, we are working on our creative individuality which can be taking us further into uniqueness—until we suddenly hit the Full Moon and must immediately begin to consider the possibility of a new unity within a larger context.

The full phase Sun and Moon models are physically as far apart space-wise from one another as possible, and as the reader may also be metaphorically from another individual. Rudhyar's new solution to our modern time is to get a larger viewpoint, one that sees your personal polarization within a still larger environment. A mundane example is simply finding an overarching common interest or passion within which you and another can relate. Another solution appears when you are climbing a mountain. The higher you climb on a mountain or skyscraper (the more experience you have) the more you see. You see what a thing is, and how it relates to the rest of its surroundings, and suddenly its meaning changes. Your relationship to it is now different than before—more truthful. Perspective is changed. This is what consciously following the phases does—it changes our perspective from narrower to broader as we move through a cycle.

As you were heading toward the Full Moon, you probably anticipated the completion of a project which would invite a personally desirable response. If you are well-grounded and knowledgeable, in control of your ego, there is a good chance that you will have a satisfying, encouraging and supportive experience. At the peak of the mountain you have been climbing, you may turn around and be met with a grand view as described above. This is your Full Moon illumination—a new perspective that can change how you understand your life and how you interact with the world outside yourself.

The Field as Full Moon in Our Time

Lynne McTaggart's *Field* as a symbol deeply enriches the prehistoric harvest field of Full Moon. It is the Field of all possibilities out of which everything emerges. It is up to us to sow, plant, and harvest our corner of the Field. At the simple Earth-level the archetypal and quintessential orange Autumn Full Moon[2] shines above the field of harvest. It behooves us to attach value to Field by knowing that what we have created out of the infinite energies of the universe (including ourselves) comes to fullness at this phase. One, we used universal energy and intelligence to bring our personal New Moon intent to completion. Two, each of us within humanity is also an integral part of the collective, and of the universe. What we co-created is part of that collective, either contributing to or detracting from, the experienced degree of unity. Three, if we believe these ideas are true, we must recognize that everything is sacred: the essence of the Great Mystery behind the Field, is that out of which we co-created. We do not keep all of what we create, nor do we give up all to the collective. What we create produces seed, out of which we save some for the Field so that our creations grow, harvest and produce more seed. We become the Moonflower, multiplying our blossoms and seeds infinitely if the universe so allows.

Harvest and Field, Then and Now

The quintessential Harvest Full Moon, the archetype for all Full Moons, timed the most important Neolithic, Bronze, and Iron Ages' celebrations of the year. These ancestors instinctively understood that the harvest field which the people planted and harvested together was a subjective unity with the universe. The Ancestors saw their harvest field as sacred and therefore as including a higher dimension beyond the physical world. They believed it offered them unlimited power to give things form (create more harvests etc.), so long as they saved out their seed, and shared the grain with all those who planted, those who could not, and the Lunar and Solar spirits

---

2   In the field of art therapy, colors in a spontaneous drawing define the emotional quality of the expression; the color orange suggests social anxieties and feelings of vulnerability in relationship. Who has not seen the huge, low-hanging orange harvest full moon and not felt a moment's apprehension without knowing why?

who granted their harvest. Thanksgiving was an inherent part of the harvest ritual. Now the universe is much larger and further from our normally limited personal grasp. We must climb a mountain and take ourselves into that larger universe; we must give a little in order to understand our relationship or idea or attitude, within the larger context.

Lynne McTaggart says that this energetic "field" is central to our beingness and our consciousness (remember that Sun represents Being and Moon represents Doing) the fundamentals of our existence.

The Field (my cap.) in the second initial quote is an objective description of the earlier and ancient subjective universe. It is no longer a metaphor, but now theoretically an objective fact. It stretches our mind to the limits, just as the harvest field with its gods stretched our ancestors' minds toward the world of the gods, beyond what they understood. But by that definition's very nature we are still embedded within the universe, as were the ancients. Only the conscious boundaries are pushed back, and with a new perspective we now regard it in our conscious minds as outside ourselves. Is that the polarity? Some of us are attempting to re-integrate the subjective with the objective side; and even now science and philosophy are beginning to report on their explorations of the newly recognized wholeness, the critical factor being that we, ourselves, emerge out of the Field. In simpler terms, what we are saying is that in some strange way, humanity is at a kind of Full Moon where we are seeing the ultimate results of our past and are forced to look at ourselves as functioning parts of a world whole. The news gives us the raw picture, and science gives us the first glimpses of the potential of the picture—a fully polarized complexity of the negative and the positive threads of development from the past.

The idea of Field gives me the odd sensation that time is multi-dimensional—like space, infinite in all directions; what we think of as our history, cast in ink and paper, actually may not be separated from us in time but exist on a web that connects us with our history in both space and time. Joseph Chilton Pierce explains how this happens in his astonishing book *The Biology of Transcendence*[3]. He explains that the heart contains a major brain function that makes us aware of others at the feeling level, and affects our relationships with them. At the same time it also is the physical, biological channel

---

3   *Biology of Transcendance* by Chilton Pierce. See Bibliography

through which we connect with the Divine. In this consciousness there is no time, and we are connected to all-that-is and possibly all-that-was.

In the present context, the Mystery behind the Field is the source of our life-energy and ability to create; it provides the bounty of the universe out of which we can harvest everything we need, if we put part of the seed back into the soil. For the ancestors, it was the field of grain, planted and harvested by the community and a gift everyone gave to each other. They understood that unity is the result of flowing with the natural patterns of nature's energies, and that all the work they contributed to the community was as sacred as the community and life itself. There was no "me" and "them"; there was experienced unity.

The concept of charity grew out of the early Shamanic practice of sharing the harvest with those who could not plant. Later, this idea was behind the widespread early middle eastern religious custom of leaving the edges of the field uncut, for the poor to harvest as they wished.

For us now there is the desperate need for humans to recognize consciously that the Field actually is "us", which includes "them". Religion has already stated this, but we have not listened. But if we believe science we must work together consciously, as the ancients did intuitively, to bring back the unity and generosity we lost in our scientific universe-as-object. The ancestors gave a value or meaning to their field, associated with their deity. Science is only now finding a contemporary value to Field—the value being that it is our ultimate source of bounty and if we do not change our relationship to it we will destroy both ourselves and our world. We apparently can only be generous when we come to know deeply that we collectively participate in the infinite power to create more out of the Field— more of anything including everything we have created to this point, but particularly compassion and non-judgmental love. Whatever the shamanic Great Mystery may be called, it is the intelligence or creativity behind the Field; and the Field is the interstice between the uncreated Mystery and the created universe. Therefore, since Deity is generous with us, we, too, must be generous, recognizing our unity, making better choices. The Mystery, and the knowledge—that we as co-creators have created the present imbalance of giving and receiving through rampant taking—should clearly point the direction of change. Nowhere is this signpost clearer than at the Full Moon. As a great teacher asked, "The field is ripe with the harvest and where are the workers?"

The Golden Link

Astrology calls this phase the time of completion, fulfillment, and illumination of our situation. The illumination, when the Moon receives and reflects the full light of the Sun, reveals either fulfillment of relationship or a taste of unity—as opposed to fragmentation or the inability to go on with it. If we get the illumination, then we get (and give) the fruits of the relationship; if not, there are... *crystallization and disintegration* according to Rudhyar. We have created something physical, material, mental, emotional or spiritual in the waxing phase—perhaps even a new part of ourselves. In some obvious or obscure way, people now become involved with what we did, whether through current relationships, or long past ones. If it was from the past, then it may now be the feeling that something is finished so that one can go on. Our ancestors live on in us, we speak to them with everything we do, and at times they seem to speak back. Or it could be as inconsequential as completing a report during which you have a new realization about yourself that makes you feel more whole or competent concerning your current life. Reports of course are made to others, who may or may not pass judgment with which you have to deal, favorable or unfavorable. Externally or internally, people are involved at your Full Moon and you find yourself face-to-face, aligned or pushing away, contributing of yourself to something larger than your individual self, or else unable to do either or any of the above. If the latter, the Full Moon energy contains the beginning of a more perfect answer down the line.

The early image of gathering the community to bring in the harvest is still the image of fulfilled relationship, where the individual joins his/her energies within the context of the collective. Literally, in some early cultures, the harvested field became the field of planting new human seed during the festival, or choosing a life-partner, to be followed by marriages. More literally, the specific crop (human or otherwise) yields the seed for the next year's crop so that each crop is connected both to the preceding crop and the one to come. For humans, that golden link shines from shamanic time to present time, in the new physics concept of the word Field. The ground of all creation past and present is a field out of which all things emerge, disappear and re-emerge out of what was previously harvested. Perhaps we are all recombinant creations. Field asks us to integrate our earthly field of joint creation with the greater universe—to accept into ourselves the possibilities of a Universal Field from which unknown new harvests can be reaped, far beyond our present imaginations[4]. The single key to this phase is, in plain and simple terms, the Full Moon request of us to join intent and action with others, or an other, by seeing our differences unified within a larger point of view.

Personal realization and achievement are the goal of a New Moon's intent—it is where we are going. The Full Moon's message or illumination (the Sun's message on your dial) is the message of messages—too simple, substantial, obvious, yet too mystical for the power-mongers—leaders of the world—to understand. It has always been about this message. You have heard it said: it begins with one person taking one step.

Your Personal Seed Power

Whatever harvest we reap at Full Moon contains what Dane Rudhyar called the second seed. It contains your personal "seed power," like the plant in full flowering, containing its own seed. The Sun or spirit planted the first seed at New Moon. The completed project (or step of a larger project) contains our own seed-power. It is shown by the Moon in the sky and our charts at Full Moon. Whatever of value we put out there will provide a new beginning, which will germinate and become the new seed-intent of the next cycle. Something in the Message of the Moon at this time will give us a clue to the larger purpose of the month, and possibly to the coming cycle.

By Full Moon, the physical and psychic energies of the cycle are being used up, but they can be replaced with new energies created by the sharing of purpose and will within a group of human beings. Sometimes rituals play this role. In any case, social power energizes the individual's consciousness and mind, which hold together one's organism. You know how energized you feel after a meeting with a group of like-minded people.

The Moon, our personal organism, is re-energized by this collective power. The house of the Full Moon's Sun shows the nature

---

4   Unified Field Theory (word coined by Albert Einstein) is an even more direct and symbolic statement of what Field is about. It is a physics theory that attempts to bring all the laws of physics together into a single framework. Although still only a theory, it is a remarkable testament to the universality of the possibility of the unity of everything.

of the seed-power and the area of your life where it is channeled through you; the Moon shows where you manifest the power, and how. Some of the power is ours to keep (from the general harvest). Some of it is the seed to be saved out, as did my own ancestor-grandparents, for planting the next season. The Old Woman's Corn Seed to be saved out will be returned to the earth with the promise of renewal at the next cycle. At the human level this is often the ego-sacrifice everyone has to make in working within relationship, and without which there can be no renewal at the next cycle. Each ancestral marriage promised that renewal, and each demanded the sacrifice of total separateness. In our time there is much argument about the meaning of marriage, currently focused on family values. Our overgrown individualities are causing the problem. The Full Moon is coming into potential alignment with the Sun—the marriage partner is coming into potential alignment with the other partner, or your little self is coming into alignment with your Higher Self. This is the basic meaning of the Full Moon. The confusion in hospitals and jails, as mentioned in an earlier chapter, is caused by human misalignments in many forms.

In early Shamanic, Chinese, and Hebraic traditions, family values were already in place. They knew that the wider meaning of personal polarity was the acceptance of the married couple into the community as working, cooperative, mature members, contributing their own seeds of co-creativity to the community. Whether we marry or remain single, or use an emergent new form of marriage, all marriages could add seed power to the collective and should be recognized and welcomed into their new role in the greater community, especially in terms of their own creativity and personal contributions to the life of the community. It is our hope and vision that when society finally dissolves its separative non-productive patterns and decides "who it is", this fundamental principle of duality in the service of creativity and new seed will re-emerge with new understandings and commitments. Relationship is in need of re-energizing.

Shadow Realizations Possible at Full Moon

Where does the shadow go at the full Moon? What actually happens to an individual's shadow at Full Moon? Remember we said that the dark side of the Moon is the collective unconscious where the archetypes are. The shadow on the Moon is our personal shadow, strangely gone at this moment. Or is it? The light on the Full Moon is the light of conscious, rational, objective mind. It reaches such a peak at this time that it behaves as though there is no shadow—do you see one? Of course not! But you and I know that can't be true.

While the bright Moon denies the shadow's presence, our personal shadow is being polarized to the extreme behind the light. Whatever it contains, that content is connected to an archetype (or sub archetype) behind the Moon. The Full Moon energy is so powerful, and our shadow is so polarized behind the reflected light, that it *must* express itself but cannot. The ultimate dark-side power of the shadow archetype projects this shadow piece onto something or someone outside ourselves in a way that we cannot miss the signal.

A decision must be made, to accept or deny what we see. It is one aspect of the illumination which can be judged as good or bad, but which is actually neither. It requires the courage to recognize and/or step out of some personal addiction or aversion—one's cherished separateness, or limiting parental pattern—the hidden power of which can then be consciously reintegrated into ourselves, increasing our wholeness. This is our greatest opportunity of the month to find and release a piece of imprisoned patterning and become freer through an unexpected blessing of compassion, self-understanding, or recognition of unity with others.

How can we do that? We weren't taught by anyone, or we forgot. Pearce's book on transcendence suggests that, by focusing on the physical heart the very minute we encounter a disharmony inside or outside ourselves, we open to that greater perception or to what he calls "the heart-mind". The impact of what the heart perceives is powerful enough to transform in an instant the old patterns and the misperception of the old emotion.

We have seen how a seed perpetuates the nature of its source, the flower for example. The flower is whatever we personally co-created with the New Moon intent or vision. The flower carries its own seed which contains the possible perpetuation of itself beyond the personal, to a whole garden of new flowers. The seed's success depends upon your nurturance. Our creation's success depends on what we did with the piece of shadow that came with it. The shadow made itself known at the 1st Quarter Moon, triggered by the challenge to our individuality. Did we release into our conscious self or our work, at that time, a new sense of integrity; of connection to the soul or spirit sides of ourselves; of true creativity? Or were they negative desires and addictive thoughts, words, actions—resistances or denial of the new soul-intent? Such diametrically opposed inner ideations profoundly affected the flower. Consider the plant and the ground it was growing in. The coming flower, malformed or weak, overwhelmed by darkness or lack of Sun or water may reproduce that deficiency at the next New Moon. Ideally, it will be a perfectly beautiful or useful flower, nurtured along by your own self-work, creating a new seed of new potentiality. If we have recognized and released some of our "god-goddess-self" into our inner and outer work, the flower promises healing to others, and they will be attracted to it. If we released our creativity, then the blueprint for a house we designed will attract others and eventually stand in full view of many—our offering—containing seed for other and greater designs.

The flower with its seed or offering is the connecting link between you and the collective. At Full Moon the offering, which is a word more relevant to our time than the ancients' word "sacrifice", means that one lets go of some of the individual control of the completed intent, realizing that it may be changed by someone else, such as a publisher changing your manuscript, or a partner changing a joint plan. If this is too difficult for you it may be a sign that you have a piece of your separate self that is not ready to freely offer your finished project. (At the same time, it goes without saying that you also must stand up for your truth.) This is a time when, if you wish, you can free up the hesitant shadow part by letting the full light of consciousness see it. Look inward and ask yourself why this is so hard. If this Full Moon is about connections within yourself, then perhaps you are struggling with old beliefs or memories, or your personal ancestors. The ability to align the Moon house activity, thoughts, or feelings, at Full Moon, with the Sun house activities, thoughts or feelings so that they track and enhance each other will be successful both outwardly and inwardly. You may be changed in some way.

These seeds bear results in the future. They evoke in the individual and collective more needs that must be fulfilled in another cycle. The seed is in the plant and the plant is in the seed. The growth thereof is innate, certain, and contains our destiny, which is colored by our Full Moon experience and our ability to integrate the shadow.

At this Moon we get feedback whether we want it or not, as others comment on our product or realization. Very sensitive personal feelings are often involved at the Full Moon, when questions must be answered. The light shines on us for a few moments and the truth is simply what it is. We are seen, or see ourselves, in the light of truth, and we may or may not be ready to accept it for what it is. But the greatest promise is that we can learn and grow from the seed we cultivated, and a new intent can be invoked at the next New Moon.

We can't tell you how to facilitate transformation if your lunations are troublesome, but we can tell you that.. . .

> Conscious intent,
> Dedication,
> Love,
> Trust in your own process...

are the four keys that allow you to use the shadow at Full Moon for growing and expanding consciousness. That's rather nitty-gritty and dull, perhaps, but the lights do go on at some point. You find an event, a phrase in the Degree Symbol, or some other piece of truth that feeds your spirit or soul, or invites the shadow out to be seen as it really is—either an ephemeral ghost of the past, or a shining angel wing. Passion to continue the journey returns. The wonderful thing about this is that you are one-of-a-kind; creation is creativity; the adventure never ends; you live and write your own absorbing mystery tale. Nothing we can write will exactly describe your experiences. You are unique, and we hope that you will find more and more of your own uniqueness through the Lunar Path.

In the deepest sense, we expand our own personal work by dedicating the waxing phase to a greater purpose than our own and thus making it sacred at the Full Moon. All of life is sacred, and when we follow the cycles with the intent of dedicating ourselves to expressing personal individual integrity, impeccability, love, and responsibility in every stage of the cycle, the Full Moon will always hold a great truth for us. Sometimes it is a greater understanding of a relationship, a creation, or ourselves; or sometimes it is truly a lesson that stretches us to our limits. What spirit (Sun) shows us of the original intent and how we are able to express it (Moon), are sometimes very far apart, struggling to reach each other. But the path between is straight and clear, and alignment brings the two together instantaneously, creating the mystical second seed within ourselves as the connection between heaven and earth.

As a society and a world, we have lost the sense of the sacred in all our affairs and the sky-knowledge of as above so below. The wisdom of Full Moon is a fulfillment of light and revelation to those who willingly offer something of themselves to the larger purposes around them. The phases show us how to restore our wisdom if we choose to take it.

Shadow as the Valley Spirit

Throughout pre-history and history, Moon-shadow, particularly during eclipses, was often considered evil. But the ancestors may have projected their own collective shadow onto a figure embodying that evil, so they could have a relationship with it.

The most striking fragmentary example of that comes from the Chinese Neolithic as the Dark Animal Goddess or Valley Spirit, a mare[5], who almost literally gallops into this bright harvest gathering. She seems to have some characteristics of our modern "Shadow", as well as the nurturing qualities of The Mother of the World. According to *The Way-Power Classic* quoted by Stephen Karcher[6]:

> The Valley Spirit never dies. It is named Dark Animal Goddess. The door of the Dark Animal Goddess is called the Root of Heaven and Earth. Like an endless thread she endures. You can call upon her easily. He who has found this mother understands he is a child. When he understands he is her child and clings to her, he will be without danger when the body dies..._____ *Dao De Jing by* Lao Tze:

Stephen Karcher adds that she is divine and clairvoyant; she is the opening that receives the seed of Force, and therefore is closely related to women's fertility. And, finally, she creates our bodies and receives the dead. She is clearly an early major feminine aspect of Deity, and represents the manifestation principle, psychic abilities, cycles and so forth. She was probably the first World Mother. She is suspiciously like the Moon! And she is the mother of the second seed.

---

5   From very early times, the horse represented the animal part of a human, and the connection between body and mind. Horse was also associated with early forms of the Tree of Life, which was a symbol for the human as a connection between the upper and lower worlds. In other connections we can see the mare as representing a specifically feminine connection between body and soul, the body being earth or the lower world, and sky being the upper world. This female horse has an unbroken tradition from the Neolithic, morphing through Pagan shamanism to modern religions that have historically developed the ideas of evil and the devil out of the feminine and the earth.

6   Quoted by Karcher in *Total I Ching: Myths for Change*.

Initially, she seems a strange contrast to the all-bright and celebratory harvest images above, a paradox like the Full Moon pair itself as the embodiment of both Yang and Yin. All of the Dark Goddess's work was done in darkness, but all of it was considered beneficial, including receiving the dead. Was she the invisible shadow from behind the brightness, or the archetypal image of the collective unconscious from the eternally dark back side of the Full Moon, projected as a deity? We know so little about her, but her form on the outer surface of the earth—a mare— is still one of the most potent of all feminine symbols. I strongly suspect that her role at the Full Moon celebration was to preside over the sacrifice, which in our time is the ego-sacrifice offered from our own shadow.

I am struck by her welcomed presence in that early time, as such a clear projection of the positive power of the unconscious.

Where does the Moon's shadow (our unconscious) go in our time, when the face of the Moon has nothing but light upon it? Can we see it in ourselves? Like the wake of the collective invisible boat, we do see it outside of ourselves in increased activity in emergency rooms, police departments, and other public places, most of us half-believing this is some strange, predictable phenomenon caused by the Moon. It seldom occurs to us to recognize it as our own unconscious which is also part of the collective unconscious. But in our time we do not want to acknowledge or take responsibility for it, so we project it on the human "others" who lurk in dark alleys waiting to be caught in the ultimate social nets. We do not have a collective dark goddess upon which to put it, giving it a meaning, credibility, and a way to neutralize it. The Dark Goddess held both the ancestors' hopes and fears, and made them sacred[7].

We need to repeat something here that we have stated before in other words. Those "dark" things that have been trapped in our unconscious are there because we imagine that they are "bad". Some forgotten parental or societal image once taught us to judge them so in the long past. In reality, most of them were at the worst social blunders. The first step in transforming them is to accept them unseen whatever they are. This is what the Dark Goddess might have done. This is what many of us believe is a divine quality—non-judgmental

---

7   This is an amazingly precise symbol of what we are discussing. At Full Moon, our illumination may be positive or negative, but either way it provides a step in growth if we allow it. If we were "an ancient" from the late Neolithic, we would project upon the Valley Goddess, a piece either of our demonic or divine shadow and allow her to "be" it for us.

acceptance. It is our own spirit which must apply that acceptance nonjudgmentally to ourselves, thus bringing our own god-goddess spiritual aspect into play. There may be instances where one needs to call upon the Divine to overshadow the personal. But there are also instances where our own sense of the divine is imprisoned and we are afraid to let it out. Most of these dark things, in other words, are bogey men. We need not alwas to take ourselves so seriously.

Many people now have no trusted divine being to embody and make sacred our dark secrets, to carry them for us, and to keep us safe in their presence. We do have in religion a forgiving aspect of deity, but no revelation of the unconscious aspect of what is being forgiven. Without that we cannot use and transform these energies, even though we are forgiven. So what can we do in our time? In actuality, we do project them onto others and thus make those others the focus of our paranoia; so, we must learn to recognize ourselves in our projections of fear, hate, love, guilt, or fascination. .. Oh, I feel so guilty; oh, that's his fault; oh, she did that to me—how awful! Oh, I love her/him so much I will die if he leaves me. The ancients had a way of making that darkness divine. We don't have that, and we know that projected darkness can be used for harm. There is a principle that what we send out comes back to us threefold, so if we are forgiven and do not recognize that piece of darkness inside, we may continue to spread darkness. We will continue to feel sad, afraid, and angry and so forth, wondering why.

Something we do have is the magic of words, which we have written about earlier in the book—enticing the unconscious with potent words to offer up its contents (see Chapter 5). Ultimately, we have the Moon phases which give us the opportunity to work on a small dark piece each month. If we work honestly with ourselves, we can gradually clear out the darkness and reincorporate our lost powers of consciousness.

Again we have to remind the reader that this is not about religion, but about psychological realities. Religions, as we know them in this time, provide aspects of the divine that can forgive our dark moments, and we may indeed need forgiveness, for comfort at the very least. But we need both forgiveness and the hard work of recognizing our shadow. Otherwise it eventually gets out of control because it remains unconscious. (Here we remember Jung's directive: what is unconscious rules you!)

Psychological Realities at Full Moon

What keeps us from seeing our shadow other than through the wake of the invisible boat is that in this phase we are operating most strongly in our logical brain. Rules and logic and personal preference tell us we have no shadow; and because in our modern society Yang or left-brain function is valued over Yin right-brain function, we have learned to imprison much of our Yin side. Is it possible that early man, who is said to have undeveloped boundaries between conscious and unconscious, left and right brain, used the ritual and sacrifice of the Full Moon as an external protective boundary between the outer goodness of the harvest and the fears so close to the surface? Do we fail to notice in our time that the moment of harvest that guarantees food for the winter, is the precise moment in which the mare appeared? Are we sometimes reminded that we have failed to trust the universe even when it provides what we need. Our fears of starvation, destruction, death, or other "evils" arise at Full Moon just when we think we have mastered them once and for all. Better that we face those fears and resolve them now, than let them continue to haunt us.

Like us, the Ancients certainly feared death, had homicidal thoughts, envy, etc. At the moment when mind and emotions were equally powerful the ancestors did not build boundaries in their minds that would hide their shadow-emotions but instead projected them onto a mythical figure that represented everything they feared or hated including their own frightening emotions over which they did not have mental control. We who do have internal boundaries still do something very similar; we also project our dark side—not on to a familiar goddess, which was socially acceptable, but on to our own personal external reality, which is neither acceptable nor safe. So how can we on the Moon Path safely make our shadow visible?

We suggest that there are five ways our shadow can become visible (or conscious) and therefore we can have a relationship with it.

(1) Through transformative processes at work, in dreams, visions, and synchronicities, as we attempt to understand ourselves.

(2) through watching our invisible boat we can observe our projections on others outside of ourselves. Since we have no socially or humanly acceptable container for them, as did the ancients, the unconscious dominates us. Dominance and imprisonment are qualities that do not encourage working together, individually or collectively, even within our own selves. The same goes for the

realities of law enforcement and jails, by which our projections are punished.

(3) During a mental break in which emotions irrupt chaotically. Those who become emotionally unstable at Full Moon do not have balance between the two sides of the brain. The emotional dark side breaks through weak boundaries in chaotic expression. Objective help may be needed here.

(4) Through psychic ability, dream work, guided imagery, active imagination, and other related personal work.

(5) Divination. Those who practice one of many forms of divination gradually open up their sensitivity to their intuitive side and to a view that includes more than the five senses alone.

These five channels of the unconscious have been observed as collective phenomena as well as personal phenomena. The human organism functions at the individual level in much the same ways as societies and humanity in general. If you read history from that point of view you can see different societies playing out the same shadow conflicts as those of individuals, and deciding on similar ways of dealing with them. These channels are not meant to divide us into two parts, but to allow the right brain equal time, so to speak. We need to listen to these channels to the unconscious, which are accessed by the right brain. We dislike or fear the shadow, which wants to express through the right brain, emotional, non-logical half, from which also come great music, poetry, compassion, and other deep and moving human expressions. Our challenge is to align or integrate both sides of ourselves in the process of creating and offering the Second Seed.

It is time we appreciated the shadow for what it is. Consider the aspects of the Valley Goddess—all those wonderful aspects of life and death that operate at the unseen levels: conception, nurturing, feeding, protection, security, refuge, clairvoyance, dying as being carried safely into an unseen world. It seems that in the light of the Full Moon we need to acknowledge the dark side of ourselves for all of the life-giving qualities that must by nature function outside of our conscious view. Most of all we need the quality of compassion for both our own and others' repressed shadows. This is nature, the 99% darkness of the modern Field which contains the energy that we know, plus infinitely more—the energy of creation and creativity. What if the dark matter currently acknowledged by science turns out to be our own collective darkness?

That which needs transforming comes out as demonic or divine—but always something we feel disconnected from. We ourselves originally put it out of sight, where it obstructed our appreciation; but with compassion we can recapture and begin to reintegrate it into our conscious selves during this fifth Window, perhaps finishing at the Balsamic. The Full Moon energies are specifically for releasing what is imprisoned, and increasing our power and ability to nurture and give form and creativity to our lives in alignment with spirit. A piece of something aversive, with its roots in the unseen personal self, can be recognized and released. (Read the Voices of the Elders below.)

Strangely, the dark unacceptable contents of our unconscious usually become powerfully creative when released in their transformed state. The universe's dark energy is now becoming understood as the fertile chaos out of which comes creation. While taking my certification studies for alcohol and drug addiction, I had the incredible and exciting privilege of listening to a number of the most dynamic and creative people I have ever met. They were in the forefront of the field both here and abroad, but unbelievably they originally came from the very pit of addiction as society's "lost souls."

We have to repeat that how this comes about is a mystery. It happens naturally if we are willing to let it. Making intents, being open, compassionate with ourselves and others, ritualizing each phase in some personal, private way, all these give our dark side messages that we are open to receive it without judgment. We already have built into us the mechanism by which bit by bit this other side transforms. Trust your process. Follow your highest intent. Moon phase work, we often tell ourselves, is the best therapist we know.

An ancient Spiritual Technology Re-Visioned in Modern Terms

This phase is the peak point in the cycle that both ancients and moderns celebrated as the most important and precise statement of nature on our interconnectedness. It is at the core of our practice and that of the ancients. This is where "we do it"—we fully connect ourselves within, with the outer world, or with the heavens. The ancients established this landmark in personal cycles through their most important Full Moon ritual; we promised something similar but different. They were operating in a different mind-frame than we, one perhaps more right-brained and less left-brained, as we have been explaining all along in various terms. We have suggested in the chapter on ritual, various ways of creating our own rituals and elsewhere other personal rituals. Now we must look at the basic principles that underlie our modern mental-set for getting past our endless left-brain chatter to a structure we can design according to our own emotional needs.

How can we find better ways to intentionally project or celebrate our demons or angels, or   secrets, safely, both for ourselves and others. How can we do what the early shamanic people did, without endangering the integrity of our own beliefs? We believe there are a number of modern ways familiar to everyone that can help us work the admittedly psychological aspects without actually needing a therapist, if we are basically stable and whole, and without creating a mythical figure for ourselves, such as the Dark Goddess. It is a matter of allowing our right brain and personal unconscious to operate without interference from the left side. We do it all the time, in fact. Listening to background music or doodling on the telephone pad are two ways. I know someone who doodles the most interesting and sometimes beautiful designs on that pad, but denies she is artistic. At the same time I have noted that they often parallel new insights.

We made a list of activities that we find tend to lessen or eliminate the left-brain chatter, all of which are common parts of our contemporary lives. You will find at least one item here that will work for you.

Yoga
Swimming
Dancing
Meditation
Chanting mantra silently or aloud
Drumming or clapping to the rhythm of 210 beats per minute
Watching one's breathing for five minutes
Free expression writing in a journal
Practicing active imagination or guided imagery[8]
Communicating deeply with a good friend
Games using free association
Petting a cat
Listening to music or creating it
Doodling or creating spontaneous art
Intent

8   See the book, *Psychosynthesis* by Roberto Assagioli (Bib.)

Divination
Prayer

Any of these may be incorporated into personal ritual if desired. The arts are especially useful; educators have determined that the arts are something called primary expression as opposed to secondary which involves language. Primary expression very closely describes the ancients' deep involvement in their own ritual. (Educators tell us that in our time primary expresssion is creating music and art, not speaking or writing.) However developed the ancestors' language was, it was not as significant as the experience itself. It was only when the shaman announced the divination that it became important, since only the Shaman received the divination and had to communicate it to the community. This is because language is an interpretation of an experience—a secondary expression, not the experience itself.

Listen to the Voices of the Elders

The Egyptian Guardian of Phase Five: *Bast*, the Planet Mercury, the living power of the Sunlight. Bast is the archetype that represents the conscious bringing of the task into its fullness of life and form. Here we are at our personal, most fully conscious, in the month. The little self receives from spirit the most light it is able to receive. What one does with that light is the foundation of one's evolving soul and spirit conscious-ness. This is what you have done. Is what you accomplished created out of the living power of Sunlight?

The 8-Fold Path, Aversion: *bad reputation*. As we bring full light to bear on our situation, we are vulnerable to exposing to ourselves and others those parts we most would like to keep hidden. It goes with the territory. Aversions are obsessive or compulsive, like addictions in reverse. If they truly are an obsessive issue (a shadow characteristic), they may be exaggerated under the intense light of this moment. Your ancestors are not coming to eat you, but your feelings may be so out of proportion that you could believe something equally terrifying. Just keep in mind that this is a test.

So you made a social blunder. It usually turns out that few are shocked, most never notice, and others are appreciative of our courage. Those who react negatively are likely to be projecting their own shadow upon you. It is a good thing to learn that aversions are unnecessary energy-sappers that slow down our progress. Besides, at least half of all Full Moons bring "good reputation" experiences.

"Reading" the Full Moon into Your Own Chart Wheel.

1. The Sun sign of the Full Moon phase _____.
2. The Full Moon's sign_____.
3. Place different-colored sticky-dots on the two houses of the signs above_____.
4. Note the activities of the Sun's house, using the house keyword tables. _____.
5. Note the activities of the Moon's house, using house keyword tables_____.

We can now ask the following questions:

1. In what area of my life (Moon's house) is my initial intent perfected and reaching for its place in the outside world? _____.
2. What sign characterizes the manner in which the work needs to be done?_____.
3. From what area of my life (Sun's house) does meaning and purpose come? _____.
4. What is the nature (sign) of the Full Moon Sun's message? _____.
5. What is the nature (sign) of the Full Moon Moon's message? _____.

The Process

"Ed's" example chart. The Full Moon phase in Ed's cycle began on August 16, 2008. Moon was at 24 Aquarius in Ed's 4th house, and Sun was at 24 Leo in his 10th house. This Lunation was also a Lunar eclipse. Note: the Earth's shadow completely cuts off the Sun's light to the Moon, just as the Moon approaches the full phase. The intensity of the eclipse varies according to the degree of darkening. Not all eclipses are complete and actually more are partial than not.

In diagram II the soul is closest to the personality now. Here we have the second eclipse of the half-year. If it could speak, this eclipse would tell Ed that he needs to "clean up his act" in the Moon's area of life, along with the usual meanings of a Full Moon.

The Houses. Whatever Ed's project was for this month, it comes to a head at this point. The Moon's position indicates the area of life where that happens. 4th house is home, family, foundations, security. This area being opposite the Sun 10th house, it exerts the strongest push/pull energy possible. Are Ed's personal foundations strong enough to support the demands of the career change? Does the Moon's eclipse indicate that a change of attitude and behavior is needed in his home and family area? Are the career and home in alignment or do they conflict? How could the home hold this month's second seed—a contribution to the collective? These are questions that must be answered by the signs involved, the degrees, and finally Ed's own reactions.

The signs. Moon in Aquarius in the 4th house suggests either that the home has a progressive energy, open to improvement and productive change, or even geographic change as in moving to accommodate the job. It also tells us that this area of personal security involves the collective itself. Perhaps Ed lives in a multiple dwelling. If so, it must have a connection of some importance to the career. Another interpretation may be that his home situation contains something that is bizarre, unkempt, or otherwise unsuitable if seen by others involved with the career. Aquarius rules rehabilitation and the bizarre, as well as foreign countries or people, New Age influences, or non-traditional ways and personalities. A Leo career person tends to be traditional and self-oriented which suggests that nontraditional or humanitarian foundations are necessary to balance the strong self-orientation. In essence, a Full Moon confronts the career house with an opposite needed to balance home/foundations with career.

Beyond this our information does not go. But given the Full Moon and natal Suns in Leo, we can restate from the Transpersonal Full Moon table below, that the following: personality issues of pride, leadership, sensitivity, and over-emphasis on appearances, in the 10th house…need social integration, and group involvement in the 4th house. In the best of all possible worlds, Ed's home or family is socially benefited by the probable career change, indicating it could provide a suitable foundation from which Ed can operate in the career situation, once he takes care of the deficiency indicated by the eclipse. Knowing the person here would make it easy to know which word to use, and what the home situation is actually like at the time.

The Degrees. The Sun degree theme (read 25 Leo) is *a large camel crossing a desert: Self sufficiency in the face of a long and exhausting adventure.* Roche describes this degree as courage, endurance and overcoming of outer limitations. We could fantasize many scenarios here. Perhaps the new or transformed job requires unusual living situations (4th house). "Unusual" is often the simple word for Aquarius. Or it might mean that, given the present living situation, Ed is about to embark on some strenuous personal activity in which he can depend only upon his own internal resources for accomplishment.

According to Roche's image, the negative aspect of this degree and therefore suggesting Ed's experience, can be deplored by pessimists because it is about *elimination or the sweeping away of all that has no further use or value.* In truth that *is* what the degree is about. But how do you choose to perceive the experience?   Al Gore, Sr., is said to have answered such a question this way: *Every adversity, every failure, and every heartache, carries with it the Seed of an equivalent or greater benefit.*

The Moon's degree (read 25 Aquarius) is: *A butterfly with the right wing more perfectly formed—the capacity to develop the rational and fully conscious aspect of the mind ahead of normal evolution.* What an interesting degree that is, since the butterfly is a universal symbol for metamorphosis. It fits very well with a choice of 4th house meaning as an aspect of the inner self that involves internal security. It suggests that the rigors of the new job can push him to a period of extreme internal endurance, or challenge to his inner strength, that ends with some transformation of his very consciousness. Meanwhile, we need to remember that this area of his life also needs some fixing.

While we could imagine other scenarios, what would happen if the actual situation was as follows?   Projecting from his 9 Leo New Moon, we had tuned in on this following Full Moon to see how it fulfilled the original prediction that the energies were moving forward toward transformation. That is the theme here, indeed. But what does Ed expect from "transformation"?   What if Ed does not encounter the transformation he expected—a step up the ladder to what he thought was promised. Instead, what if he encountered a stripping of material things, a serious setback to his material career. Can we imagine his words?

> So I got an eclipse [9 Leo New Moon]. My life was in the pits, but the New Moon had promised [so he thought] an upward sort of energy. I read ahead to the Full Moon, which had a scary degree symbol. It

sounded spiritual, but way beyond the level I thought I could handle or even understand. So much for me being in a better place, and all transformed in 14 days. Within the week, someone else less qualified than I got the job I was prepared for, and on the Full Moon my own job was eliminated and I was offered a lesser one in another department, with lower salary, which will require me to cut back on all but the most essential spending. What does all this mean? How can I find that my life has been moving forward and upward? Where is this divine perfection everything is supposed to unfold to?

For the first time in Ed's life, and in the lives of most people in this country, times are universally hard, and life is stripping from us so much of the external, ego-satisfying materiality we have taken for granted; and yet for the first time, in the degree symbols, here are the clues about what can result from such stripping, beyond the fear, anger, depression, that so many have, and apparently rightly so. Is it always someone else's fault? We don't think that is the largest picture. Maybe we can have that life of divine perfection, but maybe not right now in the material world; and maybe it won't look like you expected it to. Are these experiences bumping us up to the next level of consciousness? The question is—what part do we each have to play in this? What does this transformational degree mean to you?

Traditional spiritual teachers tell us that in such a state of bare reality (the desert journey,) it is possible to contact the essence of our own individual being. This is, indeed, the spiritual goal of the sign Leo (in everyone's life.) Shakespeare's 73rd sonnet (referred to previously) images this truth by comparing the barrenness of old age to the bare limbs of winter trees, where you can actually see the complete fundamental shape of the tree. As we have mentioned earlier, Aquarius is the goal of Leo, just as every sign is the goal of its opposite. Leo (individual consciousness) needs to integrate the opposite features of Aquarius (group consciousness) in order to fulfill itself. So this concept also implies the possibility of Ed's seeing himself as an innate facet of humanity when superficialities are stripped away.

This eclipse affected everyone on the planet, each person according to the Leo house of that person's chart. In the recent past, it has been interesting to see the many public changes of perspective after 9-11 and Katrina. For example, consider the number of Hollywood actors (strong Leo types) who have come forward to the aid of people in disaster areas all over the world; or people who lost everything and simply turned around and began helping others. With this eclipse happening at the beginning of a major recession, Ed cannot be blind to the fact that he is not alone in his experience, "but" Ed may say, "I don't have any money." He and others do need to change their perspective in such situations. We must use what we have. At this point he needs to fall back on his own resources as the camel tells him. These two Full Moon degrees have information for him. It appears that he is unfamiliar with the spiritual laws of transformation and therefore at a loss and very disappointed. It is likely that his home situation contains something that could help him see his personal world in a meaningfully larger context. His revelation may be that there is value in living through a "desert" period in his life, gaining courage and a greater viewpoint through persistence and reliability. Right now, he needs to focus on his home and family and use his time or energy toward its "rehabilitation", whatever that means to him.

If not a job loss, others will also be experiencing various losses affecting their Leo houses—a loss of one's highly esteemed expensive computer system (3rd house), a house foreclosure (4th house,) a loss of the sense of pride when a child (5th) house gets into trouble. The degree symbols are principles that underlie a piece of all of life. They hold not only the clues about what is happening at the moment, but the clues about what one can do with the experiences. Any one of these experiences are being experienced in the personal lives of many others in some recognizable ways. If one reaches out, there will always be others to help, or that need help, and there are always "elders" close at hand, who can offer advice. Every cycle we have the degree symbols that never fail us if we are able and willing to see what they offer. *In this case, the desert journey experience shows us a deeper truth about who we really are.* It may single us out as individuals like the man on the camel's back, but only to open us up to the truths of our own greater existence, which is the collective.

To define oneself as part of a universe, of all the millions of others having the same experience, which itself is part of something greater, is to give meaning to oneself. It allows us to participate in it, seeing it and ourselves as a participating unit. To define ourselves as a separate entity, seeing the Universe as an objective scientific fact, is to see ourselves and the universe without apparent meaning, or with no meaning implied other than that of size, weight, speed, distance, etc. As soon as people can qualify that definition with a greater meaning such as living energies informing or creating the universe, or myths mirroring their own psychological or religious insights, then whatever is included in those qualifications is perceived at a higher level, the level of meaning. As soon as you can see yourself as part of something larger, your situation will begin to have meaning, and you will have changed that individual perspective into a higher form. This is how unfolding consciousness comes about, one step at a time.

Field is still the same ancient universe, of the ancestors, created by something greater, now showing us its scientific wonders. One can participate consciously, viewing the Sun and Moon as a great clock, timing the release of meaning step by step. We are free to choose our own definition of meaning, and of its purveyors. Meaning is universal, but through the houses, signs and degree symbols we can begin to step it down to our own level of understanding.

Below is a table of the transpersonal energies of the Full Moon, showing how the energies flow between Sun and Moon during each month of the year, or sign of the Zodiac.

ENERGY THE SUN'S POSITION	FORCE FIELD THE MOON'S POSITION
ARIES: The birth of a new idea…	LIBRA: Precipitates decision
TAURUS: The conscious refinement of desires…	SCORPIO: Adds fuel to the testing fires—challenges new behaviors.
GEMINI: Weaving the web of co-service relations…	SAGITTARIUS: Marshals companions on your path
CANCER: Manifesting one's deepest values…	CAPRICORN: Leads to peak experience
LEO: Integrating personality issues…	AQUARIUS: Promotes social integration

VIRGO: Nurturing form and consciousness of the Spirit within	PISCES: Clears the way to the unknown
LIBRA: Pausing to weigh, choose, decide…	ARIES: Benefits the next beginning
SCORPIO: Tests of courage, strength, and silence…	TAURUS Releases light through your speech.
SAGITTARIUS: Exerting toward goal after goal…	GEMINI: Stimulates companions' growth
CAPRICORN: Your peak experience…	CANCER: Nurtures yourself and others on the path
AQUARIUS: Developing a sense of universality…	LEO: Increases your group sensitivity, expands selfhood into group-hood
PISCES: Walking away from the dead past…	VIRGO: Frees your spirit to fulfill its intent

Table 13. Transpersonal Full Moon Energy Flow

19

Disseminating Phase: Bringing New Light into the Core
A Time for Digesting and Sharing the Full Moon Realization

A time to absorb assimilate integrate incorporate,
Distribute disseminate circulate,
A time to digest,
A time to share,
The realization of the Full Moon,
Light seed-Dark seed

—-VLM

Transitioning between Full and Last Quarter Moons

The transition is between the revelation of the meaning of the first half of the cycle, and the place of absorbing it into your core values (3rd Quarter). You cannot adequately fulfill the 3rd Quarter's task until you have tested the new information by sharing it with others and deeply imprinting it upon your consciousness. This phase demonstrates conscious intent to carry out the Full-Moon vision, another reflection of the need to carry out spirit's message into one's life.

You have heard the phrase, "to really learn something, teach it to another". Disseminating is a teaching phase and a teaching word. This is the phase where you begin to disseminate or distribute something of value into the collective. This is your Full Moon seeding. You may have a new sense of meaning concerning whatever you completed in the two weeks of working on the New Moon message, even though it is not finished until the last day of the cycle. No matter what you did in the outside world, it is your inner level of beingness or consciousness that has been at stake. It is how you are in the world, not what you do that is the lesson of each and every cycle, which could be as invisible as sending good thoughts to someone who needs that kind of support. Is the wholeness of the Full Moon operating fully in this phase? Are you taking down into your deepest self the values or understanding you received at the Full Moon? What is that? Sometimes you have to reflect in order to know it. The question you ask at the Disseminating Moon is "What impressed you most, at the *feeling* level, from the previous 3-day period?"

According to *the Scribe*—the Egyptian guardian of this phase— your illumination is being placed on "the organic record," perhaps the cellular memories? From another point of view, our personal illumination is also recorded in the Field which may be the same thing. From either "place" it contributes to the energy of changing archetypes, which is so central to the evolution of collective consciousness. Consider how small such a contribution might be, without diminishing its significance. You have an altercation with a policeman over a minor traffic violation. In the Disseminating Moon you realize that you handled it differently than your usual way with such confrontations—"Oh, I never could have handled it that way before the last two weeks!"

While Full Moon was the flowering of the plant, Disseminating is the fruiting state. This may not be an exact symbol of botany, but it is a good symbol of our process. You have created a new seed either purged of its clinging shadow or carrying the shadow on to be perpetuated. Either way the seed is being dropped into the collective, where it may or may not take root depending on the quality of the soil. At the same time it is being taken deeply into the core of your own self during these three days. Small or great, this learning is your second seed. This seems to be the hardest of all the phases to "read" for yourself. It requires clear inner reflection. The answers here have no clarion messengers, and according to Blaschke, the messages here may offer gentleness and love that alleviates fear in others, and emotional bonding that often happens through mutual laughter. If you were the alcoholic whose story is told below, you offered hope to a fellow addict. Imagine how valuable that experience was, once written into the Field. Once you recognize your seed, you may never again ignore or lightly pass over your Full Moon insights in the Disseminating phase.

Sharing the Seed, Light or Dark

The Zodiac degrees of Sun (Self) and Moon (personal self) describe how a true partnership between self and Self, or self and others, can grow and expand by sharing personal wisdom. The Sun degree provides the archetype for the Self's wisdom. Moon's degree shows how the self's efforts can best reflect the new Self's ideal. The individual's social and personal values can expand as old limiting boundaries are crossed. And, consider, if you believe your illumination was negative, someone out there may make a better choice from having heard your story; or another may offer you the hope you need. Maybe this is the bread you had cast on the water in the past, returning to you increased. This can change your dark seed into light seed in the twinkling of an eye.

There is an implicit decision to be made here. "Why should I share dark seed and pollute the world outside of me, embarrassing myself and others?" Sharing that can have greater outcomes than the momentary mistakes. It is like two alcoholics who fell into the gutter on the Full Moon. The following day they awoke to reality. One picked himself up, went to the nearest pub and had a hair of the dog. Life went on and at the Disseminating Moon he gathered some friends and they had a great binge and enjoyed themselves mightily, telling their stories. The other alcoholic said grimly to himself, "maybe next time I'll wake up dead." He went off and asked for help. During the Disseminating Phase he gathered together his friends and told them he was quitting and asked them to quit with him. A few of them did. Reality wins again. That was the moral to the story of the month. Even if you screw up badly or lose something important at the Full Moon, the meaning is available. Recognize your mistake and go share what you learned from it, helping others and yourself to let go of some ego-patterns and make better choices.

On the other hand, maybe you or the alcoholic had an *epiphany*. So share and inspire others.

Do Not Underestimate Listening

If this is the time to tell your story, so is it time for everyone else. Will someone find you as the next listener? The following example demonstrates the importance of listening at this particular phase, in a different context than at any other time. Sometimes these experiences seem eerily destined.

A produce person in my local grocery store is from Tibet. Tibetans are not allowed to leave Tibet despite the terrible living conditions there. However some managed to escape across the border without being caught, tortured and jailed. This man went across four times.

I always have a brief conversation with him if he is present when I am shopping.

While shopping, on the first day of a recent disseminating Moon (of which I was not then aware,) I saw him and stopped to inquire about his health and any news from Tibet. I was unprepared for the torrent of "story" this unleashed. Although as always he characteristically spoke in a measured and careful manner, avoiding all negative statements concerning China, the emotional pressure behind the words was palpable. For half an hour he spoke about conditions in Tibet in grueling detail, things that never reach the press here—shocking first-hand details of people being tortured for attempting to leave, or simply possessing a picture of the Dalai Lama, land being gradually stolen from the Tibetans leaving them without a means of livelihood, and so on.

Overwhelmed, I finished my shopping and went home. It was not until a month later that I realized the consequences to me of this moving and very disturbing story. It had brought about a change in my value system; and values (particularly social values) are the substance of the Last Quarter phase just following this one. In this case my social values were subtly changed in a lasting way.

The reader may wish to read the Moon's degree for that disseminating experience. It was 11 Aries[1], in my 4th house (I was shopping for my household—4th house). This degree happens to be one degree away from the degree of my birth Sun which is in another sign; any Zodiac degree close to one's Sun degree is always an aspect. Sun represents character and this degree speaks to the danger of ignoring things you would rather not have to face. I was planning a pleasant family birthday meal and would not have chosen to include such thoughts, which were sobering, indeed.

The story was so compelling that it was difficult to identify which fragments of the Moon degree belonged to me and which to the Tibetan; which shows how a degree can apply to everyone. I found my personal interpretation in some fragments of the description, and the Tibetan's interpretation in others, but they overlapped. You will easily see these applications if you look up the degree in Roche's book.

---

1   11 Aries (Roche) A *flock of white Geese.* The symbol....*suggests a yearning for light-hearted freedom...but eventually, like migrating geese, every individual who achieves such a state must eventually come back down to earth and take up where he left off...you may be dreaming of faraway places or feeling a need to get away from it all and do something light and fun...Responsibility weighs heavily on your shoulders...*

Don't be afraid to pick and choose just those parts that are yours, in any degree books; and don't be afraid to interpret liberally or freely.

So we see how important this phase is, concerning what others plant in us as well as what we share with others during this transitional three days. Is there someone out there who has something important to share with you? With me? Will someone else's new insight reframe my own if mine was lacking or negative and vice versa? Very possibly. The energies are open; group spirit is ready to connect. Consider carefully where and how you will cast your seed abroad, and intentionally look for seeds from others.

This Second Seed is the Seed of the Next New Moon.

The Full Moon insight is the seed to be germinated at the next new Moon. It is the product of our own co-creation. Right now you are laying groundwork for the next cycle. As you follow the cycles for a while you may be able to trace the threads of how you co-create your life step by step at each phase of a cycle.

It occurs to us that this may be one of the greater personal ways of encouraging the transformation of society. Consider what happens when you release something you thought, felt, created, organized, built, wrote, into the hands of the Other or the Collective. It may seem to take on a life of its own. As you share it, it becomes more universal and so do you. Everyone changes over and over as we pass through the next three days. You take on qualities of the Other or Others take on yours. If you are socially isolated, it may be that your seed is meant only for yourself at this time, but ultimately it will change your group connection, or you will seed society in some way unknown to you at this point. The "no man is an island" concept is true and nowhere will you find it functioning more truly than here. We add that this is happening every month whether we know it or not.

One of the core beliefs which we and many others share is that whatever expands your own consciousness adds to the ultimate total of consciousness out there, even if you are isolated. This is being proven as we write, by—now well-known—studies of isolated sick people who have recovered more quickly when they were prayed for or held in the light or whatever form others chose to use in their meditations and intentions

Internalizing the Realization

If you look closely, you will see that the Full Moon message grew organically out of the task begun at new Moon and as the message became a true part of you, it also carried you deeper into your core self. Perhaps at this time you will realize how valuable it was for you to have worked the waxing phases faithfully and persistently—or didn't, as the case may be.

As you share your understanding with others, it is helping you absorb and "digest" it. You are dropping the new seed, which will grow. Is it a vital healthy seed that will produce, in others as in yourself, a healthy plant—a healthy new value? Or is it a bitter or hard-shelled seed? A bitter understanding at full Moon does not necessarily mean that the seed will be bitter; nor does an experience that "hardens your heart" have to produce a hard-shelled seed. The mirroring process of a full Moon that was hard or bitter can be transmuted by another's *understanding*—the larger meaning of the mirror's message, and a keyword for this phase. Often the degree image or its explanation will offer a clue to reframing the experience. I have heard people say, "I can stand anything if I know what it means, or why it is there". Degree symbolism defines meaning at the archetypal level. It is our task to reframe its message in terms of our personal life, house and sign.

Recognizing the Phase Energies

We wish to remind the reader once again, that these phases most often have subtle effects. Once in a while one of us will say, "It sure feels like a Full Moon today—just crazy out there." or "yesterday I felt like so listless and today I have my energy back, it must be the New Moon." There are other times, as when I unknowingly taught a class on a Disseminating Phase. It went so well, with such exciting participation! It was one of these events that so obviously belong to a phase that it generates a "Serendipity" rush. These usually happen spontaneously when the Sun or Moon is close to a planet in one's natal chart. If you have a natal chart and can read it, you can predict each month which phases will affect you most strongly.

It can take a while to recognize how the energies *feel*, especially for those whose perceptions are not based in the body. Other signals may more easily trigger recognition, as for instance, a rush of ideas and phone conversations, a sense of being more emotional than usual, or even a lack of emotional responsiveness. This is not important other than for your own satisfaction. What is important is that our intentions are aligning with the nature of a phase. This is why I try to take a few minutes the evening of or before a phase, check out the positions of Sun and Moon on the wheel, and make a conscious intent to align myself with the interpretations as I understand them in my life. Even if you forget the next day, your unconscious remembers and that intent is working in your life.

Listen to the Voices of the Elders

The Egyptian Guardian of Phase Six: *Thoth, the planet Mercury.* The guardian of wisdom and learning—the cosmic scribe—writes the message of the task in the book of soul records. You are taking down or imprinting your new awareness into your core values and living out what has impressed you most at the very human level.

The Eight-Fold Path—Aversion: *Blame.* This aversion just naturally follows after a less-than-desirable enlightenment. It is only too easy to place blame somewhere for whatever is displeasing to us. This goes both ways. Others may blame you for a misdoing, in their view. You may do the same to others. This is an opportunity to upgrade your responses, or to think before you speak.

Locating the Disseminating Moon on Your Own Chart Wheel

Arrange the following information in your own manner in the journal. We repeat from earlier: you will not have the information without the software, unless you use our website calendar page or a website that features the current signs and/or degrees. Using our rough method given in Chapter 15, find the Sun by adding 84 hours' movement from the previous, 1st Q phase, position. Place Moon 45 degrees ahead of the Sun position. Use only sign positions. Keep in mind that the Moon changes signs every 30 degrees.

1. The Disseminating phase Sun's sign (yellow dot)

   _____.

2. The Disseminating phase Moon's sign (blue dot)

   _____.

4. Note the activities of the Sun's house

   _____.

5. Note the activities of the Moon's house

   _____.

6. The Sun's and Moon's degrees if available

   _____

Notice that when you observe that you have had an insight, which you are now sharing with another, you are actually communicating with your soul and that soul is not something separate from you. You are always aware of soul communication but may never have known, simply because there is no disconnect. You simply have not defined as such the thoughts coming into your mind that are from the soul <u>level</u> and not from another entity.

The Process—Putting It Together

<u>Ed's example chart.</u> The Disseminating Moon phase in our sequence began on August 20, 2008. Moon was at 12 Aries in Ed's 6th house, and Sun was at 27 Leo in his 10th house.

<u>The Houses</u>. Moon tells us where Ed will be disseminating his Full Moon experience—Aries 6th house—with spiritual direction from Sun in the career house. Moon's house is nine houses from the Sun's career house, counter-clockwise around" the dial.[2]

6th house is work, health, and service. We will assume that health is not an issue here, with the whole month being about career. Work is what we do to fulfill a career, and is therefore the area of life where this Full Moon experience is primarily shared. We now presume that he had lost his job before the Full Moon, and subsequently took the offered new one tentatively. (We created this story before we did this cycle to see how it would work. It proves our own experience that the degree symbols and phase meanings will work for every possible living situatiaon. We suggest you try changing the story and see what the phases would say about that.)

<u>The Signs</u>. Leo and Aries are fire signs and therefore the houses they rule are especially compatible. The fire signs are good for high aspirations, creativity and eagerness to move ahead. The negative side is that anger operates externally and actively in fire signs. We know that Ed did not want this new job, so he is not dancing with excitement. However, Aries indicates abilities to take leadership in new endeavors and Moon in Aries is emotionally exciting and often hard to control. If he is angry, it is hard to keep it under control. Also, wherever the Moon goes, she carries a lesson with her. Here she cautions Ed to keep his emotional fervor within boundaries and check details in whatever he does (the Virgo background influence in the 6th house). With two fire signs at work, it would be easy to

---

2   Rule for counting houses: count the house you start with as "one", and include the house you end with in your count. Thus, beginning with house ten and counting to house six results in nine houses (10, 11, 12, 1, 2, 3, 4, 5, 6).

miss things or to be ungrounded. We refer you here to Table 6 from Chapter 9, for quick reference to the elements.

Whenever you find Moon and Sun both in the same element, you could find a lack of control of the energies of that element.) Grounding is very important here since Moon is supposed to ground the Sun's message, and 6ᵗʰ house is supposed to ground the career.

The Degrees. In this example, the Sun was at 27 Leo and the Moon 12 Aries (August 20, 2008). The theme for the Sun degree (read 28 *Leo*) is: *"Birds on the limb of a large tree. Ramification....* Birds symbolize thoughts, communication, inspiration and the spiritual and mental realms of being. Trees symbolize knowledge, stability and protection or security. Thus the image of many little birds suggests a confusing array of possibilities requiring self-limitation to avoid overwhelm. It could also lead to a learning situation in which insight into the possible consequences of hasty decisions or emotional reactions to unforeseen events may be gained through group discussion and viewing things from a higher perspective.

Notice how this degree symbol fits into the more general information gained from the house/sign readings. This is specific, detailed advice from spirit through Ed's 10ᵗʰ house Sun degree that provides purpose or meaning for the Moon's degree and action.

The theme for the 6ᵗʰ house Moon degree (read 13 Aries) is: "An unsuccessful bomb explosion. *Impetuousness"*. It emphasizes the possibility of carelessness and unpredictability. The full degree reading leaves the outcome open, ending with "Your greatest advantage lies in being patient and thorough."

The above degrees are very clear and precise for Ed's situation. Both degrees caution against impulsive action at a time when phase energies seem to encourage it. The probable situation is that Ed has either been erupting in anger, or has seen some exciting possibilities—either in the alternative job or elsewhere, and he must be patient and thorough in evaluating them for action. The Moon suggests he may not do this and therefore jumps too previously into something work wise he could regret later. Since this is a Disseminating Moon, he is probably sharing his experiences and questions among fellow-workers. Again, he needs to be circumspect about this because whatever is heard in this phase may affect others as well as himself

Apply these interpretations to your own Solar dial to see if you can interpret your own Disseminating phase.

20
Third Quarter Phase:
Establishing the New
Internal Crisis and Reorientation as New Values Emerge

Metabolism versus Catabolism
Revelation versus Vision
Past versus Future

Compassionate Understanding or Implacable Regret?
— Marilyn Busteed et al.[1]

He makes my feet like hinds' feet, and sets me on my high places.
— 2 Samuel 22: 34

<u>Why</u> Was This Cycle Valuable?

Here the Seed withers and seems to die. The previous three weeks have brought us to this point. Now there is rebellion against— and breakdown of— old forms. Is this the seed withering? Yes, but that is an illusion. The outer shell (the form of the old values) has to die in order for the inner core to be born. Deep underground in our unconscious we have creatively visioned a new form of the seed for the next cycle.

This phase is about achieving as much as we are able in at least some small collective context, and the revelation was about that, as a realization. It is also about evaluating what has been achieved in light of the new values, and deciding if we want to take what we learned into the next cycle. If we don't like what we see out there— those old values we want to get rid of— then do we rebel against them? We may need to. It is also a time when we may be recognized for any achievement, and judged positively or negatively for it. Here

---

1   *Phases of the Moon* by Marilyn Busteed et Al

is the crisis in consciousness because in the face of that recognition the energies are urging us to stand on the new values behind what we learned, while the past ways of being are still more familiar and comfortable. If we are pro-active we will commit to carrying the new values out in our actions. If we feel unable to change our way, there will be internal conflict. The new values if established will help us to live out at a future time what we have achieved this month. We need to take the one step toward the next cycle, which Dane Rudhyar called "re-orientation". We need to make the commitment to turn our minds and feelings toward the coming cycle, taking the new with us and leaving the old behind. The real value of this cycle is how clearly we see the old values, how effectively we internalize the new ones, and how definitively we then turn our attention toward the next cycle, leaving the old values (shell) to disintegrate during the Balsamic.

Taking the World inside Ourselves

Since full Moon, the shadow has begun growing on the right side of the Moon's face. Once again it reaches half shadow, half light. It signals that for those born under a Last Quarter Moon the soul is ready to disengage from the personality's focus, and trace its steps toward the junction with the Sun/spirit's path[2]. Once every month we get a mini-practice in this experience. Meanwhile you are "taking the world inside yourself". While you were doing things on the outside during the disseminating phase, inside you were absorbing values and ideas (your own and others') which will help you make your changeover to the coming cycle. A critical struggle now goes on which determines whether or not you can meet the New Moon on the next higher level of the spiral. Your need—probably only half conscious—to be a different person because of your experiences, is coming from your core self. It determines whether you will "drop the mask" of the unchanged person and be who you really are now. In ancient Chinese times this was equated with the Mandate of Heaven—cosmic change which affects the very essence of a human being. This phase allows us to see how our consciousness evolves, watch it happening, and make the conscious decision to evolve.

---

2   This refers back to Diagram I, note that there is not a clear separation between soul and personal consciousness in our daily life. But the greatest spiritual distance between soul and personality is at New Moon, where soul begins its journey back toward spirit at 3rd Quarter. This is the actual turning point of reorientation, which we live out in the external world.

The Western world understands this type of struggle, in larger time cycles, as a periodic social breakdown of idols, images, or values. What is important is how well we can understand this as the larger period of time we presently find ourselves in, in the first decade of a new century! We see around us all sorts of people pushing issues on the basis of some important principle they see as needed in moving toward "the new society", or simply their own agenda. We are pulled by the future which we can only see as a mist or fog, a fearful destruction or a hopeful vision, while we are still anchoring in the past, hanging on to it for safety. That breakdown causes physical and social crises, illness (epidemics), and revolts. Dane Rudhyar claims that even the catabolic forces [3] of the body increase at this time in this part of the Moon cycle. In individual terms, that planetary moment divides and endangers our personal perspective. We can then look at this social phenomenon in terms of the Last Quarter Moon in our own daily lives.

This phase is often hard to describe or see it happening, but easier to see in the planetary perspective. There are several tasks required in order to complete this phase fully, as you will see below. It is interesting to note that "9-11" happened on a last quarter Moon, as well as several lesser critical world events to follow; it is tempting to reflect on this event's phase meaning to the general USA state of consciousness, and then to the personal consciousness of the perpetrators. Again, anything can happen during any phase, but the phase will tell the meaning it has at that time for those involved. Speculatively speaking, the 9-11 perpetrators were completing a process of immersing themselves in the dark purposes of a larger collective and had irreversibly chosen their path. They had, in Freudian terms, "swallowed" the terrorist propaganda. The birth of a baby born at first quarter will have a different meaning to the parents (as well as the baby's own personality) than a birth on the last quarter.. Speculating on societal events in this way helps one develop a clearer understanding of the role of phases in one's own life. We believe that the changing Moon phase energies are already part of every person's psyche, and you will be able to create your

---

3   Catabolism: "A metabolic change from complex into simple molecules, accomplished by an energy release" (Webster). As the light-energy is giving way to the dark, our actual physical energies are diminishing, although not everyone is aware of the small difference that can be objectively felt. Both anabolic and catabolic forces are always present together in living beings who are changing balances.

own interpretations of their meanings after while—like the phrase in the Paul Simon song: "When You Begin to Remember..."

Establishing One's Place in the Group, and One's New Beliefs

One's "name" or public identity is established as one stands on what one believes and faces the larger whole on equal terms. The successful individual (vis-à-vis this phase) faces the as-yet-unknown future, in his/her own present strength, ready for a new approach, or something a little better. The 3rd Quarter Sun sign and degree describe the ideal; the Moon sign and degree describe the manner and area of life in which this will be acknowledged in the external world. In this seventh phase, a kind of premonition of the new phase enters the awareness as the unconscious invokes a feeling of need for a new beginning. Conscious faces the unconscious, either as a welcome partner or with a fearsome sense of being overwhelmed by the darkness (one's concepts of evil, bad, wrong, chaos, etc., usually in the world out there).

Both 1st and 3rd quarter phases refer to expansion of identity: the former, the expansion of personal identity and the latter, the expansion of social identity. We have to choose here. Will I cling too tightly to my old personal identity or will I allow it to be blended with an upgraded social identity? This can be very scary at times. Like midnight, this is a magical "witching hour", when half the Moon's reflected light is gone and life is not clear, but flashes of intuition shake our limits to open them up. Shall we take what opportunities exist for us "out there" even though expanding our social base could feel insecure? Can we share or expand our authority, our control, whatever it may be?

What Do We Need To Do to Fulfill the "Cosmic Mandate?"

We believe that those who understand the recent cycle can most effectively turn toward the vague future cycle. But it requires some hard work, this time on the inside. The personality trusts what it knows, and is comfortable with its old value system. The inner crisis is between the outer personality's learned values (Moon) and the growing inner spirit-filled part of us (Sun). Its successful resolution increases our connection to the Higher Self. This time-period puts us in touch with sometimes very deep conflicts, between old ideas and beliefs and something new we added to our value system at Full Moon (Watch your Moon- and Sun-occupied houses on your dial, for clarification). Intentional, non-judgmental self-review will help us to turn away from whatever limitations the personality wants to cling to.

We need to look back over the last 3 weeks and see what we accomplished, or failed to accomplish (where we need to try letting go of regrets). We need to evaluate what we have gained or learned from what we did or didn't do. We need to "judge" or assess the value of our efforts and the meaning of them, to understand ourselves in those terms.

Paralleling the Zodiac phase background, we are in a *Capricornian* or 10th house situation. We have reached the highest point we can in this cycle, externally. Spiritually, this is Capricorn's *revelation on the mountain top,* or anyone's peak experience.

As we had enlightenment or insight at the Full Moon; we have revelation or "*hind*-sight" at the last quarter. That phrase is related to the word "hind," the word for a female deer. The one referred to in the biblical quote above is the one described here. An interesting and unique ability of any *hind* is that its hind feet track exactly in the tracks of its front feet. With this ability it can traverse dangerously narrow pathways higher in the mountains than any other related animal is capable of. She sees where she came from—a greater expanse than from the base of the mountain.. This has been noted by a few spiritual writers who parallel this ability with human spiritual ability to traverse physically, psychologically and spiritually narrow or dangerous situations in life. It is about staying "on track" because your outer self is in sync with your inner intentions, unconscious, or spirituality.

We can traverse high dangerously narrow pathways: that view may an ideal or a vision as the result of our learning of the month. If so, one might in this last week before new Moon, be looking for others who share the same vision. Reorientation is the key to this phase. At the point where your thoughts/feelings turn toward the future, you have reoriented. Up to this point of reorientation toward the future, the "background music" has been Capricornian. Now, once we have reoriented we are in the last third of the 3rd Quarter phase, looking toward the future in Aquarian background music— forward-looking, Promethean, perhaps idealistic, maybe rebellious. It wells up and you can't resist. Aquarius can teach us to decisively turn our backs on the past. You have to be "a little weird" (Aquarius) not to find that distasteful at times, at least in the eyes of others more traditional.

In another framework, some Southwest Native American tribes have a custom they call *The Turquoise Lady*. They honor a recently bereaved wife by giving her a beautiful dress decorated with turquoise. She is to wear it to welcome all visitors to the tribe, with gracious smiles, for a year following her bereavement. She becomes the "welcome lady". During that time she is honored both for her loss, and for her services to the tribe, and her new position in the tribe as a widow. At the end of a year, she surrenders the dress along with her grief, back to the tribe. Meanwhile she has also experienced and anchored her new identity. The tribe would find it offensive if she continued grieving overtly. While working in the area of grief and loss, I found widows of 20 years still grieving their loss as though it were fresh and new. These women were all depressed to some degree, many on medication, and also grieving a life of lost opportunities. It is regretful that we don't provide a custom to honor the bereaved, to offer them a bridge to the future, and to clearly set the stage for the resolution of grief in the structure of that custom.

Turquoise Lady suggests that at some point one must turn one's back on the past and live toward the future, or cease to grow as a part of society and as a person with an identity. We may sadly remember a loss for a lifetime, but we must also have the courage to live our future in spite of this, or lose opportunities we will later regret. It seems to us that in this microcosmic 3 ½ day Moon phase, we add another brush stroke to our new social identity in some way.

Of course there are the never-to-be-forgotten once-in-a-lifetime Last Quarter Moons where one truly finds revelation on the mountain top, and anticipates the coming cycle as an opportunity to live out a vision of a lifetime. Some will gain a public honor for some achievement, or find a new responsibility.

What New Future Needs Have Been Generated? What New Tools Gained?

Whatever we decide we have gained, and how we decide to change will both generate needs and provide us with new tools. What new values and needs do you have to take with you as you move through the next cycle?

Revelation and expansion invariably open our eyes to new needs.

You internalized the new values in the disseminating Moon. Now you are pressed from inside to express those values through some kind of action in the next cycle, but the foundation is laid now. You have decided to take a new step. That can stir up internal conflicts from old fears, as the old "shoulds and should-nots" rise again." To some extent, you now must "put your money where your mouth is", and act on your new direction.

Because of the many possible kinds of struggles here, there is an important observation that needs to be made. At this turning-point of the month, personal plans and group activities tend to coalesce. Something you contributed to a group may bring you together with others.

The most power for good or evil is here. "9-11," which occurred on a Last Quarter Moon, is one example worth meditating on. On the other side of that, public acknowledgement may be given to an individual, or people with appropriate capabilities may be asked to take a responsible position. Barack Obama took the inauguration oath on a Last Quarter Moon [4]

Others whose work is behind the scenes, quiet or inward people, or those dealing with serious illnesses might experience a peak in their own perhaps equally significant personal achievements. The ability to physically stand alone may be an awesome achievement, one with impact not only on themselves, but on their caregivers as well, and down the line upon others in wheelchairs.

Don't imagine that we are telling you such great events happen every month. Nor do they or the example above always happen at the 3rd Quarter. There may be specific characteristics of such events which tie them to other phases, such as a New Moon when they signal the beginning of a new stage in one's life or a Crescent when they signal the forming of a previous idea or intention.

Major events may happen a few times in one's life, but every month is a practice preparing one for such important life experiences. Small acknowledgements from friends or family, or a brief moment of wondering why such acknowledgement did not happen, might be there. It took us four years to complete this book, because we

---

[4]   On January 20, 2009, Barack Obama became the 44th US President. The Sun had just moved into 1 degree of Aquarius the sign of humanity, progress, and universality, also his Rising Sign. It was the last day of the 3rd Quarter phase before entering the Balsamic. Perhaps this is the indication of a transitional presidency, where he would be leading the US into a world-wide period of change.

were learning so much during the process that every little while we had to rewrite everything and expand our vision each time. But our experiences of writing the book always took on the character of the phases, and at Last Quarter Moon we often had those "visions" that took us beyond the current view. Our examples are inadequate to describe all of the ways one can experience a 3rd Quarter Moon. However, two points stand out. If you have been consciously doing your inner and outer work on the New Moon intent for the month, there will be at least some small sense of accomplishment or coming-together of whatever your theme has been; there will be some acknowledgement, personal or otherwise, and/or some sense of a wider vision for something to come.

If you are beginning a life work, it may be years before the results (last quarter) will become evident. Meanwhile you will have many small expanding visions (last quarters) as you go along. A doctor working on medical research might have a paper published on preliminary findings. A mother of a handicapped child might speak to a small gathering of other mothers with similar situations, to share her successes and pull together all the mothers' ideas to form a permanent group which could go on to help others. In a sense, the mother entered the group, and the group began to enter the larger collective. For all these 3rd Quarter experiences to happen, many more very small ones were needed to build the final structure.

The Work behind the Peak of the Last Quarter

This 3rd Quarter Moon is in polarized relationship to the first quarter Moon. If your action at 1st Quarter Moon did not contribute to the development of your individuality and self-reliance, your core self's vision peak during the 3rd /Quarter will be smaller or negative—If your 1st Quarter was met with "they won't like this", "I could never do that", "I'm a failure", "nothing ever changes", you will not build the muscle to complete your task at the Last Quarter Moon. The new seed now dormant in the ground, to be germinated at the following New Moon, will not thrive well in the spent soil of denied core selfhood. Fortunately, this seventh window contains the energy of wisdom and understanding, and the eighth gives one a last chance at letting something go. Each phase is forgiving of past commissions and omissions, etc. Fully realizing one's more-or -less helpful choices increases the past month's value to yourself and your growth. It will contribute a new energy to the seed to come, one that will thrive, and balance what has already been.

Growing and strengthening the core self and being willing to let go of old patterned self-limitations at the 1st Quarter, brings its power to, and finds its reward at, the 3rd Quarter.

How Do We turn Away, Reorient?

Once we have realized the WHY or VALUE of the last quarter, and its process, it is time to mentally turn away from the activity and experience of the cycle, with expectations toward the new phase. The old energy is fading, soon to be laid to rest either in the collective memories or that mysterious place where released emotions, thought patterns, and other discarded, non-substantial "things" go.

I once knew an artist who collected all his watercolors he felt were not up to his standards and put them in a pile. Then he invited all his friends to a party at which he burned the paintings. His friends were aghast—"why didn't you give that one to me—I love it!" I was one of those friends, and shared their dismay, later realizing that all individuals handle repolarization in their own way. Our own ways of letting go of old values may be misunderstood. May you be as brave and creative as this artist! He taught me a lesson I did not understand until many years later, and probably I will never do it quite his way, but perhaps some of the readers will find this example helpful.

Taking It with You

Marilyn Busteed's book (See footnote page 1 of this chapter) gives the wonderfully insightful key words of the response to the question, "what is the result of this phase?" *Compassionate Understanding or Implacable Regret?* Who cannot relate to both these phrases? These are the gifts each third quarter can leave you with. Even the regret is a gift because at some future time it will attract to you a new experience in which you may learn then to let go of it and be truly gifted with new energies and more wholeness. We need to emphasize that letting go of old values, and finishing unfinished business are not the issue here. Third Quarter is about <u>turning away from</u> the past, and turning toward the future. It is not about letting it go as much as it is about the idea of letting go. The Balsamic phase is about <u>walking away from</u> the past., and letting go of it.

Of course there will often be regret taken into your Balsamic phases. What you did or didn't do may well be the cause. That applies, again, to how you handled the first quarter. What you really need to take with you is what you are learning from those regrets. That may be as important to the core self as the compassionate understanding you might have gained. In any case, you might well apply compassionate understanding to yourself as you consider what you have learned or not learned. Since the last phase will be the healing window, compassionate understanding will be a special gift for whatever healing you or others need.

The old energies are waning and we are turning our attention (energy, focus, intent) away from the efforts of the past cycle. Our 3-week journey has generated new experiences, and new needs wait to be filled. But we can't fully turn away from this cycle until we finish what can be finished. We are already sensing, unclearly, the new seed-impulse to come in seven days. Time is short and we may need to push some issues we feel a sudden need to uphold before this month is left behind. Perhaps something inside or outside needs to be re-formed— perhaps this is the *Aquarian* tinge to the last day of the *Capricornian* period. Both are ruled by Saturn, and Uranus always speaks with finality. Something we always believed, a value we always held—taught to us or gained from earlier experience—clutches its position in the psyche. A new learning struggles to outbalance it. If the new is something we really value, and we let the old win (*Capricorn*), then we will be seen, or see ourselves to be, as inflexible and closed to the transformative energies (Aquarius). If the new wins, others may not understand what happened to us, or may be unable to relate to our change. This is a test; do we trust our individuality enough to handle either one? That is why the effort we applied to the first quarter phase was so important. We needed to establish early on a new level of independent thinking and feeling, strong enough to support the 3rd Quarter struggle. The self-work of the waxing phases is meant to strengthen and develop or define our individuality. We don't lose that to the collective on the waning side. We simply use it to remain our own person, while blending with the collective in some way.

So, at the door to the Balsamic we must decide or not decide to go inside, be with the new value, and follow a new vague direction that leads toward the new cycle. There are no flashlights here, no familiar guidelines. We the authors do not know which path you or I will take. It is cloudy and unclear in this territory, the light is waning, and you must know what you trust before you walk. Once you begin moving you may find new responsibilities awaiting you, related to the coming new phase. You could join others who hold similar new values. Or you could completely change how you are in a relationship, even if it means leaving the relationship. Or perhaps that relationship is between your Higher Self and your personality self (Does your intuitive self persistently nudge you in one direction? Does the familiar tug you in another?). Either way trust becomes the issue. But you can be sure that making the decision for change and reorientation makes way for the Balsamic transformation—if the decision is true to your inner integrity and appropriate for the collective. I once met a professional psychic who helped many people with her readings. She frequently repeated the idea that whatever you choose, it must be for the greatest good of everyone.

The Importance of Trust in Yourself and the Future

Even though a month by month walk on the Lunar path gives us the sense that changes are often so small as to be negligible, the changes are there. This is a sure and certain way to become the best of what we can be at any given moment, which is often recognized or expressed at the last quarter Moon. Each step is one more step on the way. We can trust and keep all the gains we make. In the Last Quarter phase there are three days to do this most significant work before its energies fade out at the doors of the Balsamic Moon. Rigidity is brittle and foundationally weak, with temporary comforts that will ultimately shatter something in our lives; reorientation is flexible and powerful, with long term rewards. But that energy is Aquarian in nature and you can naturally step into that energy and experience a different you, finding you don't really care if others think you are strange.

You are getting ready to store what you have achieved in your memory banks during the Balsamic. Psychics tell us that growth experiences are thus stored so that when we come into our next life, they will already be operable in that life. In the monthly Moon cycles, what you take in underneath, now in the Last Quarter, will take on physical form in the next Moon cycle as well.

Listen to the Voices of the Elders

The Egyptian Guardian of Phase Seven: *Sebek* the planet Uranus, the transformer. Spirit, as the destroying power of the Sun, is preparing to leave the vehicle. In terms of the lifetime, this is preparation for death of the body. In monthly terms, the energy you had for the task of the month is fading. The task here was to transform the vehicle that was embodied with your energy. Either you want to enter a new phase of this task or you want to avoid it. Or, you want to focus on something else, which is called denial. The effects of the real transformation—a new influx of mental, emotional, and physical energy—will be seen in the New Phase.

The Eight-Fold Path—Aversion: *Pain*. We work hard to avoid pain, physical, emotional or mental. Unfortunately there is plenty of it to go around, particularly regarding any losses, physical, material, emotional, mental, or spiritual. All unresolved losses will pile up and add to future losses, and many people who have unresolved (un-grieved) losses from childhood through adulthood may be prevented from dealing with further losses, by losing memory, or having other issues that block the feelings of loss that might come up at this phase. We can't emphasize enough here that avoidance or denial of pain, regardless of its source, only stores it up for worse problems later. We make the argument for dealing with life as it happens, to prevent its losses from being saved till the end of life. I learned this early, about the same time as the landmark lesson on gravy, when I learned to eat vegetables first, so I could really enjoy the potatoes and gravy! From the point of view of old age, I can now assure the reader that there are always things that get left behind and come up during the waning phases of the monthly cycles. But they are doable, and I'm not sure the larger earlier ones would have been doable at this point in my life. So do the Last Quarter work, knowing that with the Balsamic Moon phase comes the gift of multiple healings.

The Last Quarter phase is the "workshop" where the willingness to release can be triggered. If it involves something from the past, well, the pain of looking at it and releasing it allows it into the Balsamic for healing.

On the other hand, if you were given a new position, or some honor, or you discovered a new exciting direction or ideal to follow, your work is leading you to a completely different experience, perhaps a long-awaited adventure, as this book has been for us. The Balsamic will be a preparation for that. There are also those who will tell you that all of it is an adventure, "good or bad".

"Reading" the Last Quarter Moon into Your Own Chart Wheel

Collect the information listed below and find your own way of putting it together that makes sense to you. It may be easier to start with only the houses, or only the signs, or only the degree symbols. If you do that, then connect the pair you choose with the energy flow table statements.

1. The 3rd Quarter Sun's sign _____position _____
2. The 3rd Quarter Moon's sign _____position _____
3. Mark the two houses on your dial with the colored sticky-dots.
4. Activities of the Sun's house, using our houses keyword tables
   _____
5. Nature (sign) of the Sun's activity _____
6. Sun's Message degree symbol _____
7. Activities of the Moon's house _____
8. Nature (sign) of the Moon's activity _____
9. Moon's Response degree symbol _____

The Process: Putting It Together

Ed's Last Quarter Moon was on August 23rd, 2008. Sun was at 1 degree Virgo, Moon was at 1 degree Gemini. As often happens, the Sun changed signs just as we started this phase. The Sun can change signs at any point during a cycle, depending upon how close the New Moon degree was to the beginning of a sign. The overall New Moon purpose does not change, but it is a signal that the original purpose is being altered in some respect. After two eclipses, that is not surprising. One message could be, "Now it's time for Ed to get down to business or get to work on the basics." This phase could be described as "establishing his social foundations" as opposed to the first Quarter's "establishing his personal foundations."

Ed's Chart. This phase is about choosing between the past and the future in terms of values. Ed's Higher Self or Spirit (Sun) is challenging the incarnated personality (Moon) to make a decision between new attitudes or values learned this month, and old values from the past.

The houses. Ed's Sun is in his 11th house of friends and associates. His Moon is in the 8th house of Changes. If he has old values to be left behind, they probably will be found in the Moon's house. Perhaps he has some old issues around the subject of change, itself

The signs. Leo and Scorpio played major roles this month, and they are fixed signs, which have a hard time dealing with change. Gemini is notorious for changing its mind and vacillating over what it thinks about anything. On the negative end of the spectrum, this house could contain clues to old values that need to be changed.

On the positive end, it could be bringing opportunities for Ed to network more with 11th house associates, which normally is not his "cup of tea" (his natal Sun sign of Scorpio tends to want things to be done his way).

Now the New Moon Leo Sun is suddenly in Virgo. It wants Ed to re-focus his attention toward friends and associates (originally Leo-oriented) now toward Virgo—in other words, toward ideas or values of service. This is the second time this month that the 11th house has been highlighted. The degree symbols will give us the details.

The Degrees. This 3rd Quarter Sun degree of 1 *Virgo* (read 2 *Virgo*) gives us a picture of a large white cross upraised. It is an ambivalent-sounding degree that at first looks like a kind of sacrificial experience, but with the theme of "Glorification". Roche tells us that the cross alludes to a moral courage and fearlessness that inspires others to stand up for what they believe in and move toward higher expressions of their values and ideals. She says it is about dedication to improving the lives of others through some special service. Remember that Virgo is about letting the spirit radiate through your work.

His Moon degree of 1 *Gemini* (Read 2 *Gemini*) has the theme of *Prodigality*. This is about giving as though there is no end—that the universe will continue to provide no matter how much you give. This degree appears to be about the reciprocity of prodigality—that it works both ways, and Ed can expect that giving leads to receiving, "*Someone may express his gratitude by surprising you with a gift*". It is interesting that the 8th house is also about joint resources, debts, legacies and other people's resources.

Given Ed's preceding phases, one might guess that his new work is about service and giving at several levels. He has realized some new values this month, perhaps about giving and networking and flexibility. Old values about being either too unwilling to change, or unwilling to talk about change (*Gemini*) instead of doing it, may be asking to be left behind. Sun is asking him to apply his personal attitudes (Moon) toward change to a wider world out there (11th house).

At this point, Ed may be asking himself, "why did this happen to me? I did everything right; I've been a good employee; I was well-qualified beyond my present position." He needs to look at a larger picture at this point—the whole cycle as a major change in career direction due to the eclipse in his 10th house. The cycle did not fulfill his expectations and personal desires; instead it essentially demoted him from his present position to a lesser one with lower salary. What message could that be conveying? The complete story is not unveiled until the Full Moon, when as we often say, the axe fell. Nor will we deny that the outcome seems quite undeserved. So we have to look at a still bigger picture, that of spirit in the stories of our lives.

Major life-changing events cannot be argued with, and most probably are part of one's destiny. The change of the 8th house in the Last Quarter refers to the change required of Ed to adapt (a Moon keyword) to the career change of the Full Moon. If you reread the Disseminating Moon you see that two fire signs give him an enormous challenge in dealing with this change—two fire signs operating at once—anger flaring, most likely, and the advice from several sources that he needs to control himself. If we look objectively behind the scenes we might see that under other circumstances the new diminished job had some very interesting possibilities that could have engaged his creativity big-time. Spirit's choice was that he would have seen that, but Moon was giving him a lesson about unbridled emotions. Did Ed listen? We leave the reader to fill in the gaps here, since this is primarily about how to interpret the phases in the context of a New Moon, with an initial established situation.

If Ed listened to spirit, he may by the 3rd Quarter phase be ready to see that his earlier values are turning from self-actualization toward service as a career goal, and in the final Balsamic phase he will need to let go of the older values. This was a major step in in some way for everyone on the planet during this cycle.

21
Phase Eight: Balsamic Fragrance
Realignment, Conscious Transformation, Healing, Closure

Raven Moon

In the shadows of the dark moon,
winds of destiny are calling you,
Raven Moon, Raven Moon,
you are the messenger of change,
seeker of truth, speaker of wisdom,
healer of our troubled and wounded past,
giver of fearless courage,
singer of celestial songs,
bringer of magic moments,
diviner of time, star time.
Traveler between the worlds
with your Raven wings,
soaring to greater heights,
past the edge of time, into the spirit world,
where you become the spirit messenger,
the keeper of the great mysteries,
meet the faceless, nameless one,
feel everywhere spirit,,
hear the voice of the
Great Spirit speak,
"When we set aside our differences,
Together as rainbow warriors,
We can be the bringers of a new dawn"
—Marcia Moonstar [1]

---

1   www. MarcyMoonstar.com: Performance Poet, Seattle, Washington

The Transition between Last Quarter and New Moon

The theme of this phase is transition between death and rebirth, or transformation. The Sun (by sign, degree, and house) describes the nature of this final phase as a closure. The Moon (by sign and degree) describes where that closure is needed and the way you can deal with it. Such a simple statement leads us into the most complex of all the phases. The symbol of the Balsamic Moon degree is said also to express the need of humanity to which the New Moon will speak. We begin with the meaning of the number eight itself.

The Power of Number Eight and the Spiral

Remember from Chapter 11, where we discussed the number eight in its horizontal position as the infinity symbol—the cycles continue on their spiral infinitely, and the *old woman never dies.*

In biblical Judaism the eighth step in the temple was the symbol of the end of the mundane and the beginning of the spiritual level. The number 8 in Western philosophy is also, in its vertical mode, a symbol for transformation and "as above, so below". The eighth Tarot card, Strength (in the Rider Waite Deck), is about the alchemical transformation of the Sun-Moon cycle. In Astrology, the eighth Moon Phase is about personal transformation. The transformation, of course, is the rebirth of the old Moon, the eternal return. Nothing is ever repeated exactly the same on the other side of any interstice.

In numerology the number 8 is the most powerful of the first nine numbers. So here we are in phase 8. How can a foggy, dark end of a worn-out cycle live up to the number 8's reputation? We see that power in the transformative renewal of life energies. Perhaps it is a joint phenomenon between Balsamic and New phase. In any case, what could be more powerful than the ability to renew what is old and worn-out?

If we achieved something in the outer world by choosing a new value—and realized how our actions can benefit us—as we enter this last phase we discover ourselves anew in preparation for a new experience.

The Nature of the Balsamic Energy

This phase opens briefly with the Aquarius background music encouraging a feeling of the coming future, which is followed by the whole sign of Pisces, sign of the unknown future itself. We are opening to the Unknown, a window in time when the old is almost gone, the new has not yet arrived. Some writers have called it the phase of the prophet. I had a client born under the Balsamic Moon, who was a telephone repair supervisor of many year.s before being promoted to traffic director (coordinating the interactions between departments in the phone company.) He said that while he loved his recent position, it was so frustrating because he had so many ideas that would save the company money and benefit the employees, but to which the company turned a deaf ear.. He felt he was forced to operate in an outdated system that he could have easily fixed.

At the mundane level, in the monthly Balsamic phase, there is often a sense of being held back, or waiting for something to happen. Some feel caught in the collective and not yet able to feel their own selves within it. Or they may feel alone in the midst of multitudes. The collective unconscious is close to our own personal unconscious at this time. Strange dreams invade our sleep. In our society, the usual anxiety-driven questions go something like this: If the past was good, what will the future bring that could endanger that? If the past has been difficult, will the next month be worse? The problem is that any action (and life is action) generates mistakes—this is what we are here for.. Mistakes are to be learned from, and all action or movement through time creates change, by its very nature. Despite our dislike of it, the ability to change, in itself, is the hope and the promise for anyone who desires to learn from a mistake, or begin anew. Never forget that we usually make mistakes because we don't know everything yet, or we don't know something deeply enough.

In the shamanic and quantum physics worlds this phase represents the breakdown of systems into the final chaos out of which came the creation. Nothing truly new can happen until enough of the old boundaries and structures have dissolved. Do you remember this: "and the spirit of God moved over the face of the waters?" In shamanic tradition and in modern physics, all form emerges from the unformed creative soup of the ocean, the Field, or the spiritual waters of the sky. (Meanwhile, according to many ancient shamanic teachings, our present universe was destroyed and recreated four times, which speaks to the ancientness of the modern concept as an early philosophy.) Something in us or our lives dissolves in the Piscean depths in order that a new form can emerge in the next cycle. As shamans, we may sacrifice (offer up, let go) something we no longer need in order to receive the new connection to spirit. But we don't have to be shamans or scientists. All religions and science as well tell us the same story. This is the end and beginning of all cosmic, and all natural and human rhythms. Nevertheless it arouses old fears, lost hopes, or other signs of loss. The death of a poor self esteem has its own pain and fear—who am I now, and how can I handle the responsibility this loss gives me? What excuses do I now have for not taking on the responsibility?

The shaman handled this by identifying with the chaos and *letting go into it,* in the clear knowledge that with the new cycle would come a new connection with sources of help and guidance, and a new creation of his world. In translation, it might mean that he would visit the land of the dead, or journey to the Milky Way, divesting himself of his daily consciousness and personal ego. For everyone, an experience of chaos, confusion, and loss can be navigated by staying in one's center and focusing on the here and now, whether that be in this middle world, or in one of the other realities. Ability to respond in this way implies accepting or letting go into the chaos. This is the universal key. Don't confuse ego with core self, however!

So greater winds are blowing through this window, beyond personal feelings of fear or hope at the moment. How we look at our lives *every day* determines whether we enter the Balsamic with negative or positive thoughts about the future. On a deeper level, this is a time of personal sacrifice. One is giving up an old value in order to move on. Sometimes one can feel a sense of danger or even death here, signaling "ego-death" or even physical death. It has been said that our fears of death come from the fact that our cells die every day, at a deeply unconscious level, in order to be replaced with new ones. We are unconsciously aware of all our body functions, even at the cellular level. Ego-death happens all the time in big and small ways, and this triggers the cellular fears, perhaps in turn triggering a more conscious fear. These are the catabolic (yin) forces mentioned in the Last Quarter Moon chapter, continually at work breaking down the cellular structures so the anabolic (Yang) forces can renew them.

To the ancient Chinese, this was not only subjective or figurative. They saw this time of the moon as a dangerous place, like a precipice or a trap or pit. Their diviners would tell us there is swift water running through the gorge and we must take the risk either of going into the water (Yin) and going with it, or falling and falling until the bottom is reached, in order to overcome the danger.. In all cultures

Yin was the dissolver of structures and form—we remember the Hindu goddess Kali the destroyer.

We know that in the part of Neolithic China from which the Yang/Yin concepts came, the landscape was like that—high rugged mountains (Yang)and fertile valleys (Yin), rivers rushing through deep gorges, canyons, swift rapids, and cliffs, along with bitter seasonal weather. No doubt there were many physical dangers in their time unknown to us city dwellers, providing ample symbolism for their lives. However, the human race seems quite capable of generating fear under almost any circumstance. The message of the Chinese Shaman is at the core of Balsamic moon. "Let go", "go with it". Risk danger, venture falling, falling until a bottom is reached, overcoming the danger of the pit. Remember, too, that the whole sign of Pisces finishes the Balsamic, which began with the last third of Aquarius. These words, like "let go", are the signal to be carried through the phase rather than to struggle with it. Perhaps The Dark Valley Goddess has another message for us as she gallops in the background both of full light and full darkness, carrying us into life and out of it, and monthly, into a phase of our life and now out of it. What might that message be?

A family member went to a fire-walking demonstration in which observers were invited to participate. First they were required to put on blindfolds and fall backward into someone's arms. When and if they were able to do this without fear, they could then walk the glowing coals. He did the walk, and finished with only a small blister on the side of one foot. We think this kind of trust in oneself could be the kind of trust one sometimes needs here, the ability to trust that the new month is bringing us exactly the experiences we need and that we have the tools to deal with them. There is a cautionary point to the story however. It is that, like the firewalker, we need to know ourselves to know whether we should tackle a task once we are confronted with it. If one's trust is only at the ego-level, one will be burned.

There will always be some kind of option in the Balsamic. Maybe all you really have to do is learn how to fall backwards and trust someone is there to catch you. Another option is always the one of intentionally "going with it". If the future is out of your control physically, then you can consciously let go of control and intentionally go with it, which is extremely difficult, but an option we all will need at sometime in our lives. Balsamic is a time to practice these tools, and walk on coals if necessary.

How to Walk Safely through the Unknown of Change

The moon's path is more about eternal change than death itself. Change as well as death is associated with the Unknown, there are many kinds of death, and death itself is only change. We fear it in its many forms. The makers of the early I Ching understood the universal human need for a way to walk safely through the unknown of change. For them the essential way was *sacrifice.* Now that is a word most of us choke on if we try to say it out loud, unless it is in the non-personal ritual-speak of a religion. But as we mentioned in an earlier chapter it also means *offering,* an easier word. The ancient peoples since Stone Age times understood that the sacrifice or offering connected their world with the world of heaven. It had to do with *weaving the warp of living energy (from heaven) into the weft of history.*[2] Sacrifice or an offering of ourselves to the mystery was, in truth, the way to walk through the unknown to the other side. Perhaps we can apply that concept to our time.

Why do we sometimes feel discomfort, dissonance, often incompletely suppressed fear, unexplained sadness, at the end of a Lunar month? What does that have to do with sacrifice, and are we dimly aware that there is a chasm called the unknown that we are crossing? Could it be that we hold memories and parts of ourselves in that deep well of the shadow, which were already and long ago sacrificed in reverse form and buried, at the price of a less complete consciousness—things we are afraid to look at? Or perhaps some even deeper layer of physical or emotional loss.

If this is the case, we may find another way of safely crossing the chasm, described in the following fragment of poem originally by Emily Dickinson, and adapted by a friend for use in a religious service. We do not have the reference on this.

> *There is a pain so utter –*
> *-it swallows substance up-*
> *Then, it covers the Abyss with Trance—So we can*
> *walk around, across, upon it*
> *as one within a swoon goes safely—where an*
> *open eye would drop in, bone by bone.*

Perhaps such memories have helped shape our present situations and left their dark mark upon them. During the Balsamic

---

2   S. Karcher, *Total I Ching: Myths for Change*

window of time the unconscious becomes permeable to the cellular breakdown, allowing the cellular fears through, and we are close enough to touch and heal past memories if we choose. But the poem gives us assurance that we are not expected to do what is the impossible for us at a given time. The trance or the swoon allows us to experience only what we are ready for, like novocaine at the dentist's office.

Not in every Balsamic or in everyone's life are the above ways of crossing the abyss relevant. But these days far too many lives need ways to cross seemingly unnavigable chasms. Those things that give rise to sadness, fear, and dissonance tend to come up in the Balsamic Moon: the Dark Unknown too often leads to the idea of sacrifice or either to giving up our dreams or giving in to our demons. But still…when they do come up they are ready to be addressed., and the timing will likely be related to the house and sign of the particular Balsamic Moon. Often the experiences arouse programmed emotions, and you remember the saying, "the devil you know is preferable to the one you don't". That is the pit into which you do not want to fall.

Most of all, Balsamic is about closure, making peace, releasing, healing, which is perhaps the reason these feelings come up here so often. They need final peace or healing. We need to comment here that the foregoing paragraphs are telling us that for healing we may need to fall into, let go into, allow ourselves to feel the depths of, whatever emotion is being triggered. It is not commonly understood that once the old feelings are fully felt and acknowleged they no longer have power over one.

Situations not as desperate as those described above may be dealt with more easily. There are greater things in the Unknown than fears; there are the great archetypes, evoked by movement in and out of the unconscious in ritual, prayer, and true reverence. Touching them can bring effortlessly the deep relief of letting go of a burdensome piece of ego-restriction, a giving up of some limitation we just stumbled over, with which we had identified unknowingly. How good it is to give that up in order to make space for change or a larger identity, or being regenerated. It seems to us that willingness to give up the sources of our physical sickness and emotional demons by recognizing and then offering them up or accepting them back into ourselves, healed, are two sides of the same final Moon phase.

Some Ways of the Balsamic Path in our Personal Lives

We need to repeat that a primary Balsamic theme is about the feminine Divine Presence invited into our lives and celebrated, wherever we are. From ancient Jewish tradition, families invite the Shechinah (Jewish feminine Divine Presence) to every Friday evening meal, the evening of the last day of the week, and often with a healing ritual. In Christianity, members practice a similar ritual yearly on Good Friday. Everyone can do this at the Balsamic phase, by whatever name we call it. The darkness is complete here; we are in the domain of the feminine, the un-locked emotions, and the great feminine archetypes. For healing we must go back to the shadow containing the un-healed, but most important is this: *our shadows contain both the divine and the human, and the former is often rejected by us as well the latter. The essence of the Balsamic says of the rejected parts: "divine or demonic we need to view them with compassion."* Yin-Feminine compassion is the only way we will tease the shadow into giving up its closely guarded imaginings, and its broken fragments of light, past the equally closely guarded limits of the Yang-conscious ego-mind. This is the sacrifice at the conscious level at the same time it is the healing at the unconscious level. This was the role played by the Dark Goddess of the Valley, who brought both death and life to the Ancestors.

In early shamanic times, the ancestors' fears appeared to them in the outside world, in the masks of the shamans, or a vision of the Dark Goddess herself, that .taught them how to relate to the shadow. In our time, we have left behind these ways of life, but have done little to replace them. Our mental objectivity has opposed or avoided the reality of the unconscious and we are split. We repeat an earlier quote of Richard Tarnas, who says that *unless we rediscover our unconscious we are lost.* If one mistook their fears for outer reality, one could be destroyed. We need to recognize both outer and inner reality, and allow our inner reality to reconnect with the outer—to see how our personal, emotional vision is entwined in the events of our outer lives.

Some contemporary ways we learn to do this part of the Moon path are by speaking and listening to others at the heart level. Or, perhaps one could write in a journal. Reach inward and pull out some small rejected lump of clay or coal or worse. Ask, "What is its gift?" What shall I do with it? Recognize it, honor it, grieve it if that is called for, and suddenly it is no longer what it seemed. The gift becomes part of one's personal power.. Perhaps it once held you prisoner to a belief that you "can't", "shouldn't", "aren't", whatever. The veils are thin here; the soul is getting rid of memories it does not need, in the personal unconscious, before it stores the genuine learnings in the memory banks. Let the Balsamic Moon work its magic. By compassionate intent, allow the energies to transform your offering behind the veil of inner boundaries and return it to you as a greater consciousness, power, or definition of your own identity. Let me share what Judy and I did at one point while writing this book.

At one particular Balsamic moon, a month after Judy had experienced a death in her family which triggered a mass of un-finished grief from previous losses, she suddenly felt overwhelmed with anger from a seemingly unknown source, at the same time she was having serious energy-loss. I was trying to deal with a serious physical problem that was looking very much related to some childhood issues at which I should legitimately have been angry but was not. Judy's and my childhoods were similar. We were both taught not to express our anger.. Now, our bodies were giving us messages…we needed to release these memory-blockages. With each of us listening to the other, and watching our charts, both of us received startling insights into the anger we still held, and the effect it was having on our bodies—less and less energy and physical problems arising! Our individual tasks were to go back and revisit the child in ourselves and then validate, offer up, sacrifice, let go, etc., the held anger and tell our unconscious we no longer needed to hold anger in. Then we needed to feel the compassion due this child. It turned out, as so often happens, that Judy's anger, though a perfectly legitimate part of the current grief process, had a source in her childhood also. These insights were so major that we felt a ritual would be appropriate, involving actually burning something like paper with an intent written upon it, or cornmeal (don't try it—cornmeal doesn't burn!) which would be designated as the ego-part we were offering.

Emotions and memories held at the cellular level are well known to respond to therapies involving the body. This is what ritual is about—using a physical symbol of the spiritual intent to take our bio-psychological issues down deep into the body level, getting the message to the unconscious through the body. It is good solid fact that the unconscious *is* our connection to the body. That is part of the efficacy of shamanic healing. We can do much for ourselves by "talking to our unconscious" aloud so the body can hear, and doing an action that represents what we are saying.

Imagery triggers the right brain which is a two-way channel to the unconscious, which is our connection to the body. Imagery may be a more powerful way for this contemporary time than writing things down. Drawing free or spontaneous images in reverie, or drawing dream images, is one way to pass over the abyss with our eyes open. Images are direct messages which end up in the outside world, one step away from our sensitive inside world. They also become universal once they are drawn, and perceived by another person. Then we know we are not alone.

Balsamic Moon as Preparation for New Moon

Transformation, being in the interstice between worlds, is never conscious, but conscious intent that is present with ritual is an important beginning of the transformation process. The first task of Balsamic Moon is often the sacrifice of the ego-part—the past, so that we can turn fully toward the next phase. This part is best done the first day, under Aquarian energy. For both Judy and me there is often physical or mood change, relief after we deliberately combine a symbolic action with the words that express our intent about the past. If we neglect the release of the past, it will hold us back at the coming Crescent moon when the new seed-intent takes outer form.

The Final Step of the Balsamic

If you let go of whatever you need to, you can "surrender" your worries and stresses in the second and third days. (Some religions provide ways to do this.) These last two days are Piscean in background energy—emotional, feminine, unfocused, imaginative, and creative. True to form, these days are full of mystery. Use them as that. You wrote your story of this past month in your memory or your journal, and made peace with it in some way. Now, what do you want to write for next month's story? What do you most need next month? Turn your attention to the New Moon's house because you know that is where the focus of next month will begin and you know it will answer some need that has arisen out of this past month. Begin to image what you would like to see happen, or better still, feel your need, invoking the power of the new seed in the New Moon area of your life. Then simply open yourself to accepting what new purpose is being downloaded into the physical body-heart-brain. Like the vision of the Moon-weaver of destiny, this Balsamic process weaves your personal energies and your "connection to heaven" into the unfolding history of your physical existence; it heals the dissonance, and realigns you with your destiny, which is also the unfolding history which you create within the context of co-creating human history. Know that all before you is new, clean, and ready for your creative touch.

Ritual for those who resonate with it is one of the most helpful tools we know about. Lighting a candle is always a good beginning, or maybe the whole of it. Creating sacred space is another step. Shamanic work "calls" the directions. Religious work may use prayers, which can be made more effective by including the body as in sacred dance or music. Incense involves the body, the sense of smell, said to be the most spiritual of the five senses. Inviting helpers from the unseen is comfortable for some. Whatever space you create for yourself will intensify and focus Balsamic work. The rest is up to you and your intent.

In three days the great, universal need out there will be answered by the exactly right archetypal image for that moment. Your need is a tiny part of the world's need, and its fulfillment will contribute in that measure to the world's fulfillment. It may not be what you imaged, but if you persist in wanting to know how it will fulfill your need in that house, you will find the answer. Be careful here, though, because this is not a wish-book—objects and things may not always materialize here because your Higher Self , soul or spirit may override your ego-desires. One might best wish with a disclaimer clause, or simply be willing to take whatever the universe offers as the gift.

Transformation is change in one's nature or condition, is permanent, and affects body, mind, and spirit. It happens when one is ready on the conscious level, physically, mentally and emotionally, *and when desire is connected to spirit, life energy to heaven.* Every lunar month provides this three-day window with the opportunity and appropriate energies available to the one who deeply desires transformation. (Life is generous—we average 1,000 Balsamic phases in a lifetime!)

In spite of the Balsamic mystery, these three, and the previous 12 days have been the days of the month fullest of conscious-ness, and because they have presented opportunities for seeing ourselves more objectively, we are able to know consciously what needs transforming, and desire it. Usually, though occasionally we have a major change, these monthly transformations appear small or even invisible in the overall picture. However, over the years, they build step by step until we can hardly recognize our earlier selves. Occasionally, as in our own two cases described above, a particular Balsamic Moon turns out to be a major turning point in our lives. As Dane Rudhyar says, *It is a way of progressive illumination, of phase-revelation, of gradual perception—phase after phase of reality.*

Sometimes the past has such a strong hold upon us that we are not yet ready to accept a future which looks very different as the end result of the past we are hanging on to. Remember the phrase "one door closes in order that another may open". This closing door sometimes touches a fear or a lack of trust that a new door or a desired one really will open. One often has to carry a strong spiritual desire to accept the new and move toward it. Either that or one must be in the final depths of despair with no other way out. You lose nothing by staying open to what life might bring, and a lot by closing yourself to options that may lie waiting for you.

Re-Viewing the Whole Moon Cycle and Its Implications

The whole moon cycle is the "normal" person's psychotherapist/shaman/priest-priestess. Life and the universe, of which we are an organic part, provides us with everything we need to build or rebuild a growing and vital physical, mental, emotional, spiritual consciousness, and even sometimes a physical body. Although we do not address earth's companion planets in this book, they, too, are playing a part in this universal growth process. Balsamic phase is ruled by the planet Mars, *which is the symbol of transformation brought down to earth*[3]. We need the energy and desire for change. Action invokes the energy of transformation. Mars is *the desire that propels new forms into being, and its connection to spirit that earth dreams or intuits in order to do thi*s (Jeff Green). If we seriously worked on our phase tasks this month, our whole being will be ready, the outside as well as inside. Mental or emotional changes are incomplete unless they reach the physical and or conscious level.

We have spent little time discussing the more assertive possibilities in this phase. Mars is about action, based on the will of any person. Obviously, there is a huge amount of apparently negative action out there, which especially given this peaceable last phase raises many

---

3   Jeff Green, *The Evolutionary Journey of the Soul*

questions about the aggressive nature (Mars) of humanity and how the Balsamic can be for those involved. Mars is our desire-nature and it is said that we have to want to be changed or to change our circumstances, in order to be transformed. (For the Astrologer: it takes Pluto, the carrier of the intentions of the soul, to make the transformation. Pluto is what transforms the work of Mars, our desire-energy from ego-oriented to soul-oriented.)

Perhaps people who wage wars of destruction are creating the opportunity for regeneration. We have few answers, except that each of us is responsible for our own actions. If we are looking for transformation, our intent will be toward that, from New Moon to New Moon. With that intent in place, transformation however small will not fail us. We *will* grow. And every gain we make will affect every other person on the planet. We believe that the image from recent science about the butterfly flapping its wings in Burma affecting the weather pattern in Seattle is similar. Whether you follow the Moon Path or not, *conscious intentional living in the light*, however you perceive it, is the most-needed commodity on the planet right now. Every person is needed to become a vessel of light. The wisdom of every religion and system of divination will tell you the same thing.

So this is what we have done in 29 days:

New Moon: we began something new;

Crescent: it began to take form;

First Quarter: we struggled between our own creativity and society's old ideas;

Gibbous: we perfected the task;

Full: we had insights and illumination of the meaning of the task;

Disseminating: we shared and internalized the insights;

Last Quarter: we extracted the value of the exercise and turned away from the task;

Balsamic: we made closure on old business, surrendered ego-control, and turned toward the next cycle.

At Balsamic moon, Judy and I look over our month, ask what we need, look at the next New Moon in our symbol books, and say to each other, "I'm not sure what that means, but I could sure use some of it!" We light the candles, say the prayers, and open ourselves to the Unknown with curiosity and acceptance (of course we don't really do it every time!) That is a conscious intent, like the intent at the new moon. Curiosity is high on our list of necessary life energies.

Why is the Dark of the Moon, the Most Conscious Phase?

Repeatedly we have asked and been asked, "Everyone equates consciousness with light; so why is it that we say, "the Balsamic moon is the most conscious phase of all, when the light is entirely gone?" We want to answer that here. To answer that we must remember to distinguish between visual light and spiritual light. Being conscious and aware of physical or sun light is an everyday function of the personal self or ego. Consciousness is a spiritual faculty connected to spirit, Sun, and the use of our will.

Sun light has always symbolized spiritual light. That light is permanent and goes with us throughout our life and our lifetimes, through dark and light times. Like the physical sun, spiritual light is always shining somewhere. Just so, at Balsamic Moon, and every night, the Sun is still shining somewhere, and even a young child knows this; but during the Balsamic phase the spiritual Sun or the Higher Self is still shining. Consciousness is a core quality of our being. It determines, and is determined by, how we deal with the issues of all eight phases. The light on the Moon is the reflected light of ur conscious selves, more related to the consciousness of the ego. The darkness on the Moon is Earth's shadow—our personal unconscious, while the light is our waxing or waning personal conscious awareness. We are still fully conscious at the dark of the Moon, but we are temporarily immersed in the Unknown, the depths of which are more significant than surface consciousness. We are turned inward, introverting, and temporarily true "bearers of wisdom". So remember, no matter how dark you feel on a Balsamic Moon, your conscious-ness is at its highest then. You can be the most objective if necessary; because wisdom is the essence of the feminine and right brain, and accessible if you are in touch with your spiritual self.

How the Balsamic Moon Got Its Name

We searched a long time for how and when this curious name, *Balsamic*, was assigned to the last three days of the month. It is still somewhat of a mystery. We found some historic information, however, that may explain it in a non-direct way. First, genuine Balsamic vinegar is vinegar made by a very old, secret family recipe, in Modena, Italy. It is aged, sometimes for several years. The age is prized—I once saw a tiny ten-year-old bottle for $125.00! At first sour and bitter, the longer it is aged, the mellower and more delicious (and expensive!) it becomes. The name is associated with several aromatic healing plants called Balsam, long used in the Middle East for a universal healing balm, and mentioned in the New Testament. Vinegar in its own right is an old folk medicinal, and we personally know some people who use Balsamic Vinegar for health reasons. The makers of this famous vinegar must have had similar reasons for its unusual name—a healing vinegar? We have heard that the original recipe contains some of the actual balsam herb. The ancient herb and the vinegar (with its hint of the bitter), known for their mellowness and soothing quality, seem appropriate to the bittersweet eighth and final phase of the Old Moon, *the old woman who never dies but transforms in the twinkling of a star into the new Young Moon.*

We have also heard that balsam has been used as incense and that the energy of the Balsamic phase has been tentatively compared to the scent of incense.

The Last Word

The Balsamic Moon's opening degree of the eighth phase symbolically describes not only the eighth phase itself but the specific need of humanity for the coming New Moon. Likewise, the New Moon Sun answers that need. You will find the Balsamic degree and the following New Moon degrees both cryptic and mysterious. They are wonderful to speculate upon and see if you can guess how they fit into your life. Altogether, we found this last phase the most fascinating of all eight phases—and as delicious as aged balsamic vinegar! We continue to love a mystery!

Of all the phases, this is the one where you most easily find the mystical, or become most unfocused. We are approaching the sacred unity consciousness of the New Moon. This opens the door to the right brain and heart brain functions. However, we need to remember that we are still of the Earth and that we have a responsibility toward Earth of which we are a part, and to her wellbeing along with ours.

Listen to the Voices of the Elders

The Egyptian Guardian of the Balsamic Phase: *Mars*. Here we can pause and meditate on creation and renewal, death and rebirth. The theme is the conscious commitment to end the cycle and allow the spirit to project in a new form. Letting go of some layer of the ego here allows us to pass through the gates of the New Phase and receive the energy to carry us higher on the spiral. It takes the desire-energy of Mars for the new future to pull us through the last step, the last degree of the Balsamic.

The Eight-Fold Path Aversion: *Loss.* This aversion often follows after a less-than-desirable enlightenment. We are told that it is harder to let go of regret, a disappointment, or anger, than of a fulfilling experience. Regardless of the satisfaction or lack of it at the Full Moon, something must be left behind as we go through the final Western gates. In all cultures, shamanic paths, and mythology, it was necessary for one who desired to enter the alternate worlds to leave behind something of this world.[4] It is an eternal practice in little things in order to deal with the larger ones. Is fear of loss one of our greatest fears? Is that the real image of our fear of death? If we die, or someone else dies, either way we lose? If you have this aversion, following the Moon Path can transform it.

Locating the Balsamic Moon on Your Own Chart Wheel

Arrange the following information in your own manner in the journal. Obviously you can't work the transitional phases without this information. We strongly suggest that since this is such an important phase you check our website or call someone with the software to determine the phase signs and degrees.

1. The Balsamic phase Sun's sign (yellow dot) _____.

2. The Balsamic phase Moon's sign (blue dot) _____.

3. Note the activities of the Sun's house _____

4. Note the activities of the Moon's house _____.

5. The Sun's degree _____

6. The Moon's degree _____

The Process

Ed's Example Chart. The Balsamic Moon phase in Ed's sequence began on August 27, 2008. Moon was at 19 Cancer in Ed's 9th house, and Sun was at 4 Virgo in his 11th house. This phase is about the need

---

4   The myth of the *Descent of Inanna* is a famous early Mediterranean myth about this theme, as are also the later ones about *Persephone* and *Orpheus and Eurydice.*

of humanity (and Ed, and the reader) for a new beginning.   The Sun is spirit's reassurance that there will always be a new beginning. Moon describes our state of mind during this phase, what we need to leave behind, the area of our life most affected, and what we need most at this time. We remind you for the last time, that not all phases are equal. If there are no phase degree contacts made to the Sun or Moon or a planet, in your natal chart, a cycle may seem insignificant. At least, it may not seem significant, but remember that the Signs and degrees operate at a physical, emotional, mental or spiritual level. The significance will be there no matter how subtle, although we hope you do not frustrate yourself trying to see it. There is always another Balsamic down the line.

This phase is also about looking at the whole cycle and considering what we learned from it, and whether it was successful; chalk it up to Wisdom. We look at the New Moon degree symbol which was, in this case, *the exalted feeling that rises within the soul of the individual who has successfully passed through the long night which has tested his strength and his faith.* Did this statement describe your experience? Ed's? I think Ed's experience certainly describes a test of his strength and faith. If he had faith of some kind to fall back on, the messages of the phases would have been easier to understand, accept and follow. How did you find it?

The Houses. Moon's house tells us where we will be experiencing the Balsamic need at the personal level. Ed's moon is in his 9th house of growth and expansion. If all has gone well, Ed will be looking ahead to a more expansive career life. In fact, one could say that he NEEDS that, and the Solar eclipse (change of direction in the house of the eclipsed Sun) clearly indicated that that was where this cycle was going. The 9th house Balsamic Moon suggests a change of location (9th house long distance travel.)

Sun is in the Virgo 11th house of friends and associates, as well as hopes and dreams. These people in his life either share a common service goal, or they represent co-workers of a possibly more technical type of work. It is from this sector that Ed's inner spiritual guidance comes, either as a vision or ideal or dream, or in the words of an associate.   Service may be the substance of the message. As you read through the following interpretations, remember the phase interpretation above.

The Signs. Moon in the Cancer 9th house describes in a general way the need to be filled by the coming new cycle. Moon is strong in its own sign and has some control in the matter. Therefore it is here a positive sign, indicating not only that he would benefit by moving his home to another or more distant location, but that some choices are open to him in the process. Cancer is an emotional sign, and also one with a lot of imagination. Perhaps this currently unappetizing job offers him the freedom to use this ability. Or maybe he needs to move to another area for an entirely different job. He might see one of these two options as an opportunity in which he could develop his self expression and also find belonging and support. Sometimes the 9th house means higher expectations, so perhaps Ed needs to use his imagination to see the greater possibilities of his situation.

Sun is in the Virgo 11th house of friends and associates, hopes and dreams, and "the world out there." If Virgo here indicates service of some kind, then spirit's message to Moon is that he is to use his creative abilities in providing that service. Virgo is also technical and detail-oriented.

The Degrees. In this example, the Sun was at 4 Virgo and the Moon at 19 Cancer (August 27th, 2008). The keynote for the Sun degree (read 5 Virgo) is: *The opening of new levels of consciousness* and the keyword is *Imagination.* Spirit is clearly telling him that here is an opportunity for him to grow in consciousness by either looking for another job in another area, possibly through a lead from friends or associates, or by finding the opportunities for use of his imagination in the current job.

Notice how this degree symbol fits into the more general information gained from the house/sign readings. This is specific, detailed advice from spirit, pointing to the highest way of using the energies.

The theme for the 9th house Moon degree (read 20 Cancer) is: *Happiness as an overtone of social integration and conformity to custom.* Since Leo's primary goal is social integration (see Full Moon Energies table in the Full Moon chapter) this final Moon degree of the cycle appears to offer a relative degree of happiness to Ed and to the reader if one has followed the Sun's advice throughout the cycle.

The above degrees are very clear and precise for Ed's situation. Apply these interpretations to your own Solar dial to see if you can interpret your own Balsamic phase.

Meanwhile, the energies are winding down to the end of both Yang and Yin. The world is waiting for...something. You may feel quiet, anticipatory, worried, or whatever you have brought with you to the end of the cycle. You are waiting for the sunrise and the opportunity once again to be lost in the spiritual light as the moon is lost in the sun's light.

22

Reflections

Roots of the Moonflower

A Shrine for the Flowering of the Heart

In the sphere of all that we see, touch, hear,
smell, taste, feel, think, imagine and believe
There is a Sacred Space And in that Sacred Space
There is a Temple of Reflection, a Temple of the Moon
And in the Temple of the Moon
There is a Shrine of Revelation
A Shrine of Understanding
A Shrine for the Flowering of the Heart.
                    —N. Kirsten Honshin[1]

The teaching of the Moon cycles began in the Neolithic, although we can never discount the possibility of earlier, unknown, cultures. The history of the teaching has disappeared and re-emerged in many times, places, and changing forms. One of its last appearances was in the Olmec culture of Central America. The Olmecs preceded the Mayas and Aztecs, leaving few traces behind them, other than the pictorial evidence of the feathered serpent which reached prominence in the two later cultures along with a lunar calendar. What we do know is that the Olmecs provided the forerunners of the Aztec/Mayan calendar and writing. Their calendar system was very sophisticated, seemingly beyond what their presumed short history could have produced, and the 28 days of the Moon-Sun cycle were built into the calendar at the basic level.

All calendars with SoLunar cycles built in have been teaching systems. People learned from the Moon's relationship to the Sun how to count, keep track of history, and to preserve through writing

---

1   N. Kirsten Honshin. Contemporary artist and poet, Seattle, Washington. You can view his works at http://nwartalliance.com/gallery

the discoveries and inventions of their cultures. Today, the Moon in Western Astrology represents memory in all its forms.

Some believe that writing and mathematics were the means by which we lost our connection to the universe, since individualism and ego ultimately developed out of such knowledge and brought us to the critical state of our time. This ego-development is said by some historians to be attributed to the Sun's masculine influence. That belief is misleading. The Sun, and its masculine gods, is not to be blamed for the male domination of humanity for so many eons. The original Moon teachings connected us to the divine creations of both Sun and Moon, and later the universe; our own human ego-driven decisions lost that connection. It was the choice of unevolved male planetary energy which is, even now, eons later, waning in the presence of increasing planetary female energy. Also, under no circumstance do we wish to imply that all male energy is contained only by men, or that all female energy is contained by women. What we do see has actually happened is that for the last 4-5,000 years the male species was socially dominant, and managed to keep the feminine side of the species in varying degrees of subjection. Before that we believe the feminine Yen energy was more dominant. These periods exibited a separation of the sexes, we believe, that gave humans an opportunity to see the characteristics of both sides and what Yang could produce unbalanced by Yin. Now these two energies appear to be integrating at the present time within both genders of our species. Of course, if humans have not learned enough from the experience, the feminine Yin side could easily do the same thing and overbalance the Yang with dark Yin collective experiences.

The Olmecs, somewhere between one and two thousand BCE, made the Moon cycles a way for people to connect with the lower and the upper worlds. Nothing is ever lost, and now the primary sky-connection has emerged once more, in our science, to reveal a higher level. The earlier levels were about the *interdependence with*—and reverence for—animals and the elements: Earth, Sun, Sky and Water. The new level includes unity with humanity and the universe, and expanding the reverence for it all, including the gift of human life and its capacity for transformation.

Some readers will choose to use the Sun-Moon energy cycles only for divination and for the material lives we all lead; for those the phases will bring many blessings and much puzzlement. But there are other levels to experience beyond that, and following the daily path will lead to those levels.

The cycles are for everyone; at all levels, they are about how people become vessels of light—people who are able to heal the planet and the societies who live upon it. People who consciously use the Moon cycles to become better people, or vessels of light like the Full Moon, will bring the needed changes, day by day, month by month, and year by year, simply by *being* and *becoming*.

The above prose-poem, composed by N.Kirsten Honshin, expresses our final summation of the meaning we have found in the Soul-Moon's cycles as they channel the Spirit-Sun's purpose into our lives.

Our blessings to all who got this far, and to those who will go beyond,

—Virginia and Judy

THE END

The words go forth again
into the great darkness
on waves that crest and fall.
After many births and deaths
through unknown time
the words will come forth again

Bibliography

Black Elk Speaks: U. of Nebraska Press, 2000

Robert Bly, *A Little Book on the Human Shadow* Edited by William Booth: Copyright 1988 by Robert Bly. Harper Collins Publishers.

Rhonda Byrne, *The Secret* : Nov 28, 2006 (Calendar).

Joseph Campbell, *Pathways to Bliss*: The New World Library, 2004. *Primitive Mythology,the Masks of God*: Penguin Books 1987.

Doc Childre and Howard Martin, *The Heartmath Solution*: Harper Collins 1999.

Mircea Eliade, *The Sacred and the Profane*: Rowohlt Taschenbuch Verlag GmbH, 1957. *The Myth of the Eternal Return*: Bollingen Fn., Inc., 2005.

Belinda Gore, *Ecstatic Body Postures*: Bear and Company, 2005.

Mark Edmund Jones and Ella Wheeler, *The Sabian Symbols in Astrology*: Wilcox Sabian Publishing Co., 1969.

C. G. Jung, *The Basic Writings of C. G. Jung:* Bollingen Fn., Inc., 1959.

Stephen Karcher, *I Ching. The Classic Chinese Oracle of Change:* Vega, 2002. *Total I Ching, Myths for Change,* Time Warner, 2003.

Rhoda Kellogg, *Analyzing Children's Art:* 1970 Mayfield Publishing Co. O.P. ISBN# 0874841968

Helene and Willem Koppejan, *The Zodiac Handbook, Vol. 1, 2, 3,* Elements Books Ltd., 1991.

Ellias Lonsdale, *The Inside Degrees: Developing your Soul Biography Using the Chandra Symbols:* North Atlantic Books 1997

David H. Kelley, *Exploring Ancient Skies:, an Encyclopedic Survey of Archeoastronomy, 1st Ed.* Springer, Nov. 19, 2004

Lynn McTaggart, *The Field*: Harper Publishers, 2002.

Daphna Moore, *The Rabbi's Tarot.* Llewellyn Publications, 1989.

Joseph Chilton Pearce, *The Biology of Transcendence*: Park Street Press, 2002. (Other books: *The Crack in the Cosmic Egg*, and *The Magical Child .*)

Dane Rudhyar, *An Astrological Study of Psychological Complexes.: The Astrology of Personality*: Aurora Press, 1991. The Lunation Cycle: Servire – Wassenaar, 1967

Richard Tarnas, *Cosmos and Psyche, Intimations of a New World View*: Penguin Group, 2006

Richard Wilhelm, trans. T*he Secret of the Golden Flower, a Chinese Book of Life*, Harcourt Brace & Co., 1962

* * *

Beginning Summer 2009 you can find ongoing updated information about Moon phase dates, times, and positions on Grandmother Moon's website at OurGrandmotherMoon.com

For more information about worldwide Moon groups, contact: The New Group of World Servers at http://www.ngws.org/service/intro.htm

Appendices

Appendix A
The Legend of the First Corn Ceremony

Most prehistoric and later cultural shamanic rituals were patterned after what was believed to be the *same* ritual given to the first ancestor of the long ago by a god. When one was partaking of the ritual one was not only acting out an identical ritual, but *the same original* ritual created by the god who gave it to the ancestor. According to Mircea Eliade, in his book *The Sacred and the Profane,* all ritual time was sacred time and as such had no duration. All ordinary time in which one did ordinary things was profane or linear time, not sacred, and it had duration. Ritual or sacred time tapped into the no-time of *Beingness,* while profane time was a linear process of *Becoming.* The universal celebration of an annual new year was a way of eliminating the profane time of the previous year with all its possible sins or evil actions displeasing to the gods, and beginning profane time all over again, fresh and new as the first day of creation. In fact, it *was* the first day of creation. Basically many rituals and most healing rituals operated on the same basis.

The following corn ritual, though celebrated in contemporary times, is believed by the Southwest Indians practicing it, to be the original corn ritual enacted by the god who gave it to the ancestors. No one knows how old it is, but it is so similar to ancient fertility rituals practiced in many parts of the world that it seems fitting to reprint it here, as a connection to the indigenous ancestors of our own continent.

The corn ritual is not only significant for its early roots, but for the name of the goddess who gave the original ritual to the ancestors—the name of this book. It expresses beautifully the theme of what Eliade calls "the eternal return", the cyclic nature of life and creation. We are born, we live, we die, and we are born again. The source of this cyclicity is the Moon, which insists that all things return after death to live another cycle, be it a month or a lifetime. Moon is the first and longest revered symbol of the spiral-like principle of cyclicity, described as the old woman who never dies, but after three days of darkness returns again, new and thin as the first moon of creation. Some vestiges of this worldwide aboriginal belief remain in major religions. Jesus' three-days between death and resurrection, and many others such as the feathered serpent Quetzalcoatl's three (or sometimes 9) days of teaching the dead in the underworld before he rose into the heavens to become the morning star version of the planet Venus,.

We are indebted to the American Indian Heritage Foundation [1] (at *Indians.org*) for the moving retelling of *The First Corn Ceremony*. We reproduce the website's telling below.

THE CORN CEREMONY

The Corn Ceremony was held in the spring or early summer as a prayer to the spirits to grant bountiful harvests and strength to the tribe.

A man who in the preceding autumn had witnessed the ceremony in a dream, climbed to the top of his lodge. There he made a vow to the Corn Spirit, whose name, Kadhutetash means "Old Woman Who Never Dies."

"Hear me, Old Woman Who Never Dies," the man said in a loud voice. "I shall give a great feast in your honour for four reasons. I want to live to see another season. I want my people to become strong and prosperous. I want our harvest to be bountiful. And I want our children to become as abundant as the flowers in the spring."

All of his people would hear him, and he would hear a murmur of approval throughout all the village. He then began to collect robes, clothing, horses, and other things of value, to be given away as presents or exchanged as medicine bundles.

When everything was in readiness, he took a gift and a pipe to a man whom, he believed, had greater supernatural strength than himself. He requested this man to act as priest in the Corn Ceremony. If the man accepted the invitation and smoked the pipe, he became the Medicine Maker, the chief medicine man of the ceremony. The Medicine Maker soon went to the lodge of the Singer, who knew all the songs

---

1   American Indian Heritage Foundation, P.O. Box 6301, Falls Church, VA 22040

and secrets of the ceremony. When the Medicine Maker offered him a robe and invited him to participate in the Corn Ceremony, the Singer gladly accepted. They then smoked the pipe together.

When the Medicine Maker had left the lodge, the Singer dressed and painted himself. Taking a piece of charcoal, he made three motions, as if he were painting his face. The fourth time, he drew a mark across his face as he sang:

"I am walking. I am walking."

The words meant that he was still following the instructions that the Old Woman Who Never Dies gave to the first priests of the first Corn Ceremony. He then placed a necklace of corn ears about his neck as he sang, "Yellow, Yellow," meaning "corn." Taking an ear of corn in his hand, he chanted:

"I am standing. I am walking."

Putting on a cap of the head-skin of his medicine animal--the kit-fox, for example--he sang:

"Kit-fox is walking. Kit-fox is asking."

When he was ready to depart, he addressed Old Woman Who Never Dies by singing:

"Young Woman, your fire-smoke I see;
I am coming. It is here."

The Singer then went to the lodge of the Medicine Maker, where those who were to participate in the ceremony were seated. They had been invited because their medicines were various birds that were thought to be the children of Old Woman Who Never Dies, and were therefore particularly appropriate for this ceremony. Their medicine bundles were laid in the centre of the lodge.

The Medicine Maker burned incense, and then all started for the lodge of the man who had made the vow. He was called the votary. The Medicine Maker led the group, carrying the head of a deer. The others followed, with the Singer in the centre.

As they approached his lodge, the votary came forth with a pipe, which he offered to the Medicine Maker. He took a few whiffs and then returned the pipe. This stopping and smoking occurred four times before the group reached the votary's lodge.

In the place of honour in his lodge, a very fine buffalo skin had been spread as an altar. Upon it the Medicine Maker placed the deer's head he had carried. The Singer sat behind it, and at his right sat the Medicine Maker, the votary and his wife, and the other participants. Buffalo robes had been spread in front of the positions taken by the assisting medicine men. Each of them placed his medicine bundle upon his particular robe.

The Medicine Maker raised the deer's head and touched the body of the votary's wife with it. Then each of the medicine men touched her body with his bundle and laid it in front of the altar, on robes that had been spread out for that purpose. This part of the ceremony was to give to the woman the strength and the power contained in the medicine bundles.

The votary and his wife then seated themselves on the side of the lodge at the left of the Singer. The Singer said to the votary, "Bring a live coal from the fire in the centre of the lodge and lay it on an earthen bowl."

Near it was a special bowl that was considered a symbol of Old Woman Who Never Dies. From it, the Singer took a handful of sage. After making a slow motion toward each of the Four Winds, the Singer lowered the sage to the hot coal, made four circles over it, and let the handful of sage fall.

The Medicine Maker waved a large bundle of sage over the smoke. Everyone was silent. The Singer took up the bowl in which the incense burned and passed it back and forth over the medicine bundles. As he passed it, he sang, again and again:

Sage is good.
Sage is good.

When he had set the bowl down, all the people stretched their hands toward it and rubbed themselves as if they were receiving its power. The votary filled a pipe and handed it to the medicine man at the end of the row. After inhaling a puff or two, he passed it to the one seated at his left.

When all had smoked, the Singer raised one of the medicine bundles, perhaps the raven, and sang as its owner came forward:

Raven is walking. Raven is walking.
Pedhifska didahuft.
Raven is walking.

The Raven man took the bundle from the Singer's hands and danced backward and forward between the altar and the fireplace. He held the bundle in his hands and swung it back and forth and from side to side. As he danced, he and the Singer chanted:

Raven is dancing back and forth.
Raven is dancing back and forth.

The Medicine Maker brought choice bits of meat and pretended to feed the Raven bundle! The votary then gave it back to him, and he returned to his seat. His wife gathered up the presents offered to his medicine by the votary.

The Singer thus called, in the correct order, each of the medicine men, and learned the songs as he had learned the Raven songs. When all these songs had been repeated, the votary and his wife brought food and placed it before the altar. The Singer chanted the prayer to The One Who First Made All Things:

Madhidift, Ifdihkawahidith.
I am walking in your path.

The votary brought a dish of choice parts of meat and laid it before the Singer. He sang:

"Old Woman Who Never Dies, I am walking in your path."

Lifting the dish, he extended it to the Four Winds and then threw the meat among the medicine men while he sang:

I take; I offer; it is done.

This was allegorical of the feeding of her birds by Old Woman Who Never Dies. The people scrambled for the food, chirping like blackbirds, ravens, and chickadees. The votary and his wife distributed the remainder of the food among the participants and the spectators. When the feast was finished, the owners of the medicine bundles advanced to receive them, while the Singer chanted:

I am walking; I have finished.
The land is green,
The land is yellow,
The land is gray.

The Medicine Maker took a bundle of sage and waved it toward the Four Winds and toward the door, as if to rid the lodge of evil spirits. The Singer brushed himself with sage, removed his cap and his necklace of corn ears, and then washed his face with water brought by the votary. His last song was this:

Kadhakowift; huft--
It is done; come--.

This song meant that the vow had been fulfilled and asked the Corn Spirit to answer the prayers for a bountiful harvest.

The Indigenous Peoples' Literature pages were researched and organized by Glenn Welker.

Appendix B
Sedna's Myth

There are many versions of Sedna's story. The Inuit's most major myth, it belongs to the original native migrations who brought it across the Bering Strait from the Eastern coast of Siberia. Variations occurred as groups settled and became isolated from other groups over many thousands of years. The version we chose to use in our book is the one which seemed most resonant to our time, since the minor planet's orbit has approached closely now, 5,500 years after its last close approach when humanity underwent its largest known transition in consciousness. It seems to tell us that from time to time we have to return to basics, let go of our outworn values or customs or wrong ways of thinking, and transcend ourselves to another level. We need to do this in the interests of the group or nation or collectivity. We here retell the story in our own words, as close to how we think it might have been told as we can.

It is not a children's fairy tale as you will soon discover. You will also see that although the shortcomings of the characters are very specific, they can be understood as representing many other problems we share with these characters. The meaning is about the egoistic individualism that plagues our planet, and particularly that of Western culture. Sedna goes through a transformation from her own narrow point of view to that of a goddess, who becomes responsible for the food of her people.

Sedna was a young woman of an Inuit seacoast fishing village. She lived with her father, who was constantly bringing young men to offer her in marriage. However, for reasons we are not told, Sedna rejected all of them and preferred sitting and combing her long, luxuriant hair in front of a mirror. Finally her father, who could no longer support her, said "Enough! You will go with the next suitor who comes."

A "next" one soon came and Sedna, realizing that her father meant business, looked him over. She said, "Well, he is dressed well and appears to be a decent sort of man. I suppose one is as good as another. I'll go with him." [Of course, the reader should realize that it was terribly cold and the man was dressed in heavy furs up to his eyes, so she didn't see much of him.]

He took her away, to a big rock on the cold sea, in which there was a cave. The cave floor had some sticks and other debris. The story offers nothing more. That was the first shock. The second came when the "man" undressed and showed himself to be a large bird. After that, every day he flew off to find fish which he brought home for Sedna to eat raw.

In great despair, Sedna screamed and called out to her father to save her. Across the waters, he heard her cries, got into his boat, and rowed valiantly to her cave, put her in the boat and raced back toward his land.

Birdman, meanwhile, discovered Sedna's defection and flew after her and her father. He tried to get Sedna out of the boat, but she hung on so tightly to her father and the boat, he could not. So he flapped his wings and stirred up a terrible storm. The boat took on water and the father realized that he couldn't save either of them with both in the boat, so he pushed Sedna out of the boat. However, Sedna clung to the edge of the boat for dear life and could not be detached. Her father then took his fishing knife and cut off her fingers. The fingers fell into the ocean and became the small fish. Still she hung on with her wrists, so he cut off her wrists which fell into the ocean and became the whales. Finally Sedna herself sank to the bottom of the ocean.

Sedna sat on the ocean floor, crying and bemoaning her state. After a long period of time of which the story again tells us nothing, Sedna, having apparently gone through a transformation, became a goddess. She then controlled all the fish and the whales of the ocean, in other words the Inuit's food supply. When the fisher people were not behaving, she cut off their supply and a shaman had to take the dangerous journey down to Sedna. He would appease her by soothing her with soft words and combing her long hair, which had become tangled with seaweed, and which she could no longer comb without fingers. Eventually, she would forgive the people and send the shaman back with the news that if they behaved themselves their fish supply would return.

Some versions say Sedna burned down her father's village in revenge and others say she forgave her father and granted his village an eternal supply of food. Both conclusions are equally applicable to the way people behave now all over the world.

Appendix C
Eclipses: Phases Extraordinaire

Many people are unclear about just what it is that creates an eclipse. It is as simple as New and Full Moons. In fact, every solar eclipse is a New Moon and every lunar eclipse is a full Moon. We already know that a New Moon is a Moon between the Earth and Sun, aligned almost in a straight line. A Full Moon is earth lined up between the Moon and Sun, almost in a straight line. What makes an eclipse is a more exact alignment of the three bodies, in a straight line in each case. The body in the middle is always the one responsible for the shadow causing the eclipse at one end.

A Solar Eclipse is Always a New Moon

Eclipses occur twice a year in pairs six months apart: a solar eclipse is followed in two weeks by a lunar eclipse, or vice versa, with an occasional addition of a 3rd eclipse. Many eclipses are partial, because alignments of the sun, moon and earth are not always exact. For simplicity we are discussing all eclipses, but the principle is always the same, total eclipses being more intense or impactful.

At New Moon we know Moon and Sun rise together in the sky, although the Moon is visually lost in the Sun's rays for about three days, the period called "the dark of the Moon". New Moon is not seen in the day because the Sun's rays obscure it. It is not seen at night, because for three days the Moon's path is following the day path close to the Sun (visually) and at night it is where the Sun is, on the other side of the earth. The Moon—if it were not obscured by the Sun's light—would not appear in front of the Sun, but just to one side of it, during those three days.

Twice a year, creating a solar eclipse, Earth, Moon and Sun are in exact or nearly exact alignment, with Moon exactly aligned between Earth and Sun. From that position, the Moon cuts off not only the light from the Sun to the earth, *but the Sun itself,* since the Moon from Earth's perspective is perceived as the same size as the Sun. The Sun appears completely black, but what we are really seeing is not a "black Sun" (as the ancients, such as the Aztecs, believed) but the Moon without light on its face. In actual fact, the only time we ever see a new Moon is during a total solar eclipse! The Moon itself, between us and the Sun, is fully cutting off the light from the Sun, which is then lighting up only the Moon's backside which we

341

never see. Sometimes the Moon appears smaller, being on the far end of the long arc of its elliptical orbit and therefore farther away. Then we see the impressive *ring of fire,* the black disk of the moon against the fiery outer edge of the sun. These and other astronomical factors provide us with symbolic information about our selves and our own lives. I am reminded of Johnny Cash's song "Ring of Fire". Perhaps a "ring of fire" eclipse emphasizes the possible dangers of our passions and the fateful possibilities of moving in their direction if they are not coming from our spiritual center.

A Lunar Eclipse Is Always a Full Moon

Unlike normal full Moons, during lunar eclipses the Earth is aligned exactly between Sun and Moon. Earth cuts off the Sun's light on the Moon, but *not the Moon itself.* We can still see a dark red disk, slightly lighter than the night sky.

But, you may exclaim, the moon can not emit light! True, but let us see what actually happens with light, between the Sun and the Moon just before and during a normal full Moon. *Infra-red* light is generated by heat. The Sun radiates lots of infra-red (heat) as well as *visual* red and all the colors of the visual spectrum. For several days before every full Moon, the Sun's infra-red light has been heating up the moon's surface, which reaches beyond boiling temperature. During any Full Moon, the Moon becomes so hot it generates more of its own infra-red than it receives from the Sun, but since infra-red is invisible to the naked eye we are not aware of this.

Science tells us that during an eclipse the full Moon's surface temperature quickly drops way below freezing, as both Sun's light and its heat (infra-red) are cut off by the earth. The Moon stops emitting infra-red entirely of course, because now it is freezing. But strangely, though its normal light is cut off, and it is freezing, we do see a dark red disk! So we have to ask, why does it look red? We know absolutely that the Moon has no light of its own. Or does it?

The surprising answer is that the eclipsed Moon is still receiving red light from the Sun! The longest wavelengths of the Sun's light are *visual* red. During total lunar eclipses, Earth's atmosphere grabs the Sun's *visual* red light waves, and bends and wraps them around the Earth where they then project toward the Moon. Since *visual* red light can reflect, it reflects back to us from Moon, and we see a dark red disc.

Infra-red can emit but can not reflect or "bend".
Visual red can reflect and "bend" but not emit.

The Moon's Nodes

The Nodes are important to the eclipses, even though you can't see them in the sky. But you can imagine the path of the Moon as we see it around the earth. You can also imagine the path of the Sun as we think we are seeing it going around the earth, at a plane tilted from that of the Moon. (This is not astronomically correct but in Alice's Looking glass WYSIWYG, it seems to "work"). You can put two wire hoops together, then tip them in relationship to each other in such a way that they only touch or intersect each other in two places, the plane of one tilted from the other. That is basically the idea of what the nodes are—those two intersection points of the circular paths of Sun and Moon. It's more complex than that, but this gets the idea. All solar eclipses occur when Sun and Moon are together near one of the nodes. In all lunar eclipses, the Sun will be near one node and the Moon will be near the other. The closer they are to the nodes, the more total will be the eclipse. The nodes in your chart have much to say about your life as moving from the past (south node) toward the future (north node).

Eclipses and Lunar Nodes

As we have stated, the nodes are points on the apparent orbits of the Moon and Sun where the two orbits intersect. They do this twice a day. The Moon twice daily crosses the (imaginary) path of the Sun, once when the Moon rises in the east and once when it sets in the west. Except for eclipse times, the Moon's path appears to be quite independent of the Sun's path, rising sometimes in the day and sometimes in the night. But the cycle always begins, at new moon, with the Sun and Moon rising together. A solar eclipse always occurs very close to a north or south node, which also affects the way we interpret an eclipse, although we don't need that piece to interpret the eclipses at this point.

The ancients called the *north node* the *dragon's head*, and the *south node* the *dragon's tail*. An image of the dragon with its tail in its mouth has become a universal symbol for the completion of a circle of the zodiac, of the calendar year and other cosmic complete cycles. Many of our readers will have seen the great Aztec Calendar Stone or a facsimile, in a museum or in Mexico, with the snake symbol around the outside.

Eclipses are recorded in 19 year cycles. There are over a hundred sets of these cycles, called Saros cycles. Each cycle began at a different time in history. Each cycle has its own astrological meaning. What may interest you now is that when you have a solar eclipse followed in two weeks by a lunar eclipse, both of which are followed in six months by two more eclipses, these eclipses are not related. Each one is in a sequence on its own Saros cycle with its own meaning, parallel to all the others but separate. The fact that they progresss slowly through your houses over many years' time is what connects them at the personal level.

Normally we have four eclipses a year, a solar eclipse followed two weeks later by a lunar eclipse. Then in six months a similar pair will occur in opposite signs. It takes 19 years for the two pairs of eclipses to go through all the signs of the zodiac.

During that time, over the years, several changes occur so (1) the order of a solar eclipse, followed in two weeks by a lunar eclipse, is reversed; and (2) the solar/lunar pairs change signs. Due to these variables, sometimes an eclipse is skipped or there is a 5th eclipse in which cases various changes occur in the rhythms of eclipses. Basically the effects on the individual chart are the same, but one finds unusually longer or shorter periods of time between solar and lunar eclipses. One astrological difference important to our own charts is that whereas a solar eclipse has been preceding the lunar eclipse by two weeks, in the order of Signs, the lunar eclipse will now precede the solar eclipse by two weeks.

Eclipses never ceased to interest the ancients, and they never cease to interest us. They are one of the strongest expressions of Divine guidance through the astrology chart. Even the most scientific minds pause in awe before an eclipse. Read the next appendix to find out how to interpret all these scientific facts. Many of the facts have not been interpreted in books on astrology, and we guaratee you that if you spend a week working out one major interpretation of an eclipse in your chart, you will get very deep into some amazing self-knowledge.

Appendix D
Signatures of "Fate": Interpreting Eclipses

A solar eclipse deals with the cyclic urge of the spirit to manifest. Behind the dark curtain of the New Moon, as usual, her desire energy is implanted by the sun with a seed of spirit-purpose. This eclipse seed, however, carries much more creativity and drive of purpose. It is one of those astrological timings that refer to the free will of spirit, not the human ego. It acts as a timed reminder of how easy it is to let our highest best intentions yield to Moon's needs and desires which then overbalance our larger purpose. Solar eclipses have great power to return us to our spiritual direction in spite of our overbalanced needs and desires.

A lunar eclipse deals with the moon's habituated reactions, desires, and neediness, and with the convoluted ramifications those things represent for each of us. Moon holds the karmic reason for incarnating—the need to live out our unfinished business from before this life as well as the need to live out a future new purpose or goal for this life. At eclipse time we have the opportunity to understand and work through these karmic needs and desires. If we have rationalized or repressed our emotions and desires we may be in trouble with denial and justification. Lunar eclipses, like it or not, make us live out our denied life-needs—which like spoiled meat, may be unsavory after several lifetimes on ice. Nevertheless, their purpose is to restore balance with spirit. In Medieval and ancient times, eclipses were merely labeled as evil or dangerous, without interpretation. The farther back one goes in history, the more they were primarily used as predictors of earthquakes, floods, plagues and destruction. As history got closer to Greek times, rulers' lives were subject to eclipses, also negatively. Now we are in a position to consider what the scientific facts of an eclipse might mean to our own lives.

Eclipses are mysterious phenomena, surrounded by myth, ritual, magic, fear, and ancient politics. Their deeply embedded heavy mythologies and powerful rituals over thousands of years are still with us, even though most Westerners do not believe in the stories or practice the rituals any more. Eclipses have been and still are strongly associated with the ideas of fate, on which we prefer to cast some light. Fate is better understood as that which happens outside of our ability to make other choices—things controlled by our spirit's free will over our ego's will.

From childhood many generations of us have known scientifically that an eclipse of the Moon or Sun does not harm or diminish either. Nevertheless, a blackened sun in a day sky, or a dark red disappearing moon in the night sky, can be deeply, if subtly, disturbing. Even in our own time some people have thought the red color on some lunar eclipses was prophetic blood on the moon. Some of us may still have deep-seated, perhaps genetically stored, memories of mystery or primal fear upon seeing an eclipse.

Consider the concept of the dark night of the soul, a personally intense, often transformative, experience many people have at least once in their lives, when they feel cut off from the very Source of their being. During a solar eclipse we are, in fact, cut off from the Sun, which is our earthly and visible source of spirit, life, and vitality, and historically the universal symbol for Deity. A night-time eclipsed moon, our only source of light at night, leaves us open to the demons of long-forgotten terrors of the dark. Such images are powerful emotional triggers. These are fundamental archetypes from an ageless past. They may still be in our very genetic structure after more than 100,000 years. Did they have a lesson to teach us? Can they tell us something about our own Dark Nights of the Soul? About our fears?

Without looking further, the Balsamic phase of the moon cycle might offer us a microcosmic image of the dark night of the soul. Twice a year we can watch our state of mind when (and if) the balsamic moon precedes a solar eclipse. If we still feel the connecting thread of the ancestors within us, we know instinctively that the Sun will be cut off from us within a matter of hours. Since solar eclipses are sometimes felt and manifested to some extent up to a week in advance, we are in a position to sense even our personal meaning of the coming loss of the Sun. If our personal timing resonates in some way, there will be a true microcosmic dark night—an experience of great value when it occurs.

Why would we wish to experience such a deep sense of darkness? Are we not following faith, astrology, divination, and other gifts of spirit in order to feel positive? Ah, but that is exactly what we feel we are losing. We say, "It's darkest before dawn", and other such phrases designed to offer hope, and now our god of science even guarantees that the Sun and Moon will be back. But if we would honor our feelings, we may find that sometimes we do actually feel that we cannot connect with spirit and that may be frightening.

If we look back at those writers who have described a dark night of the soul we see that this is a soul terrain that must be crossed by everyone at some stage in their incarnations, and can never be circumnavigated, risen above or otherwise avoided. Such soul transitions lead to the light of spirit and to an inevitable expansion of Self (Sun) and self (Moon). The need is to let go into whatever that dark time brings in order to fully make the crossing of the dark valley from a lesser life to a greater. Fully experiencing the Balsamic phase preceding a solar eclipse, provided it is your time to resonate fully to the dying energies of both Yin and Yang cycles, prepares you for other, greater transitions through a true dark night of the soul. Science tells us the dark matter of the universe is 99% of the universe. It is out of that dark matter that everything was created. Just so out of our darker moments come our own creations stronger than before.

Some Myths about Eclipses

An eclipse was considered by the ancients to be a bad omen at the very least. They perceived it as a great sky dragon taking bites out of the Sun or Moon and swallowing it. If this aggression had persisted the ancients believed the evil dragon would have destroyed earth or all life on earth. Traditionally, eclipses were believed to herald disasters, wars, and diseases, and in early Chinese city-states, eclipses were very political. If the official astrologer neglected to forecast a coming eclipse, thus endangering his country, he was usually executed. Even now, mundane astrologers (who predict or explain current physical, social, and political events) place great emphasis on eclipses.

Eclipses are still thought to foretell earthquakes, invasions, epidemics, floods and other natural disasters. Not to worry, most eclipses (being partial) are not much stronger than new and full Moons; and they apply strongest mainly to the areas over which they occur. Further cutting the risks, in personal astrology an eclipse has to have a close aspect to a planet in your chart, particularly a conjunction, to affect your life strongly. It does happen, and there are many of us to tell the tale, though most of us have lived long enough to tell you that it was the best thing that ever happened to us.

The dragon theme is related to the Moon's nodes. The south

347

node or dragon's tail represents the past and is related to the Moon; the north node or dragon's head represents the future and is related to the Sun. As you remember, during eclipses the Sun and Moon are very close to the nodes. The closer they are, the more impactful the eclipse. The nodes hold important information concerning your past and your destiny in the natal chart. The north (latitude) node represents where you are headed in terms of your destiny and what new things you need to learn in this life; and the south node represents where you came from (past lives) and some talents and abilities you bring with you.

Each eclipse is on a continuous thread of meaning from a different time in history, the Saros cycles mentioned earlier, which can last as long as a thousand years. If a cycle were traced back it would be found that there is some relationship between earth's current affairs and the affairs at the time of the initial eclipse of its cycle. This is just one more thing that shows how many different ways we are connected to all humans, in time as well as space. We have checked out the above statement and found it to be accurate to our personal satisfaction. Astrologers have been using this information in chart readings for a very long time, and we think that in some cases an eclipse that is close to a planet in your chart may, by its Saros cycle, indicate a past life you are connected with.

Sun relates to men and rulers, and to the north node, or future. Moon relates to women and the past, and therefore according to the ancients, to evil, as was the south node. (We note, however, that in India and Tibet the south node was the most spiritual point in the chart.) We guess that the male supremacy attitude that has dogged the footsteps of women for so many millennia was related to this connection of Moon to women, darkness and evil. In the long past, the Sun always referred to the emperor or whoever held the male leadership role, which ironically was responsible for rather large chunks of evil throughout history, while the Moon, or women, often took the blame.

As modern astrologers, we no longer believe that eclipses *cause* the disaster and disease, or growth of crops or babies. They are cosmic timing tools, letting us know when it is time to redirect our course in life (sun), and when it is time to let go of past attachments and behaviors (Moon). They might well predict disaster or disease, but they will only be timing the natural results of earth changes or collective wrong living over time. The effects of eclipses, whether we like them or not, are intended to move things toward healing personal, social or earth imbalances or disharmonies. Their reputation for disaster is often truth in action, as we well know that human beings who set out to change the pendulum, turn the tide, or make any kind of major social or personal change, often manage to commit a lot of carnage in the process. Or, at another level, a person who eats too much sugar may get diagnosed on an eclipse with diabetes (Full Moon revelation) unnecessarily, because he/she ignored the warning signs of their own bodies. A positive note is that in our experience, eclipses have less negative effects in the lives of people who are taking their own responsibility to turn their experiences into positive ones, through personal transformation. Spirit gives us signs in many ways, besides astrology, that we need to change our ways. In astrology, a lunar eclipse will give you a warning that the house in your chart in which it occurs is in need of some cleaning-up because the next solar eclipse is going to let the axe fall. If you are ready, the event will be easier. If not, then the readers beware.

Modern keywords for eclipses are "they balance inequalities", or "right wrongs". One can see that when we allow the masculine Sun part of ourselves to become overbearing or self-obsessed, even to the point of neglecting personal or relationship needs, events of a solar eclipse can force us to see that and remedy the imbalance. When the learned behaviors and needs of the Moon part of ourselves go out of control with addictions or outdated reactions to life, lunar eclipse events can force us to see that, too, and remedy it. Over millennia as the pendulum swings, eclipses have specifically contributed to the rebalancing of male/female in humanity and individuals. This is important both at the individual level in understanding our own personal growth process, and in terms of the socio-political world-level imbalances.

How Do We Look At Eclipses in a Chart?

Usually a lunar eclipse occurs in the same sign/house polarity as the solar eclipse. The solar eclipse of course occupies only one sign/house, but is always considered to be in polarity with its opposite sign/house. For example, a Capricorn solar eclipse is in the Capricorn/Cancer polarity. The following lunar eclipse usually falls in the same Capricorn/Cancer polarity, with the Sun in the same Capricorn sign/house, and the moon in the opposite Cancer sign/house.

However, occasionally a Lunar eclipse two weeks later crosses over to the next polarity, dragging the sun with it into the next sign in the middle of the lunar cycle, and continues that pattern for a number of months after which the solar eclipse polarity progresses into the newly established sign of the lunar eclipse.

Following the original example, with the solar eclipse in the Cancer/Capricorn polarity, let's say the lunar eclipse has moved out of Cancer into Leo, with the Sun opposite it in Aquarius. This mixed pattern continues for a number of months after which both eclipses occupy the Leo/Aquarius polarity.

When we see this changing polarity pattern, we know that we are preparing to transition from one major set of lessons being learned, (Sign) to another. The Houses of the eclipses in our own chart or Solar dial will show the areas of our life where the emphasis is beginning to change. The lunar eclipse always begins that process. It "takes the heat off" one area of your life but opens up another area for a spell of personal work.

A solar eclipse tells you that your purpose and direction in its house needs more expansion, growth, development, or personal recognition of your selfhood and purpose. You need to change or expand the direction you are going in here. The physical, emotional, mental or spiritual area in which this growth is needed can be determined by the element the eclipse is in: <u>earth = physical, water = emotional, air = mental, fire = spiritual</u>. That turns out to be an exceptionally useful piece of information which can be generalized elsewhere in chart work. Basically the message is "time for an update or upgrade here".

A lunar eclipse is Scorpionic in some ways. It signals a time to actively release deep-seated, old, perhaps unconscious or at least semi-conscious, learned behaviors or addictive patterns. These are specific to the House of the lunar eclipse and specifically ones that are limiting you from focusing or manifesting the Sun's purpose into your life. That purpose is described by the opposite Sign, where the Sun sits. In other words, at a Full Moon eclipse the Sun-Moon Sign polarity is out of balance on the Moon side. In this House you are not keeping up with the side of yourself that is moving ahead toward various life goals. Generally it is the outdated or early social-parental patterning that blocks you from hearing and manifesting the spirit's message.

Another metaphor for the relationship between Solar and Lunar eclipses was created by Jansky[2] using the image of a supervisor coming around to review these areas and giving warnings about the next review. <u>You are the supervisor (Sun)</u>—the core self that should be running your life.

Isn't the organization of our cosmos an amazing structure? The sky contains all we need to figure out what is happening and why and even peek in on our future.

There is nothing in astronomy that does not reveal an astrological meaning. Infra red and visual red contribute to the meaning a total lunar eclipse has for you personally. Throughout the book, every astronomical fact you read can suddenly become personal if you dig deeply enough.

The visual red of a lunar eclipse comes from the Earth and is reflected back at us. It is an aspect of human energy related to Mars. Mars has been called the god of war, but in fact it has a much deeper, more significant meaning of strong ego-desire which can be transmuted from physical desire and actions to spiritual desire and actions. Either way, we can do nothing without Mars. At a lunar eclipse, we may have our earthly actions and reactions mirrored back to us, which gives us an opportunity to change.

The infra-red represents spiritual energy. It is unchangeable and cannot be bent or changed because it is of the Divine. It is said that Pluto, the planet of transformation, holds the intentions of the soul, while Mars carries them out. Thus Pluto is connected to the infra-red, while Mars is connected to the visual red. The six months following a lunar eclipse is thus a time in which we might expect transformation of some sort.

How Long Do the Effects of Eclipses Last?

The effect of a solar eclipse is traditionally considered to be as long in years as the hours the eclipse lasts. The effect of the lunar eclipse is considered to be as long in months as the minutes the eclipse lasts. Some astrologers now suggest one year for the solar eclipse and 6 months for the moon, although in actual fact the effects of both can last several years, in terms of astrology, which complexification most astrologers ignore.

We will not be venturing into that argument in this book, other than to say that for practical reasons, we ourselves routinely only look at the effects from one solar/lunar eclipse pair to the next of like

---

2   Jansky, Robert Carl. *Interpreting the Eclipses*, ACS Publications, Inc., 1979, San Diego, CA.

kind. During these 6-month periods the greatest emphases of life will be in the houses of the eclipses, interpreted according to the nature of the eclipses. While the effects may continue past 6 months, we will have a new six months of potent house emphases to consider, which overlaps and sometimes the overlaps overlap more overlaps. Remember also that the Sign-polarity emphases continue for years in the same areas of life, but with the Sun and Moon alternating occupation of Houses, and of the ends of the polarities, and holding different degree symbols. Thus we work through the problems of life and humanity over many years through each Sign and its polarity, step by step. It takes 19 years to complete a whole cycle of eclipses. Through the eclipses we are each responsible for one tiny part of humanity's growth in consciousness.

We leave further refinement to astrologers who specialize in mundane and political astrology. However, we would add that transiting planets, aspecting an eclipse point during that interval, will often activate an aspect of the eclipse meaning. Again, this is for another book.

Positions of Eclipses on the Natal and Solar Wheels

There are six positions on both the natal and solar wheels, which are of major importance in eclipses, but different in nature from each other. They are the Sun, Moon, and four directional points called "Angles". If you draw an equal-armed cross on a circle, you have a symbol for Earth which in the chart is always opposite the Sun. All four points represent significant turning points at various levels, and are considered the most powerful "sensitive" points in *your relationship to earthly reality*. The four Angles are:

Ascendant (cusp of 1st house or house 1 on the solar wheel) *personal* (East)

MC or Midheaven (cusp of 10th solar house) *career* (South)

IC or Imum Coeli (cusp of 4th solar house) *family* (North)

Descendant (cusp of 7th solar house). *Relationships* (West)

This image is sometimes called "the cross of matter" which symbolizes the four major lessons of living life in this reality, and the spiritual reward for giving it your "all" in the process. It also represents in shamanism the sacred space—for you the chart is your personal space in history and on this planet, which may, in itself, be sacred.

In a solar chart these angles refer to your Sun's relationship to your power of essential being and self-expression in this world. In a natat chart the angles are about your whole relationship to the world you live in: the 12 areas of life experience in your world environment.

If an eclipse falls close to one of these points, in either chart, it assumes a greater, more intense influence (at one of the four levels of being). It is said that changes related to an eclipse will be more dramatic or impactful than in in-between houses, and will be permanent. The Ascendant and Midheaven points are considered the most important, but we do not accept that other than as a statement that they are more obvious because they deal with the external world. The 4th and 7th House cusps are more about family relationship, and social or collective relationship, which may be, for some, far more personally important because they are the foundations for living in a spiritiually expanded external world.

An eclipse falling on an angle in a natal chart indicates a change in how you relate to one of the four points:

Ascendant = very personal, having to do with the self image one projects

Midheaven = one's position in the community, reputation, honors

IC = One's foundations in life—family, roots, inner strength, support

Descendant = One's partnerships, audiences, clients

An eclipse in a solar chart indicates by sign changes in how you express, or relate to, your personal power in the house it occupies:

Ascendant = Consciousness, vitality, self-expression, pride, ability to **love**

Midheaven = one's desire or ability to be honored by the outer world

IC = the foundations of one's individual self-hood: self-acceptance, self-respect

Descendant = How you integrate your selfhood with others; shadow-projections;

An eclipse near the Sun and Moon indicates critical personal changes in the house it occupies.

Sun = Your purpose in life, will, vitality, and consciousness. How you express your purpose and will in your life experiences.

Moon = Your emotions, memory, form-building ability, needs, health. How you react or respond to life experiences,

You may want to get out your wheel, the tables of signs, houses, and New and Full Moon energies. Locate the most recent pair of eclipses in the front material of your "Celestial Guide", and mark the Houses in which they fall with small re-usable colored dot labels. As you read through the material keep checking your eclipse Sun and Moon signs and houses to see if the information resonates for you.

Because we have found eclipses so difficult to pin down into useable information for ourselves, we created five sets of key words/phrases to keep ourselves on track when working with eclipses in our own lives. We re-phrase in many ways, because repeating in different terms reinforces the learning process. Experimenting initially in different ways with these simple statements makes it easier to "read" an eclipse into our own lives.

1. Eclipses of the Sun indicate that our direction and expansion into the future has gotten out of balance with our personal emotional lives.
2. Eclipses of the Moon tell us that we need to clear out outdated patterns of behavior and needs in preparation for the next solar eclipse.

1. In the House of a solar eclipse we need to give more, and
2. In the House of a lunar eclipse we need to receive more

1. In the House of a solar eclipse we need to expand our territory, and
2. In the House of a lunar eclipse we need to clean up our act.

1. In the House of a solar eclipse the past cuts off some part of the anticipated future,
2. In the House of a lunar eclipse the future direction cuts off the continuance of a part of the past

1 & 2. Eclipses right wrongs.

It should be clear that the Sun and Moon functions must be in balance together in order for us to become all that we can be. The two are both responsible for our successful experience of. In terms

354

of giving and receiving, eventually the Sun must receive wisdom from others to grow in its own wisdom, and Moon must nurture or give to others as he/she has been nurtured.

Meanwhile, the Sun can only fulfill its purpose through the Moon's form-building. Sun's purpose must have strong enough self knowledge to convey the monthly images clearly to the Moon's consciousness and the Moon must throughout the lifetime continually release learned thoughts, beliefs, inhibitions, outworn griefs, addictions, patterns, etc, from the past, in order to be personally free enough of limitations to know its own truth and build the forms of the future.

Doing Your Own Eclipse Interpretation

The basic interpretation of an eclipse is no different than that of any New or Full Moon. Initially, if this is too much information, just use the regular interpretations and consider that they are likely to be more intense. That is what most astrologers will tell you anyway.

Find the New and Full Moon Signs, Houses, and interpretations in the tables elsewhere in this book, and consider what they are telling you about your direction in a solar eclipse House. One of the difficulties you might have if you are new to astrology is that there are so many interpretations of Houses. We have included in the appendices a large wheel with many interpretations of each of the Houses. If the table descriptions don't resonate, read more from this wheel, or read astrology books about Houses. When you have decided what you were doing, planning or wishing for before in the most recent solar eclipse House, write that down in your journal. You, like we, may find it hard to remember these things exactly if we are not keeping regular journals. One way to trace memory back is to consider one's most pressing current problem to see if it relates to the last eclipse. If not, go further back to the preceding eclipse.

Now, in your journal describe your situation in terms of the House and Sign interpretations, and the key words in this appendix. You may not at first be satisfied with these statements, but part of the Moon path work is learning from experience what Signs and Houses mean for you individually. In that process you also define more clearly what the aspects of your life mean to you.

In-Depth Interpretation of the Red in a Lunar Eclipse

We saved this part of the eclipse information to last because of its involved, complicated nature, and because it is, to us, very special.

We have never seen this interpreted anywhere, although perhaps we just missed it. Here it is:

The Earth's shadow shuts down the infra red, freezes the Moon's surface, and blocks the objective reflected Sun's light. The monthly Full Moon needs to balance the needs of our individuality with the needs of society. We see a dark red disk, almost obscured by the earth-shadow. Immediately, we need to know that visual red is the color of Mars, the urge to action, anger, or the drive toward spirit. The personal unconscious (blackened red) is bared and vulnerable, and robbed of its thin veneer of conscious awareness and its protective censors.

Infra-red is associated with Pluto and the transformation of Mars' actions. Infra red is out of this picture—our urges to act on old emotions are coming to the surface and will inform us of the old patterns of emotional action that need transformation. They may cause us to act externally, or to react internally, and there will be no doubt that they are outdated and unhelpful. Where Mars has been transformed to its true meaning, the drive toward spirit, actions and reactions will be for the good of all.

The Earth-shadow, the black mixed with the red, are the hard facts of material life. They can block our ability to apply what objectivity we have developed, in the current situation. Psychology tells us that in a struggle between the unconscious and the conscious, the unconscious always wins. This operation is what ancient societies called "fate", long associated with eclipses. Our conscious is receiving an unconscious message projected on the external world in all its primal power, and can not avoid it. Now either the unconscious individual or the outer world claims its due. Consider the increased reception of patients into mental wards and felons into jails during lunar eclipses. If you are an addict will you take a larger dose, with all its possible consequences, or will you check into a rehab?

Let's take another look at the image of that eclipsed Moon. How does the Full Moon message get through to us? That red light from the Sun, wrapped around the earth as it stands in the way of direct sunlight, projects toward the moon. Our "shadow" is clearly looking back at us, but out of that shadow we see a faint touch of its contents. Something we are meant to change at this time is saying, "Here I am, come get me". As happens so often, the unconscious manifests in the outer world, and we may see either our least desirable qualities or our denied spiritual qualities projected onto our environment. We are at the point of sharing whatever we created from the Sun's intent, but the environment of the self's (moon's) unconscious may often appear threatening. A mountain of reality is in our way. Perhaps we are afraid of being embarrassed, guilty, attacked, whatever—which definitely does not feel like being recognized for the individual we are. Perhaps someone is in trouble and we are in a position to help but that would be dangerous. We might be on that proverbial cliff with a snapping wild boar behind us and a lion at the bottom. What to do? The mountain in front of you is the key. Listen to your gut here, but keep your eyes open and be very conscious about what you are experiencing. There is wisdom on the outside at Full Moon. There is a mirror to see yourself in. There is another in your chart, in the Sign, House and degree.

The Earth is bathing the black Moon in the Sun's faint red light. Of course. We cannot join with another person or with society and retain our ego intact. Some of it has to go. We need Mars (red) reaching out beyond ourselves in action. It is not possible to let go of something trapped in the unconscious without action. Transformation cannot be had without action being taken. Mars acts, Pluto transforms.

Every action transforms us ever so little, either toward the angelic or the demonic. During the eclipse there is no transformative energy coming at us with the chunk of reality, but there is the unconscious image of our past actions revealed for all to see! We must choose to do something but we can choose to do nothing, to blindly "act out" of our unconscious, or to act consciously in a different and *new* way, not an action mucked up with ego-stuff.

But Mars is also the activating red of life-blood, which carries the soul, mixed with our unconscious. The questions asked are: can I separate my un-purified unconscious (darkened Moon) from my conscious Sun-self? Can I use my Sun-intelligence to act in a way that will simultaneously transform that un-redeemed part of me and integrate it into my consciousness? All unconscious urges that cause us trouble become increased personal power once they are made conscious through action, recognized, and transformed.

We face the inner reality described by the eclipsed Moon's Sign and degree symbol, and we reach for the Sun's intent at the opposite Sign to find an answer. The degree symbol of the Sun/spirit contains the spirit's intent at that moment. Read these symbols in terms of the elements as described earlier. (Ex. Cancer is water--emotions, Capricorn is earth—physical)

As we have noted before, eclipses do not necessarily show us the full situation at the time. It could be weeks or months before we know more than the area of our life being affected. That is why transiting planets aspecting the eclipse point down the line so often trigger the meaning of the eclipse. Action is required and only then the opportunity. This is also demonstrated by the fact that only visual red is available during the eclipse, but afterward infra-red (release or transformation) manifests.

In Other Words

The hardest thing we have to do is take responsibility for our old patterns and emotions and find a safe way to let go of them, continually upgrading the Moon-past. So we have the ordinary Full Moon covered with the light of consciousness, showing us these patterns and emotions. The Full Moon Sun-message shows us how to release them safely so they do not stand in the way of clear, objective understanding. We are free to follow these messages or not. For many that objectivity is not yet well developed and Full Moon is a time to deny, drown themselves in alcohol or sugar treats, kick the dog, go out and pick a fight, or fall down the stairs. High blood pressure patients take note! Stay home in bed if your psyche is loaded and you don't have a good therapist!

However, a lunar eclipse can change all this. Real problems await those who ignore the eclipse messages. Not that we don't receive the messages from the world around us all the time. This is simply a more precise and focused way of seeing what our life needs. Seeing it on a chart, and reading it in a book often makes us more open to hear the message, since we don't like hearing it from others.

Since Moon is about doing what the Sun directs, the actual process of rebalancing your self with relationship can be exciting and wonderful or sometimes really shockingly awful. To some degree you may not have been impeccable, in the eclipsed Moon area, about carrying out the Sun's directives toward participating in outer relationship and you need to clean up your act. Since virtually no one is always impeccable, this applies to everyone. So look at your reflection in the outer world, see the wake of your invisible boat, and move fully on the wave of opportunity to rebalance. The reward is there, the gift is in the experience, whatever it might be. Transformation is the permanent reward.

Appendix E
The Original Degrees Of The Zodiac And "Sabian" Symbols

By Marc Edmund Jones
As excerpted from
The Astrology Of Personality, Dane Rudhyar, 1991,
Aurora Press, Santa Fe, NM
with permission of publisher

Any fraction of a degree is to be considered as a whole degree. Aries 15° 0' is to be read as Aries 15°; but Aries 15° 1', as well as Aries 15° S9', represents Aries 16°. The symbols are the expression of a span of activity, a cycle, the significance of which is released at once, the moment it begins.

ARIES I. THE SPAN OF REALIZATION

1° A WOMAN HAS RISEN FROM THE OCEAN; A SEAL EMBRACES HER
Potentiality of selfhood: the individual is emerging from the collective and realizes self for the first time.

2° A COMEDIAN IS ENTERTAINING A GROUP OF HIS FRIENDS
Objective understanding through extracting salient elements of being. Joy of life's discovery; or escape through humor.

3° A MAN'S PROFILE SUGGESTS THE OUTLINES OF HIS COUNTRY
The individual self as an avatar of greater collective reality; as participant in the larger scheme of society or life.

4° TWO LOVERS ARE STROLLING THROUGH A SECLUDED PARE LANE
Fullness of conscious participation in life without responsibility. Closing of a cycle of activity, implying satiation.

5° A WHITE TRIANGLE, WITH GOLDEN WINGS ON ITS UPPER SIDES
Evolution of values in the sphere of inward self, but at a stage not yet substantiated. Eagerness for a spiritual goal.

6° A BLACK SQUARE; ONE OF ITS SIDES IS ILLUMINED RED
Primal effort toward individual selfhood. First and uncontrolled interest in any given thing. Great inner restlessness.

7° A MAN EXPRESSES HIMSELF AT ONCE IN TWO REALMS
Conscious duality by which man first really differentiates himself from the animals. Versatility in work. Self-expansion.

8° A WOMAN'S HAT, WITH STREAMERS BLOWN BY THE EAST WIND
First real attempt at self-exteriorization and embodiment in consciousness. Individualizing Eastern forces are suggested.

9° A SEER GAZES WITH CONCENTRATION INTO A CRYSTAL SPHERE
Direction from within. Taking advantage of all factors in a given situation, and knowing when to make decisions. Assurance.

10° A SCHOLAR CREATES NEW FORMS FOR ANCIENT SYMBOLS
Deep understanding, beyond normal means. Abstract seership, integrating the inner and the outer. Interpretative gift.

11° THE RULER OF A COUNTRY IS BEING OFFICIALLY INTRODUCED
Fine stewardship of collective racial ideals. Good and necessary, but unimaginative conformity to standards. Idealization.

12° A FLOCK OF WHITE GEESE FLIES OVERHEAD ACROSS CLEAR SKIES

A soul as yet socially immature and unadjusted; not come down to full and steady concrete expression. Self-discovery.

13° A BOMB WHICH FAILED TO EXPLODE IS NOW SAFELY CONCEALED
Intangible fears of nascent selfhood: the creative stirring up of a new perspective and a new identity suddenly revealed.

14° A SERPENT ENCIRCLES A MAN AND WOMAN IN CLOSE EMBRACE
Power of higher wisdom manifest in the bi-polar nature. Protection by the higher genius of Self. Fulfillment in truth.

15° INDIAN WEAVING A BASKET IN THE GOLDEN LIGHT OF SUNSET
Full and conscious realization of selfhood, through the memory of all the powers acquired in the past. Retentiveness.

ARIES II. THE SPAN OF EXAMINATION

16° BRIGHTLY CLAD BROWNIES, DANCING IN WARM DYING LIGHT
Relationship between conscious and unconscious sides of life. Invisible assistance often entailing obligation to outer forces.

17° TWO PRIM SPINSTERS ARE SITTING TOGETHER IN SILENCE
Poised and dispassionate outlook, involving either great dignity and integrity of self, or inability to live life fully.

18° AN EMPTY HAMMOCK IS HANGING BETWEEN TWO LOVELY TREES
Rest after some notable achievement. Capacity for consciousness after the act, for reaping fruits of activity. Detachment.

19° A MAGIC CARPET HOVERING OVER AN UGLY INDUSTRIAL SUBURB
Capacity to transform everyday life by the power of creative significance; or escape in idle fancy.

20° A YOUNG GIRL FEEDING SWANS IN A PARK ON A WINTRY DAY
Participation of self in a life larger than any conception of selfhood. Protection, or the need for it.

21° A PUGILIST, FLUSHED WITH STRENGTH, ENTERS THE RING
Complete immolation of self in things purely physical. Intense self-assertiveness, physical and psychological.

22° GATEWAY OPENING TO THE GARDEN OF ALL DESIRED THINGS\
Joy and utter lack of inhibitions in objective life. Self-exaltation or bondage to the craving for happiness.

23° WOMAN IN SUMMER DRESS CARRIES A PRECIOUS VEILED BURDEN
First maturity of conscious life in any phase of experience. Sense of value and delicacy—or wastefulness. Innocence.

24° A WINDOW CURTAIN BLOWN INWARD, SHAPED AS A CORNUCOPIA
Good fortune attending upon the putting forth of effort. Rush of spiritual forces into the conscious ego. Protection.

25° A DOUBLE PROMISE REVEALS ITS INNER AND OUTER MEANINGS
Fortuitous cooperation between inner and outer elements of being. A sense of responsibility to self or to society.

6° A MAN, BURSTING WITH THE WEALTH OF WHAT HE HAS TO GIVE

Supreme endowment, and inexhaustibility of resources in all possible life realms. Sometimes obsession by potentiality.

27° THROUGH IMAGINATION, A LOST OPPORTUNITY IS REGAINED
Beginning of mental maturity and slow growth of the creative faculty. Revision of attitude. Mental house-cleaning.

28° A CROWD APPLAUDS A MAN WHO SHATTERED A DEAR ILLUSION
A new light is shed upon cherished ideas. Fearless, constructive and public facing of the facts of existence. Adjustment.

29° A CELESTIAL CHOIR HAS ARISEN TO SING COSMIC HARMONIES
At-one-ment of consciousness with cosmic powers. Harmonic understanding and faith in the order and meaning of life.

30° YOUNG DUCKLINGS DISPORT THEMSELVES MERRILY UPON A POND
Essential social cooperativeness and appreciation of selfhood. Also a sense of inner restriction. Contentedness.

TAURUS III. THE SPAN OF EXPERIENCE

1° A CLEAR MOUNTAIN STREAM FLOWS THROUGH A ROCKY DEFILE
Purity, excellence and immediate availability of the strength and power of being. Refreshment. Self-sustainment.

2° AN ELECTRICAL STORM BRILLIANTLY ILLUMINES THE SKIES
A sensing of the power and wonder of nature's forces. Complete transformation of the implication of all being. Awe.

3° NATURAL TERRACES LEAD UP TO A LAWN OF CLOVER IN BLOOM
The invitation extended by all nature to man for self-expression. Inspirational possibilities in all experience. Hope.

4° THE RAINBOW'S POT OF GOLD GLOWS AMIDST THE SPARKLING RAIN
Unlimited resources. Overflowing sense of power. Prodigality of spiritual love showered upon seekers for the highest.

5° A YOUNG WIDOW, TRANSFIGURED BY GRIEF, KNEELS AT A GRAVE
Revelation of meaning behind fleeting appearances. Restless quest for understanding. Birth from illusion into reality.

6° A CANTILEVER BRIDGE IN CONSTRUCTION ACROSS A DEEP CANYON
Conquest of difficulties and limitations by intelligence. Directed effort toward solving a problem. Channel-ship.

7° WOMAN OF SAMARIA COMES TO DRAW WATER FROM THE WELL
The gaining of perspective by a return to ancient sources of being. Introspective approach to collective unconscious.

8° A SLEIGH SPEEDS OVER GROUND AS YET UNCOVERED BY SNOW
Independence of the will of the self from outer circumstances. Power to mould life upon the pioneer's prophetic vision.

9° A CHRISTMAS TREE LOADED WITH GIFTS AND LIGHTED CANDLES
A symbol of the promise which outer life offers to the pure in heart; of immortality through giving of self to the race.

10° A PRETTY RED CROSS NURSE HURRIES ON AN ERRAND OF MERCY

Natural, unrestrained pouring of self in service to one's fellowmen. Self-expression through compassionate understanding.

11 ° A WOMAN WATERING ROWS OF FLOWERS IN FULL BLOOM
Man's and nature's creative partnership of service and beauty. Nature's rich response to man's care or lack of care.

12° YOUNG COUPLE WALKS DOWN MAIN STREET, WINDOW-SHOPPING
Inner interest in outer life which leads to whole-souled participation and achievement. Self-projection. Estimation.

13° A PORTER IS CHEERFULLY BALANCING A MOUNTAIN OF BAGGAGE
Joy of effort put forth. Faith in the eventual results of a simple plunging ahead in things. Extreme of self-reliance.

14° CHILDREN SPLASH IN RECEDING TIDE AMID GROPING SHELLFISH.
Need for a realization of life's unity in the multiplicity of its forms. Unconscious contact with higher stages of being.

15° MAN WITH RAKISH SILK HAT, MUFFLED, BRAVES THE STORM
Supremacy of conscious mind over brute nature forces. Full appreciation of outer difficulties. Great inner resources.

TAURUS IV. THE SPAN OF ENJOYMENT

16° OLD MAN TRIES HARD TO IMPART HIDDEN TRUTHS TO A CROWD
Conscious possession of greater knowledge and potentiality than can be used. Great inner fullness. Spiritual loneliness.

7° A SYMBOLICAL BATTLE BETWEEN "SWORDS" AND "TORCHES"
Struggle between might and enlightenment, physical desires and higher inspirations. Self-orientation. Divine enthusiasm.

18° A WOMAN IS AIRING A LINEN BAG THROUGH A SUNNY WINDOW
Revolt against musty, dark corners of being. Psycho-analysis. Self-dissatisfaction. Strong will for self-transformation.

19° A NEW CONTINENT, FRESH AND GREEN, RISES OUT OF THE OCEAN
Potentiality for tangible self-manifestation in all beings. Overflowing originality. Spontaneous, rich creative urge.

20° WISPS OF CLOUDS, LIKE WINGS, ARE STREAMING ACROSS THE SKY
Exalted state of consciousness; lightness and breadth of being and understanding. Mystical and ecstatic self-expansion.

21° MOVING FINGER POINTS TO SIGNIFICANT PASSAGES IN A BOOK
Symbol of spiritual discrimination, of capacity for getting to the heart of any matter. Good memory. Perspicacity.

22° A WHITE HOMING PIGEON FLIES STRAIGHT OVER STORMY WATERS
Freedom of understanding; strength based on the possession of a real mission. Transcendent activity. Self-extrication.

23° A JEWELRY SHOP FILLED WITH THE MOST MAGNIFICENT JEWELS
Abundance of permanent spiritual values; or social display of traditional racial achievements. Profusion of inner gifts.

24° INDIAN, HUMAN SCALPS HANGING AT HIS BELT, RIDES PROUDLY

Forceful intrusion of elemental energies in over-conscious selfhood. Return to primal values. Conquest of inhibitions.

25° VAST PUBLIC PARK DISPLAYS GLORIOUS AND INSPIRING VISTAS
Social strength of collectivities. Power of traditional culture. Faithfulness to established achievements. Immutability.

26° A SPANISH SERENADER AT THE WINDOW-GRILLE OF HIS BELOVED
Power of well-defined desire which assures success in all life- contacts. Imaginative power that compels manifestation.

27° A WITHERED OLD SQUAW, SMILING BRIGHTLY, SELLS TRINKETS
Dignified offering of fruits of wisdom to exuberant youth. Patient understanding of destiny; or else meddlesomeness.

28° MATURE WOMAN REAWAKENED TO ROMANCE ADMIRES HERSELF
New perspective on life, genuine rejuvenation. The compelling charm of mature experience. Rebelliousness of inner hopes.

29° TWO GARRULOUS OLD COBBLERS WORK SEATED ON AN OLD BENCH
A symbol of discursive reason, the battle of "pros and cons" within the inner being. Analytical, recapitulative judgment.

30° PEACOCK DISPLAYS ITS PLUMAGE ON LAWN OF OLD ESTATE
Personal magnificence or unconscious splendor. Sure retreat for the solitary soul where it can reveal its inmost glory.

GEMINI V. THE SPAN OF ZEAL

1° GLASS-BOTTOMED BOAT DRIFTS OVER UNDER-SEA WONDERS
Depth of realization in a consciousness constantly in touch with the sources of life. Sensitiveness to collective images.

2° SANTA CLAUS IS FURTIVELY FILLING CHRISTMAS STOCKINGS
The natural beneficence in any normal human heart. Alertness to the wishes of others; the often hidden pride of benefactors.

3° LOUIS XTV'S COURT IN THE GARDENS OF THE TUILERIES
A degree of genuine aristocracy and perfection of behavior. Self- fulfillment in form and tradition. Collective strength.

4° HOLLY AND MISTLETOE BRING CHRISTMAS SPIRIT TO A HOME
Holiday spirit as an attempt to preserve for individuals the wealth and power of racial background. Social warmth.

5° A RADICAL MAGAZINE DISPLAYS A SENSATIONAL FRONT PAGE
The compelling power of social propaganda. Exteriorization of emotional sympathy in organized reform. Efficiency.

6° NIGHT WORKMEN DRILL FOR OIL AMIDST NOISE AND CONFUSION
Exaggerated activity in pursuit of material wealth. Capacity to drive oneself in view of future and speculative gains.

7° AN OLD WELL, FILLED WITH PURE WATER, SHADED BY TREES
Deep and mature relationship between man and the basic life- giving reality of his environment. Inner assurance; poise.

8° AROUND A CLOSED-DOWN FACTORY STRIKERS MILL DEFIANTLY

A stirring of the collective, unconscious factors of being toward the repolarization of the conscious ego. Idle protest.

9° A MEDIEVAL ARCHER, WITH BOW AND ARROWS, READY TO FIGHT
Superiority and ease based upon training. Sure marksmanship. Certain self-direction. Preparedness. Invisible help in trouble.

10° AEROPLANE, AFTER A NOSE-DIVE, RIGHTS ITSELF GRACEFULLY
Capacity to plunge into experience without surrendering one's principles or self-control. Self-expansion through sacrifice.

11° NEWLY OPENED LANDS OFFER VIRGIN REALMS OF EXPERIENCE
New vista of concrete, conscious development. Renewed and enlarged opportunities. Nature's call for the pioneer spirit.

12° A BLACK SLAVE-GIRL DEMANDS HER RIGHTS OF HER MISTRESS
The will to rise above racial conditioning and limitations; or a sense of the need to conform to things as they are.

13° WORLD-FAMOUS PIANIST BEGINS TO PLAY TO A HUGE AUDIENCE
Extreme exaltation of social standing. Reaching of climax in selfhood. Ghastly sense of emptiness at the end of the quest.

14° TWO PEOPLE, LIVING FAR APART, IN TELEPATHIC COMMUNICATION
Conscious mastery of space-time limitations of ordinary existence. Realization of basic realities in all situations.

15° TWO DUTCH CHILDREN ARE STUDYING THEIR LESSONS TOGETHER
Conscious approach to spiritual truth and underlying meanings. Open-mindedness. Clarity of thought along traditional lines.

GEMINI VI. THE SPAN OF RESTLESSNESS

16° WOMAN AGITATOR MAKES AN IMPASSIONED PLEA TO A CROWD
Rising of the human soul in demand for the recognition by the outer nature of the needs of inner being. Self-assertion.

17° HEAD OF A YOUTH CHANGES INTO THAT OF A MATURE THINKER
Progression from robust participation in outer things to a realization of deeper realities. Inborn wisdom. Steady growth.

18° TWO CHINAMEN CONVERSE IN CHINESE IN AN OCCIDENTAL CROWD
Alienness, but also independence from environment. Conscious self-sustainment in spite of all conditions. Individualization.

19° LARGE ARCHAIC VOLUME ON DISPLAY IN A MUSEUM'S ARCHIVES
Reserve of collective knowledge and wisdom beyond true individual self-expression. Deference to past experience.

20° A SELF-SERVICE RESTAURANT DISPLAYS AN ABUNDANCE OF FOOD
Prodigal distribution of life-resources. Inner wealth. Satiation, or discriminative use of natural energies. Rich supply.

21° A LABOR DEMONSTRATION THRONGS A LARGE CITY SQUARE
The impetuous onsurge of natural instincts within the field of the conscious ego. Blind struggle. Compelling power of fate.

22° DANCING COUPLES CROWD THE BARN IN A HARVEST FESTIVAL

Richness of life in associations based on natural instincts. Warmth of simple living. Normal fulfillment of self.

23° THREE FLEDGLINGS LOOK OUT PROUDLY FROM THEIR HIGH NEST
Conscious self-establishment in the soul and its threefold nature. Innate self-confidence. Superiority of real being.

24° CAREFREE CHILDREN SKATE OVER A SMOOTHLY FROZEN POND
Capacity to use every opportunity, even in the hardest of environment, for self-recreation or relaxation. Appreciation.

25° A GARDENER TRIMS BEAUTIFUL PALM TREES WITH UTMOST CARE
Capacity in man to control his environment and the impulses of his most intense nature. Active care for possessions.

26° FROST-COVERED TREES, LACE-LIKE, AGAINST WINTER SKIES
Creative bestowal of significance upon all things. Transforming power of beauty. Keen appreciation of natural processes.

27° YOUNG GYPSY EMERGING FROM THE WOODS GAZES AT FAR CITIES. Growth of consciousness from the instinctual to the intellectual. Anticipation and mounting self-confidence. Deep longing.

28° BANKRUPTCY GRANTED TO HIM, A MAN LEAVES 113E COURT
Release of self from collective pressure impossible to bear. Determination to regather forces for new attempt. Protection.

29° THE FIRST MOCKING BIRD OF SPRING SINGS FROM THE TREE TOP
Recapitulation of past opportunities at the threshold of a new cycle of experience. Realization of new potentialities.

30° A PARADE OF BATHING BEAUTIES BEFORE LARGE BEACH CROWDS
Use of individual vanity in raising racial standards. Examination of intellectual values for use in the soul life.

CANCER VII. THE SPAN OF EXPANSION

1° SAILOR READY TO HOIST A NEW FLAG TO REPLACE OLD ONE
The nascent desire to align oneself with a larger and more significant life trend. Compelling decision. Repolarization.

2° A MAN ON A MAGIC CARPET OBSERVES VAST VISTAS BELOW HIM
Broadening of perspective. Supremacy of intelligence over circumstances. Conscientiousness. Objective self-control.

3° AN ARCTIC EXPLORER LEADS A REINDEER THROUGH ICY CANYONS
The pioneering, trail-blazing instinct urging man to get out beyond all things. Plunge into virgin possibilities of life.

4° A HUNGRY CAT ARGUES WITH A MOUSE, BEFORE EATING HER
The urge to self-justification through intellectual sophistry or social-ethical considerations. Sense of self-righteousness.

5° AUTOMOBILIST, RACING MADLY WITH A FAST TRAIN, IS KILLED
Individual man is brought to account for his obligations to society. Curbed recklessness. Tragic escape from emptiness.

6° INNUMERABLE BIRDS ARE BUSY FEATHERING THEIR NESTSInstinctive preparation for mature and full expression of the self. Subconscious planning or dreaming of idle dreams.

7° IN A MOONLIT FAIRY GLADE TWO LITTLE ELVES ARE DANCING
Man's recognition of the elusive play of underlying forces in nature. Cooperation with the invisible. Unusual good luck.

8° RABBITS IN FAULTLESS HUMAN ATTIRE PARADE WITH DIGNITY
Reaching out to participation in a higher order through imitative behavior. Willingness to grow; also self-exploitation.

9° NAKED LITTLE MISS LEANS OVER A POND TO CATCH A GOLD FISH
First curiosity of being; innocent reaching out for understanding. Untiring eagerness. Unsocial or infantile cravings.

10° A WONDERFUL DIAMOND IS BEING CUT TO A PERFECT SHAPE
Spiritual fulfillment or the acme of civilized being. Actualization of potentialities and outpressing of real selfhood.

11° A CLOWN CARICATURES MERRILY ALL KINDS OF HUMAN TRAITS
Sharp discrimination and understanding of human nature. The light touch of masterful living; self-control; or frivolity.

12° A CHINESE WOMAN NURSING A BABY HALOED BY DIVINE LIGHT
The promise to all men that God may take birth within their souls. Personality integration. Illumination; or frustration.

13° A HAND WITH PROMINENT THUMB IS HELD OUT RECEPTIVELY
Strong, active and self-certain will, or persistent yet blind plunging ahead into reality. Freedom from soft illusions.

14° AN OLD MAN, ALONE, FACES THE DARKNESS IN THE NORTHEAST
Fearlessness; and noble, self-perpetuating strength arising from knowledge. Courage in the facing of spiritual problems.

15° MERRY AND SLUGGISH PEOPLE RESTING AFTER A HUGE FEAST
A turning to superficial things for self-strengthening. Self- indulgence in sensations. Unintelligent satiation; dullness.

CANCER VIII. THE SPAN OF INGENUOUSNESS

16° A MAN HOLDS A SCROLL. BEFORE HIM, A SQUARE IS OUTLINED
Underlying tendency to revert to root patterns of being: "squaring" oneself with everyday reality. Control over life.

17° THE ARCHETYPAL SOUL BECOMES FILLED WITH LIFE-CONTENTS
Gathering of all life values and experience in the perfectly formed consciousness. Spiritually integrated knowledge.

18° IN A CROWDED BARNYARD A HEN CLUCKS AMONG HER CHICKENS
Constructively practical, natural approach to life and its simpler joys. Concern over things. Child-like group devotion.

19° AN ARISTOCRATIC AND FRAIL GIRL WEDS A PROLETARIAN YOUTH
Blending of the cultural fruition of the past with the impetuousness of new blood. Assimilation of unconscious contents.

20° A GROUP OF SERENADERS MAKE MERRY IN A VENETIAN GONDOLA

Exaltation of social intercourse in the traditional manner. Sentimental clinging to old life-ideals. The will to romance.

21° AN OPERATIC PRIMA DONNA SINGS TO A GLITTERING AUDIENCE
Elevation and popularization of human values through art as a social factor. Supreme realization of the life-ambition.

22° A YOUNG WOMAN DREAMILY AWAITS A SAILBOAT APPROACHING
A longing to live life as a great adventure. The compelling power of all sustained desire and of the dreaming of dreams.

23° A GROUP OF INTELLECTUAL INDIVIDUALS MEET FOR DISCUSSION
Interchange of ideas among any élite as a basis for the cultural development of the whole. Mental or physical fellowship.

24° WOMAN AND TWO MEN CASTAWAYS ON A SOUTH SEAS ISLAND
The three "souls" in man—actional, emotional, mental—"exiled" in the body. Potential fulfillment. Sense of being lost in life.

25° LEADER OF MEN WRAPPED IN AN INVISIBLE MANTLE OF POWER
Support of unconscious elements in every fearless and positive stand of the ego. Restoration of strength; or self-discovery.

26° GUESTS ARE READING IN THE LIBRARY OF A LUXURIOUS HOME
Emergence of consciousness upon higher levels of being, once life has been fulfilled at normal levels. Conscious fruition.

27° A FURIOUS STORM RAGES THROUGH A RESIDENTIAL CANYON
Intensification of elements necessary to arouse latent possibilities. Rising to the occasion. A descent of cosmic power.

28° INDIAN GIRL INTRODUCES COLLEGE BOY-FRIEND TO HER TRIBE
The human soul as intercessor between primordial natural forces and the intellectual order. Self-integration. Linkage.

29° A GREEK MUSE WEIGHS IN GOLDEN SCALES JUST BORN TWINS
The revelation of latent worth in all things through the power of creative imagination. Piercing beyond appearances.

30° A LADY OF ARISTOCRATIC DESCENT PROUDLY ADDRESSES A CLUB
The will and ability to maintain a social supremacy based on thoroughly established tradition. Inner or outer aristocracy.

LEO IX. THE SPAN OF ASSURANCE

1° UNDER EMOTIONAL STRESS BLOOD RUSHES TO A MAN'S HEAD
A basic symbol of Man: forceful, dangerous entrance into the Soul realm. Irresistible outpouring of self. Activity per se.

2° THE SCHOOL CLOSED BY AN EPIDEMIC, CHILDREN PLAY TOGETHER
Constructive result of inconveniences of life in developing communal values. Self-sensitiveness. Subtraction from things.

3° MATURE WOMAN, HER HAIR JUST BOBBED, LOOKS INTO MIRROR
Sense of freedom from age and realization of the value of youth. Self-creation and independence from fate. Will-power.

4° ELDERLY MAN GAZES AT MOOSE HEAD ON CLUBROOM'S WALL

Self-development through the culture of masculine activities. Subservience of individual to social pattern of behavior. Taste.

5° SUGGESTING FIGURES, GRANITE MASSES OVERHANG A CANYON
Permanence of basic elements in nature underneath temporary changes and emphases. Endurance. Steadiness of self-knowledge.

6° OLD-FASHIONED BELLE AND FLAPPER ADMIRE EACH OTHER
Realization of changeless subjective worth beyond changing appearances. Interchange of sympathy. Enhanced self-awareness.

7° THE CONSTELLATIONS GLOW IN THE DARKNESS OF DESERT SKIES
Sense of primordial wonder and awe before life. Unquenchable faith in a spiritual being complementing our own. Realization.

8° PROLETARIAN, BURNING WITH SOCIAL PASSION, STIRS UP CROWDS
Leavening of the inchoate materials of a new order by a forceful vision born of repression and misfortune. Revolution.

9° GLASS-BLOWERS SHAPE WITH THEIR BREATH GLOWING FORMS
The formative power of the soul in moments of emotional intensity. Controlled self-expression. Art as a spiritual fact.

10° EARLY MORNING DEW SPARKLES AS THE SUN FLOODS THE FIELDS
Freshness of spontaneous response to life and emotions. Uplifting lightness in experience; or else superficial glamour.

11° CHILDREN PLAY BENEATH HUGE OAK, SHELTER FROM THE SUN
The sustaining and protective power of ancestral background against emotions. Appreciation of inborn cultural restraint.

12° A GARDEN PARTY IS IN FULL SWING UNDER JAPANESE LANTERNS
Easy intercourse of human souls in moments of relaxation from strain. Examination of, or self-loss in social values.

13° OLD SEA-CAPTAIN RESTS IN NEAT LITTLE COTTAGE BY THE SEA
Reward of growth from outer to inner realms. Serenity through the overcoming of storms. Self-gained mellowness. Retirement.

14° CHERUB-LIKE, A HUMAN SOUL WHISPERS, SEEKING TO MANIFEST
The desire to be, to suffer and to grow which brings Spirit to Earth. Whole-souled self-giving. Yearning for experience.

15° THE MARDI GRAS CARNIVAL CROWDS NEW ORLEANS' STREETS
Spectacular, dramatic release of subconscious energies. Self- exaltation for social approval. Self-indulgence and license.

LEO X. THE SPAN OF INTERPRETATION

16° REFRESHED BY A STORM, FIELDS AND GARDENS BASK IN THE SUN
A return to values after a major life-crisis. Cleansing power of suffering overcome. Mastery of strain—or indifference.

17° VOLUNTEER CHURCH CHOIR MAKE SOCIAL EVENT OF REHEARSAL
Utilization of normal human instincts as a foundation to high endeavor. Lay-participation in Mysteries. Joy in faith.

18° CHEMIST CONDUCTS AN EXPERIMENT BEFORE HIS STUDENTS

Practical application of principles to ordinary life. Active enlightenment; or forced awakening to inner potentialities.

19° A BARGE MADE INTO A CLUBHOUSE IS CROWDED WITH REVELERS
The transforming power of pure joy over routine existence. Human fellowship in the effort to make life happier, freer.

20° AMERICAN INDIANS PERFORM A MAJESTIC RITUAL TO THE SUN
Man's instinctive or traditional call upon basic life-energies for sustainment. Sense of fitness in behavior. Worship.

21° INTOXICATED DOMESTIC BIRDS FLY AROUND IN DIZZY ATTEMPTS
Unsteady first realization of spiritual being. Forced inspiration which the ego cannot sustain. False self-intoxication.

22° A CARRIER-PIGEON ALIGHTS AT DAWN BEFORE HIS OWNERS
The return of the soul-energies to the central Self after a significant experience. Adventuring. Practical enlightenment.

23° THE BAREBACK RIDER IN A CIRCUS THRILLS EXCITED CROWDS
The supremacy given to the man who has mastered his senses and his emotions. Full utilization of inner powers. Audacity.

24° A YOGI, WITH TRANSCENDENT POWERS-YET UNTIDY, UNKEMPT
Spiritual emphasis at the expense of outer refinement. Interior focalization of energies. Self-abnegation. Character.

25° A MAN, ALONE, DARINGLY CROSSES THE DESERT ON CAMELBACK
Superiority of knowledge and will over hostile nature. Mental self- control. Spiritual strength in facing past Karma.

26° AS LIGHT BREAKS THROUGH CLOUDS, A PERFECT RAINBOW FORMS
Promise of conscious immortality after the death of useless things. Spiritual linkage through emotional stress. Blessing.

27° IN THE EAST, LIGHT SLOWLY INCREASES, WIPING OUT THE STARS
Transforming power of creative impulses as they bring ideas to concrete manifestation. Stirring to opportunity. Soul-power.

28° MYRIADS OF BIRDS, PERCHED UPON A BIG TREE, CHIRP HAPPILY
Social nature of experience as man finds sustainment in a larger whole of being. Normal, collective self-expression.

29° MERMAID AWAITS PRINCE WHO WILL MAKE HER IMMORTAL
Pure longing for a new order of selfhood. Critical point in "emergent evolution." Perspective; or a sense of incompetence.

30° AN UNSEALED LETTER FULL OF VITAL AND CONFIDENTIAL NEWS
Basic faith in the goodness of all life. Unthinking trust in, or desire to see to the bottom of all things. Confidence.

VIRGO XI. THE SPAN OF IDEALIZATION

1° IN A PORTRAIT THE BEST OF A MAN'S TRAITS ARE IDEALIZED
The shaping power of idea or ideal over outer form and behavior. Completeness of realization. Pure aggrandizement. Intent.

2° A LARGE WHITE CROSS STANDS ALONE ON TOP OF A HIGH HILL

Dominance of environment through individualistic self-realization. Eminence at the cost of struggle. Full self-assurance.

3° TWO ANGELS BRING PROTECTION TO FAMILY IN THE WILDERNESS
Divine guarantee to man of supply of all his needs. Divine help when human efforts fail. Unconscious sense of strength.

4° NEGRO CHILD PLAYS WITH WHITE BOYS UNAWARE OF RACE LINE
Underlying fellowship of all life underneath social creeds. Stimulating sense of distinctness. Rising above contrasts.

5° IRISHMAN DREAMS OF "LITTLE PEOPLE" BENEATH A TREE
Constructive imagination as it reveals unconscious realms of being. Creative fantasy. Contact with inner life-energies.

6° EXCITED CHILDREN RIDE ON A BLATANT, GAUDY MERRY-GO-ROUND
The culture of pleasure as a transmuting force. Unfearing plunge into life. Endless and futile repetition of experience.

7° IN A PALATIAL HAREM BRIGHT-EYED WOMEN LAUGH HAPPILY
Early stage of development of individual soul, with full yet binding life-protection. Freedom from responsibility or restraint.

8° ARISTOCRATIC FIVE-YEAR-OLD GIRL TARES FIRST DANCING LESSON
Early social conditioning of the superior elements of being. Proper start in self-discipline. Conventional development.

9° A MODERN EXPRESSIONISTIC ARTIST PAINTS A STRANGE CANVAS
Original genius of every individual soul unconcerned with collective values. Absolute, tradition-less self-expression.

10° A MAN WITH TWO HEADS IS SEEN LOOKING OUT TO THE BEYOND
Consciousness functioning in inner and outer realms. Competence in understanding. Over-sensitiveness to life-currents.

11° A TYPICAL BOY, YET MOULDED BY HIS MOTHER'S ASPIRATIONS
Efficacy of overtones in life; of ideals in giving reality or depth to outer material things. Conformity to inner light.

12° A BRIDE, LAUGHING, SCOLDS THE GROOM WHO LIFTED HER VEIL
Disclosure of the hidden fruitions of nature to him who dares and who loves. Full appreciation of life. Penetration.

13° A POWERFUL STATESMAN WINS TO HIS CAUSE A HYSTERICAL MOB
Power of personality as incarnation of subconscious race ideals. Sublimation of motives. Transmutation of energies.

14° A SPLENDID FAMILY TREE ENGRAVED ON A SHEET OF PARCHMENT
Importance of ancestral background in all accomplishments. Power to experience deeply. Cultural sensitiveness. Heritage.

15° OLD LACE HANDKERCHIEF; SOME RARE PERFUME; A MIRROR
Ultimate fineness of material values shading into the spiritual. Schooled and aristocratic delicacy. Cultured restraint.

VIRGO XII. THE SPAN OF EXPERIMENTATION
16° CHILDREN CROWD AROUND THE ORANG-OUTANG CAGE IN THE ZOO

The lesson which the very old can give to the very young in all realms. Vicarious experience. Inertia of instincts. Poise.

17° A VOLCANIC ERUPTION RELEASES POWERFUL TELLURIC ENERGIES
Irresistible outbursting of pent-up impulses, creatively or regeneratively. Breaking up of "complexes." Will to wholeness.

18° Two EXCITED YOUNG GIRLS EXPERIMENT WITH A OUIJA BOARD
Human desire for contact with the beyond. Inquiry. Restless questioning of superficial facts of being. Immature curiosity.

19° A SWIMMING RACE NEARS COMPLETION BEFORE A LARGE CROWD
Social sustainment of individual accomplishment. Encouragement. Competition as a means to create group-consciousness.

20° A GROUP OF SETTLERS START ON THEIR JOURNEY IN OLD CARS
Rising to achievement in spite of an inadequate equipment. toying in meeting life's challenges. Venturing with faith.

21° TWO TEAMS OF GIRLS ENGAGED IN A CONTEST OF BASKETBALL
Physical wholesomeness as prelude to inner integration. Self- evaluation, or refusal to face self. The rhythm of instincts.

22° A JEWEL-SET ROYAL COAT-OF-ARMS IS DISPLAYED IN A MUSEUM
Preservation of ancient race values for healthy veneration by youthful individuals. Certification of merit. Aristocracy.

23° A LION-TAMER RUSHES FEARLESSLY INTO THE CIRCUS ARENA
Readiness to face the aroused energies of one's nature and test one's moral strength. Faith in self. Valor and mastery.

24° A BOOK FOR CHILDREN PICTURES LITTLE MARY AND HER LAMB
Freshness of viewpoint un-inhibited by social intellectual preoccupations. Vibrant simplicity. Spirit-born imagination.

25° A FLAG AT HALF-MAST IN FRONT OF LARGE PUBLIC BUILDING
The ability to carry a task through to consummate completion. Deference to past achievement. Cultivation of public spirit.

26° RAPT-EYED, A BOY SERVES IN A MASS READ BY AUTOMATONS
Ability to find inspiration in daily routine. Hope arising in the midst of all deadness of heart. Rejuvenation of spirit.

27° ELDERLY LADIES DRINKING AFTERNOON TEA IN A WEALTHY HOME
Preservation of social and cultural values. Inward, unobtrusive superiority, or else pure smugness. Prestige of position.

28° BALD-HEADED MAN DOMINATES GATHERING OF NATIONAL FIGURES
Driving power of real personality in moments of crisis. Capacity for hard work. Compelling manifestation of inner self.

29° ARCHAIC MS. DISCLOSES TO SCHOLAR THE OLD MYSTERIES
The understanding which is built on patient steady work and persisting aspiration. Fecundative power of ancient wisdom.

30° AN EMERGENCY CALL FREES HOUSEHOLDER FROM ROUTINE DUTY
Joy of enlisting in a task which broadens the life-horizon. Willing rising to the occasion, or escape from narrow destiny.

LIBRA XIII. THE SPAN OF EXPECTATION

1° PIERCED BY A DART OF LIGHT A BUTTERFLY IS `MADE PERFECT"
The symbolical death that is initiation into spiritual reality and wisdom. Sudden awakening. Craving for inner light.

2° A SYMPHONY IS PLAYED DRAMATIZING MAN'S HEROIC ASCENT
Inspiration through creative identification with the large sweep of cycles. Spiritual expansion. Renewed encouragement.

3° A NEW DAY DAWNS, REVEALING A WORLD UTTERLY TRANSFORMED,
Transforming power of periods of silence and darkness, which lead to stirring revelations. Real touch with cosmic process.

4° PILGRIMS GATHER ROUND CAMP-FIRE, IN SILENT COMMUNION
Fellowship of higher ideals that sustains the individuals on their arduous path to Reality. Mellow participation in life.

5° INSPIRED DISCIPLES LISTEN TO THE WORDS OF THEIR TEACHER
Knowledge and experience put to the test. Greatness calling its own to itself. Ordered seeking. Distrust of appearances.

6° IN A TRANCE, A PILGRIM BEHOLDS HIS IDEALS MADE CONCRETE
Inevitable confrontation with the concrete results of one's ideals. Lessons to be learned from it. Willingness of heart.

7° WITCH FEEDS CHICKENS FRIGHTENED BY A HAWK SHE HAD TAMED
Control of natural forces by the higher intelligence. Taming the strong, uplifting the weak. Transmutation through service.

8° A FIREPLACE BLAZES MYSTERIOUSLY IN A DESERTED FARMHOUSE
Constant presence of unseen, sustaining agencies in every worthwhile activity. Great depth of initial effort. Providence.

9° THREE "OLD MASTERS" HANG ALONE IN AN ART GALLERY
Efficient cohesion of the three "souls" of man; of mind, feeling and instinct. Integrated wisdom. Sagacious behavior.

10° A CANOE LEAVING NARROW RAPIDS REACHES CALM WATERS
The reward of all sincere and daring outreaching of self in life. A sure Destiny. Reliance upon skill and circumstances.

11° KINDLY OLD PROFESSOR IS TEACHING A CLASS OF YOUNGSTERS
Cooperation of genuinely superior agencies with beings less evolved. Glad willingness to assist and protect. Kindliness.

12° MINERS ARE EMERGING FROM A DEEP WELL INTO THE SUNLIGHT
Depth of participation in the world's work. Whole souled giving of self to service; or inability to bring self to effort.

13° CHILDREN ARE BLOWING SOAP-BUBBLES AT A YOUNGSTERS' PARTY
Healthy stimulation through play and joy of human intercourse. Creative fantasy; spinning of idle dreams. Relaxation.

14° RICH LAND-OWNER TAKES A SIESTA IN HIS TROPICAL GARDENS
Proper adjustment to the rhythm of nature. Faith in the ordered scheme of things; injudicious dependence upon others.

15° A STACK OF MACHINERY PARTS; ALL ARE NEW AND ALL CIRCULAR

Perfect and effortless participation in the universal order. Smooth approach to self-expression; inert self-satisfaction.

LIBRA XIV. THE SPAN OF REVELATION

16° A HAPPY CREW IS RESTORING BEACH PIERS WRECKED BY STORMS
Constructive results of apparently destructive forces; stimulation to new accomplishment. Glad response to needed work.

17° RETIRED SEA-CAPTAIN IN UNIFORM WATCHES SHIPS SAIL AWAY
Vicarious or mellow participation in life. Transfer of activity from physical to mental; or self-involvement in the past.

18° TWO MEN PLACED UNDER ARREST ARE BEING BROUGHT TO COURT
Responsibility of individual to society in terms of normal behavior. Return to values. Obligation to face objective facts.

19° ROBBERS ARE HIDING, READY TO ATTACK HEAVILY ARMED CARAVAN
Protest against the perpetuation of unearned social privileges and wealth. Repudiation of bondage. Challenge to custom.

20° OLD RABBI SITS CONTENTEDLY IN ROOM CROWDED WITH BOOKS
Interest in permanent rather than transient values. Accumulation of ancient wisdom brought to use. Competent service.

21° HOT SUNDAY CROWDS DELIGHT IN THE COOL SEA BREEZE
Fundamental popularity of natural values. Communion in objects of real and universally recognized worth. Association.

22° CHILD LAUGHS AS BIRDS PERCH ON AN OLD FOUNTAIN, AND DRINK
Intuitive understanding of simple souls in spiritual matters. Youthful life-enjoyment. Fresh grasp of the soul's needs.

23° CHANTICLEER SALUTES THE RISING SUN WITH EXUBERANT TONES
Capacity for self-refreshment at the inner sources of ever-reviewed life. Anticipation of opportunity. Security in Self.

24° A BUTTERFLY SPREADS ITS WINGS, SHOWING AN EXTRA LEFT ONE
Potentiality of new forms and opportunities in every life. Instinctive expansion of self; or submergence in the not-self.

25° FALLING GOLDEN LEAF TEACHES LIFE TO REBELLIOUS SCHOOLBOY
Discovery of deeper elements of wisdom after intellectual knowledge wearies. Growth through awareness of basic meanings.

26° AN EAGLE AND A WHITE DOVE CHANGE SWIFTLY INTO EACH OTHER
Necessary cooperation between mind, will, spirit—and heart, love. Power of psychological balance and compensation. Unity.

27° A SPOT OF LIGHT IN CLEAR SKIES, AN AEROPLANE SAILS CALMLY
Dwelling above the normal stress of existence. Superior mental vision. Calm objective observation; quiet inner strength.

28° A MAN IN DEEP GLOOM. UNNOTICED, ANGELS COME TO HIS HELP
Spiritual sustainment given to him who opens himself to his full destiny. Slow realization of betterment. Unsolicited help.

29° VAST MASSES OF MEN PUSH FORWARD REACHING FOR KNOWLEDGE

Intense desire to overcome the blind life of passion and to uplift others. Intellectual vision. Tense mental outreaching.

30° A PHRENOLOGIST DISCOVERS MOUNDS OF KNOWLEDGE ON A HEAD
Ability to read spiritual meanings in concrete objects. Objectivication of abstract truths. Cleverness in understanding.

SCORPIO XV. THE SPAN OF RETENTION

1° SIGHT-SEERS IN A BUS STRAIN TO SEE CROWDS AND BUILDINGS
The perspective which leisure gives to everyday affairs. Appetite for larger things. Seeing life as whole. Social Intercourse.

2° FROM A BROKEN BOTTLE TRACES OF PERFUME STILL EMANATE
The fine scent of deeds well done as it persists in the memory of men. Stimulating recollection. Spiritual immortality.

3° HAPPY HOUSE-RAISING PARTY AMONG WESTERN PIONEERS
The constructive sharing of experience which builds social values. Interchange of efforts. Necessity to learn cooperation.

4° YOUTH CARRIES A LIT CANDLE IN HIS FIRST CHURCH SERVICE
Beginning of spiritual participation in the world's work. Sustained inspiration. Conscious linkage to inner realities.

5° A MASSIVE ROCKY SHORE UNCHANGED BY CENTURIES OF STORMS
Revelation of absolutely stable elements in all life. Strong confidence born of fundamental perception; or spiritual inertia.

6° CALIFORNIAN HILLS: THE "GOLD RUSH" SHATTERS THEIR PEACE
The passionate quest for universal values, destructive of cultural ease of living. Leaping to opportunity. Avid seeking.

7° DIVERS OF THE DEEP SEA ARE BEING LOWERED INTO THE WATERS
Purposeful, daring plunge into life-mysteries. Fulfillment of individual selfhood through study of unconscious energies.

8° A HIGH MOUNTAIN LAKE IS BATHED IN THE FULL MOONLIGHT
Illumination of the soul by transcendent wisdom. Quiet touch with cosmic strength; or wayward moody effort at greatness.

9° A DENTIST IS REPAIRING TEETH RUINED BY CIVILIZED HABITS
Mechanical inventiveness and control over nature needed to balance man's emphasis on mind and self. Applied creativity.

10° A FELLOWSHIP SUPPER REAWAKENS UNFORGETTABLE INNER TIES
Companionship rooted in past performance. Group-personality emergence. Fraternity of ideals uplifting individual efforts.

11° A DROWNING MAN IS RESCUED, BROUGHT BACK TO THE CROWD
Outreaching warmth of human character. Saving power of social restraint for too emotional souls. Humanitarian ideals.

12° HIGH OFFICIALS ARE GATHERED AT AN IMPORTANT EMBASSY BALL
Social recognition of accomplishment as the substance of a ritual of human association. Certification of rank. Ambition.

13° IN AN IMPROVISED LABORATORY AN INVENTOR IS NEAR SUCCESS

Driving power toward achievement, as featured in all benefactors of mankind. Self-sufficient activity. Clever outwitting.

14° WORKERS PUSH A TELEPHONE LINE ACROSS FORBIDDING RANGES
The will to association regardless of time and space. Linkage of separate realms. Spiritual living "in spite of" nature.

15° LAUGHING CHILDREN PLAY UPON FIVE MOUNDS OF WHITE SAND
The world of the five senses as the playground of God and Soul. Honesty in self-expression. Bondage to sense-patterns.

SCORPIO XVI. THE SPAN OF APPRECIATION

16° A GIRL WITH ARISTOCRATIC FEATURES SMILES ENTRANCINGLY
Fervent outreaching of self in moments of the purest beauty. Leaping to meet the potentialities of life. Blossoming forth.

17° WOMAN, FECUNDATED BY HER SPIRIT, IS "GREAT WITH CHILD"
Fullness of self-reliance and individual destiny. Cooperation between spiritual and material agencies. Pure self-revelation.

18° A WINDING ROAD LEADS THROUGH GLORIOUS AUTUMNAL WOODS
The light which transfigures the soul after passions have faded away. Revelation of inner wealth. Radiant consummation.

19° A WISE OLD PARROT REPEATS THE CONVERSATION HE OVERHEARD
Dependence upon inner or outer environment for the substance of understanding. Transmission of knowledge. Channel-ship.

20° WOMAN FLINGS OPEN DARK CURTAINS CLOSING SACRED PATHWAY
Courage needed to enlarge sphere of being. Readiness to press beyond self. The "woman" within, opening the gates to Spirit.

21° SOLDIER READY TO FACE CHARGES OF DESERTION FOR LOVE'S SAKE
Conflict between old and new perspectives. A willingness to face chaos for the sake of a new order. Yielding to emotions.

22° HUNTERS SHOOTING WILD DUCKS WALK THROUGH A MARSH
Aggressive quest for outer or inner sustenance. Purposeful satiation of desire. Tragic incorporation of ideals. Exercise.

23° PLACID WHITE RABBIT METAMORPHOSES INTO A DANCING ELF
Revelation of unexpected vital urges latent in all beings. Great creative potentialities. Capacity for self-maintenance.

24° CROWDS, STIRRED BY A GREAT MESSAGE, RETURN HOME
The power in well-formulated ideas to become actual facts. Practical inspiration; or else inability to face a vital challenge.

25° THANKS TO A FINE X-RAY DIAGNOSIS, A MAN'S LIFE IS SAVED
Penetrating power of reality. Dependence of outer facts upon basic structures or causes. Sharp and applied discrimination.

26° SWIFTLY, INDIANS ERECT THEIR TEEPEES. CAMP IS BEING MADE
Ability to feel at home in any outer or inner environment. Efficient functioning. Retreating into the familiar and the known.

27° A MILITARY BAND, FLASHY AND NOISY, MARCHES ON POMPOUSLY

Desire to impress upon others the glory of one's social eminence. Materialization of normally subjective values. Show.

28° THE KING OF FAIRYLAND IS SOLEMNLY WELCOMED TO HIS REALM
Necessary respect for symbolic values holding vital forces integrated. Self-realization through devotion to the One.

29° PRINCESS PLEADS BEFORE INCA KING FOR HER CAPTURED SONS
The soul's mediation between spirit and matter. Sustaining power of instincts. Self-awakening to the need for action.

30° HALLOWE'EN GIVES SOCIAL RELEASE TO YOUTHFUL IMPISHNESS
Need for giving free rein to unsocial instincts within the pale of social traditions. Planned release of inner pressure.

SAGITTARIUS XVII. THE SPAN OF RECEPTIVENESS

1° RETIRED ARMY VETERANS GATHER TO REAWAKEN OLD MEMORIES
Cohesive power of social experience. Comradeship, born of collective achievements, which quickens the self. Fervent reunion.

2° WHITE-CAPPED WAVES DANCE RHYTHMICALLY UNDER THE WINDS
Glad response to a vital call to activity. Power to stir and to impress one's own rhythm upon materials. Proud adornment.

3° TWO SEDATE MEN, SMOKING PIPES IN COMFORT, PLAY CMS
Re-creation of a world of manifestation through symbols and intelligence. Schooled confidence in the judgment of self.

4° WATCHED BY HAPPY PARENTS, A CHILD TAXES HIS FIRST STEPS
Life's kindliness in creating safe opportunities for growth. Full appreciation of opportunity. Crisis in self-development.

5° HIGH ON AN OLD TREE, A SOLITARY OWL IS GRAVELY PERCHED
Poised observation upon the drama of life. Mellow judgment. Ingrained confidence in the situation and worth of the self.

6° A CRICKET GAME IS BEING WATCHED BY A COLORFUL CROWD
Socialization of man's competitive impulses. Instinctive solidarity building race consciousness. Capitalizing on skill.

7° CUPID KNOCKS SMILINGLY AT THE DOOR OF THE HUMAN HEART
The happiness which awaits every man willing to accept its fulness. Rounding out of experience. The call to love's feast.

8° IN THE CAULDRON OF THE UNIVERSE THE METALS ARE FORMING
Irresistible determination to be. Infinite capacity for hard work. Crystallization of purpose and will out of experience.

9° A MOTHER IS LEADING HER CHILDREN UP A BROAD STAIRWAY
Conscious advance of selfhood from plane to plane. Real courage in all approach to life. Inner guidance in all growth.

10° A STAGE SYMBOLIZATION OF THE "GODDESS OF OPPORTUNITY"
Power of creative significance, as it transforms mere facts into universal symbols. Exteriorization of inner impulses.

11° AN EVER-BURNING LAMP THROWS LIGHT UPON AN ARCHAIC IDOL
Influence of social mass upon the individual. Power of "primordial images of Unconscious." Activity dominated by fate.
12° A FLAG BECOMES AN EAGLE; THE EAGLE A PROUD CHANTICLEER
Development of consciousness from abstract to concrete, from general to personal. Mounting mastery. good fortune.
13° A YOUNG WIDOW IS SURPRISED INTO A NEW BIRTH OF LOVE
The eternal call for fulfillment through love which overcomes personal sensitiveness and set patterns. Revision of attitude.
14° SPHINX AND PYRAMIDS STAND, REMAINS OF A GLORIOUS PAST
Achievement based on past greatness. Power of the countless dead upon the living. Vast resources in selfhood. Antecedents.
15° GROUND-HOG, OUT OF ITS WINTER SLEEP, LOOKS FOR ITS SHADOW
Revelation of basic life-purposes and cycles through omens. Universal patterning of life-relationship. Keen divination.

SAGITTARIUS XVIII. THE SPAN OF DETACHMENT

16° A CALM OCEAN; A MOTIONLESS SHIP; LAZILY SOARING SEAGULLS
The moments of pause which sustain and presage change. Alert readiness to act; or distress at not knowing what lies ahead.
17° PEOPLE GATHER BEFORE DAWN FOR AN OUTDOOR EASTER SERVICE
Spiritual living in conformity to natural law. Coming out of doubt and despair. Unwavering faith in a near higher power.
18° ON THE HOT BEACH CHILDREN PLAY, PROTECTED BY SUNBONNETS
The protective agency which safeguards the free behavior of individuals. Vivifying contact with collective life-energies.
19° PELICANS, DISTURBED BY MEN, MOVE TO PLACES UNKNOWN
Inward re-emphasis of foundations. Recuperation by retreating within. The introvert's escape. Moving about in reorientation.
20° MEN CUTTING THE ICE OF A FROZEN POND, FOR SUMMER USE
Depth of operation necessary to prepare for next phase of life. Sacrifice of present to future. Thoroughness of action.
21° CHILD AND DOG PLAY GRAVELY, WITH EYEGLASSES ON THEIR NOSES
Usefulness of make-believe. Rising to situations through the imagination. Assuming a part ahead of natural development.
22° THE SHOP CLOSED, CHINESE LAUNDRYMEN REVERT TO RACE TYPE
Retreat to the inner world of self after outer achievement. Safe return to ancestral patterns of behavior. Easy poise.
23° IN NEW YORK, ELLIS ISLAND WELCOMES THE IMMIGRANTS
New openings that come to all who are willing to risk self for the sake of greater selfhood. Reorientation. Presumption.
24° THE SYMBOLICAL "BLUE BIRD" ALIGHTS UPON A LITTLE COTTAGE

The blessings bestowed upon all those who are true to themselves. Unexpected assistance. Happiness. Sheer good fortune.

25° RICH LITTLE BOY RIDES UPON HIS BRIGHT-COLORED HORSE
Growth through vicarious, imaginative experiences, which life might deny us. Detachment from reality. Self-conservation.

26° FLAG-BEARER DISTINGUISHES HIMSELF IN HAND-TO-HAND BATTLE
Exaltation of physical valor as necessary support to lofty race ideals. Spectacular effort. Endowment beyond realization.

27° THE SCULPTOR'S VISION IS TAKING FORM UNDER HIS HANDS
Mastery of formative intelligence over substance. Sure characterization and understanding. Permanent self-expression.

28° ANCIENT BRIDGE WITNESSES TO THE SKILL OF FORGOTTEN MEN
Enduring elements in understanding as symbols of the community invisible of man, dead and living. Steady coordination.

29° PERSPIRING FAT BOY, EAGER TO REDUCE, IS MOWING A LAWN
Desire for fitness inherent in all living beings. Consciously built, thus dependable determination. Persistent endeavor.

30° THE POPE IS HOLDING AUDIENCE IN A HALL OF THE VATICAN
Wealth of spiritual resources which can be tapped for the glorification of every relationship. Concrete form of ideals.

CAPRICORN XIX. THE SPAN OF ILLUSIVENESS

1° INDIAN CHIEF CLAIMS POWER FROM THE ASSEMBLED TRIBE
Mastery of a situation through purposeful planning and venturing. Bold rising to opportunity. Extreme of self-confidence.

2° ROSE-WINDOWS IN A GOTHIC CATHEDRAL; ONE, DAMAGED BY WAR
Underlying resistance to change in life foundations. Faithfulness to self. Testimony of beauty against brute force.

3° THE SOUL, AS A HOVERING SPIRIT EAGER TO GAIN EXPERIENCE
Inner and pure motivation. The power to remain superior to physical limitations; to demonstrate free will. Detachment.

4° MERRY-MAKERS EMBARK IN A BIG CANOE ON LANTERN-LIT LAKE
Externalization through individuals of the collective urges of the race. Foolish love for pleasure. Exploitation of self.

5° AN AMERICAN INDIAN CAMP: A FIERCE WAR DANCE BEGINS
Mobilization of latent energies for determined self-exertion. Obsession by elemental forces. Violent awakening to reality.

6° TEN LOGS LIE UNDER ARCHWAY LEADING TO DARKER WOODS
Illimitability of experience, as man moves from completion to ever greater fulfillment. Keenness in knowing. Thoroughness.

7° A HEAVILY VEILED HIEROPHANT LEADS A RITUAL OF POWER
Gathering together of the power of a group to one purpose and into an individual will. "Avatar"-ship. Responsibility.

8° IN A BIG LIVING ROOM FLOODED WITH SUNLIGHT CANARIES SING

The happiness that radiates from an integrated personality. Firm self-establishment in social comfort or respectability.

9° AN ANGEL CARRYING A HARP COMES THROUGH A HEAVENLY LANE
The basic harmony of fulfilled selfhood. Realizing harmony in everyday life through detached and lofty understanding.

10° ON A SAILBOAT THE SEAMEN ARE FEEDING A TAME ALBATROSS
Overcoming of instinctive fears through gentle persuasion. Kindly conquest. Culture of spiritual values. Harmlessness.

11° PHEASANTS DISPLAY THEIR BRILLIANT COLORS ON A VAST LAWN
Latent richness of natural resources brought out through selective processes. Capitalization upon opportunity. Luxury.

12° NATURAL WONDERS ARE DEPICTED IN A LECTURE ON SCIENCE
Piercing through appearances; disclosing the magic splendor of the core of things. A universal living touch. Keen vision.

13° BENEATH SNOW-CLAD PEAKS A FIRE-WORSHIPPER IS MEDITATING
Firm establishment upon immemorial principles. Consciousness of absolute unity. Depth of soul-penetration. Self-conquest.

14° IN DENSE JUNGLE, A PERFECTLY PRESERVED MAYAN BAS-RELIEF
Man's power to leave permanent records of his achievements. Personal immortality. Fecundation of future by past. Assurance.

15° IN A HOSPITAL, A CHILDREN'S WARD FILLED WITH PLAYTHINGS
The goodness of life in the tragic trials of first attempts at self- regeneration. Administered responsibility; or escape.

CAPRICORN XX. THE SPAN OF DEPENDENCE

16° SCHOOL GROUNDS FILLED WITH YOUTHS IN GYMNASIUM SUITS
Normal dependence upon physical stimulation. Robust enthusiasm in approaching life's contests; or immature impulsiveness.

17° REPRESSED WOMAN FINDS A PSYCHOLOGICAL RELEASE IN NUDISM
Escape from bondage to social inhibitions. Readjustment of relation of spirit to body. Self-purification. Self-confrontation.

18° THE UNION JACK FLAG FLIES FROM A NEW BRITISH DESTROYER
Extreme of objectification of inner resources. Challenge to life. Splendid self-realization. Full awareness of competition.

19° FIVE-YEAR-OLD GIRL PROUDLY DOES HER MOTHER'S MARKETING
Capacity to take place ahead of normal standards. Increased self- confidence. Waiting for conditions to catch up with self.

20° THROUGH THE EMPTY CHURCH, THE CHOIR IS HEARD, REHEARSING
The unrealized fullness of life even in the emptiest hours. Preparation for activity. Ray of hope through all difficulty.

21° A RELAY RACE. EACH RUNNER SPRINGS EAGERLY INTO PLACE
Extreme of cooperation and give-and-take in life-relationships. Full surrender of self to service. Planned group-behavior.

22° DEFEATED GENERAL YIELDS UP HIS SWORD WITH NOBLE DIGNITY

Apparent defeat that spells real spiritual victory. Bowing to custom. Conquest through conformity to established norm.

23° A SOLDIER RECEIVES DECOROUSLY TWO AWARDS FOR BRAVERY
Reward offered by society for the fulfilling of individual responsibility. Recognition of worth; unearned good fortune.

24° A WOMAN WALKING TO THE SURE HAVEN OF A CONVENT
Protective kindness of life to weary hearts. Quiet undercurrent of real existence. Compelled assistance. Timely rescue.

25° LITTLE BOYS FROLIC UPON SOFT RUGS IN AN ORIENTAL STORE
First realization of cultural values through sensuous enjoyment. Refinement of sensations. Psychological enrichment.

26° RADIANT SPRITE DANCES UPON THE MIST OF A WATERFALL
Transcendence of spirit over body and environment. Lightness of understanding. Inexhaustible soul resources. Effervescence.

27° MEN CLIMB A SACRED PEAK: BELOW, THE WORLD-ABOVE, PEACE
Necessary linkage of above and below in the seeker's personal experience. Balanced dualism of subjective-objective life.

28° THE AVIARY OF A RURAL MANSION, FILLED WITH SINGING BIRDS
Enhancement of personality by familiarity with spiritual values. Joying in the significance of things; or mental confusion.

29° A GYPSY READS FORTUNES IN THE TEA-CUPS OF SOCIETY LADIES
The quest for inner understanding through all life-conditioning. First approach to reality. Desire to transcend routine.

30° THE DIRECTORS OF A LARGE FIRM MEET IN SECRET CONFERENCE
Activity of inner formative elements of real personality. Massing of soul-energies in an emergency. Spiritual leadership.

AQUARIUS XXI. THE SPAN OF DEFENSIVENESS

1° OLD ADOBE MISSION NESTLES IN CALIFORNIA'S BROWN HILLS
Mastery of man over environment while becoming an integral part of it. Recognition of established values. Impressiveness.

2° UNEXPECTED THUNDERSTORM BRINGS RELIEF TO PARCHED FIELDS
Liberation from adverse conditions through violent spectacular developments. Galvanizing to action. Cosmic visitation.

3° A DESERTER SUDDENLY REALIZES THE FALLACY OF HIS CONDUCT
Ability to regrasp past experience and turn it to account. Sharp self-examination. Awakened new fearlessness. Decision.

4° A HINDU PUNDIT REVEALS HIMSELF SUDDENLY A GREAT HEALER
Supremacy of the unsuspected faculties hidden deep within. Conscious utilization of divine potency. Revelation of self.

5° A WORLD-LEADER IS SEEN GUIDED BY HIS ANCESTORS' SPIRITS
The rich ancestral heritage of every individual, which is the potent foundation of character. Direct, real inspiration.

6° IN AN ALLEGORICAL MYSTERY RITUAL A MAN OFFICIATES ALONE

Compelling urge in every soul to express the unknown and the more-than-physical. Sensitiveness to high purpose. Conflict.

7° OUT OF THE COSMIC EGG, LIFE IS BORN FRESH AND VIRGINAL
New actuation of effort by the power of unrealized purposes. Self-expression beyond all expectation. Spiritual protection.

8° WAX FIGURES DISPLAY BEAUTIFUL GOWNS IN STORE-WINDOWS
Need for public presentation of virtues and life standards. Exteriorization of value, that it may be shared with others.

9° IN MEDITATION, A FLAC IS SEEN, WHICH CHANGES INTO AN EAGLE
Process of spiritual realization as it progresses from outer to inner standards. Rebirth, or rebellion against drudgery.

10° UNSPOILED BY POPULARITY NOW WANING A MAN PLANS ANEW
Ability to rise above vicissitudes of passing fortune. Faithfulness to self. Dependence upon native endowment. Projection.

11° ARTIST, AWAY FROM THE WORLD, RECEIVES A NEW INSPIRATION
Creative power in man: its relationship to social behavior. Self- crystallization in a form of power; or else self-exploitation.

12° LIFE'S BROAD STAIRWAY: EACH LANDING, A NEW GRADE OF LIFE
Points of pause and transition, where the soul can evaluate its progress. Graded effort. Necessity for divorcing the past.

13° A BAROMETER HANGS UNDER THE PORCH OF A QUIET RURAL INN
Vantage point in consciousness whence life may be observed and measured in peace. Inner retreat of a soul seeking truth.

14° ON A STEEP CLIMB, A TUNNEL OFFERS SHORT-CUT TO A TRAIN
The way within to outer success. Sure relief to the toiler ready to face facts. Penetration and direct accomplishment.

15° TWO LOVE-BIRDS ON A FENCE SING OUT THEIR PURE HAPPINESS
Contagiousness of happiness in human associations. Revelation of constructive reality. Radiation of spontaneous faith.

AQUARIUS XXII. THE SPAN OF PERSPECTIVE

16° BUSINESS MANAGER AT HIS DESK STUDIES A COMPLEX PROJECT
The central control of operations needed in all organized enterprise. The head-function. Surety in decision. Management.

17° WATCH DOG ON GUARD AS GOLD-MINER SLEEPS NEAR HIS STRIKE
Nascent protective faculties in all men as they adjust themselves to new conditions. Competent organization of affairs.

18° AT MASQUERADE, THE LAST MAN UNMASKS, URGED BY THE GIRLS
The introvert's desire to protect himself from social judgment. Clinging to self-valuation. Conservation of experience.

19° A FOREST FIRE SUBDUED, THE WEARY FIGHTERS FEEL JUBILANT
Exaggeration of life-problems, which reveals to man his real stature and which expands him. Impatient challenge. Ascendancy.

20° WHITE DOVE CIRCLES OVERHEAD; DESCENDS, BEARING A MESSAGE

The blessing of every effort by the "Holy Ghost" of revealed significance. Exaltation of all individual efforts. Celebrity.

21° A WOMAN IS DISAPPOINTED, AS A MAN LEAVES HER BOUDOIR
Capitalization upon misfortune by which spiritual justification is gained. Supremacy over experience. Inward retirement.

22° CHILDREN REVEL UPON A SOFT NEW CARPET IN THEIR NURSERY
Life's warmth and richness given to those who eagerly learn to live. Luxurious self-knowing, or self-appreciation. Comfort.

23° A BIG TRAINED BEAR PERFORMS, SITTING ON A HUGE CHAIR
Need to build an adequate concrete vehicle for cosmic power. Performance beyond native endowment. A striving for balance.

24° NOW FREED FROM PASSION, A MAN TEACHES DEEP WISDOM
Utilization of experience and passion by the intelligence that remains un-involved. Self-conquering. Genuine dispassion.

25° A BUTTERFLY EMERGES FROM ITS CHRYSALIS, RIGHT WING FIRST
Necessary advance of volition over reflex elements. Willing approach to problems of being. Fitting to alien ideas. Choice.

26° A GARAGE MAN IS SEEN READY TO TEST THE BATTERY OF A CAR
Capacity of self to take up and deliver spiritual power. Controlled release of power through the emotions. Measurement.

27° AMID RARE BOOKS, AN OLD POTTERY BOWL HOLDS FRESH VIOLETS
Reality of spiritual or esthetic values, linking generations of seekers for the highest. Addition or commitment to value.

28° HUGE PILE OF SAWED-UP WOOD INSURES HEAT FOR THE WINTER
Rich contribution of nature to all who work with foresight. Intelligent preparation. Calm yet potent faith in Providence.

29° METAMORPHOSIS COMPLETED, A BUTTERFLY SPREADS ITS WINGS
Immortality of the real self. Graduation into a new realm of being. Confident projection of self; lack of self-confidence.

30° MOON-LIT FIELDS, ONCE BABYLON, ARE BLOOMING WHITE
Soul-refreshing inner poetry of being. Spiritually nurtured sentiment which illumines the heart. Voices from the past.

PISCES XXIII. THE SPAN OF INNOCENCE

1° LATE SATURDAY AFTERNOON: CROWDS FILL THE PUBLIC MARKET
The social nature of human responsibilities. A last-moment, joyous rallying to a task. Seed synthesis at end of cycles.

2° SQUIRREL, SHOWING HUMAN ACUMEN, HIDES FROM HUNTER
Instinct of self-preservation as a basis for greater realization. Lifting of self to surer foundations. Transference.

3° A PETRIFIED FOREST: PERMANENT RECORD OF ANCIENT LIVES
Mastery of form over substance. Archetypal immortality. Conscious handling of existence. Participation in race impulses.

4° CARS CROWD A NARROW ISTHMUS BETWEEN TWO RESORTS

Linkage in activity of all community values. Free flow from ideas to consummation. Sense of significance in relationship.

5° A WARM-HEARTED CROWD GATHERS AT A CHURCH BAZAAR
Interchange of spirit and understanding on which groups are built. New self-development. Discouragement mastered. Commerce.

6° A PARADE OF WEST POINT CADETS IS HELD AS THE SUN SETS
Self-exaltation through consecration to the task of defending collective values. Self-testing. Perception of high goals.

7° FOG HIDES THE SHORE; BUT ON A CLEAR ROCK A CROSS RESTS
Concentration of values amidst the chaos of outer living. Clear light of high realization. Acceptance of life's limits.

8° GIRL-SCOUT, IN CAMP, BLOWS HER BUGLE TRIUMPHANTLY
Fullness of life as it manifests in service to the whole. Spiritual socialization. Call to participation in the race work.

9° THE RACE BEGINS: A JOCKEY SPURS HIS HORSE TO GREAT SPEED
The capacity of man to throw himself fully into any type of activity. Self-quickening. Premature expenditure of energy.

10° THE AVIATOR SAILS ACROSS THE SKY, MASTER OF HIGH REALMS
Transcendence of normal problems. Gaining of celestial responsibilities. Consummation of the highest ideals. Coronation.

11° SEEKERS FOR ILLUMINATION ARE GUIDED INTO THE SANCTUARY
Introduction of conscious mind to the intuitive soul-realms. Self- dedication. Self-awakening; or surrender to inner fears.

12° CANDIDATES ARE BEING EXAMINED BY THE LODGE OF INITIATES
Inner ordeal before every true seeker. The individual facing collective wisdom. Re-affirmation of purpose. God-revelation.

13° OLD WEAPONS IN A MUSEUM: IN A GLASS CASE, A SACRED SWORD
Courage and fearlessness needed in the quest for spirit and real understanding. Real faith in self; or emptiness of dread.

14° A YOUNG LADY, WRAPPED IN FURS, DISPLAYS SUPREME ELEGANCE
Necessary superficial advertisement of inner worth. Certification of true merit. Schooled esteem. Embarrassing wealth.

15° AN OFFICER IN UNKEMPT CAMPAIGN UNIFORM DRILLS HIS MEN
Subjection of outer appearances to real necessities. Potent compulsion of a great task to be performed. Opportunity seized.

PISCES XXIV. THE SPAN OF PROTECTION

16° IN A QUIET MUSEUM, AN ART STUDENT DRINKS IN INSPIRATION
Subjective source of strength around all manifestation. Communion with accumulated race power. Deep, vibrant realization.

17° EASTER: RICH AND POOR ALIKE DISPLAY THE BEST THEY OWN
A symbol of "high moments" in life, when man challenges himself and renews his faith in circumstances. Self-improvement.

18° IN A HUGE TENT A FAMOUS REVIVALIST CONDUCTS HIS MEETING

Reinforcement of faith which can open up a new environment. A revision of ideas back to source. Critical survey of life.

19° MASTER AND PUPIL COMMUNE IN STRENGTH IN A LONG WALK
Body-strengthening function of the soul. Release from race karma. Transmutation of everyday facts into intelligence.

20° IN THE QUIET OF EVENING THE FARMER'S SUPPER AWAITS HIM
Encompassing richness of experience whenever a particular ordeal is over. Spiritual nourishment. Ingathering of forces

21° CHILD WATCHED, BY CHINESE SERVANT CARESSES A WHITE LAMB
Eager probing of the soul into its many potentialities and higher reaches. Self-expansion: or refusal to grow in Spirit.

22° DOWN A SYMBOLIC MOUNTAIN OF INDUSTRY COMES A NEW MOSES
Man's success in meeting the challenge of a new order. Codification of new values. Holding oneself to highest standards.

23° A "MATERIALIZING MEDIUM" SUMMONS WEIRD GHOSTLY SHAPES
Display of powers which, though physical, transcend our normal awareness. Subjective mastery of, or passivity to life-forces.

24° IN A TINY LOST ISLAND MEN BUILD HAPPILY THEIR OWN WORLD
Adaptability and inherent creativeness of man. Extreme of surety in self-expression. Centralization of supernal forces.

25° AFTER DRASTIC REFORMS A PURIFIED CLERGY OFFICIATES ANEW
Ability periodically to cleanse from all selfish dross the channels for spiritual service. True vision. Soul-reformation.

26° TWO RAPT LOVERS AND A PHILOSOPHER WATCH THE NEW MOON
Polyphony of values as man lives at various levels of consciousness. Inner call to realization. Transmutation of meaning.

27° THE HARVEST MOON RISES IN TRANSLUCENT AUTUMNAL SKIES
The power of creative visualization by which great Dreamers transcend outer reality. Complete dominance of circumstances.

28° UNDER THE FULL MOON THE FIELDS SEEM STRANGELY ALIVE
Normally unnoticed powers released at the fruition of natural processes. Call of universal mind to the heart. Fullness.

29° SCIENTIST IS MAKING TESTS BY MEANS OF SPECTRUM-ANALYSIS
Capacity of mind to transfer its powers to machinery. Enlargement of perception. A closing-in of vision. Subtle analysis.

30° A SEER'S DREAM NOW LIVES: A FACE CARVED INTO HUGE ROCKS
Eventual concrete manifestation of all higher poetic images and enduring truths of the race. Sure culmination of effort.

Appendix F
More Houses

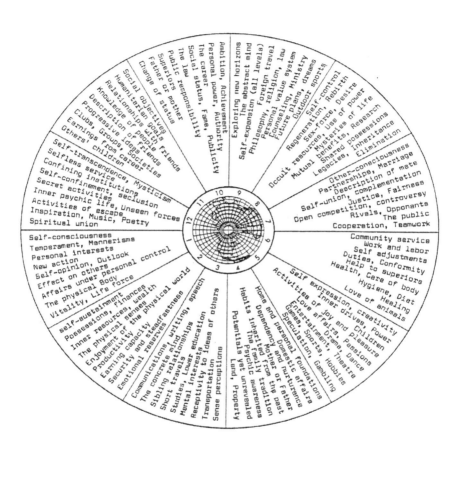

16616658R00232

Made in the USA
San Bernardino, CA
10 November 2014